The Place of Landscape

The Place of Landscape

Concepts, Contexts, Studies

edited by Jeff Malpas

The MIT Press
Cambridge, Massachusetts
London, England

For information about special quantity discounts, please email special_sales@ mitpress.mit.edu

This book was set in Stone Sans and Stone Serif by Graphic Composition, Inc., Bogart, Georgia. Printed and bound in the United States of America.

Library of Congress Cataloging-in-Publication Data

The place of landscape : concepts, contexts, studies / edited by Jeff Malpas.
    p. cm.
Includes bibliographical references and index.
ISBN 978-0-262-01552-3 (hardcover : alk. paper)
1. Landscapes. I. Malpas, J. E.
BH301.L3P48   2011
700'.46—dc22

                                                                2010040932

10 9 8 7 6 5 4 3 2 1

Contents

Introduction

Jeff Malpas

In 1994, W. J. T. Mitchell published a groundbreaking set of essays on land-scape under the title *Landscape and Power*. In the preface to the second edi-tion of the volume, published in 2002, Mitchell wrote: "If I were given a chance to retitle *Landscape and Power* today, some years after its first appear-ance, I would call it *Space, Place, and Landscape*."[1] The change of perspec-tive that Mitchell records here reflects an important shift, or set of shifts, that has occurred over recent years within the various discourses in which the idea of landscape figures—shifts that also lie at the heart of the current volume, whose own title, *The Place of Landscape*, connects two of the three terms that figure in the revised title preferred by Mitchell.

In its originally published form, the significance of *Landscape and Power* was in marking an earlier shift in the critical engagement with landscape away from the "innocence" (Mitchell's term) exemplified in Kenneth Clarke's Oxford lectures, published in 1949 as *Landscape into Art*. Clarke's focus was on the character of landscape art as part of a cycle "in which the human spirit attempted once more to create a harmony with its environ-ment."[2] Mitchell, on the other hand, along with his contributors, took a much darker view, arguing that the appreciation of landscape "must be the focus of a historical, political and (yes) aesthetic alertness to the violence and evil written on the land, projected there by the gazing eye . . . [and that] landscape is the medium by which this evil is veiled and natural-ized."[3] The way in which landscape can operate to embody, conceal, and support forms of power, especially the power of money and class, remains a theme in many current explorations of landscape. Yet the way landscape functions in this way is itself indicative of the deeper significance of land-scape—a significance that is not restricted merely to landscape as a genre of painting, but is directly tied to the interconnection of human life with the spaces and places in which that life is lived. Recognition of this aspect of landscape was not absent from Mitchell's original 1994 volume, but it was not its main theme, and it is the explicit shift to this broader perspective to which Mitchell appears to allude in his 2002 preface.

Mitchell argues that, despite their differences, both the "phenomenological" and "experiential" traditions "agree on the primacy of 'space' and 'place' as the fundamental categories of analysis,"[4] and he notes the development of spatial and topographic concepts in the work of theorists such as David Harvey, Michel de Certeau, and Henri Lefebvre, and the application of those concepts to landscape as this is articulated in the new essays added to the 2002 edition of *Landscape and Power*. Nevertheless, Mitchell also acknowledges that landscape remains "relatively underanalyzed" and that so far as the triad of space, place, and landscape are concerned, "no one has really attempted to think the three terms together."[5] Mitchell does attempt some explicit clarification of the concepts at issue here, but such a conceptual investigation is not his primary interest, and this reflects the more general state of affairs in discussions of place and space, as well as landscape, across most of the disciplines in which these concepts figure. Indeed, often the investigation of these concepts amounts more to an exploration of certain particular configurations of the phenomena to which they refer than of the concepts as such.

The present book aims to contribute to the enlarged analysis of landscape that Mitchell envisions here, including its conceptual clarification (although this remains somewhat obliquely addressed), and especially to the thinking of landscape in connection with *place*. In focusing on the *place* rather than the *space* of landscape (where place, I would argue, must encompass both the spatial and the temporal), this volume aims to explore some of the issues that Mitchell originally raised in terms of the role that landscape plays in relation to other concepts and structures, including power, but also in our own relation to the world as that is already an issue in more traditional approaches to landscape such as that of Clarke. In this respect one might say that the aim of the volume is to explore the "conceptual topography" of landscape and so to explore the connections and disjunctions between concepts as they also form part of a larger conceptual domain.[6] Moreover, in asking after the place of landscape, what is also brought into view is the manner in which landscape itself functions topographically—what is the place (what are the places) that it opens up, to which it allows entry, within which it appears?

The focus on place here is no mere rhetorical flourish. Although place and space are indeed connected, the thematization of place is not intended, as is so often the case, simply to indicate the adoption of a more spatially attentive mode of analysis. Elsewhere I have argued for the importance of distinguishing between space and place, for taking place to be the more overarching concept, and for maintaining the connection of place with both space and time.[7] Some of the essays in this volume (Casey's is a notable example) can be seen as contributing to the further elucidation of the concept of place that this implies—the title of the volume thus indicates the way in which what is at issue here is both place and landscape. In emphasizing the "place" of landscape, the intention is also to indicate an approach to landscape that is not to be construed only in terms of the spatial or, indeed, of the visual. There is a widespread tendency for discussions of landscape to privilege both space and vision, and this is partly a result of the centrality in discussions of landscape that is given to the pictorial and the filmic (and this volume contains a number of essays that attend to such modes of representation, especially the essays by Benjamin, Steiner, Donald, and Gibson). In framing these essays in terms of the "place" of landscape, the emphasis is also on opening up the possibility that the place at issue here is one that encompasses more than the visual alone, one that combines the spatial and the temporal and constitutes a mode of *engagement with*, rather than merely *separation from* (an issue directly thematized in my own contribution—see chapter 1 below).

The volume is divided into three parts: *concepts of* landscape; *contexts for* landscape; and *studies in* landscape. As with all such divisions, there is a certain arbitrariness about the way this structure fits the essays themselves—they are not intended to provide a neat set of categorizations, but rather to indicate something of the way each set of essays should be positioned with respect to the others. The idea of dividing the volume in this way, and the way the essays were chosen to fit within those divisions, was to ensure a range of approaches to landscape that was, first of all, multidisciplinary in character. Consequently, the essays included encompass philosophy, literature, geography, anthropology, theology, sociology, art history, ecology, landscape and garden history, and contemporary social and political critique. In addition, the aim was to include a range of different types of inquiry. The volume thus begins with investigations of the concept of landscape—which is where the relation between landscape and place is most directly taken up—moving through explorations of the way landscape emerges in particular contexts and with respect to specific problems, and ending with a number of studies of landscape within specific generic, historical, and geographic formations. One further, and final, consideration was to assemble the contributors so as to include not merely a range of disciplines or of modes of inquiry, but also a range of perspectives that would open up the issue of landscape in ways that would contrast with, as well as complement, one another and what is present within the already existing literature.

The essays that fall into the first of these three parts, "Concepts of Landscape," start from my own characterization of a general tension that seems to be embedded within the contemporary treatment of landscape and that concerns its supposedly "pictorial" character. Wesley A. Kort explores the concept of landscape as it connects, primarily through its literary exploration, with ideas of character and identity. Adopting a specifically Australian perspective, John J. Bradley explores the relation between the "whitefella" concept of landscape and indigenous Australian understandings of the relation between identity and place or "country." Theodore Schatzki sets out a view of landscape as more than just spatial or temporal, but rather as a phenomenon of "time-space," and he illustrates this through a particular formation of landscape, namely, that of the "bluegrass" landscape of the Kentucky horse-farms. Finally, Edward S. Casey explores the "liminal" aspect of landscape—its borders and edges—and since every edge defines as it also delimits, so the question of the unity of landscape also emerges here.

Part II, "Contexts for Landscape," moves from geography, through photography and garden history, to theology. Nicholas J. Entrikin's discussion considers another of landscape's darker sides, although one seldom explored—a dark side found in landscape's "natural" rather than "human" character. Bernard Debarbieux examines the implication of landscape, not merely in the construction of power, but in the articulation of civic and political life. Through the sustained analysis of a single photograph, Andrew Benjamin explores the character of landscape through a reworking of the idea of the sublime, showing how landscape operates through the interplay of spacing and distancing, thereby also exhibiting something of the spatial and topographic formation of landscape. From within the framework of garden history, as well as contemporary environmental sensibility, Isis Brooke reexamines the idea of the picturesque, while Philip Sheldrake considers the role of landscape in the Christian religious imagination. Although, among the essays assembled here, only Sheldrake talks specifically, and at length, about the connection between landscape and imagination, it is clear that this is a theme that runs throughout almost all of the essays contained here. The geographer Doreen Massey has explored the concepts of space and place specifically in terms of their discursive and imaginary potential.[8] It is just this potential that is at issue in the political and social function of landscape, in its operation as a mode of self-formation and self-articulation, in its expressive and representational character.

One might go further and say that it is out of the connectedness to landscape, our embeddedness in particular spaces and places, that imagination
itself arises, on which it draws, and to which it also gives shape and form.
It is thus not merely the *concept* of landscape that is taken up here, nor
merely the contexts and studies in which landscape may figure, but the
image of landscape as well as the *imaginary* to which it belongs.

The final part of the volume, "Studies in Landscape," includes a series of
more focused studies that deal with particular instances or forms of landscape from medieval landscape painting through to landscape as it appears
in contemporary film and even television. Reinhard Steiner explores the
emergence of landscape within the conventions of late medieval painting
in which space appears as homogeneous and nonperspectival. What form
does landscape take here? Stephanie Hemelryk Donald and Ross Gibson
each explore the filmic appearance of landscape, although in quite different
manifestations. In Donald, the exploration is part of a larger consideration
of landscape in contemporary Chinese society and culture, whereas in Gibson it is the thematization of landscape in the classic American Western,
specifically John Ford's *The Searchers*, that is the focus. In Katie Campbell's
essay, the concern is with the shaping of landscape through both a physical
topography and a literary heritage. Landscape is not only formed in the
geography of a place, but also in the cultural context that belongs with
that place, and that derives from as well as contributes to it. The two clos-
ing essays bring us back closer to the themes of Mitchell's *Landscape and
Power*, as Michael Rosenthal and Nigel Everett examine the appearance of
landscape in discourses of nationality and identity in Ireland and England.
These essays draw landscape more directly into the domain of the political,
but one might say that they also draw politics into the domain of landscape. Moreover, they make salient what is no less important, and which
is a recurrent theme throughout the essays contained here, namely, the
equivocity, multiplicity, and indeterminacy of landscape. At the same time
as landscape allows its discursive appropriation, it also gives the lie to any
attempt to identify it with its appropriated image. Landscape may provide
the site in and on which political power is inscribed and articulated, but it
also retains the potential to resist such inscription and articulation, to render it unstable and uncertain.

While there can be no doubt of the political character of landscape, just
as there can be no doubt of the political character of place, neither can
place or landscape be understood as wholly taken up within the political
alone. Landscape is thus not exhausted by its character as political, nor by
any other aspect under which it may be interpreted or to which it may be

appropriated. Landscape opens out to a multiplicity of different genres, forms of practice, and modes of analysis in a way that itself reflects the multiplicity of perspectives that are present in every landscape. The question of the place of landscape is thus not the sole preserve of any one field or discipline. Just as "landscape" can no longer be used, as it once was, to refer to a particular genre of painting, so "landscape" does not belong to the art historian or the aesthetician alone—nor indeed is it the special preserve of the landscape architect or designer (the latter being one of the few fields that is not represented in the essays included here). The question concerning the place of landscape is thus not only a question of how landscape relates to forms of power or to modes of representation, but of how landscape functions in relation to place itself, in relation to human being in place, and of how place may be said to function in and through landscape. In responding to such a question, and to the full range of issues that it encompasses, it cannot be sufficient to offer just one answer from within a solitary frame of thought—only a plurality of answers and approaches can begin to do justice to the iridescent and often opaque character of landscape and of place. In this latter respect, the essays that make up this volume do not aim at providing a single definitive account of landscape, whether in terms of specific studies, contexts, or concepts, but are instead directed at offering what might be thought of as a series of "views" on the "landscape," the place, that landscape itself opens up.

Notes

1. W. J. T. Mitchell, *Landscape and Power*, 2nd ed. (Chicago: University of Chicago Press, 2002), p. vii.

2. Kenneth Clarke, *Landscape into Art* (London: Readers Union/John Murray, 1953), p. 1.

3. Mitchell, *Landscape and Power*, pp. 29–30 (same pagination as in original 1994 ed.).

4. Ibid., p. viii.

5. Ibid.

6. See my *Place and Experience: A Philosophical Topography* (Cambridge: Cambridge University Press, 1999), pp. 39–41, for an exploration of the idea of topography that is at issue here.

7. See again my *Place and Experience*. In his 2002 preface to *Landscape and Power*, Mitchell writes that "If a place is a specific location, a space is a 'practiced place,' a site activated by movements, actions, narratives, and signs, and a landscape is that

site as encountered as image or 'sight,'" p. x. There is much that remains obscure in this characterization (most significant, perhaps, is the fact that it leaves "place" almost entirely unelucidated, and yet it is "place" that seems to underpin "space" and "landscape"), and Mitchell's discussion immediately following this passage suggests that there remains a real question as to how these terms should be understood or how they should be connected.

8. See Massey, *For Space* (London: Sage, 2005).

I Concepts of Landscape

1 Place and the Problem of Landscape

Jeff Malpas

Landscape is like revelation / it is both singular crystal and the remotest things
—Geoffrey Hill[1]

I

Although it seems to me mistaken to treat "landscape" as a term referring only to a particular artistic genre, it is nevertheless with a landscape
painting that I want to begin—a work by the painter, John Glover, who
immigrated to Tasmania from England in the 1820s. The painting is *Mount
Wellington and Hobart Town from Kangaroo Point*, painted in 1834.

Thought for many years to have been destroyed in London during
World War II, the painting seems to have acquired some significance for
contemporary Tasmanians—so much so that the Tasmanian Museum and
Art Gallery combined with the National Gallery of Australia to purchase
the painting for a record price of AUD $1,762,500 (approximately €1 mil-
lion) when it reappeared in public view at Christie's in November 2001.
It is a landscape painting, a painting of a place—Hobart Town seen from
across the Derwent River with Mount Wellington behind it.

The significance of the work undoubtedly derives from the all-
encompassing view of early Hobart and its immediate surrounds that the
painting presents to the viewer, as well as the record it provides of the
town at this point in its history. It is through its presentation of this view
that the work contributes to the sense of the town's history and identity.
Of course, the view that is presented appears within an idyllic frame—one
that romanticizes the town along with its setting. Not only does Mount
Wellington appear in the background as loftier and more imposing than in
reality, while the town itself appears bathed in a swathe of light that cuts
across the painting, but the foreground of the work is occupied by happy
scenes of Tasmanian Aboriginal life that were impossible at the time the

Figure 1.1
John Glover, *Mount Wellington and Hobart Town from Kangaroo Point*, 1834. Oil on canvas. Tasmanian Museum and Art Gallery and National Gallery of Australia.

picture was painted. There is, in fact, a cruel irony here, since, by 1836, the real plight of the Tasmanian Aboriginal people was one of destruction, displacement, and death. The rosy presentation of the developing town, and the idealized scenes before it, can thus be seen to mask the dispossession and desolation that accompanied that very development—although one might also say, and perhaps this might have been Glover's reading, that the painting portrays the Europeanized present alongside the Aboriginal past, and if both are placed within the same romantic glow, it may also be significant that the Aboriginal scenes are cast into relative shadow compared to the sunlit town across the water.[2]

Glover's painting presents a particular place, and a particular landscape, to us. It does so in a way that also modifies the landscape it presents. Indeed, it achieves much of its effect, in a manner characteristic of such paintings, through just such modification—the way in which the modification of landscape in pictorial presentation enables the assertion of relations of power and subjectification is a large part of what W. J. T. Mitchell thematizes in his important collection *Landscape and Power*.[3] So here we have a painting *of* a landscape, and so *of a place*, that is, as a painting, also itself a landscape. The way in which the landscape painting presents the landscape that is painted involves, however, the inevitable modification of the landscape so presented—it involves the adoption of a particular view or views (Glover seems actually to have incorporated multiple perspectives into the same work) that, in this case especially, invoke the past as well as the present, while also pointing toward a future (the prosperous appearance of the sunlit town is itself an indicator of the hopes and aspirations of both town and painter).

While the painting presents a place or landscape, and presents it in the form of a landscape, what is it that is shown or revealed in such presenting? Is it a real landscape that is revealed here? Or is it purely an imagined landscape—in which case, what is revealed but the artist's own imaginative creation? Yet there is a relation, not merely of presentation, but of *re*presentation here, which is to say that the painting is indeed a painting *of* Hobart Town. Moreover, if we take note of the two senses that are contained in the word "landscape," and we admit that there is both the landscape represented, and the landscape that is the representation, then what is it that is revealed in and through either of these senses of landscape other than a place—a place that itself encompasses the artist's own situation in, or in relation to, that landscape?

Edward Casey has written that "Landscapes are, in the final analysis, placescapes; they are congeries of places in the fullest experiential and represented sense. *No landscape without place*; this much we may take to be certainly true."[4] The relation between landscape and place will be the focus of my explorations here. But in looking to this relation, I also want to explore the question of the "revelatory" character of landscape, and the matter of what is revealed in the connection between landscape and place. One of the underlying questions here concerns not only the relation between landscape and place, but also our own relation to both. Before I go any further, however, there is another question that lurks in the background, which is already evident in one of the questions I asked immediately above: what is meant by the term "landscape"? It is already clear that landscape can refer to a mode of presentation or "representation," such as a painting, as well as to that which is presented, namely a place. To some extent, every use of the term carries something of both these senses, since for a place to be a landscape is already for it to appear in a certain way—there is, consequently, an inevitable equivocity that attaches to talk of "landscape." The question as to the meaning of landscape is thus always an issue in any and every discussion of landscape—it is not a matter that can be taken as simply decided from the very start. Moreover, to ask about landscape is also, therefore, to ask about the nature of representation, since the equivocity evident in the term "landscape" is an equivocity that also affects the idea of representation as such.

What lies behind my inquiry into landscape is a fundamental problem. It is a problem already adumbrated in the equivocity I have noted here, and although it is not a problem that emerges in any clear way in Casey's work, it is certainly present in much contemporary discussion of landscape, as well as in contemporary reactions and practice in relation to landscape. To some extent, this "problem of landscape" is expressed in a common conception of landscape according to which landscape is the product of an essentially "representational" construal of our relation to the world that always involves separation and detachment. This conception takes landscape to involve the presenting of the world as an object, seen from a certain view, structured, framed, and made available to our gaze. Such "views" may well affect us, and we may well take them to be important in a variety of ways, but precisely because they are already seen as "views," so they are separated from us, and our involvement with them is based purely in the spectatorial—in a form of visual or pictorial presentation in which we remain mere observers of the presented scene. The "representational" character of landscape as an art form is often taken to underpin the "dark side" of landscape—its complicity in exclusion and oppression—since it is precisely in and through the representational character of landscape art that landscape art is seen as constructing the landscape that it presents in ways that reinforce the relations of power and authority that hold sway within it.

There is an implication here, seldom spelled out, in which visual presentation is itself understood as entailing a more passive relation to what is viewed than might other modes of presentation, and that this passivity itself functions to enable power to operate through representation (and also to conceal that operation). Such an implication of passivity in relation to vision is surely mistaken—vision, as with all modes of sensory engagement, presupposes activity (and not only on the basis of Gibsonian considerations alone[5])—but it nevertheless seems correct to say that there is a sense of *separation* between the viewer and what is viewed that is more strongly and immediately evident in visual than in other modes of presentation.[6] Thus, although the spectatorial does not belong to the visual alone (every sensory modality allows of more or less spectatorial modes of engagement), the visual is more inclined, we might say, to a spectatorial construal. The problem that concerns me here is that the construal of the visual often leads us to disregard the fact that the visual and the spectatorial are not the same, and that the visual always implicates more just than the visual alone.[7]

It is the "representational" or "spectatorial" character of landscape that will the primary focus of my discussion. My claim will be that landscape, while often understood in purely visual terms, is inadequately understood if construed as merely a "view," and that even landscape painting, although certainly employing a visual mode of presentation, presents more than the visual alone. Landscape is a representation of place, and as such, it is the re-presentation of a relatedness to place, a re-presentation of a mode of "emplacement." The argument may also be put in terms of a claim, itself implicit in Casey's work, regarding the visual and the pictorial: Every view carries with it more than just a view narrowly conceived, but is itself the expression and representation of a relation to place—if every landscape is a place-scape, then so is every "view" an entry into place.

II

In his famous essay on the country and the city, Raymond Williams put the point regarding the essentially spectatorial character of landscape as follows: "a working country is hardly ever a landscape. The very idea of landscape implies separation and observation."[8] Something like the same idea also appears in Stephen Daniels and Denis Cosgrove's important collection on the "iconography" of landscape. In a much-quoted passage, they write that:

A landscape is a cultural image, a pictorial way of representing, structuring or symbolizing surroundings. This is not to say that landscapes are immaterial. They may be represented in a variety of materials and on many surfaces—in paint on canvas, in writing on paper, in earth, stone water and vegetation on the ground.[9]

The idea that it is the "representational"—and especially the visual-representational—character of landscape that underpins its ideological character is often seen as tied to the way in which landscape "objectifies," and even "commodifies," that which it presents. The external environment, or aspects of it, is thus treated as an object made amenable to human purposes and interests—whether as an object available for enjoyment or contemplation, or for production, development, or exchange. Indeed, the art historian Enzo Carli claims that it is only when landscape has been transformed into something *useful* to human beings that it can become an object of aesthetic appreciation:

before man could begin to appreciate landscape, or rather, the elements that constitute a landscape, he had to put his mark upon it. Only when he has planted his orchards and fruit trees and gardens does it become for him a source of delight for the senses; then it commands aesthetic appreciation and he makes pictures of it.[10]

On this account, the character of landscape as already embodying certain relations of power and production comes before its appearance as aesthetically valuable. Moreover, in both cases, the character of landscape *as* landscape is grounded in the objectification of the environment, or aspects of it, and so is grounded in its appearing as separate from, while also available to, the viewer.

It is no accident that the rise of landscape painting, and of a glorified concept of Nature and "the Natural," was tied, in England, to the rise of the enclosure movement, and, in Europe more generally, to the shift away from a primarily rural mode of life. The idea that there is a close relation between the rise of landscape and changes in social and economic conditions has been well documented, especially as this occurs in literature, by works such as Ann Bermingham's *Landscape and Ideology*.[11] Similarly, John Barrell has argued that the rural poetry of John Clare, a poetry tied to a very specific landscape and the evocation of that landscape, and to some extent Clare's own breakdown, can only be understood against the background of the destruction of his familiar Northamptonshire countryside through its gradual enclosure in the early 1800s.[12] In a way more directly relevant to the discussion here, Barrell also emphasizes the way in which the more distanced appreciation of landscape and place found in the work of writers such as Thomas Hardy arises only with the breakdown of the rural life that Hardy depicts. Moreover, the rise of landscape in eighteenth- and nineteenth-century literature is itself closely tied to the rise of landscape art, and so the literary engagement with landscape is thus often seen as drawing on, as well as contributing to, paradigmatically visual modes of representation. It is no accident that Wordsworth's immortalization of the Lake District in poetic form plays such a role in the shaping of that place as a site, not only for the making of landscape paintings, but also for touristic appreciation. The Lake District becomes a site, but also, so it would seem, a site for sights.

The visual-representational character of landscape is thus taken to imply a conception of landscape as inevitably tied, not merely to the rise of landscape and also landscape art as themselves commodities (so that the production of landscape, whether through tourism or through the making of pictures, becomes an industry in itself), but to new forms of land ownership and economic usage based on the exploitation of the nonpropertied classes or on the dispossession and oppression of indigenous populations. John Berger's *Ways of Seeing*, first a television series and then a book, provides a paradigmatic example of such an approach to landscape painting,[13] but the approach also carries over, as the work of critics such as Bermingham makes clear, to the analysis of landscape poetry and literature, and even landscape design. Since such analyses are often undertaken from a "progressive" political perspective, whereas landscape itself is taken to be expressive of the existing order, and thus to be politically "conservative," so the very concept of landscape is often taken to be politically "tainted." In an Australian context, for instance, landscape has thus been tied to a colonialist past that is an ongoing source of negotiation and often conflict[14]—and this, of course, is what is evident in the Glover painting with which I began.

Yet the content of a work, including a work of landscape, cannot be *limited* to its political content or effect. Moreover, while any account that takes our relation to landscape as a significant one must also be committed to the necessarily *political* character of landscape—all forms of human activity embody and express aspects of the political and social context out of which they emerge—such politicization cannot be taken to undermine the viability or significance of the idea of landscape, or of the practices associated with it.[15] The politics of landscape is itself a reflection of the way that landscape operates, in much the way Casey claims, as an articulation of place, and of the relationship to place. Indeed, this is a point that W. J. T. Mitchell's analysis of the relation between landscape and power can itself be taken as both reinforcing and exploring—although the question Mitchell also raises is whether landscape art, as a particular genre of artistic practice, still has the same capacity to function in the manner in which it has in the past (one might wonder, however, whether this decline is indeed specific to landscape art as such or whether it reflects a broader crisis in traditional modes of artistic practice).

III

The idea that landscape comes into view, as an explicitly thematized element in artistic and poetic representation, only when there is a certain separation between landscape and the human that enables a spectatorial relation is not merely a feature of the discussion of modern art or literature—it also appears in Vincent Scully's famous discussion of Greek temple construction. Scully writes that the absence of landscape representations in classical Greece did not mean that landscape was not important in Greek culture, but rather that landscape was simply not experienced in that represented form—landscape was experienced in the full, says Scully, rather than as something merely to be "viewed":

the Greeks of the archaic and classical periods are not supposed to have cared much for landscape, since they did not carve it or paint it or describe it at length in their literature. . . . The statement is of course not strictly true . . . there is . . . a deep sense of the action and effect of landscape to be found among most Greek writers from Homer on. Similarly the very absence of landscape background in most, in the larger sense all, vase paintings and reliefs may better be taken as indicative of the fact that the archaic and classical Greeks experienced the landscape only as it was, at full scale.

Scully goes on to claim that the appearance of landscape as a theme in Greek art and culture arises only when landscape is no longer experienced this latter sense:

it is only when the older, more intense belief in the gods tends to flag by the fourth century B.C. that romantic, picturesque poetry, nostalgically descriptive of landscape delights, like the idylls of Theocritus, makes its appearance, to be joined later by some tentative landscape painting. Again, it is only when the gods finally begin to die completely out of the land and when many human beings begin to live lives totally divorced from nature—at the beginning, that is, of the modern age—that landscape painting, picturesque architecture, and landscape description, like that of the romantic rediscovers of Greece itself, become the obsessive themes of art.[16]

Here Scully seems to argue for a transition in the Greek experience and conception of landscape that might also appear to be present in the rise of modern landscape art out of an experience of dislocation in the human relation to landscape in the seventeenth and eighteenth centuries. Only when our relation to landscape comes into question, one might say, does landscape come to be an explicit artistic theme.

Yet although it is almost certainly true that the idea of landscape often arises, at least in European culture, out of a certain sense of actual or potential alienation from the physical surroundings in which one lives, and the structure of particular landscapes cannot be divorced from social and economic forms, the idea of landscape as essentially tied to a representational, that is, spectatorial, way of relating to the world seems to neglect crucial elements in the very experience of landscape out of which any such representation or "viewing" arises. Although writers such as Williams advance a view of landscape as essentially spectatorial, and although landscape painting may seem to be restricted to the presentation of a view, the experience of landscape would seem not to be restricted to the visual alone. The experience of landscape is as much of the sound, smell, and feel of a place as of anything purely visual.

The anthropologist Tim Ingold has taken up this very point in relation to the passage from Daniels and Cosgrove I quoted earlier. Having quoted Daniels and Cosgrove's comment that "landscape is a cultural image," Ingold writes:

I do not share this view. To the contrary I reject the division between inner and outer worlds—respectively of mind and matter, meaning and substance—upon which such distinction rests. The landscape is not, I hold, a picture in the imagination, surveyed by the mind's eye; nor however is it an alien and formless substrate awaiting the imposition of a human order . . . neither is the landscape identical to nature, nor is it on the side of humanity against nature . . . it is *with* us not *against* us.[17]

In contrast to the view of landscape as spectatorial, Ingold argues for a view of landscape as the embodiment of a set of dynamic elements and interactions. The landscape that is represented visually in landscape painting, then, is the collapsing of that dynamic interaction into a set of visually represented forms and features. To illustrate the underlying dynamic and involved character of landscape, as this may be present even in the painted representation of landscape, Ingold takes a painting by Pieter Bruegel the Elder of 1565, *The Harvesters*, suggesting that we understand the landscape that is represented in that painting, not merely as something experienced visually, but in terms of a set of actions and involvements relating the various elements—hills and valley, paths and tracks, tree, corn, church and people—that appear within the work.[18] As Ingold sees it, landscape is to be construed in terms of a confluence of influences and interactions; it is essentially temporal and historical, and this applies, so his analysis of Bruegel would seem to suggest, even when we look to the landscapes that appear in art.

This latter point is an important one, since one might be tempted to say of Ingold that his account simply misses the point that "landscape" can refer both to an artistic form—the form exemplified by the works of Bruegel as well as Glover that we have just seen—as well as to that which those artistic forms aim to depict or represent. Whereas Ingold is interested in what is depicted as it is itself constituted—that is, in the landscape as it is lived—Daniels and Cosgrove are interested in the nature of the depiction. Yet, of course, part of Ingold's argument is that we can only understand the depiction if we understand what it depicts; moreover, in arguing against the idea of landscape as spectatorial, he is also taking issue with the conception of landscape as indeed primarily based in a "representational" or spectatorial relation to the world, and as therefore inevitably associated with a backward-looking conservatism.

Ingold's argument is not based in a misconstrual of the issues at stake here, and what he advances is not merely a claim about the nature of the "lived" as opposed to the "represented" landscape, but rather concerns the relation between the two. Much the same conclusion as that reached by Ingold can also be arrived at, however, by a slightly different route. Even considered in relation to artistic production alone, landscape does not first appear only in terms of visual depiction. The landscape artist is indeed typically concerned with a certain view, a view that is already given in her own appreciation of a stretch of country or a particular scene, and with the representing of that view. Strictly speaking, however, this means that landscape art, and especially landscape painting, should not be construed as merely the presentation of a view, but as rather the view *of a view*; hence its properly representational—which need not yet mean "spectatorial"—character. But the very possibility of such a view in the first place already depends on having a place, and so an experience, that is within the landscape so viewed. Every such "view" is of this character: It always already depends on an involvement and orientation with respect to some particular place or locale. Landscape as art derives from such involvement and orientation, and is a representation of it—although *as* a representation, so it also presents only a certain view of that original and originary involvement.

This point is perhaps best illustrated by looking to the work of landscape artists themselves. If we return to John Glover, for instance, and specifically to the paintings from the period after his arrival in what was then Van Dieman's Land, in 1832, one sees a body of work that is directly connected with specific sites and reflects his own increasing engagement with the Tasmanian landscape—although as such, it is *his* engagement that is primarily evident here, with all that entails. Glover wrote that "there is a thrilling and graceful play in the landscape of this country which is more difficult to do justice to than the landscapes of England."[19] Part of the significance of Glover's work for the history of Australian art, a significance for which David Hansen persuasively argues,[20] is that unlike many other early artists who attempted to render the Australian landscape in European terms, Glover seems to have been much more open to the influence of the landscape in which he found himself. The works Glover painted in Tasmania were thus not the product of a passing and detached "view" of the landscape, but of a sustained interaction with it, an interaction based in his own living and working in that landscape (a living and working itself tied, of course, to his socioeconomic status as a free settler and landowner—and so also reflective and expressive of it with all the sociopolitical consequences that entails), as well as his artistic engagement.

The connection between the work of the landscape artist and involvement in the landscape itself is also evident in the life and work of one of Glover's now more famous contemporaries, John Constable, whose work was almost exclusively focused around places in his native East Anglia, and who is a major focus for Casey's discussion. There is no difficulty in finding other such examples. One of the most notable can be seen in the engagement between that central figure in the history of modern painting, Paul Cézanne, and the landscape of Provence to which his work is inextricably bound. As Cézanne writes, "within us they have not gone to sleep for ever, the vibrating sensations reflected by this good soil of Provence, the old memories of our youth, of these horizons, of these landscapes, of these unbelievable lines which leave in us so many deep impressions."[21] For Cézanne, the landscape that he paints is not a terrain standing apart from him, nor is his engagement with it that of the detached spectator. In his paintings of Provence, Cézanne undertakes an exploration of his own experience, his own memories, his own self. Casey directs our attention to examples from Chinese art, specifically to landscape painting from the pre-Han (1030–256 B.C.E.) and Northern Sung periods (960–1120 C.E.). Here, as in Cézanne, there is an explicit sense of art as arising directly out of the artist's own involvement in the landscape, and Casey quotes the painters Kuo Hsi, who tells us that "An artist should identify himself with the landscape and watch it until its signification is revealed to him,"[22] and Shen Kua, who writes that the great painters of previous centuries "had streams and rocks in their vitals, and clouds and mists as chronic illnesses."[23] In this latter respect, the experience of landscape, both as that on which the artist draws and is also represented in the work, is as much of wind and sun, hill and plain, sound and smell, as well as the movement and feel of a place, as of anything purely visual. Thus Seamus Heaney's two-line evocation of an Irish village: "Inishbofin on a Sunday morning / Sunlight, turfsmoke, seagulls, boatslip, diesel"[24] is as much a work of the representation of a landscape (and one that is, it should be noted, not restricted to the landscape of nature), as is any simple visual portrayal.

Raymond Williams and others aside, then, there is a significant sense in which landscape does not imply separation or observation, but quite the reverse. Moreover, while the emphasis is on human responsiveness rather than active engagement, the idea that landscape is no less about connection than separation is already present even in conventional theories of landscape such as to be found in the work of Kenneth Clarke, who writes that "Landscape painting . . . depends . . . on the unconscious response of the whole being to the world which surrounds him."[25] Landscape only arises as landscape out of our original involvement with the place in which we find ourselves as that place affects and influences us through its sound, smells, feelings, and sights, and also, we might say, through our own, and others', actions. The artistic representation of landscape, just because it is a *re*presentation, may itself allow a certain distance from the landscape so presented, but the appearance of landscape as landscape in the first instance, and its capacity to engage our attention is itself based in the prior engagement out of which the experience of landscape arises. Much of the interest in our own engagement with landscape art is surely in coming to understand the modes of engagement that particular works may present to us—modes of engagement that always possess multiple aspects, both dark and light, and that are revelatory of ourselves as well as the places they present.

IV

To experience a landscape is to be active within it, since it is by means of such activity that landscape affects and influences us—the nature of the place determines what is possible within that place. Understanding landscapes means understanding the forms of action out of which they arise, to which they give expression, and to which they may also contribute. It is thus that landscape finds its connection to structures of power and authority, as well as to modes of self-formation and identity, of topographical exploration and articulation. In this respect, all landscape already presupposes involvement in it and influence by it. In fact, what is properly represented in the artistic representing of landscape is a not a mere representing of a scene or mere "view," but rather a representing of the particular influence and involvement—different in each case—of the landscape (and of the place) in the life and modes of life that arise within and in relation to it.

The founder of American landscape studies J. B. Jackson writes that "it is only when we begin to participate emotionally in a landscape that its uniqueness and beauty are revealed to us."[26] This seems to me to be fundamentally correct, although I would add, and I think Jackson would agree, that such emotional participation is itself always based in the full engagement of the senses and of action. Indeed, in the same essay, Jackson writes that:

This is how we should think of landscapes: not merely how they look, how they conform to an aesthetic ideal, but how they satisfy elementary needs: the need for sharing some of those sensory experiences in a familiar place: popular songs, popular dishes, a special kind of weather supposedly found nowhere else, a special kind of sport or game, played only here in this spot. These things remind us that we belong—or used to belong—to a specific place: a country, a town, a neighborhood. A landscape should establish bonds between people, the bond of language, of manners, of the same kind of work and leisure, and above all a landscape should contain the kind of spatial organization which fosters such experiences and relationships; spaces for coming together, to celebrate, spaces for solitude, spaces that never change and are always as memory depicted them. These are some of the characteristics that give a landscape its uniqueness, that give it style. These are what make us recall it with emotion. Not necessarily agreeable emotion: the military landscape provided us with a spatial order dedicated to sudden and violent movement, a set of relationships based on total subordination and anonymity, and a sensory experience based on death and the premonition of death; it was the ugly caricature of a landscape. Nevertheless, it functioned, and even its horrors instructed us in what a good landscape, and a good social order, should be.[27]

If landscape is always a mode of involvement that encompasses us and our world, then in landscape art it is that prior involvement, and the mode of that involvement, that is represented to us—and what it represents will likely include a set of social and political elements as much of anything that is purely "aesthetic." Moreover, precisely because it aims to represent that mode of prior involvement in a way that thematizes it in particular ways—and so presents a particular *formation* of landscape (every landscape can be understood as a formation of landscape)—so it will almost inevitably present that involvement in a way that reinforces certain relations of meaningfulness, certain ways of seeing or modes of revelation, certain structures of power and authority.

The way in which the representation of landscape constitutes an articulation of our prior modes of involvement with place is evident even in the construal of landscape as wilderness that is so prevalent within much contemporary Australian and North American engagement with landscape. Jackson himself argues that the American conservation movement has its origins in a frontiersman mythology and rhetoric that posited a idealized conception of forest and woodland tied to an idealized conception of the relation between the human and the natural, and so to an idealized conception of place and our relation to it. One of Jackson's concerns is that the tendency for the preoccupation with and valorization of wilderness landscapes leads to a misconstrual of our proper relation to landscape, to a neglect of certain forms of landscape, especially the urban, and so to a certain detachment from the actual places in which we live.

There can no doubt that one of the problematic aspects of the idea of landscape as wilderness is the way in which it sometimes seems to reinforce the very conception of landscape that I have been arguing against—of landscape as based in the separated and narrowly "spectatorial." Wilderness landscapes are often presented as standing resolutely apart from the human, and, to some extent, this is given additional emphasis by the enormous popular impact of wilderness photography. The work of photographic artists such as Olegas Truchanas and Peter Dombrovskis in Australia (two notable chroniclers of the Tasmanian wilderness), and of Ansel Adams in the United States (whose images of Yosemite, in particular, have had such an impact on the popular imagination), while indisputably of great artistic and political significance, also continues a tradition of artistic engagement with wilderness that can be seen, whether deliberately or not, to emphasize the natural to the exclusion of the human, and thereby to stress the apartness of wilderness landscapes, and sometimes, even, their apparently timeless (if nonetheless vulnerable) character. Significantly, the way in which the works of such as Truchanas or Adams function in this way is not merely through their visual-representational character, but also (as writers such as Mitchell, for instance, would surely stress) through the specific manner in which the subject matter is framed, and especially, in the case of wilderness photography, through the absence of any reference to the human within the work (unless it be the very absence of the human).

This mode of presentation of the wilderness landscape often feeds into a position according to which the only possible way of responding to wilderness is to preserve it in as pristine a condition as possible, and this may extend into an attitude to the landscape in general that tries to isolate it from human activity—Raymond Williams's emphasis on landscape as indeed spectatorial in character may thus be seen to return in perhaps unexpected fashion. Yet such a view of wilderness, and of landscape with it, gives rise to a deep contradiction between the self-evidently human character of wilderness itself (even the grounding of wilderness in a certain form of human experience), and the desire to maintain wilderness as something apart from the human, as well as between the desire for perpetuation of wilderness as it now is, and the character of landscape, including wilderness landscape, as a changeable and changing form.[28] Thus, the specific case of wilderness art seems to embody, in especially clear terms, the more general tension that arises between the supposedly spectatorial character of landscape and its underlying character as reflecting our own engagement in and with landscape, in and with place.

Inasmuch as all landscape presupposes involvement and influence between the human and the natural (so that these categories lose any absolute character), then landscape may be said only to become landscape through the way in which it is implicated in human lives as both affected and affecting. Even the wilderness landscape is made what it is, as wilderness, through the way in which it establishes a certain set of human interactions in relation to it and the way in which those interactions themselves establish the particular form of landscape that is wilderness. This is not to say that landscape is somehow a construction of the human—as if it were some form of cultural or social artifact. Although it is true that even the landscapes we most often think of as natural are typically products of the interaction between human, environmental, and other factors,[29] this does not mean that the human somehow plays the determining role here.

Landscape may be shaped by human involvement, but the human is itself shaped by landscape, and neither has the upper hand in this relationship—each is appropriated by and to the other. This is a large part of what lies behind Ingold's rejection of a purely spectatorial conception of landscape and his insistence that the human and the natural are not opposed, and that nor is landscape something that is either purely natural or purely constructed.[30] For this reason, too, we cannot think of landscape as merely that within which human activity is located and in which human lives are played out—as if it were merely some form of stage set, a very well-painted one to be sure, against which we act. Instead, landscape is, as W. J. T. Mitchell writes, "the medium in which we live, and move, and have our being, and where we are destined, ultimately, to return."[31]

As landscape will take on different forms according to the nature of the involvement that is contained within it and that it both expresses and enables, so the way in which landscape comes into art will also vary according to such involvement. Vincent Scully, in the passages I quoted earlier, talks about the way in which the Greek experience of and involvement in landscape shifts from the archaic and classical periods onward. Scully's claim is that the experience of landscape is not absent from archaic and classical Greek culture, but that it takes a form that is very different from its explicit thematization in nature poetry and landscape painting. Instead, the representation of landscape is achieved through acting architecturally or sculpturally, we might say, upon the landscape itself. Thus, Scully writes that:

The mountains and valleys of Greece were punctuated during antiquity by hard white forms, touched with bright colors, which stood in geometric contrast to the shapes of the earth. These were the temples of the gods. . . . the temples were not normally intended to shelter men within their walls. Instead they housed the image of a god, immortal and therefore separate from men, and were themselves an image, in the landscape, of his qualities. . . . the temples and the subsidiary buildings of their sanctuaries were so formed themselves and so placed in relation to the landscape and to each other as to enhance, develop, complement, and sometimes even to contradict, the basic meaning of what was felt in the land.[32]

In Greek temple construction, then, we seem to have an art form that establishes and articulates not separation between the human and the landscape, but rather their necessary interconnection. This is not to say, of course, that such an outcome was itself an explicit element in the design that lay behind Greek temple construction, nor is the mode of relation or the manner of its expression one that can be understood as given in "picturesque" or aesthetic terms. The form and placement of the Greek temple was undoubtedly determined by more immediate considerations, including those deriving from topography, engineering, religion, and politics. Yet these considerations can be understood as themselves already shaped in and through the landscape, in the broadest sense, the place—which must here be understood to include both the *polis* and its *chora*[33]—within which Greek life was situated, and in which the temple was itself sited. Moreover, one might also argue that this more prosaic, but also more fundamental, sense of the relatedness to place was itself something embedded within Greek thought as such. To repeat the words of the Greek philosopher Archytus: "to be is to be in place."[34]

The experience of landscape, and its articulation in art, need not take any one form. Moreover, similar forms may also arise in quite different ways. Indeed, within the European tradition the recognition of landscape, and of its importance to us, often arises out of certain forms of dislocation in relation to landscape in general, or to specific and otherwise familiar such landscapes. One comes to understand and to know a landscape through movement within it, and often one comes to understand and know a landscape as a landscape through the journey "there and back again" that takes one from one landscape to another—from the familiar to the strange and from the strange to the familiar—or that shifts elements of the landscape itself. In this respect the dislocation and disruption of the traditional landscape, especially in England, that occurred in the seventeenth, eighteenth, and nineteenth centuries is indeed an important element in the rise of landscape art and landscape appreciation over that period. Recognition of this point also enables us better to understand why it is that landscape is associated, in so much contemporary discussion, with a detached and spectatorial gaze.

In contemporary Australia, the recognition of landscape, and the questioning of what it may be and what it may signify, has often been directly tied to the changes in the way in which the landscape is brought into salience through journey and return, whether it be the journey and return that occur within the landscape through processes of disruption and change, or the journey and return that occur as individuals, and sometimes whole communities, move within landscapes, across country, between places. This is so both for the European experience of landscape and also the indigenous. While indigenous Australians have always engaged in the representing of place through rock art, and the construction of topographic and other patterns using sand, rock, and other natural materials, the rise of a distinctive indigenous practice of landscape art, and especially painting, has arisen through the interaction with European art practice, materials, and styles—and also, perhaps, because of the challenge to indigenous conceptions and culture that European culture brings with it. Yet perhaps what is most notable about recent and contemporary indigenous Australian landscape depiction is the way in which it too involves a mode of representing that derives from a particular mode of emplacement in "country," in the landscape. Kathleen Petyarre's work, for instance, which often employs patterns and delicate shadings composed of multiple dots and lines, is often compared to that of abstractionist painters such as Mark Rothko.[35] What is most interesting in the present context, however, is less the character of abstraction in the work than the way the work derives from a particular way of experiencing and understanding the landscape as such—as Ian North puts it, what Petyarre offers through her painting is "a complex, energized reading of the land in its multiple dimensions."[36] Work such as Petyarre's is based in indigenous representings of the fundamental elements of landscape—of "country"—and of totemic figures within the landscapes—waterholes, animal tracks and trails, hills, rocks, seeds, the fall of rain, and so on. If this gives rise to a mode of abstraction, it is a mode of abstraction based in the concrete.

"Landscape," whether we understand it as referring to the lived country or to the created work, is always a matter of active involvement and experience. It may sometimes, as a form of art or a theoretical concept, arise out of a feeling of separation or an experience of dislocation, but our involvement with landscape, and so with the places that are found within it, is fundamental to the way we find ourselves in the world. In our engagement with landscape through art we also, therefore, engage with our own mode of being in the world. In the case of an artist like John Glover, this engagement with the landscape is, as I noted earlier, evident in his art in important and surprising ways. Glover's Tasmanian work takes on a character that is not matched by European landscape of the same period—having originally worked within the format of the Claudean "picturesque," Glover's Tasmanian paintings develop a character that appears quite distinctive.

In the very late painting, *"Cawood" on the Ouse River*, from 1838, we see a landscape that, as David Hansen points out, is not merely the

Figure 1.2
John Glover, *"Cawood" on the Ouse River*, 1838. Oil on canvas laid down on board
75.5 × 114 cm. Tasmanian Museum and Art Gallery, Hobart.

transplantation of the English or European to the Southern hemisphere,
but instead offers a new and open, and more idiosyncratically "antipodean" vision.[37] There is no doubt that one can find political or even
ideological elements in this work (if my argument is correct, then such elements will be inevitable); but there is also a new experience, a new set of
possibilities, a new "world" that is presented to us.

In the encounter with landscape, and with place through landscape,
we do not merely encounter something apart from ourselves, but rather
we come into contact with the place in and through which we ourselves
come into being. As the contemporary landscape and new media artist
Char Davies says of her immersive virtual environments *Osmose* (1995)
and *Ephémère* (1998), "I see [them] as a means of return, i.e., of facilitating
a temporary release from our habitual perceptions and culturally-biased
assumptions about being in the world, to enable us, however momentarily, to perceive ourselves and the world around us freshly."[38] Davies's
"virtual" landscapes thus function to reengage us with the world rather
than separate us from it, although they do so through an engagement with

a landscape that is indeed created by means of digital technology. Landscape as it appears in Davies's work is thus very different from previous traditions of landscape art—very different from the art we encounter in Glover's work—and yet it is nonetheless continuous with it.[39] Moreover, inasmuch as part of what occurs in landscape art, including art such as that of both Davies and Glover, is the exploration and representation of our own interaction, and our mutual constitution, in and through place, so such art is concerned with the fundamental character of what it is to be human as well as of the nature of place itself.

V

What, then, of the "problem" of landscape to which I referred at the beginning of this chapter? The contemporary Tasmanian artist Jonathan Kimberley writes of landscape that

The term "landscape" is symbolic of an outmoded cultural paradigm, and is no longer adequate to describe the complexity of relationships that people have with place in Australia. Something more reciprocal exists at the interstices and intersections of landscape and non-landscape conceptions of place.[40]

Kimberley's comments reflect a widespread view of landscape among many contemporary artists and critics—not least of whom is perhaps W. J. T. Mitchell.[41] It is, however, a view of landscape that I would, to some extent, contest.

The problem of landscape arises precisely because landscape, whether it appears in literary or painterly form, whether thought of in terms of the presented or that which presents, is indeed a function, and a representing, of our relationship with place. Is the term "landscape" inadequate to describe the complexity of that relationship? If we treat landscape purely in terms of the narrowly spectatorial and the detached (or as associated with a single historical formation or artistic genre), then perhaps it is. Yet the argument I have advanced here is that this conception of landscape is itself inadequate to describe the complexity of landscape as such. The problem of landscape is thus that landscape represents to us, not only our relationship with place, but also the problematic nature of that relationship—a relationship that contains within it involvement and separation, agency and spectacle, self and other. It is in and through landscape, in its many forms, that our relationship with place is articulated and represented, and the problematic character of that relationship made evident. In this respect, the continued engagement with landscape, including that by artists such as Kimberley, is indicative of its continuing significance, even if the mode of that engagement—its style and conventions—has changed, and even if the meaning of "landscape" as a term of artistic practice can no longer be taken for granted.

In a painting such as Glover's *Mount Wellington and Hobart Town from Kangaroo Point*, both the problematic character of landscape *and* its continuing significance are revealed to us through the way in which what appears there, whether deliberately presented or implicitly invoked, encompasses a multiplicity of perspectives—the real and the imagined, the present and the absent, the remote and the near, the remembered and the forgotten— rendered into the singleness of a view. In such a painting—such a work of pictorial representation—we are presented not merely with something that stands apart from us, but, if we choose to attend to what is there, with a mode of relatedness in which we are inextricably implicated; not merely the simple appearance of a single place, but something of the complex working of placedness as such—something of the complex and multiple happening of landscape. Landscape is indeed like revelation: like revelation, landscape draws things together, connects them, allows them to appear; like revelation, landscape also hides things, removes them, obscures them from view; like revelation, landscape is both singular crystal and the remotest things. Landscape is where we find, and also lose, ourselves.

Notes

1. "The Mystery of the Charity of Charles Péguy," in Geoffrey Hill, *Collected Poems* (Harmondsworth: Penguin, 1985), p. 188.

2. This second reading is not entirely inconsistent with the first. While the juxtaposition of the European and the Aboriginal could be seen as an acknowledgment of prior occupation, it can equally be seen (and perhaps should be seen) as an assertion of the European over the Aboriginal—as an assertion of current possession. On this general theme in Australian and New Zealand art, see Nicholas Thomas, *Possessions: Indigenous Art/Colonial Culture* (London: Thames & Hudson, 1999).

3. See W. J. T. Mitchell, *Landscape and Power* (Chicago: University of Chicago Press, 1994; 2nd ed., 2002).

4. Edward S. Casey, *Re-Presenting Place: Landscape Painting and Maps* (Minneapolis: University of Minnesota Press, 2002), p. 271.

5. See, for instance, chapters 4 and 5 of my *Place and Experience* (Cambridge: Cambridge University Press, 1999). Although this issue is approached there from a rather different direction, the main claim that is developed is that all experience presupposes activity, since all experience presupposes a complex grasp of spatial and other relations that can only be worked out in and through embodied agency.

6. This sense of separation arises, first, from the fact that vision does not require immediate physical proximity (unlike touch), and, second, that it seems to lack the same quality of internalization or of envelopment that may obtain in relation to some other forms of sensory engagement (taste, smell, sound, proprioception). One must, however, remain cautious about such phenomenological distinctions between senses, since often apparent phenomenological differences are actually reflective more of particular modes of habituation than of anything specific to the senses as such.

7. Of course, the same point might be made in relation to the spectatorial—that it too only arises out of a mode of prior engagement that is not purely one of passive observation. Rather than undermining the argument, however, this point reinforces it—even if it also complicates the matter. Of course, while the visual always implicates more than the visual alone, this does not rule out the possibility that, in at least some cases, undue emphasis may be placed on the mode of visual presentation to the exclusion of others. I have argued elsewhere that this often occurs in architecture (see my 'Truth in Architecture' forthcoming), and that it is problematic precisely because of the way in which it is actually in tension with the character of the architectural as such—architecture thus appears as if it operated primarily visually, when, in fact, it encompasses a complex of sensory and spatial modes. On the other hand, the visuality of, for instance, landscape painting is not in tension with the character of such painting—painting is, indeed, a primarily visual mode of presentation—and the visuality of the painting need not imply a separation of the visual from other modes. Where the visuality of painting becomes problematic is precisely in those instances in which it is presented as separated and detached– where painting is construed in *narrowly* 'spectatorial' terms.

8. Raymond Williams, *The Country and the City* (London: Chatto & Windus, 1973), p. 120. He goes on: "It is possible and useful to trace the internal histories of landscape painting, and landscape writing, landscape gardening and landscape architecture, but in the final analysis we must relate these histories to the common history of a land and its society." His point, of course, is that it is common history, rather than landscape as such, that is crucial here (although one might ask to what extent history can be divorced from the landscape to which it belongs or the landscape from the history).

9. Stephen Daniels and Denis Cosgrove, "Introduction: Iconography and Landscape," in *The Iconography of Landscape: Essays on the Symbolic Representation, Design, and Use of Past Environments*, ed. Denis Cosgrove and Stephen Daniels (Cambridge: Cambridge University Press, 1988), p. 1.

10. Enzo Carli, *The Landscape in Art* (New York: William Morrow, 1980), p. 17.

11. Ann Bermingham, *Landscape and Ideology: The English Rustic Tradition, 1740–1860* (Berkeley: University of California Press, 1986).

12. John Barrell, *The Idea of Landscape and the Sense of Place, 1730–1840: An Approach to the Poetry of John Clare* (Cambridge: Cambridge University Press, 1972).

13. See John Berger, *Ways of Seeing* (Harmondsworth: Penguin, 1972).

14. See, once again, Nicholas Thomas, *Possessions*, for an exploration of the way this problematic can be seen to play out in visual art, including contemporary art, in the "settler" societies of Australia and New Zealand.

15. There is a larger issue here that affects more than just the idea of landscape. "Place" itself, and the idea of attachment to place, is commonly taken to bring with it a fundamentally conservative orientation—such attachment is supposed, for instance, to lead inevitably to an exclusionary and often violent politics. My argument here can thus be seen as a small part in a larger project aimed at a "defense" of place, and the concepts, like that of landscape, that are associated with it—a defense that aims at showing both the impossibility of any abandonment of place and the necessity of attending to place as a key element in the articulation of a viable, and also "progressive," ethics or politics—see my *Ethos and Topos: On the Ethics and Politics of Place*, in preparation. This is not to say, of course, that ideas of place and landscape will always and only be deployed in politically benign ways. The very significance of place means that it will be called upon as a key element in political and ethical discourse of every shade. Indeed, only if we recognize the significance of place can we understand the power that can be exerted through it.

16. Vincent Scully, *The Earth, the Temple, and the Gods: Greek Sacred Architecture* (New Haven: Yale University Press, 1962), p. 2.

17. Tim Ingold, "The Temporality of the Landscape," in *The Perception of the Environment: Essays on Livelihood, Dwelling, Skill* (London: Routledge, 2000), p. 191.

18. Ibid., p. 204; the temporal character of the painting is also indicated by the way in which the work includes within it a series of activities that encompass different aspects of daily human life: working, eating, playing, resting. These activities are portrayed in a roughly circular order within the space of the painting.

19. John Glover, handwritten note on "View of Mills Plains, Van Diemen's Land," Art Gallery of South Australia.

20. See David Hansen, "The Life and Work of John Glover," in *John Glover and the Colonial Picturesque* (Hobart: Tasmanian Museum and Art Gallery, 2003).

21. "Letter to Henri Gasquet, Paris, 3 June, 1899," *Paul Cézanne Letters*, 4th ed., ed. John Rewald (New York: Da Capo, 1976), p. 271; see also Philip Conisbee and Denis Coutagne (with contributions from others), *Cézanne in Provence* (New Haven: Yale University Press, 2006).

22. Kuo Hsi, *An Essay on Landscape Painting*, trans. S. Sakanishi (London: Murray, 1949), p. 38, quoted in Casey, *Representing Place*, p. 107.

23. Shen Kua, citing the biography of the seventh-century painter Ti'en Yu-yen, in *Early Chinese Texts on Painting*, ed. Susan Bush and Hsio-yen Shih (Cambridge, MA: Harvard University Press, 1985), p. 120, quoted in Casey, *Representing Place*, p. 107.

24. Seamus Heaney, "Seeing Things," *Seeing Things* (London: Faber & Faber, 1991), p. 16.

25. Kenneth Clarke, *Landscape into Art* (London: Reader's Union/John Murray, 1953), p. 134.

26. John B. Jackson, "Learning About Landscapes," in *The Necessity for Ruins* (Amherst: University of Massachusetts Press, 1980), p. 18.

27. Ibid., pp. 16–17.

28. In so doing it may also give rise to problematic forms of politics—it may, for instance, involve the implicit denial of the claims of indigenous peoples to the landscapes declared as wild; it may function to reinforce rigid oppositions between the interests of conservation as against those of "development."

29. See, for instance, Simon Schama's discussion of Yosemite National Park as the archetypal wilderness that is nevertheless the product of human activity—*Landscape and Memory* (London: HarperCollins, 1995), pp. 7–9.

30. See also Ingold's discussion in "The Temporality of Landscape," pp. 190–193, and his emphasis on the way landscape relates to embodiment.

31. W. J. T. Mitchell, *Landscape and Power* (2002), p. xii. In a discussion that also tries to do justice to both the political problem of landscape and its continuing significance, Stephen Muecke seems to arrive at a similar conclusion, if by a somewhat different route, to which is evident here—see Muecke, *Ancient and Modern: Time, Culture, and Indigenous Philosophy* (Sydney: UNSW Press, 2004), pp. 71–79.

32. Scully, *The Earth, the Temple, and the Gods*, pp. 2–3. See also Robin Francis Rhodes, *Architecture and Meaning on the Athenian Acropolis* (Cambridge: Cambridge University Press, 1995), pp. 10–18. Like Scully, Rhodes does not invoke any picturesque notions here, but is instead concerned with the power that landscape seems to carry with it, and the way that power is expressed in and through the temple site—although Rhodes also acknowledges other factors, including past settlement and construction, in temple construction.

33. The relation between these too is particularly important in the understanding of the complexity of Greek sacred architecture—see, for instance, Susan Guettel Cole, "Demeter in the Ancient Greek City and Its Countryside," in *Placing the Gods: Sanctuaries and Sacred Space in Ancient Greece*, ed. Susan E. Alcock and Robin Osbourne (Oxford: Clarendon Press, 1994), pp. 199–216.

34. The line is repeated by Aristotle in *Physics* IV—see Edward S. Casey, *Getting Back into Place: Toward a Renewed Understanding of the Place-World* (Bloomington: Indiana University Press, 1993), p. 14.

35. See, for instance, the reproductions in Christine Nicholls and Ian North, *Kathleen Petyarre: Genius of Place* (Kent Town, South Australia: Wakefield Press, 2001), p.

82. The delicacy of the works makes them unsuitable to the purely monochrome reproduction available here.

36. Ian North, "The Kindness of Kathleen Petyarre," in *Kathleen Petyarre: Genius of Place*, p. 82.

37. See David Hansen, "The Life and Work of John Glover," p. 227; see also p. 98.

38. Char Davies, "Virtual Space," in *Space: In Science, Art, and Society*, ed. François Penz, Gregory Radick, and Robert Howell (Cambridge: Cambridge University Press, 2004), p. 69.

39. Davies's current work continues the concern with landscape, but whereas previously her work had focused on the creation of immersive virtual landscapes, it is the very land itself, and especially the land comprising the property that she has named "Reverie," that is her main focus. Although Davies sees her own work as aiming to shift our engagement with landscape away from a narrowly spectatorial perspective, and on to a fully immersive engagement, it can also be read, in the manner I read it here, as a rethinking of landscape as such, and a demonstration of its continuing significance.

40. Kimberley, *Jonathan Kimberley—Ur-Landscape: Post-Landscape (Blue Tier)*, exhibition catalog (Hobart: Bett Gallery, 2005).

41. Kimberley's comments can be seen to echo Mitchell's claim (in "Imperial Landscape," in Mitchell, *Landscape and Power*, p. 5) that "Landscape is an exhausted medium, no longer viable as a mode of artistic expression" (Thesis 8 in the "Theses on Landscape" with which Mitchell's essay begins), although Mitchell also makes clear that the term "landscape" as it figures in this claim means "a particular historical formation associated with European imperialism" (Thesis 6). One way of reading Mitchell's position is to take it as actually rendering uncertain the very idea of landscape—in spite of the historical specificity that he also takes to be associated with it. Thus, rather than say that "landscape" is now an empty term, one might ask what landscape might now mean given the exhaustion of landscape as "a particular historical formation associated with European imperialism."

2 "Landscape" as a Kind of Place-Relation

Wesley A. Kort

Consider Ishmael. He begins, in *Moby-Dick*,[1] with comments on the lures of water, especially vast water. Denizens of "your insular city of the Manhattoes," he tells us, are drawn by water from their daily places, "pent up in lath and plaster—tied to counters, nailed to benches, clinched to desks." Why?—Water "is the image of the ungraspable phantom of life; and this is the key to it all."[2]

Ishmael launches his narrative this way to explain why he is drawn, especially in melancholy states, to the sea. He is also luring the reader into his tale, one that, though vicariously, takes the reader out on the oceans that encompass human societies. He is appealing to what he takes to be a common impulse or need, namely, to exchange relations to social and personal spaces for a relation to the natural, comprehensive context of human life. Ishmael does not immediately explain the irresistible attraction that draws "landsmen" to the sea and why he finds so many people standing close to water and gazing out at it. But later the reader is told that the exchange of a relation to social sites for a relation to comprehensive space is so compelling because it corresponds to an internal exchange of a secure for a truer self: "so in the soul of man there lies one insular Tahiti, full of peace and joy, but encompassed by all the horrors of the half-known life."[3] For Ishmael and for Melville, persons require place-relations not only to social "Manhattoes" and personal Tahitis but also to a capacious and ungraspable natural space, and they will not be satisfied until their potential for that kind of place-relation is actualized.

Although Melville's assumption of a correspondence between the vastness of the sea and the potential of human internality is a noticeably Romantic one, it is also a realization of something basic about persons or groups and their environments. Locations are not simply incidental or instrumental. They have consequences both of force and meaning for persons and groups. People, then, have relations to places, relations, as

Jeff Malpas has made clear, that contribute to personal and group identity and are analogous to the relations that persons and groups have to one another.[4] Although relations to places can, like relations to other people, be negative, they are, in and for states of human well-being, positive.

The kind of place-relation to which Melville defers is comprehensive and natural. To suggest its positive qualities, it could also be called "landscape" or, in this instance, "seascape." "Landscape," often standing as background, can, while being positive in its relation to human well-being, yield to more particular human relations and places. However, attention can and even needs to be given to it. "Landscape" connotes a particular but comprehensive space that is given, that supports human activities, that is worthy of an attention that it does not often receive, and that, as Malpas puts it, "does not entail a dispersion of elements, but rather enables their 'gathering together'—their interconnection and unification."[5]

The question raised by Melville's great epic of the sea and its relation to human potential is whether or not "landscape" can still be suggestive of a relation to natural space. Increasingly we live in a humanly constructed and controlled world, and it becomes common to refer to social, political space as comprehensive. One speaks, for example, of "urban landscapes," and rightly so. People can feel included in a spatiality that is vast and unifying and has positive effects on personal well-being but also is humanly constructed and maintained. However, I think that it is important to see that Melville's evocation of natural space as the comprehensive setting of human potential and interests has a strong and complicated culture behind it. We should, however briefly, reconstruct those cultural warrants and then ask why this kind of space or place-relation has become questionable in our own, late-modern time. We then will be in a position to ask whether we can retain or retrieve natural, comprehensive place-relations in and for the repertoire of human spatiality. Can we restore or, at least, project a connection between landscape and a human potential, if not need, for relations with comprehensive natural spaces?

I

Melville, in his orientation to the natural context of human life, is a recipient of two cultural strands that have a single source. The two strands are a Calvinist or Reformed doctrine of scripture, and modern culture's orientation to nature as both an object of study and a moral/spiritual resource. These two strands find a single source in interests of the sixteenth century epitomized by the work of Francis Bacon.

Bacon took Calvin's doctrine of scripture, which is a doctrine not of the text or of its origins but of reading scripture, and applied that theory of reading to the reading of nature. Nature already was well established as a text to be read. The trope of nature as a book came into Renaissance culture from classical and medieval sources, and it was taken up by Calvinists early on. The Belgic Confession of 1561, for example, refers to "the creation, preservation, and government of the universe" as "a most elegant book," which can be read for contemplating the "invisible things of God, namely, his eternal power and Godhead." The belief in nature as a second scripture offering knowledge of God was not something Calvinists invented but something they emphasized. This they did because the Old Testament generally and the Wisdom literature of the Old Testament particularly had an important place in Calvin's work and subsequent applications of it, and this textual location grounded the strong doctrine of Creation for which Calvinism, in comparison to other forms of Protestant theology, such as Lutheran and Anabaptist, is noted.

Among the many characteristics of Wisdom literature in the Old Testament, a particularly noticeable one is an emphasis on the natural context of human life as a locus of divine wisdom and a text of moral instruction for its readers. The student of Proverbs, for example, is led to observe natural creatures. Job is told to consider the cosmos and animal life in order to come to some sense of divine power. Nature in the wisdom literature, then, is a text, and reading it is a moral and spiritual discipline. Bacon altered or expanded this practice in two ways. First, he applied, as I said, the theory of reading embedded in Calvin's doctrine of scripture to reading nature. Second, he elevated reading nature to a level equivalent to reading the Bible as scripture. That is, reading nature as scripture was not for Bacon secondary or optional but primary and necessary if one is to form an adequate understanding of who God is and who human beings, as part of the Creation, are.

In his implied theory of reading nature as scripture, Bacon, following Calvin's doctrine of reading scripture, is a minimalist. Reading nature brings to attention and makes available the basic laws by which the world was created and is maintained. In addition, as for Calvin, Bacon sees this kind of reading as undercutting the primacy of human authorities, institutions, and assumptions. Reading nature is not determined by ecclesiastical and philosophical directives; it even subverts, for Bacon, the authority of human language: "Here therefore is the first distemper of learning, when men study words and not matter . . . for words are but the images of matter; and except that they have life or reason and invention, to fall in love with them is all one as to fall in love with a picture."[6] Reading requires divestment of preconceptions, inherited understandings, and language itself for the sake of recognizing the traces of God left behind, so to speak, in the Creation and maintenance of the world. This knowledge is then applied to a more general understanding of the world, resulting in beneficial consequences for the reader and for society. Bacon compares these two sides of reading, concentration and extension or centripetal and centrifugal directions, to two conjoined planets, Saturn, the planet of contemplation, and Jupiter, the planet of action. Knowledge is drawn from nature and used for the "relief of man's estate."[7]

It is important to note that what subsequently happens to reading nature is that its standing becomes elevated above reading the Bible as scripture. One can see this in a transitional figure like John Locke, who had strong interests in reading the Bible but gave primacy to knowledge gained in experience or in reading nature. Reading the Bible, rather than reading nature, supplies certainty only in those areas that the reading of nature leaves as merely probable.[8] The primacy that Locke gives to the text of nature and the certainty to which that reading leads sets the conditions for reading the Bible as scripture. This shift of primacy allows for such directions as that which John Toland's *Christianity Not Mysterious* (1696) takes and that so many deists in the next century followed.

By the end of the eighteenth century, this exchange is complete and widespread in the culture. No clearer statement of it could be made than is made by Tom Paine's *The Age of Reason*. Paine believed that the Bible could not be read without the help of experts, especially clerics. Nature, in contrast, is open for everyone to read and to understand. Paine is addressing people for whom the appeal of anticlericalism, even outside Quaker circles, had acceptance, for whom democratic values were current issues, and for whom nature was, as well as a religious datum, a principal characteristic of and point of distinction for the new world. He finds his conclusion irresistible: "THE WORD OF GOD IS THE CREATION WE BEHOLD."[9] Paine's argument is notable not because he claims that nature should be read as scripture—this is part of the tradition—but because he rejects Bible reading for reading nature.

Meanwhile, within more orthodox Protestant circles, the doctrine of Creation continued as a warrant for referring to the natural context of human life as a text to be read from which knowledge of God could be gleaned. However, within those circles, the doctrine of Creation also loses ground to an increasing evangelical emphasis on the evil of this world, the judgment of God on it, and the redemptive work of Christ that delivers people from it. Biblical Wisdom literature, while it becomes more important for the culture, becomes less important for dominant Christian movements and loses its role as warranting the reading of nature as scripture. Whereas the doctrine of Creation is very important for someone like Jonathan Edwards, by the time we come to Melville a separation has occurred between Christianity, in its emphasis on sin and redemption, and religious interests that, though derived from Christianity, are oriented primarily if not exclusively to nature.

II

It is against this background that the cultural category of "landscape," especially when referring to paintings in the modern period, should be seen. Supporting the attention to the natural context of human life as deserving contemplation and artistic depiction is an additional stress in Calvinism, namely, Calvin's injunction that artists, rather than depicting invisible things, particularly religiously revered figures, should attend to visible things. This prohibition was motivated not only by fear of possible adoration of the depictions of spiritual figures but also and perhaps more by the recognition that these invisible realities would be subjugated to particular interpretations and fancies that would rob them of their freedom. Calvin's prohibition, joined with the positive assessment of nature, sponsors the cultural importance of landscape painting in the early modern period, especially in Calvinist cultures.

The emergence of the sublime as a normative spiritual/aesthetic category has the cultural interest in relations to natural settings behind it. Especially in response to vastness but also to the untamed in nature, the sublime, in its ineffability, captured while it also released a particular potential in natural scenes that gave to art and to viewing it a religious or, at least, spiritual force. It was the belief not so much in nature as in something to be read in nature needing to have its potential power and significance brought into focus by art that came to dominate. Nature is epitomized in art, and it is in art that nature's potentials can be actualized. The English Romantics approached the Lake District not directly but as mediated to them by such landscape painters as Salvator Rosa and his orientation to scenes of strange or picturesque aspect. And they themselves did not so much view and contemplate nature as capture it in their physical and conceptual/linguistic frames.

The incorporation of nature into art and poetry should be seen, I think, as a step toward the demise of natural space as the locus of human place-relations. Rather than giving attention to natural spaces that divested a person of confining expectations and preconceptions, as prescribed by Bacon and embodied in the tradition, nature was interpreted and mediated by artists and poets as kinds of cultural priests. But a more important process also sets in, one by which nature becomes national. Even in the Romantics, with their emphasis on the universality of nature and the experience of the sublime, we find an emphasis on English landscapes. Indeed, it is difficult to talk about landscape painting apart from its national setting, since landscapes are locations. Landscape, then, becomes incorporated by something that, while large, is also particular, namely the nation. Van Ruisdael's work is Dutch; John Constable's, though influenced by it, is English.

In his book on the importance of natural sites for formations of American identity in the new republic, John Sears describes natural pilgrimage sites in nineteenth-century America and the complex roles that they played. Sears begins his study with the opening, upon the completion of the Erie Canal in 1825, of access to Niagara Falls. This site, along with others later, especially Monmouth Cave and Yellowstone Park, was seen as a place powerfully revealing the handiwork of deity. Indeed, these natural places were viewed as religious sites that rivaled the cathedrals of Europe by possessing the added distinction of having been made by God (however much these locations were deliberately altered to enhance their assets). But pilgrimage to these sites was also a patriotic gesture because such sites were American and because, in the spirit of Tom Paine, they were open for all to see, democratic and religious at the same time. It is not difficult to see how easily natural settings could be read not so much as texts concerning the power and oversight of God but as attributes of the nation and causes for devotion to it.[10]

It is also to be noted that pilgrimage is a commodity that adds to the stature of those who undertake it. These pilgrimage sites also became something to be owned by reason of having visited them. For this reason, the gift shop at pilgrimage sites, as later at tourist attractions, is as important as the sites themselves, since mementoes can be purchased that not only testify to the fact that the person who owns them has actually been to the places, but also allow the person to take pieces of those places into his or her home. While tours, especially of Europe's religious, political, and cultural monuments, continue to be essential commodities for building and warranting social stature, visits to notable natural sites become an essential part of that ennobling repertoire.

As the Erie Canal granted access to Niagara Falls, so railroads, beginning in Britain, provided access to natural landscapes. Not only as destinations but also as vistas viewed in passing, landscapes became broadly available and more widely viewed. Indeed, as the paintings of Augustus Leopold Egg and, later, of Eric Ravilious make clear, natural vistas and train travel form a mutuality that, as Ian Carter shows, blurs the answer to the question of which of the two is more important.[11] It is not surprising, then, that trains, as farm implements or carriages earlier had been, could be incorporated into landscape painting.

More radical alterations occur when relations to natural landscapes are dominated by the quest for raw materials. In the gradual exchange from agricultural to industrial societies, especially in England, natural locations were viewed in terms of their potential industrial and commercial value. It is consistent with this view of things not only, as Edward Said points out in fictional narratives of the early nineteenth century, that the larger world is viewed from a cultural center assumed to be England but also that the larger world is viewed in terms of England's political and economic needs and potentials.[12] This turns attention to landscape as drawing its value not from its spiritual but from its material potentials. Mary Louise Pratt, for example, working with travel books about Africa written by visiting Europeans in the nineteenth century, details how little interest was taken by these tourists in the meaning for indigenous peoples these places held and the cultural, religious relations of the people to their physical surroundings. Rather, attention was given to the landscape itself, as though it could be imagined, by virtue mainly of vastness, to be free of inhabitants and open to all.[13] Landscape becomes a seductive invitation to enjoyment and exploitation. American depictions of western expanses were, for similar reasons, eagerly consumed by eastern people of means, depictions first in paintings and then in relatively inexpensive photographs, and they were contemplated not only as places testifying to divine creativity or even as suggestive of aesthetic qualities of the beautiful or sublime but also, if not more so, as opportunities for ventures.

It is difficult, then, to separate nature as a comprehending, spatial context of human life from the subjection of it to these and similar aesthetic, political, and economic interests. One may think that Melville, in turning to the sea, brings into view something that, in its vastness and mystery, avoids these interests. However, the sea in *Moby-Dick* is also an economic resource, and the ship a kind of factory; the ventures of the narrative are torn by the contrary interests of the ship's owners, which must be satisfied, and Ahab's, his mission to do a morally and spiritually motivated battle with the sea's most sublime inhabitant. Nonetheless, it is possible to recognize that Melville thinks that, despite the inevitable presence of social and economic factors, the human need to have a spatial relation to natural vistas that complements, if it does not surpass, relations to social and personal spaces can be satisfied by contemplating or encountering the sea. And, it can be assumed, Melville thinks this because his earlier Calvinism regarding the spiritual authority of nature, added to his Romantic sense of the sublime, allows him to see, alongside the commercialization and nationalization of natural space, a lingering moral and spiritual potential in this kind of place-relation.

The cultural viability of relations with natural places narrows sharply in the post-Darwinian period, however. The consequences of the Darwinian depiction of the natural world, especially as it gained for many a totally explanatory status and a widely accepted social application by the end of the nineteenth century, are difficult to overstate. By losing its ties to divinity, nature had nothing attached to it that raised it above the political and economic interests of acquisition and exploitation. Rather than something higher to which sober attention should be given and even a form of reverence shown, nature falls under human subjugation. Rather than landscape paintings that encompass trains and even factories, as Leo Marx shows us, we begin to have landscape paintings that reveal the displacement of the natural context of human life by socially, politically, and economically constructed space.[14] Comprehensive space becomes, as Ian Carter points out concerning Claude Monet's paintings in 1877 of the interior of the Gare Saint-Lazare, cathedrals not of nature but of the urban sublime.[15] There are no longer any strong, culturally shared warrants for treating natural space as having an integrity or value of its own apart from the uses, for pleasure, power, or profit, which can be made of it. The sublime, as Henry Adams argued, and as Monet's paintings reveal, is associated with the machine, whether the dynamo or the locomotive. Comprehensive spaces become railroad stations that, like Monmouth Cave, are cathedral-like—vaulted, immense, and incorporating—but unlike the Cave or the Falls, which, as the story has it, were fashioned by God, are human constructions that incorporate the natural context within the city by means of railroads rather than being incorporated by it.

Henri Lefebvre concludes that nature, for many decades in retreat, has finally, now, been subsumed in the modern West by social, political, and economic space. Nature is a commodity; sun and sea, mountains and tropical islands are poster material and are fully subsumed by a culture of acquisition and accumulation. This loss is problematic for Lefebvre: "It is becoming impossible to escape the notion that nature is being murdered by 'anti-nature'—by abstraction, by signs and images, by discourse, as also by labor and its products. Along with God, nature is dying."[16] He regrets the withdrawal or death of nature because nature otherwise could challenge the kind of space characteristic of modern societies, namely, mental space, social space that tends to be general, uniform, and without particular qualities. Nature, in its particularities, arbitrary juxtapositions and centrifugal effects, is contrary to the prevailing tendency of social space constructed for purposes of accumulation and control. He points to the success of urban spaces to conceal their actual dependence on pieces of land and to exchange natural spaces for homogeneous volumes of architectural space. Everything, as he says, conspires to inflict harm on nature, to isolate, conceal, and destroy it: "nature is now seen as merely the raw material out of which the productive forces of a variety of social systems have forged their particular spaces."[17] Against this onslaught, nature has no recourse, has largely been defeated, and is undergoing its ultimate demise.

III

Given these prevailing attitudes toward and relations with the natural context of human life, it seems late and quixotic to propose a reconstitution of the relation between "landscape" and the natural context of human life. However, it is my belief that a possible or actual relation with the natural context of human life is, for reasons that I shall give later, an important component in the repertoire of human place-relations. Consequently, I think that an attempt needs to be made in this direction, even though we cannot anticipate a restoration, at this point in late modernity, of early modern attitudes toward and relations with nature. Before we begin this attempt, we should note a few other things, in addition to the history of the cultural demise of nature sketched above, that affect our efforts.

First of all, contemporary societies are becoming increasingly urbanized. Although at one time it may have been possible to think that non-Western societies and cultures lived in proximity to and in mutuality with the natural context of their lives, it is now clear that if such was ever the case it is now largely not. Urbanization is even more rapid and determining in cultures outside the first world. While there continue, of course, to be sites outside of cities that are relatively natural, these can be accessed only by people with the leisure and means to do so. It is unrealistic and ethically provocative, then, simply to call for a higher view of and a greater exposure to the natural context of human social and personal life.

Second, I think that an attempt to revitalize our relations to the natural context of our lives should not be undertaken by emphasizing the negative characteristics of social, especially urban, space. Urban spaces have been for too long maligned, and their treatment by the culture, especially literary culture, contributes to, if it does not warrant, the mistreatment and denigration of urban spaces that have marked far too much of their history. Literary depictions of urban life, especially in the modern novel, have been largely negative. This is because the Romantic literary movement, especially in England, was carried forward as an alternative, if not a contrary, to modern industrialization and urbanization. Indeed, literature, as Raymond Williams argues, came to be viewed as the repository of human values, transcendent of the history of rapid material change and as a moral and spiritual guide for modern life.[18] The city was perceived and depicted as a contrary to the increasingly assigned place of human spiritual potential, namely, poetry and genius. Of the many ways in which literary modernity can and should be described, one of the most important is in terms of the increasing separation and even conflict between the massive, external, and physical world epitomized by modern urbanization, on the one side, and the personal, internal, and spiritual realm epitomized by religious and aesthetic genius, on the other.

In my opinion, this history of denigrating urban space is as much a cause or warrant for the exploitation of cities as a result of it. The largely negative literary stance toward the city gets support from a line of social, economic critiques of cities, traceable, for example, from the analysis of Manchester by Engels in the mid-nineteenth century to Michael Davis's analysis of Los Angles in our own time.[19] The blending of literary and cultural studies with social and economic critiques, then, though very much a recent phenomenon, has a powerful history behind it. However, I do not think that pursuing a revitalization of our awareness of and possible relations with the natural context of human life should include use of that resource, however fashionable and convenient it may be. Theorizing the relations between social and natural spaces and place-relations need not be a zero-sum game, and the possibilities of revitalizing relations to the natural context of human life should not be advanced at the expense of social, including urban, space. It is possible, therefore, to applaud the more positive views of urban life that follow from the paradigm-altering book of 1961, Jane Jacobs's *The Death and Life of Great American Cities*,[20] and that have continued into the present, most notably through the work of feminist geographers, while at the same time to work toward the restoration of relations, in some form, to the natural context of human life.

I do not think, therefore, that the category of landscape should be reserved for natural space and not used, as it often is, to suggest relations to urban space. The primary force of landscape, it seems to me, is to suggest the borders that comprehend the human world and to suggest a positive relation to a comprehensive space. There are cultural warrants for thinking of urban locations as having these characteristics of landscape, including the second of them. These warrants, for reasons suggested earlier, are not frequently found in literary culture, but they can be found with greater frequency in the history of modern painting, especially outside the Anglophone world. France and other European countries seem to have a somewhat more positive attitude toward their cities than do people, especially in England, who tend still to idealize country living. It is, therefore, not only possible but in many ways desirable to use the category of landscape to indicate relations to urban spaces.

The question is whether or not the term can still be used, given the demise of nature, to connote a relation to the natural context of human life. Nature, while it cannot be taken as synonymous with a specific kind of place, continues to operate in our culture as a trope for a location that directs attention to what precedes, comprehends, and supports humanly constructed and controlled places. Peter Coates, for example, points out in *Nature* that the term has been used from ancient to modern times to signify what is not humanly made and what provides the comprehensive background for human life.[21] As D. W. Meinig says, "Nature is fundamental only in a simple literal sense: nature provides a stage."[22] I take him to mean by this that human spatiality requires a component that locates human constructions in relation to a space that human constructions do not themselves provide. This concept of human placement seems also to be supported by the stress that Malpas puts on an experience of place "that goes beyond."[23] Urban spaces are dependent on a space that precedes and outstrips them. Robert Sack agrees. He argues that nature, in our cultural history, has been tied closely to justice and to truth because the "natural" connotes not only what lies beyond our control but also what relates us as persons to the most extensive context of our lives.[24]

In addition, natural space counters the possible pretentiousness of social spaces, the assumption of nature's displacement by the primacy of social constructions. There is a space of which people are or can be made aware and with which they can have at least some kind of relation, which is a space that antedates and extends beyond the reaches of even the most extensive boundaries of massive social spaces. This is a kind of space that, finally, is not so much constructed or owned by anyone as it is simply there as given, a container, so to speak, for people without regard to what otherwise may separate them from one another. Unlike social space, natural space can be affirmed as free of those lines of inclusion and exclusion that Lefebvre theorizes as definitive of social, especially urban, space.

Although I do not agree with Meinig in his desire to reserve the category of landscape exclusively for relations to natural space, I do agree with his call for a category that suggests a space that is primary, fundamental, encompassing, and enduring. While I think that "landscape" can also refer to inclusive space that is humanly constructed, it is important also to use "landscape" as a category that brings to attention human locations within encompassing, inclusive spatial horizons, because comprehensive natural place-relations are experiences of something given, enabling, unifying, and supporting. Such experiences expose the possibility carried by all positive place-relations, namely, of a spiritual resonance that both confirms and challenges the way in which we are in the world.

Let us say, then, that there are three ingredients to this sense of relation with natural space implied in the category of landscape. The first is framing. Per Raberg points out that comprehensive space has an enclosing potential. We give our environment, he says, "a visual outer boundary. This boundary very often consists of existing natural formations which we label as spatial signals."[25] Yi-Fu Tuan agrees, and he argues that without a sense of boundary, comprehensive space, rather than expansive and edifying for persons "can be bewildering and threatening."[26] One can see this toward the end of *Moby-Dick* when Pip, after the great encounter and the sinking of the ship, becomes disoriented and distressed by his location in all that unframed vastness.

The second thing that is needed for "landscape" as a relation to natural space is the sense of natural space pointing beyond itself to yet more expansive or powerful possibilities. I think that this is what D. W. Meinig means when he says that natural space under the category of landscape suggests a space that "lies utterly beyond science, holding meanings which link us as individual souls and psyches to an ineffable and infinite world."[27] The point, it seems to me, is that natural landscapes not only frame and particularize but also are, as Lefebvre says, centrifugal, opening out to something more and directing attention to possible boundaries that are beyond depiction. When Meinig calls natural landscapes meaningful, I take him to mean not something specific but a sense of being related to a location that, while specific, also eludes grasp and adequate representation.

The third thing that marks "landscape" as a relation to natural space is the significance it gathers from similarities to and differences from other kinds of spaces and place-relations. I think that it is not only possible but also very helpful to distinguish between three kinds of place-relations, personal or intimate, social or political, and natural or comprehensive. I think that spaces and place-relations of all three kinds are necessary if human spatial potentials are to be actualized. I would argue, too, as we see in the scene from Melville described at the outset, that these kinds of place-relations complement one another in that the deficiencies of one are addressed by relations to one or both of the other two kinds. However, it is also important to say that, because all three are *place*-relations, there is significant continuity between the three kinds. Indeed, one can, for example, have a personal place-relation in and with a location that is outdoors or is a public or social place. And, as I have said, one can have a relation to urban space that is suggestive of a relation to natural, comprehensive space. But a relation to natural space reserves to itself the sense of a comprehending spatiality that precedes and, relative to human constructions, is distinctive because, among other things, of its primacy, anfractuosity, and unpredictability. If one is not ready to agree with Melville that the reason for the attractions of such a spatiality lies within the human spirit and its capacity for immensity, one can at least say that a relation to space of this kind has a liberating effect relative to the predictability and structuring of social space and the familiarity and particularity of personal or intimate space. Natural space is a reminder of the relatively late arrival and derivative standing of humanly constructed spaces.

Lefebvre calls for attitudes and actions that would help to retain what may yet remain of a cultural language of natural space. One is to treat nature not as a general environment but as a variety of locations that have been affected, at times occluded, by social spaces. Also, we should abstain, he thinks, from defining nature primarily in terms of its laws or design, since such notions validate the theories of planning that we so willingly impose on nature. Instead, he argues, we should emphasize the complexity and even disorder of nature, its hidden, "uterine" realities. In its retreat and even in its dying, nature continues to lure us to the limits of our sense of placement.[28]

We should not, however, be so concerned with recapturing a sense of relation with natural places as to ignore the fact that there is no clear access to them. There are no places that are natural in the sense of being non- or prehuman. This is not only because by having a relation with such places we bring to that relation a culture-laden set of expectations, needs, and potential responses. It is also because there are no natural places in the sense of their being, for example, not owned by anyone. When we are out to sea with Ishmael, we are on the owners' ship. When we look into the sky, we see not only stars and planets but also planes and satellites. Deserts are forsaken, but they are, however unused, parts of national territories. Indeed, we must resist the temptation to think of large vistas as in some way transcending their particular ties to peoples and human history. While our relation to natural landscapes is distinguishable from our relations to other kinds of places, we should include all three kinds of place-relations in an inclusive theory of human spatiality.

Since it is not possible to posit natural places as free from social and economic ties, it may be good also to think of accesses to comprehensive spaces as lying not only or primarily at the terminations of humanly con-structed space, but also in interstices and at the margins of constructed spaces. One finds architects and designers referring to SLOIP, that is, space left over in planning.[29] Such space owes its definition to the limits of build-ings and other planned areas. If we extend this term, we can think of all social and political spaces as not completely comprehensive because they are constituted by particular structures of interest and coherence. What lies between these structures and interests—at their limits and, especially, at the points of opposition between structures and interests—are accesses to something not fully available that lies behind or beyond them. All planned, constructed, and controlled places create SLOIP between them or at their edges, and SLOIP can easily suggest a significant remainder or an access where potential relations to unconstructed space are proffered.

When we think of gaps, margins, or transitions as points of access to a spatiality that precedes and outstrips human constructions, we are aided by the anthropologist Victor Turner. In his *The Ritual Process* he gives atten-tion to in-between places that participants in rituals enter, places defined by being incorporated by neither the structure that precedes the ritual nor the structure subsequent to it. His term for such places is "liminality." Lim-inality, by providing a place separable from social structures that stand on either side of it, takes on a significance and power of its own. It becomes the location from which the constructions of society arise, the potential that antedates human constructions and on which they depend. Liminal-ity exposes the always present but usually hidden base of human structures and differentiations. Liminal places, thereby, are also hazardous and threat-ening because they are unstructured and underdesignated. Turner extends liminality and its contrary relation to the structures of a society by locating it not only between structures but also at their edges, with what is deemed by society to be marginal and even worthless.[30]

I have reservations about Turner's theory of liminal space. The rhetorical force of his description is to define natural or comprehensive space not only by means of the differences between it and humanly constructed spaces but also by the suggestion that all unconstructed or liminal spaces are the same, indicating a shared base from which all human constructs are derived. However, I agree with his general point that all human constructions create margins, leave gaps, and cannot wholly contain transitions. These points or sites form potential accesses to comprehensive, natural place-relations because they grant persons the possibility to get out from under or to stand aside from the dominance and presumed inclusiveness of space determined by human designs.

Retrieving or reconstructing natural, comprehensive space and place-relations requires, let us say in conclusion, three things. First, it requires attention to the language of nature. The fact that the word "natural" helps to sell products reveals both how thoroughly the category has been secularized by the market and how tenacious are the qualities of goodness and reliability in "natural" as opposed to "artificial." Because of the importance of nature as a trope for access to comprehensive space, it should as long as possible be retained. Indeed, the moral and spiritual potentials of current environmental movements to draw attention in tangible ways to the comprehensive, natural context of our lives are as important as the long-term consequences they carry for the viability of the natural environment and our material survival.

Second, language of the natural and of comprehensive space must recapture its referential potential. Since this language does not have something specific, especially a human construct, as its signified, its referential potential is weak. It is important to affirm that when we use the language of natural, comprehensive space, as whenever our location in its widest and most inclusive terms is being described, we take that which is indicated to exist. What is needed is an imaginary of the natural as comprehensive, primarily by means of bracketing the languages of social and personal spaces. This imaginary can be reinforced by the many literary and graphic "landscapes," depictions of natural spaces and of human relations to them, that continue to come to us from our writers and artists.

Finally, the reconstitution of comprehensive, natural space requires narrative. This includes accounts of why and how people hazard the risks of venturing out to find locations that grant forceful and meaningful relations with places that, in contrast to humanly constructed and controlled places, can be taken as natural. Narratives of this kind, travel accounts or fictional depictions, can revitalize the language of comprehensive space, and they can designate the sites of, accesses to, and relations with it. The language of comprehensive, natural space needs to be delivered not only from the tyranny of the abstractions and commodifications of what Lefebvre calls "mental space" but also from the curse of vagueness in force and meaning. The narrativization of comprehensive, natural place-relations can help to do that. Natural sites and spaces need to be retrieved and revalued in and by narratives already with us and still to come and, just as much, by our attention to and regard for them.

Notes

1. Herman Melville, *Moby-Dick* (A Norton Critical Edition), ed. Harrison Hayford and Hershel Parker (New York: W. W. Norton, 1851/1967).

2. Ibid., pp. 12–13.

3. Ibid., p. 236.

4. Jeff Malpas, *Place and Experience: A Philosophical Topography* (Cambridge: Cambridge University Press, 1999), p. 13.

5. Ibid., p. 174.

6. Francis Bacon, *The Advancement of Learning*, ed. Arthur Johnston (Oxford: Clarendon Press, 1974), p. 26.

7. Ibid., p. 36.

8. John Locke, *An Essay Concerning Human Understanding*, ed. Peter H. Nidditch (Oxford: Clarendon Press, 1975), pp. 691–693 (Bk. 4, chap. 18, §5) and p. 694 (Bk. 4, chap. 18, §8).

9. Thomas Paine, *The Age of Reason, Being an Investigation of True and Fabulous Theology* (New York: Prometheus Books, 1984 [1794–1795]), p. 31.

10. See John F. Sears, *Sacred Places: American Tourist Attractions in the Nineteenth Century* (New York: Oxford University Press, 1984).

11. Ian Carter, *Railways and Culture in Britain: The Epitome of Modernity* (Manchester: Manchester University Press, 2001), pp. 261–270.

12. See especially Edward Said, "Narrative and Social Space," in his *Culture and Imperialism* (New York: Knopf, 1994), pp. 62–80.

13. Mary Louise Pratt, "Scratches on the Face of the Country; or, What Mr. Barrow Saw in the Land of the Bushmen," in *"Race," Writing, and Difference*, ed. Henry Louis Gates, Jr. (Chicago: University of Chicago Press, 1986), pp. 138–163.

14. See Leo Marx, *The Machine in the Garden: Technology and the Pastoral Ideal* (New York: Oxford University Press, 1964).

15. Carter, *Railways and Culture in Britain*, pp. 119–121.

16. Henri Lefebvre, *The Production of Space*, trans. Donald Nicholson-Smith (Oxford: Blackwell, 1991), p. 70.

17. Ibid., pp. 30–31.

18. Raymond Williams, *Culture and Society: 1780–1950* (New York: Columbia University Press, 1983), p. 63.

19. See Friedrich Engels, "The Great Town," and Mike Davis, "Fortress L.A.," in *The City Reader*, 2nd ed., ed. Richard T. LeGates and Frederic Stout (London: Routledge, 1996).

20. Jane Jacobs, *The Death and Life of Great American Cities* (New York: Random House, 1961).

21. Peter Coates, *Nature: Western Attitudes since Ancient Times* (Berkeley: University of California Press, 1998), pp. 3–4.

22. D. W. Meinig, ed., *The Interpretation of Ordinary Landscapes* (New York: Oxford University Press, 1979), p. 2.

23. Malpas, *Place and Experience*, p. 66.

24. Robert Sack, *Homo Geographicus: A Framework for Action, Awareness, and Moral Concern* (Baltimore: Johns Hopkins University Press, 1997), pp. 202–203.

25. Per Raberg, *The Space of Man: New Concepts for Social and Humanistic Planning* (Stockholm: Almquist and Wiksell International, 1987), p. 139.

26. Yi-Fu Tuan, *Cosmos and Hearth: A Cosmopolite's Viewpoint* (Minneapolis: University of Minnesota Press, 1996), p. 2.

27. Meinig, *The Interpretation of Ordinary Landscapes*, p. 47.

28. Lefebvre, *The Production of Space*, p. 71.

29. See E. Relph, *Place and Placelessness* (London: Pion, 1976), p. 23.

30. Victor W. Turner, *The Ritual Process: Structure and Anti-Structure* (Chicago: Aldine, 1966).

3 "Whitefellas Have to Learn about Country, It Is Not Just Land": How Landscape Becomes Country and Not an "Imagined" Place

John J. Bradley

Introduction

In 1988, while helping to make the film *Buwarrala Akarriya* (*Journey East*)[1] with the Yanyuwa community of the south west Gulf of Carpentaria in the Northern Territory of Australia, I stood with the filmmaker and a senior landowner Annie Karrakayn. It was a hot day: the north wind whipped the sand off the salt pans and samphire heath that fringed the savannah grasslands that marched on into the east; to the north the salt and clay pans ran on until they halted at a distant fringe of green that spoke of mangroves, and although it was not visible, the mangroves spoke of the sea. To the south lay the open woodland forests that continued to the horizon and beyond. Everywhere we looked the heat haze shimmered.

As we stood there surveying the scene the filmmaker, fresh from Melbourne, never having been in the Northern Territory before, let alone this kind of environment, pondered aloud and somewhat fearfully, as if exposed to some hellish realm, "What kind of landscape is this?" Annie heard the comment and looking searchingly at me and asked, "What is this word 'landscape'? Is it another whitefella 'wheelbarrow word'?" A "wheelbarrow word" was in Annie's view the big English words that "need a wheelbarrow to carry them"; they are words used by white, fluent speakers of English that are not known or used by most indigenous people in her community. Such a term, therefore, comprises a form of "secret" or "restricted" speech that signifies power and authority over both the land she called home and, perhaps, over herself and her family's very lives.

Writing and Thinking about Landscape

The question I am seeking to explore in this essay is the following: if for an indigenous person such as Annie, there is no understanding of landscape, then what is there? And does the word "landscape," with all it attachments to Western ways of knowing, serve a useful purpose for indigenous people? If it does not serve a useful purpose for them, then whom does the term serve?

The literature within Australia that describes how indigenous people relate to their land is rich, and has long provided a focus for analyses that have been concerned with the dynamics of people within what are described as "cultural landscapes."[2] The authors of these works all demonstrate in varying ways how people make use of the material features of their environment, and how the landscape is evidence of cosmological processes that define kinship, group alignments, and cultural practices. Increasingly there have been attempts also to explore the idea of landscape as a repository for cultural knowledge and memory. These are fine-grained attempts at trying to get the "heart of the matter," to move away from dominating Western-centered structuralist views, to an understanding of people in the land—attempts to understand something of the emotional and sensory engagements that indigenous people bring to the land they find themselves living in.[3]

Landscape continues to be a point of central discussion in writings about indigenous Australia. For the most part, however, it has remained a part of the ethnographic description rather than being seen as an integral part to social processes. Within this essay I will provide a case study that seeks to demonstrate that a discussion of landscape/country belongs firmly within a dialogue about self and necessary emotional needs, attachments, and subjectivities.

There is little doubt that the term "landscape" and derived terms such as "seascape"[4] and "spiritscape"[5] are attempts to find a way to articulate human interaction with the environment, and, increasingly, this engagement is cutting across intellectual and academic boundaries.[6] Landscape has become the conceptual tool for anthropology, archaeology, architecture, resource management, biology, geography, cultural studies, and literature.[7]

Embedded in this increasing interest in the term "landscape" there still abides the same set of older questions. With all its use, it is still important to ask if there has been a conceptual breakthrough or a new theoretical way to engage with the word, or if the academy is caught up in a drift, a fad, that will run its time and then move on. This is an important question, because in regard to the use of the word "landscape"—the way we might use it to describe lands that are not our own, lands for which we have other words to describe what we think we see, and other ways of knowing—we must increasingly face the fact that people like the Yanyuwa elder mentioned above have an ontological reality that is totally different from the view shared by myself and the filmmaker. As indigenous people strive to retain their ancestral lands, the landscape becomes embedded within issues of both social and environmental justice.

Another question that arises is how did someone like Annie Karrakayn speak of landscape; or did she? Within the Yanyuwa ontological and epistemological construct of their home, how do we find referent points of understanding? Casey offers us a beginning by his use of the term "place" as an alternative model to the notion of landscape in constructing the relationship of people to their land.[8] This follows on from Foucault where the notion of landscape has been constructed in diverse ways over the last century, each according to the dominant ideas, theories, and paradigms of the time. As such, landscape has always been a Western epistemological view of the world. Bender describes it as "the western gaze": a historically defined way of viewing the world that creates a separation between nature (the object) and culture (the people).[9] In the academic traditions of anthropology, archaeology, cultural resource management, and geography, there has been a history of understanding the landscape as another form of attributed symbolic meaning that people assign to their "worlds."[10] As such, place has become divorced from human interaction and is viewed as a manifestation of the symbolic or structured relationship between people and their landscapes. Place, however, even in it fullest theoretical sense, cannot be separated from people but rather is fully realized by the interrelationship of human existence and practices.[11] Thomas describes place as a "relational concept" that is embedded in the ontology and epistemologies of people throughout the world.[12] In this regard, then, place offers a potential to examine the interrelationship of people to their place-worlds, allowing for an exploration in the way people perceive their worlds and themselves.

Increasingly there are extensive and thoroughly researched ethnographies and oral histories of Australia's indigenous peoples. These are guided by approaches that view people and place as interrelated, where the interconnectedness of people to place is established through social, moral, and personal threads of connection.[13] This relationship is one of reciprocity, where people and place are linked through what Basso describes as "interanimation" in which people animate place through experiences, memory, and emotion—for some, a problematic subjectivity.[14] Through these lenses, place offers a way of interpretation where, following Thomas, we can "put their bodily presences back"[15] into the landscape and then attempt to interpret changes in the ontologies of past and contemporary peoples.

No landscape is static. David and Wilson note the importance of acknowledging people's changing interactions with place "to investigate changes in the construction of place, self and identity,"[16] and all of these will be linked to the ontological reality of people in place at any one time. It then follows, as Casey suggests, that conceptualizing places is not only a part of the interaction of people to their surroundings but as underlying all aspects of human practice and "habitus."[17]

In regard to developing a response to the reality of indigenous ontologies in relation to their places and being able to see clearly the limitation embedded in the term "landscape," it is important, following on from Tilley[18] and Thomas,[19] to explore phenomenological understandings concerning the experiential nature of place. Drawing from Heidegger,[20] with particular reference to his understanding of "dwelling" as well as of "being-in-the world," it is possible to locate a position for understanding the place of both the mind and body "being" in a relationship with place.

It follows, then, if we are to attempt a cross-cultural or transcultural rendering of place or even attempt to understand the intersubjective position an indigenous view of place and space offers, we must be prepared to challenge the very essence of the Western academic tradition: the objective premise. The premise of objectivity is predicated on the understanding of an unknowing subject and a social authority. Moreover, language and knowledge arrive as a "closed and already constituted system."[21] The historical development of Western modes of thought—those patterns and processes that construct our knowledge in the first instance—is concealed from view and unavailable for critical comment. "Our" knowledge exists independently of social and historical definitions and processes, and its very authority is derived from this separation.[22]

The Western observer is then urged to direct his or her gaze outwardly with very little thought for the underlying structures and unconscious presuppositions that construct our own ontological and epistemological "truths." These are all too often considered fixed and given. It is Ricoeur who points to this in a critique of Levi-Strauss's structuralism where he argues that it represents "yet another triumph of a 'Cartesian' science." Words such as "landscape," which we use as the markers of structure, then subsume history and more significantly the "speaking subject," which is then "read out of consideration."[23] What is important to note here is that the very elements that a structural reading of subjective inquiry may render as inconsequential are in fact integral components of indigenous ways of knowing.

One of the implications of this form of inquiry is that the act of speech, or in some instance no speech but body language, is considered subordinate—a mere secondary expression of deep and universal structure, available for the reading by the appropriate social authorities. The perceptions of the participants are reduced to fit this conceptual schema, while the subjective cultural and epistemological interests of the observer are concealed from view. The direct result of this exclusion of the vital link between culture and place raises serious questions regarding the relevance of these explanations for the people they purport to describe.[24] In my own work with Yanyuwa people such research methodologies lead to exasperated comments of "we don't speak like that."

It is not surprising, then, that many indigenous people consider the "findings" of such observers akin to childlike, or quaint, translations.[25] Their words are multilayered and not easily reduced to the language of objectivism where object and subject, language and speech, place and people exist as separate and autonomous entities.[26] To gain entry into those worlds, therefore, an attempt must be made to examine and deconstruct some of the basic and taken-for-granted assumptions that underpin Western knowledge systems. This means acknowledging the equal validity of indigenous accounts and that it is possible that the very systems we seek to study may stand as incommensurable with their so-called non-indigenous counterpart.[27]

We are left then with a premise that suggests that any accounting of indigenous views of knowledge must go beyond specifying geological form and ecological processes and examine the subjective and emotional interactions with the concrete and (in our "scientific" observer terms) the "imagined phenomena."

It is this understanding of "imagined phenomena" that leads me to the central thesis of this essay. In the most general terms, the source of these imagined phenomena maybe found in indigenous Dreaming, where "Dreaming" is a complex term that is used to understand the consciousness of and interactions with the physical landscape.[28] "Dreaming" in the words of indigenous people is a subtle and complex term that has little if anything at all to do with sleep.[29] According to many (but not all) indigenous cosmologies, ancestral beings shaped the landscape and imbued it with significance and meaning and value, which included the presence of humans. Humans share the essence, although, as with the multitude of other living things, they differ in form; thus the Western binary of culture and nature is unified and exists as a corporate whole. The core reality of

this is that indigenous people fuse, without critique or worry, understandings that the rational West has fought to keep separate.[30] This sense of
unity—the interdependence of all things—gives rise to a moral consciousness in regard to a positioning of constant negotiation with the past and
an animated and powerfully "enchanted" place-world, where cultural continuity and environmental vitality are codependent. As Rose suggests, it
offers a view whereby "a country and its people take care of each other."[31]

Reading Country

The key word in this phrase quoted from Rose is "country." The meanings
that indigenous people apply to this term Australia-wide are multivocal
and totally dependent on context to make sense of the meaning at any
one time. Working with ideas from Levinas, Rose draws from his concept
of *l'éspace vital*, the "vital place," and leads us to an understanding of landscape as a nourishing terrain that provides us with a way of exploring the
indigenous understanding of country. This leads Rose to comment that
"country is a living entity, with a yesterday, today and a tomorrow with a
consciousness, and a will toward life."[32] The conclusion that is then drawn
from this is that country is sentient; it has a will and a need of its own.

In my own fieldwork and travels with the Yanyuwa people over the last
three decades I have been drawn to similar conclusions as Rose. I have
come to understand that when Yanyuwa people use the term "country"
there are many implicit understandings moving through people's minds
and bodies that speak of intimacy, love, and a deep and abiding concern.
People speak about country in the same way that they talk about human
and nonhuman relatives: people cry, sometimes wail for their country,
they sing passionately and with fervor about their country and, increasingly, there is a deep concern and worry about country as they begin to
understand the values that the West places on their country. People listen to country, they visit their country, and speak with love and longing
for country that they may not be able to visit because it is part of pastoral lease, a mining development, or maybe it is just too hard to get the
boat or vehicle to visit it. In return, country listens to people; it can hear,
think, and feel about its human relatives; it can be hard or easy, forgiv-
ing or unforgiving, just as people can with each other. Close relatives will
often address each other as country, and when people see animal or plant
species that are their Dreaming, their ancestor, they will often call out,
"Hello country!" Furthermore, "Country is full of countrymen, you can

never go lonely," a senior Yanyuwa elder, Dinny McDinny, once told me as he watched the antics of a group of crows, a species he called his most senior paternal grandfather's sister. Country also speaks of loss and pain, over the course of colonial history—what Rose calls "wounded places"[33] of a contemporary landscape.

Over nearly three decades of fieldwork, I have begun to draw these conclusions about what country really is and how ontologically we are dealing with a separation from any understanding of landscape as the West may understand and experience it. Without presuming too much on the reader, I now want to explore a number of grounded experiences that allow for the color and sentiment of the term "country" to be revealed and, in doing so, lead to a position that challenges our very reckoning of how landscape may be perceived. Country is different from the way landscape is presented in normative Western education, where there is an acceptance that knowledge is abstract, the metaphysical axiomatic; and therefore landscape is not tied to place experience to nearly the same extent.

"Landscape Is Sea"

In the Yanyuwa language the surprisingly simple word *awara* is translated as country, but equally it can mean home, place, earth, land, soil, dirt, possessions, sea, or reef. What we might call a landscape can contain multiple countries, each with its own biography and meaning, so our view of a landscape in reality is a series of intermeshing places of event. Thus, over Yanyuwa country, which incorporates the Sir Edward Pellew Group of Islands and the tidal reaches of the McArthur and Wearyan River as well as the mouth of the Robinson River, there is in excess of 1,500 countries, but no one landscape.[34] I have included a "mudmap" (see figure 3.1) drawn in the ground by a senior Yanyuwa elder Old Pyro Dirdiyalma. He and I had sat before a space he had cleared in the earth between us, and he pressed his forefinger into sand: as he called the name of each country, he gave the stories that belonged to each place, and he called these places with a precision that matched the cardinal direction of a Western compass.

I want to use this map of countries as a case study and explore, albeit briefly, some of the issues that Pyro's conception of place reveals to us. It is interesting to note that on a standard Western map of this area, there appears only one English name, "Sharkers Point," which is an Anglicization of the Yanyuwa place name "Jarrka" that appears three lines below the dotted line marked A. An unusual occurrence perhaps, but not when it is

Figure 3.1
Mudmap of Yanyuwa country—redrawn by the author from the original by Old
Pyro Dirdiyalma.

considered that most of the country Pyro is talking about has never been
seen as having economic value to the West and, therefore, for the most
part was not wanted.[35]

Pyro described himself as an owner of all of these countries; they were
his by an uninterrupted paternal line of descent from both human ancestors and then nonhuman ancestors in the form of the brolga, *kurdarrku*
(*Grus rubicundus*), and the estuary cod, *wangkuwa* (*Epinephalus undulastostri-
atus*). There are other Yanyuwa people who relate to this country by virtue
of their mothers having come from these countries, their mother's mothers
or father's mothers, each line of descent marking a particular way to relate

to the countries in question. These descent lines do not mark reasons for exclusion; rather, they are indicative of a system that seeks to include all people and nonhuman entities into a weblike system of relationships. It is beyond the scope of this essay to explore the kinship and politics embedded in these comments.[36]

For Pyro, all of these countries were part of a much larger emotional geography that is concerned with the social and sensory relations that define place. His understanding of human engagement with this area has shaped his own and the countries' cultural identity, and these are dominant principles in regard to the emotional encounter that someone like Pyro can have with place. For Yanyuwa people like Pyro and Annie Karrakayn, mentioned above, a relationship with country is only possible if defined by an understanding that humans have an effect on country only to the extent that they are emotionally engaged with it. Emotion is the effective state of consciousness that is experienced in any engagement with country.

After Pyro had marked the ground for me and had watched as I had translated the indentations of his fingers into place names in my field notes, he spoke at length about what all these countries meant to him. This is a short extract from a much longer review of his country, but it demonstrates clearly the multiple narratives and emotions he deals with in his negotiation with country:

We have not been here for many years, to our country, and here [indicating the "map"] is the country we call Liwulkungka, a long time ago the old people were on this country. My father, my father's brothers and my grandfathers, they have all died but they once lived and moved through this country, such men as Mangayi, Mamudiyatha and Birribirrikama, there are many names for this country, you can see them here, to the south is Wubunjawa and Lurriyarri, the spiritual abode of the my most senior paternal grandfather the Brolga and not far to the north east is Kumbarikanyajulaki, where the feathers of the Brolga fell down, alright then there is Larlmanda and then Milundurrala where the ribs of the Rainbow Serpent lie, and then there is Marribindila, Liwukuthula, and Wangkuwala, our sacred song cycle is moving through that country, onwards and northwards to Jarrka, that island country of ours where there is a fresh water well, the place of origin of the Rock Cod. I am a descendant of all of this country, of all those men and women who have come before me.[37]

For a man such as Pyro, his recollection of country and his relationship to it—the calling of names and ancestors, both human and nonhuman—represents articulations of emotion that are not metaphorical and imagined but real, and that contribute to a both a personal and group identity.[38]

The Yanyuwa people called themselves saltwater people. In Yanyuwa this term is *li-Anthawirriyarra*, a term that translates as "the people whose

identity and emotional and cultural heritage come from the sea." The sea
is the constant reference point in the lives of all generations of Yanyuwa
people, even those who may never have visited it and have spent their
lives in urban and remote centers far from the coast. The sea provides a
point of interactive connection that results in a true spirit of place and profound sense of being, as the following Yanyuwa song illustrates:

Marnaji ngambala
li-Anthawirriyarra
layirli-nganji waliwaliyangka

We are the people
Whose spirits are from the sea
We are the people who are kin to the island country.[39]

According to the Yanyuwa people, and as highlighted in the lyrics of this
song, the sea, which is also country, and identity are inextricably linked. In
purely functional terms, this social environmental connection may be seen
as a metaphor for a rich repository of "practical" ecological knowledge, but
for people such as the Yanyuwa it means much more: it is not metaphor,
it is a conceptual anchor point for indigenous social organization, unique
cultural identity, and ontological and epistemological definition.

The country (or countries) that Pyro described in figure 3.1 is described
more generally as "saltwater country." It is coastal, and some of the names
that Pyro called are actually in the sea. However, at no time in his calling of
the names did Pyro make this distinction. I have drawn onto figure 3.1 two
dotted lines, one marked A and the other B. The place names above line A
are in the sea, and the places names between the lines A and B are on what
the West might call the mainland, but some of them also extend out into
the sea and surrounding sea grass meadows.

Technically the West would call most of the space occupied by the place
names appearing between lines A and B a landscape; it can be walked upon
(in the right season) and comprises geographic and floral and faunal species that our Western gaze believes to be landscape. In Yanyuwa, there is
a geographic term for this area of land: *narnu-ruluruluwanka*.[40] This term
defies a simple word-for-word translation: it is a word, like many in indigenous languages that, as Walsh[41] suggests, has too much attached to it to be
easily defined. It is a word enmeshed in an inextricable web of associations
where people can be rendered inarticulate, not because they are ignorant,
but because there is just too much knowledge embedded within the word.
Here is my translation of the term *narnu-ruluruluwanka*: "a geographic land
unit that consists of saltpans, clay pans, and samphire heath country. It

is country that is flooded on the king tides, or, during cyclonic surges, it is proper saltwater country. It also has numerous small raised islets with sparse vegetation such as small melaleuca trees that provide good shade for resting and camping."

This country extends for some 13 kilometers from the sea, inland to a low uprise that meets with the savannah grasslands. In a Yanyuwa conception this 13-kilometer region is still the sea, and the small peninsula called Jarrka that has as its headland the place named Liwarriya (see figure 3.1) is in Yanyuwa called *waliyangu*, an island, though a Western map or an aerial vista would see them as part of the mainland. Another Yanyuwa term for this area is *narnu-wuthan*, which literally means "incompleteness": it is country that is neither one thing or the other—only circumstances will tell; this is also the same term that is given to what the West would call the "intertidal zone." This is not to say that the Yanyuwa do not have words for sea; they do—*antha*, the sea in its generic form, *walamakamaka*, the open ocean, and *kunjurrkunjurr*, the line of the horizon and the sea, *narnu-ngawurruwurru*, the deep dark sea between and to the north of the islands, and *kurnmurr*, the expanse of "rolling" sea between the islands and the horizon—but a Yanyuwa reckoning of the *narnu-wuthan* also allows it to be called *antha*, the sea, as well.

As mentioned above, this is country that can be flooded by the sea, and perhaps the most dramatic example of this was in April 1984 during Cyclone Kathy, when all of the country between lines A and B was inundated by what is reckoned to have been a six-meter tidal surge that deposited dugong, sea turtle, large stingrays, sharks, and numerous fish species up to at least nine kilometers "inland."[42] For the Yanyuwa it made proper sense: it is not "inland," but the near limit of the sea. In the "map" provided by Pyro only the place-names Liwulkungka, Lurriyarri, and Wubunjawa (below line B) would actually be seen as emphatically mainland (*narnu-maya*). Thus the vista of landscape is no more; it is the sea, incomplete country, that can be both awash and dry.

This understanding was further evidenced for me in two ways. First, just after Cyclone Kathy, I was speaking to a senior Yanyuwa elder, Old Tim Rakawurlma, about the dugong and sea turtle having been thrown "inland." I said to him, in Yanyuwa, "Nya-mangaji lhambiji kinya-walima walya ankaya nyungku-mangaji mayangku" ("the cyclonic winds threw the dugong and sea turtle onto the mainland"). Tim's immediate response was, "Waraba mayangku nyungku-mangaji ki-awarawu ki-anthawu, antha nya-mangaji awara" ("no it is not the mainland, that country is the sea, it is sea that country"). Second, during the court proceedings of a land claim I worked on in 2000, which involved a claim to the seagrass beds of Yanyuwa country, a middle-aged Yanyuwa claimant, Nancy McDinny, was asked to indicate to the judge the sea country under claim. The expectation was that she would follow the coast as marked on the map, which constituted the legal reality of the claim. However, she immediately began to draw her finger along a line that was between 10 to 13 kilometers inland: this was for her the boundary between the mainland and the sea.

There is on Pyro's map a small river that, though not marked on any map, is called by the white locals Lousy Creek. Its mouth is marked by the two named sites of Thayinda and Wamukakali (in Yanyuwa the mouth of a river is called *narnu-walmurr*, the root). However, rivers (*na-wulangi*) extend out to sea; the channel of the river is still the river (*na-wulangi*) until it drops off into deeper water, and this river "drop-off" is also called *narnu-walmurr*, the root or mouth. Our Western gaze of land is challenged when we pause to ponder these understandings. It is further challenged when, in a Yanyuwa understanding, the ultimate way to conceive of and understand any country is through song, sacred song called *kujika*, that flows like numinous ribbon through various parts of the land.

When Pyro gave the names of his country, he began with Liwalmangka and Lidambuwa (see top of figure 3.1). Unless we were aware we would not know that these are sea countries. They are always submerged, but are still country as important as that which we can see with our gaze. I provide below six verses of the song of 200 verses, which moves between the two countries. It provides a gaze, another way of understanding the immediacy and intimacy of country:

Mirrimbukuma
Mirrmbuku

Dust rises from
The movement of the feeding dugong

Yuwamaka
Duwalyarrany

Sea grass grows thickly
On the country of Lidambuwa

Yuwamaka
Yalminji manaya

Sea grass carpets the country of
Lidambuwa

Yarikiyara lhungkarrmi
Lhungka

Large numbers of dugong cows
Their calves are following them

Wabarrku ramba
Jirrimbi ramba

The bull dugong
Sends out a warning,
He slaps the water with his tail

Ngarna wirijarra
Yumbul majarra

The bull dugong
Surfaces, he travels
Around the cows and calves

These are song verses about countries, not a landscape, not even a seascape but mostly an underseascape of reefs, sea grass meadows, and sand bars. The song flows without break from what we reckon the mainland is or should be. The content of these verses speak of what all Yanyuwa people know, young and old; there are dugong swimming in the sea over the sea grass beds of their country, and the verses speak to those who know dugong behavior. For those Yanyuwa men and women who understand the nature of the song cycle knowledge and the agency of the songs themselves, they will also understand that these verses come from the countries that exist a little way away from Liwalmangka but arrive at Lidambuwa. Talk of these songs will also bring to mind deceased kin who also knew these songs, and from there there will be discussion of living kin and their relationships to kin and country. For the Yanyuwa songs represent an objective "truth" about their country; for the West this may seem like a fairly strenuous exercise to accept because there also has to be some engagement with the powerfully enchanted space that is Yanyuwa country. It is also a dialogue with what is often referred to as "worldviews": a Yanyuwa understanding of country challenges us all and gives us cause to review and reconsider geographical renderings of land and sea, what the Yanyuwa call *awara*, country.[43]

Conclusion

The Western view more often than not sets language and landscape apart and in opposition to each other, where landscape evokes the natural world

and language the world of humanity; in the Yanyuwa case, there is a striking realignment of cultural and environmental processes.[44] A Yanyuwa
social order is articulated within the dynamics of the land through seasonal,
climatic, and geographical variations and, in this regard, often reflects the
way they are spoken about and acted upon in day-to-day settings.[45] There
is recognition also that both those social and physical landscapes are subject to change, and for this reason the production of knowledge becomes
situation-dependent. Because of this, any understanding of what may constitute landscape is never seen to represent an immutable truth. Knowledge
is embedded in social, political, emotional, economic, and environmental
discourses that constitute everyday realities that are a reflection of everyday
existence and an explicit arbitrariness of meaning.

Povinelli draws our attention to the fact that a Western view of indigenous knowledge has a tendency to create a "childlike appreciation" that
isolates material aspects of indigenous land interactions, and that this can
itself be directly linked to Western environmental perceptions. As discussed
above, for many Western observers culture and nature exist independently
of each other; therefore, human ecology is divided into either cognitive or
environmental models. There is no attempt at synthesis between the two
and, as a consequence, social systems are either a result of "a set of patterns . . . people [carry] around in their heads" or a product of the environment in which those people find themselves.[46] This conceptual separation
or binary opposition forms the epistemological basis for scientific inquiry,
and when set against knowledge such as the Yanyuwa, it begins to appear
illusory, "a figment of Western imagination."[47]

For people such as the Yanyuwa, "real" cultural identity, or sense of
place, is the outcome of effective and ongoing relationships with country;[48] without these human–country interactions people do not know
how to behave. However, just as important is the need to understand the
conceptual links between environmental and epistemological processes,
because embedded in these issues are the modern and often-demanded
two-way management relationships between indigenous land owners and
the scientific community.[49] What the West quite comfortably calls landscape, in a Yanyuwa way of knowing, excludes the sea as country; thus,
there is an exclusion in regard to a qualitative appreciation of indigenous
environmental narratives and relationships. All too frequently the objective method militates against gaining this deeper understanding.

Many indigenous people, such as the Yanyuwa, can exist with the
understanding that knowledge is never complete,[50] an idea that stands in
contrast to the Western scientific way of knowing. The Yanyuwa would

argue that their knowledge too needs to be incorporated within a totality of human knowledge; otherwise knowledge becomes limited to the production of information that is encased within Western epistemological "truths" that, in turn, can lead to a deeply reductionist materialistic view of "the world," which presents a "truth" that can be equated to a form of scientific materialism.

Yanyuwa engagement with country is about understanding a particular system of logic, which is constrained and informed by factors as diverse as authority, language, utility, aesthetics, ecology, habitat, ownership, and a deeply embedded system of relationships. For the Yanyuwa the aim of their relationship with country is not to arrive at knowledge of a particular system but rather to explore and understand the various relationships that exist within their knowledge system. Therefore, one of the defining points about knowledge of country is context and the inclusion of empirical knowledge with what the West would class as subjective and emotional states, through which is exposed a system of relatedness that is presented via a system of countries that are an ecological model of complex internal relations and understandings. An openness to other epistemological positionings and other rationalities and a critical understanding of the assumptions built into Western epistemologies and linguistic comprehension are at the heart of many of the issues embedded in the word "landscape."

This essay is dedicated to the memory of Annie Karrakayn (1930–2008), my mother, my mentor, and a grand Yanyuwa philosopher. Her words and name are used with the permission of her family who wish to celebrate her determination to impart to a wider world what it means to be Yanyuwa.

Acknowledgments

Helpful comments on previous drafts of this chapter were kindly provided by Amanda Kearney, Ian McNiven, Nonie Sharp, and Steve Johnston. I also gratefully acknowledge my Yanyuwa teachers and mentors for their continued guidance and teaching.

Notes

1. *Buwarrala Akarriya (Journey East)*, video, Marndaa Productions and Australian Broadcasting Commission, 1989.

2. See, for example, R. Layton, "Representing and Translating People's Place in the Landscape of Northern Australia," in *After Writing Culture: Epistemology and Praxis in*

Contemporary Anthropology, ed. A. James, J. Hockey, and A. Dawson (London: Routledge, 1997), pp. 122–143; H. Morphy, "Colonisation and Construction of Place: The Politics of Landscape in Northern Australia," in *Landscape, Politics, and Perspectives*, ed. B. Bender (Oxford: Berg, 1993), pp. 205–243; H. Morphy, "Landscape and the Reproduction of the Ancestral Past," in *The Anthropology of Landscape: Perspectives on Place and Space*, ed. E. Hirsch and M. O'Hanlon (Oxford: Clarendon Press, 1995), pp. 184–209; Frank Myers, *Pintubi Country, Pintubi Self: Sentiment, Place, and Politics among Western Desert Aborigines* (Berkeley: University of California Press, 1991); Deborah Bird Rose, *Dingo Makes Us Human: Life and Land in an Aboriginal Australian Culture* (Cambridge: Cambridge University Press, 1992).

3. J. Bradley, "Landscapes of the Mind, Landscapes of the Spirit: Negotiating a Sentient Landscape," in *Working on Country: Contemporary Indigenous Management of Australia's Lands and Coastal Regions*, ed. R. Baker, J. Davies, and E. Young (Melbourne: Oxford University Press, 2001), pp. 295–307; A. Kearney and J. Bradley, "Landscape with Shadows of Once Living People: Kundawira and the Challenge for Archaeology to Understand," in *The Social Archaeology of Indigenous Societies: Essays on Aboriginal History in Honor of Harry Lourandos*, ed. Bruno David, Ian McNiven, and Bryce Barker (Canberra: Aboriginal Studies Press, 2005); H. Morphy, *Ancestral Connections: Art and an Aboriginal System of Knowledge* (Chicago: University of Chicago Press, 1991); Deborah Bird Rose, *Country of the Heart: An Indigenous Australian Homeland* (Canberra: Aboriginal Studies Press, 2002); V. Strang, *Uncommon Ground: Cultural Landscapes and Environmental Values* (Oxford: Berg, 1997); Yanyuwa families, J. Bradley, and N. Cameron, *"Forget about Flinders": A Yanyuwa Atlas of the South Western Gulf of Carpentaria* (Gold Coast, Queensland: J. M. McGregor, 2005).

4. J. Bradley, "'We always look north': Yanyuwa Identity and the Marine Environment," in *Customary Marine Tenure in Australia*, ed. N. Peterson and B. Rigsby (Sydney: University of Sydney Oceania Publications, 1998), pp. 124–141; J. Bradley, "Wirriyarra Awara: Yanyuwa Land and Sea Scapes," *South Atlantic Quarterly* 98 (2000): 801–816; Buku-Larrngay Mulka Centre, *Saltwater People: Yirrkala Bark Paintings of Sea Country: Recognizing Indigenous Sea Rights* (Yirrkala: Buku-Larrngay Mulka Centre in Association with Jennifer Isaacs Publishing, 1999); I. McNiven, "Saltwater People: Spiritscapes, Maritime Rituals, and the Archeology of Australian Indigenous Seascapes," *World Archaeology* 35 (2003): 329–349; N. Sharp, *Saltwater People* (Crows Nest: Allen & Unwin, 2002).

5. I. McNiven, "Sentient Sea: Seascapes and Spiritscapes," in *Handbook of Landscape Archaeology*, ed. B. David and J. Thomas (Walnut Creek: Left Coast Press, 2008), pp. 149–157.

6. L. Rowntree, "The Landscape: A View from Geography," in *Tracking Knowledge in North Australian Landscapes: Studies in Indigenous and Settler Ecological Knowledge Systems*, ed. Deborah Bird Rose and A. Clarke (Darwin: North Australia Research Unit, 1997), pp. 1–18.

7. B. Ashcroft, "The Horizon Sublime," *Antipodes: A North American Journal of Australian Literature* 19 (2005): 141–151; K. Benterrak, S. Muecke, and P. Roe, *Reading the Country* (Fremantle: Fremantle Arts Centre Press, 1984); F. Devlin-Glass, "An Atlas of the Sacred: Hybridity, Representability, and the Myths of Yanyuwa Country," *Antipodes: A North American Journal of Australian Literature* 19 (2005): 127–140.

8. E. Casey, *The Fate of Place: A Philosophical History* (Berkeley: University of California Press, 1998).

9. B. Bender, "Introduction: Landscapes—Meaning and Action," in *Landscape, Politics, and Perspectives*, ed. B. Bender (London: Berg, 1993), pp. 1–18.

10. See P. Tacon, "Socializing Landscapes: The Long-term Implications of Signs, Symbols, and Marks on the Land," *Archaeology in Oceania* 29 (1994): 117–129; B. David and H. Lourandos, "Landscape as Mind: Land Use, Cultural Space, and Change in North Queensland Prehistory," *Quaternary International* 59 (1999): 107–123.

11. K. Basso, "Wisdom Sits in Places: Notes on Western Apache Landscape," in *Senses of Place*, ed. S. Feld and K. Basso (Santa Fe: School of American Research Press, 1996), pp. 53–70; E. Casey, "How to Get from Space to Place in a Fairly Short Stretch of Time: Phenomenological Prolegomena," in *Senses of Place*, ed. S. Feld and K. Basso, pp. 13–52; F. Tamisari, "Names and Naming: Speaking Forms into Place," in *The Land Is a Map: Place Names of Indigenous Origin in Australia*, ed. L. Hercus, F. Hodges, and J. Simpson (Canberra: Pandanus Press, 2002), pp. 87–102.

12. J. Thomas, *Time, Culture, and Identity* (London: Routledge, 1996), p. 173.

13. M. Kearney, "An Archaeology of Engagement: Yanyuwa Country and the Lived Cultural Domains in Archaeology," in *The Social Archaeology of Indigenous Societies: Essays on Aboriginal History in Honour of Harry Lourandos*, ed. Bruno David, Ian McNiven, and Bryce Barker Canberra: Aboriginal Studies Press, 2005); M. Langton, "The Edge of the Sacred, the Edge of Death: Sensual Inscriptions," in *Inscribed Landscapes: Marking and Making Place*, ed. B. David and M. Wilson (Honolulu: University of Hawaii Press, 2002), pp. 253–269; Bradley, "Landscapes of the Mind," pp. 295–307; E. Povinelli, "Might Be Something: The Language of Indeterminacy in Australian Land Use," *Man* 28 (1993): 679–704; Rose, *Dingo Makes Us Human*; Deborah Bird Rose, *Nourishing Terrains: Australian Aboriginal Views on Landscape and Wilderness* (Canberra: Australian Heritage Commission, 1996).

14. Basso, "Wisdom Sits in Places," p. 5.

15. Thomas, *Time, Culture, and Identity*, p. 88.

16. B. David and M. Wilson, "Re-Reading the Landscape: Place and Identity in NE Australia during the Late Holocene," *Cambridge Archaeological Journal* 9 (1999): 163–188.

17. E. Casey, *Getting Back into Place: Toward a Renewed Understanding of the Place-World* (Bloomington: Indiana University Press, 1993); E. Casey, *The Fate of Place: A Philosophical History* (Berkeley: University of California Press, 1998).

18. C. A. Tilley, *Phenomenology of Landscapes: Place, Paths, and Monuments* (Oxford: Berg, 1994).

19. Thomas, *Time, Culture, and Identity*.

20. See M. Heidegger, *Being and Time*, trans. John Macquarrie and Edward Robinson (New York: Harper & Row, 1962), and also "Building Dwelling Thinking," in *Poetry, Language, Thought*, trans. Albert Hofstadter (New York: Harper & Row, 1971), pp. 143–162.

21. D. Idhe, "Introduction," in *The Conflict in Interpretation: Essays in Hermeneutics*, ed. D. Idhe (Evanston: Northwestern University Press, 1974), p. xi.

22. B. Scholte, "Toward a Reflexive and Critical Anthropology," in *Reinventing Anthropology*, ed. D. Hymes (New York: Pantheon, 1972), pp. 430–457; P. Bourdieu, *Outline of a Theory of Practice* (Cambridge: Cambridge University Press, 1979).

23. P. Ricoeur, "Foreword," in *The Conflict in Interpretation: Essays in Hermeneutics*, ed. D. Idhe (Evanston: Northwestern University Press, 1974), p. xii.

24. E. Bielawski, "Inuit Indigenous Knowledge and Science in the Arctic," in *Naked Science: Anthropological Inquiry into Boundaries, Power, and Knowledge*, ed. L. Nader (New York: Routledge, 1996), pp. 216–227.

25. E. Povinelli, "Might Be Something," *Man* 28 (1993): 695.

26. J. Bradley, "How Can a Whitefella Know It All . . . ? Indigenous Science/Western Science and Marine Turtles,' in *Marine Turtle Conservation and Management in Northern Australia*, proceedings of a workshop held at Northern Territory University, Darwin, June 3–4, 1997 (Darwin: Centre for Indigenous Natural and Cultural Resource Management and Centre for Tropical Wetlands Management, Northern Territory University, 1997), pp. 25–33.

27. See J. Bradley, "Singing Through the Sea: Song, Sea, and Emotion," in *Deep Blue: Critical Reflections on Nature, Religion, and Water*, ed. Sylvie Shaw and Andrew Francis (London: Equinox Publishers, 2008), and "When a Stone Tool Is a Dingo: Country and Relatedness in Australian Aboriginal Notions of Landscape,' in *Handbook of Landscape Archaeology*, ed. B. David and J. Thomas (Walnut Creek: Left Coast Press, 2008), pp. 633–637.

28. W. E. H. Stanner, "The Dreaming," in *Traditional Aboriginal Society*, 2nd. ed., ed. W. H. Edwards (Melbourne: MacMillan Education Australia, 1998), pp. 227–238; F. Tamisari and J. Bradley, "Place and Event," in *Animal Names*, ed. A. Minelli, G. Ortalli, and G. Sanga (Venice: Instituto Veneto Di Scienze Lettere Ed Arti, 2005).

29. See P. Wolfe, "On Being Woken Up: The 'Dreamtime' in Anthropology in Australian Settler Culture," *Comparative Studies in Society and History* 133 (1991): 197–224.

30. J. Bradley, "Wirriyarra Awara: Yanyuwa Land and Sea Scapes," *South Atlantic Quarterly* 98 (2000): 801–816.

31. D. B. Rose, "Indigenous Ecological Knowledge and the Scientific Community," in *Bushfire '97 Proceedings: Australian Bushfire Conference*, July 8–10 (Darwin, Northern Territory, 1997), p. 70.

32. Rose, *Nourishing Terrains*, p. 7.

33. D. B. Rose, *Reports from a Wild Country: Ethics for Decolonisation* (Sydney: UNSW Press, 2004), p. 34.

34. Yanyuwa families et al., *"Forget about Flinders."*

35. See P. Carter, *The Road to Botany Bay* (London: Faber & Faber, 1987).

36. See J. Bradley, "Landscapes of the Mind"; Kearney, "An Archaeology of Engagement"; A. Kearney and J. A. Bradley, "Landscape with Shadows of Once Living People: Kundawira and the Challenge for Archaeology to Understand," in *The Social Archaeology of Indigenous Societies: Essays on Aboriginal History in Honor of Harry Lourandos*, ed. Bruno David, Ian McNiven, and Bryce Barker (Canberra: Aboriginal Studies Press, 2005).

37. Old Pyro Dirdiyalma, personal communication, 1985.

38. Bradley, "'We Always Look North,'" pp. 125–141.

39. Composed by Dinah Norman, Annie Karrakayny, and Eileen McDinny, 1992.

40. J. Bradley et al., *Yumbulyumbulmantha ki-awarawu-All Kinds of things from Country-Yanyuwa ethnobiological classification*, Aboriginal and Torres Strait Islander Studies Unit Research Report Series, volume 6 (St. Lucia: University of Queensland, 2006).

41. M. Walsh, "The Land Still Speaks? Language and Landscape in Aboriginal Australia," in *Tracking Knowledge in North Australian Landscapes: Studies in Indigenous and Settler Ecological Knowledge Systems*, ed. Deborah Bird Rose and A. Clarke (Darwin: North Australia Research Unit, 1997), pp. 105–119.

42. H. Marsh et al., *The Stranding of Dugongs and Sea Turtles Resulting from Cyclone Kathy, March 1984: A Report of the Rescue Effort and the Biological Data Obtained* (Darwin: Conservation Commission of the Northern Territory, 1986).

43. See Bradley, "Singing Through the Sea," pp. 17–32.

44. Rose, *Nourishing Terrains*, p. 7.

45. Povinelli, "Might Be Something," p. 690.

46. R. Netting, *Cultural Ecology* (Sydney: Cummings Publishing Company, 1977), p. 2.

47. G. Watson and D. Chambers, *Singing the Land, Signing the Land* (Melbourne: Deakin University Press, 1998), p. vi.

48. Povinelli, "Might Be Something," p. 690.

49. M. Christie, "Aboriginal Science for the Ecologically Sustainable Future," *Australian Teachers Journal* 37 (1991): 26–31; M. Christie, "Transdisciplinary Research and Aboriginal Knowledge," *Australian Journal of Indigenous Education* 35 (2006): 78–89.

50. Rose, "Indigenous Ecological Knowledge."

4 Landscapes as Temporalspatial Phenomena

Theodore R. Schatzki

Landscapes are often construed essentially as spatial phenomena. Despite this, it is obvious that landscapes are spatial-temporal entities, that is, are entities that at once occur in time and occupy or define an expanse of space. The present essay goes beyond this evident truth in holding that landscapes are not just *spatial-temporal* phenomena, but *temporalspatial* ones as well. They are temporalspatial by virtue of anchoring and being drawn into something I call the timespace of human activity. The term "timespace" is deliberately chosen: it signals that the temporality and spatiality that compose activity timespace are inherently connected and also fundamentally different from the objective space and time that are intended in the verity that landscapes are spatial-temporal entities.

The phenomenon of *activity timespace* is largely overlooked in humanistic and social theory. I have elsewhere argued that it is an important feature of social life.[1] Among other things, interwoven activity timespaces form infrastructures that run through and are essential to social affairs. To the extent, accordingly, that landscapes anchor and are drawn into interwoven timespaces, they undergird and figure in a key social infrastructure. More pertinent to the present volume, the temporalspatial character of anything, including a landscape, is that through which it is involved in place. This is because timespace is the dimensionality of human proceeding in place, where by place I mean the "open, cleared, gathered 'region' or 'locale' in which [people] find [themselves] along with other things."[2] In anchoring and being drawn into timespaces, landscapes undergird and figure in human existence in place.

This essay proceeds in two stages. I first derive the idea of the timespace of human activity from the early work of the philosopher Martin Heidegger, contrasting this idea with (1) types of space-time that dominate contemporary social theory and (2) ideas of the archaeologist Christopher Gosden that move toward it. Following this, I explore the character of

landscapes as temporalspatial phcnomena, illustrating my claims with examples taken from the horse farm landscape and practices of the Bluegrass
region surrounding Lexington, Kentucky, where I reside.

Before beginning, I must discharge two preliminaries. First, I need to
delimit what I mean by "landscapes." Although I have nothing new or
noteworthy to say about this term, clarifying my use of it is important
for what follows. As is well known to any reader of this volume, the term
"landscape" is variously interpreted. Landscapes are taken to be, among
other things, things seen, visual scenes, morphological phenomena,[3] sites
of human dwelling,[4] or cognitive or symbolic constructions.[5] I will preserve the idea that a landscape is a visible scene. Landscapes, to be sure,
are much more than visible objects alone. According to my neopictorial
understanding, however, nothing can be a landscape that is not visible.
Central among the other things a landscape is is a place of human habitation. Hence, I will define a landscape as a portion of the wider world
around that can be taken in visually where human activity takes place.
Three notes. First, a landscape is a portion of the world, not a view of it
(compare Cosgrove's 1984 notion of a way of seeing[6]). This portion can
be taken in visually, and this fact is essential to its being a landscape, but
the landscape is the thing, not the visual experience. Second, in speaking
of the world "around," I indicate that the person who takes in a landscape
is usually in it (even if off to one side): her activities are among those that
make a landscape a site of human activity. I also therewith mean to suggest
that someone who takes in a landscape is not likely to be involved with it
as spectator alone. Finally, I speak of the "wider" world around to distinguish landscapes from more constricted settings such as rooms, subway
cars, and Manhattan street corners.

The second preliminary matter is to introduce the horse farm landscape
of the Kentucky Bluegrass. The Bluegrass region of Kentucky is an expanse
of rolling hills eroded by streams and lacking any substantial river or lake.
The city of Lexington lies at the center of the region, which is otherwise
composed of farmland and small towns. Different types of farm are found
there, including commercial stock farms, family farms, and horse farms.
The overall region is dominated by the horse farms, of which there are
more than 1,000 encompassing roughly 100,000 acres of land. These horse
farms dominate the landscape owing to their size and extensive shaping
of the land. A prominent feature of these farms (for analysis see Raitz[7] and
Domer[8]) is their parklike lands divided into paddocks, pastures, and copses
by miles of plank fences. Other prominent features (see figure 4.1) include
an elaborate entrance opening on to a stately tree-lined driveway that leads

THE CONTEMPORARY BLUEGRASS ESTATE

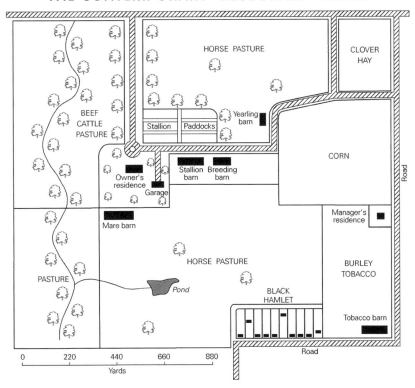

Figure 4.1

Archetypical Bluegrass horse farm. From Karl Raitz, "Negro Hamlets and Agricultural Estates in Kentucky's Inner Bluegrass," *Geographical Review* 64, 1974. Reprinted by permission.

to an elegant main residence, barns and residences distributed through the property, and a small network of private lanes.

The layouts and components of these farms are remarkably consistent, and even the state-run Kentucky Horse Park located outside Lexington among the horse farms looks much like another farm. The overall effect is of a manicured, aesthetically pleasing tapestry of enclosures, lanes, copses, and stately mansions through which streams and tree-lined roads wander.

Most horse farms are owned as an avocation, not as a profession. The owners include local families, wealthy urbanites or celebrities, and, increasingly, foreign nobles and businesspeople. Many owners do not reside at their farms, using them instead as retreats from work and city life. Profit does not govern these farms' operations. They are run for pleasure, in pursuit of a landed gentry lifestyle, or out of a love for horse racing. The Bluegrass region probably contains the largest collection of "gentleman" horse farms in the world. The appealing appearance of these horse farms is conscious and deliberate and hews to particular aesthetic tastes and ideals.[9] In part because of their beauty, not just the Bluegrass region, but the state of Kentucky as a whole, is associated by non-Kentuckians with horses and horse-farm landscapes. The beauty of the landscape also draws large numbers of visitors to the region, both tourists and buyers of the horses that are bred, raised, and boarded on the farms. The horse farms are also big business, with stud fees ranging as high as $500,000.

I   Timespace

For some time now, social theorists have studied the space of society. For even longer they have examined time as it intersects and characterizes social life. Only of late have theorists begun to ponder space-time, that is, time and space as dimensions, aspects, or components of a single phenomenon.[10] The dominant practice remains, however, to theorize space or time separately.

The Standard Accounts

Two features characterize most of the space-times that are attributed to social life in contemporary thought. The first is that they are objective manifolds, entities that persist independently of human activity, apprehension, and comprehension. Objectivity does not preclude humans from having contingent relations to space-time and its features, for example, experiencing and causing them. But the spatial and temporal properties people experience or effect persist independently of human activity, comprehension, and apprehension. In the modern era, moreover, the common denominator of conceptions of objective time is succession. Wherever events occur before and after one another, there is succession—and time; absolute, relational, and relativistic time are different interpretations of succession (of before and after orderings). For the sake of simplicity, consequently, I will equate objective time with succession in the following. I will also equate objective space with three-dimensional space, this being a pervasive modern conception of objective space.

The second prominent feature of the space-times attributed to social life is that they are conjunctions of time and space thought of as separate phenomena, that is, as phenomena that are not inherently connected. Even when time and space are treated as arising from the same processes, for example, those of the capitalist mode of production, they are conceptualized as separate. The resulting space-times lack genuine unity.

Classical Galilean space-time, though not a form of social space-time, illustrates these two features. This space-time consists of absolute time plus Euclidean space. Time and space so conceived of are objective phenomena. There is no inherent connection, moreover, between position in absolute time and position in Euclidean space. An event has a location in this time and a location in this space, and its location in objective space-time is the conjunction of these.

An important social theoretical appropriation of Galilean space-time is the time-geography of Torsten Hägerstrand and his associates.[11] In its signature representational technique, this approach treats space as an objective two-dimensional plane, across which people move. The two axes of space are complemented by a third axis, that of objective clock or calendar time. This three-dimensional system allows the locations a person occupies in space over time to be plotted in an immediately graspable graph. The resulting lines represent the paths people take in their lives. Intersections of these lines represent the simultaneous existence of people in particular locations in space and can be taken to stand for, among other things, face-to-face interactions. This technique, inspired by Galilean space-time, treats the space of social life as a two-dimensional plane and its time as absolute or relational as one pleases. Time and space are both objective and separate. An action is performed somewhere in two-dimensional space and at a particular time, and its objective space-time location is the conjunction of these. The only thing linking the two is that an action always has a location in both.

Not all the space-times ascribed to social existence combine objective space and time. They all, however, treat space and time as separable phenomena. To give some sense of this variety, consider Parkes and Thrift's splendid and comprehensive account of the formation and dynamics of place.[12] Parkes and Thrift depict places as resulting from the coalescence and coordination of multiple activities, events, and practices. A particular horse farm, for instance, might result from the coalescence and coordination of family activities and events, breeding and training practices, owner–employee relations, country government agencies and land use regulations, wider economic practices, racing events, celebrations, and so on. Space and time, too, are among the factors that determine the formation and transformation of place. As indicated, however, the spaces and times involved are not objective ones alone, for example, distance, point, interval, and instant. In particular, the authors acknowledge the pertinence of

Figure 4.2
Paddocks and passageways. Photograph by the author.

experiential time and space to place, drawing on such neophenomenolo-
gists as Yi-Fu Tuan[13] and Anne Buttimer[14] to explicate experiential time
and space. For example, among the factors bound up with the formation,
maintenance, and transformation of a horse farm are not just objective
temporal factors such as clock time, the time metal takes to heat, and the
biological rhythms of sleep and gestation, and not just objective spatial
factors such as elevation differences and distances between, as well as the
relative orientations of, buildings, but also experiential temporal and spatial factors such as perceptions of long and quick times, judgments of too
early and too late, and senses of crowdedness and spaciousness.

Parkes and Thrift make time and space real factors in the dynamics of
place. They also treat time and space as separate phenomena, which are
contingently brought together in a variety of ways. This is clearly indicated
in their initial discussion of the formation of place.[15] The authors lump
together objective and experiential spatial elements, on the one hand, and
objective and experiential temporal elements, on the other, and explain

that different combinations of elements from the two (four) sets come together in different social situations. "For any [person] a combination of the four space and time elements produces a structured space-time which is place."[16] Space-time is composed of combinations of elements of the four types. Parkes and Thrift thus treat space-time as the conjunction of spatial being and temporal being. Connections between temporal and spatial properties might be extensive, but they link separate matters.

I emphasize that I hold no brief against most versions of the idea that social life exhibits space-times that conjoin separate and typically objective spaces and times. Such space-times are important features of social affairs. Social life, however, harbors a kind of nonconjoined and also nonobjective timespace that is equally crucial to it.

Activity Timespace

This nonconjoined and nonobjective timespace is the timespace of human activity. As its name suggests, it is a feature or dimension of human activity. Before discussing it, I want to consider a conception of space-time due to the archaeologist Christopher Gosden that combines objective and activity times and spaces.

The central concept in Gosden's account of social life is that of a system of reference.[17] A system of reference is a network of actions separated in time and space. This concept is designed to highlight the interconnectedness of actions. Gosden's discussion also emphasizes that time and space are dimensions of action networks: "Space and time are not . . . abstract qualities providing the medium of social action, but rather . . . dimensions created through"[18] systems of reference. Space and time are features of social life *cum* linked human activities.

Examples of spaces are landscapes, dwellings, and other forms of material culture treated as material phenomena, physical arrangements of the world. Material configurations are spaces in the sense that they are arrangements amid which human beings proceed. Coordinated with these material spaces, moreover, are bodily skills that are acquired by learning to act in these spaces and that subtend the performance of action in them. The bodilyness of the skills corresponds to the materiality of the spaces. In fact, bodies and material spaces form complexes: "Each generation is socialized within a particular landscape and this becomes something that we are";[19] "material settings are thus internal to our social being, not external."[20] And just as a system of reference reworks spaces, such that material spaces are a product of the system, the material world acts on humans, constraining what they do and shaping their skills and opportunities.

Spaces, consequently, play three roles in human life.[21] They constitute, first, room-for-maneuver, open areas through which people can proceed and deploy their skills. Spaces, second, set bounds on movement, physically constraining what people do. These first two functions are material in nature, a matter of material opportunities and restrictions. The third function of spaces is to serve as "stage setting." Gosden writes nothing about this third function, instead stressing the materiality of spaces and the complexes that spaces form with bodily skills. He suggests only that by "stage setting" he means how spaces are the settings where humans interact. As I explain below, material arrangements are stage settings, or spaces of activity, in a more pervasive and intimate way than this by virtue of comprising entities that are drawn into human activity.

The time, meanwhile, that characterizes systems of reference has two components. The first is time-scale. When, for instance, Gosden provocatively writes that there are as "many forms of time as there are types of practice," he immediately continues by stating that "[t]hese time-scales derive partly from the nature of the materials being worked with: pottery, metal, and wood all have different time-scales contained in their production, necessitating different structures of action."[22] Time-scales are lengths of objective time.

The second temporal component pertains to the structure of human activity, not to different stretches of objective time. Gosden writes: "I used the term 'reference' to explore how every act is connected to a whole series of other acts in space. We can now see that this structure is also temporal, linked together by forms of anticipation and memory."[23] Again, "Action creates space, in this case the area to be covered by a garden, and space enables the deployment of skilled action. Time is also involved, not just in terms of the weeks that it will take to prepare a garden, but in the anticipations of the future harvest and the chain of actions the garden's produce can promote."[24] The second type of time that characterizes a system of reference is the nexus of memories and expectations that informs the actions composing the system. Because expectations often derive from memory, this nexus of memories and expectations in activity can be redescribed as the use of the past to construct the present and future. Gosden calls this use "recursiveness."[25] Time as recursiveness is a web of memory and expectation informing activity. It is also a version of activity time: time as a dimension of activity. Time *qua* recursiveness differs from time *qua* time-scale. For the use of the past—memory and expectation—has no inherent connection to the magnitude of separation between events that occur before and after one another. Memory and expectation are matters, instead, of the past and future.

Memories and expectations are ordered and connected, furthermore, in social practices. Practices, accordingly, enable, enjoin, and sustain connections between past and future that inform activity, particular orderings of time *qua* recursiveness. In city-county planning practices, for instance, memories of past land use regulations and the results they brought about form expectations about likely responses to proposed regulations, thus determining decisions that planners presently take. Practices contain numerous such couplings of past, present, and future.

Gosden claims that different times are harbored in different practices. He means this in a twofold sense: that the actions and processes that occur in different practices belong to different time-scales (contrast the practices of grooming, city-county planning, tourism, and fox hunting) and that the actions involved are informed by different couplings of memory and expectation, past and future. Still, Gosden's version of activity time is a disposition of objective time. For it is a connectedness between present activity and present states (i.e., memories and expectations) that refer to past or future states of affairs, that is, states of affairs that occur before or after present activity. Recursiveness is thus a configuration of activity, states, and states of affairs in objective time. As discussed, furthermore, space for Gosden is material space. Hence, Gosden, unlike Parkes and Thrift, fails to break with the objectivist character of most contemporary accounts of space-time. Like all theorists, finally, Gosden conceives of space-time as a conjunction of separate matters: "Possibility and limit exist in four dimensions . . . : space, time, mutuality, and materiality, all of which are both socially created and creating. I see these four dimensions as being shaped into different space-time systems, designating the spatial and temporal unfolding of social action."[26] Space-time is simply a conjunction of time (time-scales and memory-expectation couplings in action) and space (material arrangements in the world).

I want now to outline the concept of activity timespace, which, like Gosden's ideas, derives from Heidegger. According to this concept, however, (1) timespace is not objective and (2) time and space are inherently joined.

The spatial component of this activity timespace is the world around in its pertinence to and involvement in what people do. Gosden captures the idea of the world around in his notion of material spaces but fails to treat these spaces as drawn into and involved in human activity. The spatial component of activity timespace is not an arrangement of physical objects, though it is closely connected to such arrangements. Rather, it is an array of places and paths, where a place is a place to X (X is an action)

Figure 4.3
A fence is a place to watch a horse. Photograph by the author.

and a path is a path for getting from A to B. A plank fence, for example, is a place to watch a horse or to strain to get a glimpse of a mansion, whereas Old Frankfort Pike is path for getting between Lexington and home or for taking in the sights of the horse-farm landscape. Places and paths are anchored at (usually relatively stable) objects, where by "anchor" I mean object at which a place or path is located: this relatively stable object, a fence, is where places to watch exist, and this relatively stable object, a road, is where a path between city and home exists. Because objects such as fences and roads are physical in composition, where a place or path is anchored is at once its location in the physical world, in Gosden's material spaces. Note that a given place or path can be anchored in changing sets of objects: not just fences, but also windows, crests of roads, and shady trees can be places to watch a horse or to strain to get a view. Where, furthermore, places and paths are anchored is a matter of human understanding: this object, a fence, is where places to watch exist because humans understand fences as places from which to watch, whereas this object, Old Frankfort Pike, is a path to and from the city because humans understand roads as paths to destinations, and this one connects city and home.

Over the course of a person's day, she deals with objects (and arrangements thereof) as places to do so and so and as paths to such and such; it is as places and paths that objects are bound up with her activity. Indeed, over the course of the day, a person weaves through complex arrays of places and paths that affect and reflect the course, direction, and metamorphosis of her activity. Of course, she also deals with, say, the fence and the road as physical objects: she adjusts her arms and feet to the elevation of the planks as she leans on them, and she avoids potholes. Such adjustment and avoidance, however, are subservient to the activities of watching the horses, getting a view, and going to and from Lexington (or keeping her car in good condition). Places and paths are also organized into settings, locales, and regions such as, respectively, the paddocks, the farm, the farms along the Pike, Woodford county, and the Bluegrass region.

Let us now consider the time component of activity timespace. My Heideggerian conception of this component is heir to a tradition, originating with Augustine, that embraces the idea of a human time. In the twentieth century, this tradition was perpetuated by conceptions of lived, experiential, existential, and activity time. These conceptions connect time to human life, experience, existence, or activity and contrast time so understood with objective time.

The time of activity is not a figure or configuration of succession. It is characterized, instead, by past, present, and future. Of course, as the discussion of Gosden showed, past, present, and future also characterize events (and states of affairs). To order events as past, present, and future is to understand some as no longer occurring, others as occurring, and still others as not yet occurring. The past, present, and future that compose the time of activity, however, do not order events. Rather, they are dimensions of human activity. An important difference between past, present, and future events and the past, present, and future of activity is that the former form a succession whereas the latter do not follow one another; instead, they occur together, at one stroke. The past of human activity is not something that no longer exists, that trails off behind the present, just like the future of activity is not something that does not yet exist, that hovers before the present. Past, present, and future occur together. Their simultaneity will become clearer as I proceed.

Heidegger's analysis of this time is found in his interpretation of human existence as being-in-the-world.[27] Heidegger expands this interpretation by characterizing being-in-the-world as projecting, thrown being-amid entities. Projection, thrownness, and being-amid are the future, past, and present, respectively, of activity.[28] Projection is acting for the sake of a possible way of being. When people act, they do so for the sake of some way of being (for example, being a successful horse breeder, enjoying a vacation, keeping horse-farm operations running smoothly)—toward which they come in acting. This projecting–coming toward is the future dimension of activity. Thrownness, meanwhile, is people being such that certain states of affairs and not others matter to them. When something matters to someone, her actions reflect, respond to, and/or are otherwise sensitive to it. It is something given, from which she departs in acting. This departing–coming from is the past dimension of activity. Being amid, finally, is having to do with entities, that is, being engaged in the world: acting toward, with, and amid (*bei*) entities. A person, when acting, is always stretched between that toward which she is coming and that from which she is departing. This stretched-outness is the opening up of the future, present, and past of activity.

This structure can be described in more familiar terms. The future dimension of activity, coming toward something projected, is acting for an end. The past dimension of activity, departing from something given, is responding to something or acting in its light, that is, being motivated. The present of activity is activity itself. The time of activity is, thus, acting toward an end from what motivates. It is a teleological phenomenon.

The space of places and paths, however, is also a teleological phenomenon. Places and paths are of and for human activity. Their distributed anchoring indicates how the material settings through which people live house their activities and subtend their ends: Where it is sensible to perform this and that action that are components of projects carried out for particular ends. The anchoring of places and paths thus derives from the teleological structure of human activity. The fact, for instance, that fences anchor places to watch horses indicates how they can be involved in activities such as supervision and enjoyment and serve the ends pursued therein. The derivation of spatiality from teleology is also reflected in two familiar facts. The first is that use objects are defined by their uses, thus by human projects. The rough definition of a fence as a continuous built structure that divides land, for instance, indicates how fences can be involved in such activities as riding, supervision, or landscaping and serve the ends pursued therein. The second fact is that people lay out settings—fields, homes, barns, roads—with an eye to the activities that are supposed to be performed in them, thus by reference to human projects and ends. Note that spaces of activity are teleologically underpinned even when places and paths are determined not by a given person's activities and ends, but by social norms that specify how "one" acts. For instance, this object called a fence affords places to watch horses, not because Joe, say, wants to watch horses, but because this is what people do. Normativized places and paths are still teleologically underpinned because social norms that govern the use of objects reflect prevalent activities, projects, and ends. I add that the existence of such norms indicates that the rules (and understandings, etc.) that are responsible for activity space are social phenomena, that is, in this context, are properties of social practices.

I acknowledge that the significance of objects for human activity is not just teleological. Some objects, for instance, have ritual, ceremonial, or aesthetic significance. The layout of the tree-lined driveway between farm entrance and family mansion might reflect aesthetic matters as much as it does teleological ones. Similarly, horse-farm horse cemeteries are places for such activities as remembrance, meditation, and connecting with the past. Because pursuing these activities need not be oriented toward ends, the places anchored at the cemetery need not be teleological in character. Still, the institution of ceremonial, ritual, and aesthetic places and paths occurs amid and against the background of a more extensive teleological organization of space.

In any event, both the time and space of activity are teleological phenomena. In fact, they reflect one and the same teleological structure of human activity: This structure coincides with activity time and underpins the space of places and paths. Human activities thus institute and bear timespaces whose temporal and spatial dimensions are inherently, not contingently, connected. Indeed, the two dimensions are coordinately instituted together. This coinstitution contrasts with the conjoined nature of the space-times discussed above.

Any human life proceeds in timespaces that it itself opens, that exist only because life proceeds teleologically. Temporality is directionally acting toward and from events and states of affairs, whereas spatiality captures the bearing of entities about people for their directional activity. This is why it is through timespace, the dimensionality of activity, that humans proceed in place, in the open region in which they find themselves along with other things.

My discussion to this point might have suggested that the timespaces of a human life are monadic in nature. In fact, they are social. A person's actions are moments of social practices in which others participate. A practice, moreover, is organized by a set of determinations and orientations (rules, understandings, ends, projects, emotions), subsets of which help govern the actions of different participants in it.[29] Practices, consequently, delimit the teleologies that govern the activities of participants in them. In doing so, they circumscribe the timespaces of practitioners' lives.

More specifically, the timespaces of those who participate in a given practice are partly common, partly shared, and partly idiosyncratic. Common timespaces arise from the fact that, in any given practice, certain ends, motivations, and activities are enjoined. This enjoinment lays down common futures and pasts and underpins common places and paths. Enjoined in training practices, for instance, are such ends as enhancing speed and preventing injury, such motivations as sloppy turf and poor reactions to other horses, and such activities as timed sprints and giving horses days off. This enjoinment lays down common futures and pasts for trainers and riders (and also horses), as well as underpinning a common space in which they act. Common timespaces also arise from (1) the aforementioned normativization of what people do with/at certain entities and (2) the sameness of, or similarities between, the material settings in which different people carry on a given practice.

The timespaces of participants are also partly shared. This shared dimension arises when different participants contingently pursue and understand the same acceptable—as opposed to enjoined—ends, activities, and paths/places. When tourists pursue the same acceptable end, say, catching a glimpse of a famous race horse, react to the same state of affairs, say, the unscheduled cancellation of a given horse farm tour, or understand alike that a given place is anchored at a given entity, say, a bend in the road as a place to gaze at the landscape, their lives share futures, pasts, and spaces. Finally, the third, idiosyncratic dimension of timespace arises from people idiosyncratically pursuing certain purposes and activities, being motivated by particular states of affairs, and understanding the world in particular ways. Common, shared, and idiosyncratic timespaces all exist against the background of the organization of a practice and the range of temporal and spatial determinations that it carries.[30]

In sum, any human activity opens a teleological timespace. When a person acts, she usually comes toward particular states of affairs, goes back to other states of affairs, and acts amid an array of places and paths tied to the teleological structure of human activity. Since people's activities are moments of social practices, the timespaces of those who participate in a given practice are partly common, partly shared, and partly idiosyncratic. With this account of activity timespace in hand, let us now turn to examine landscapes as temporalspatial phenomena.

II Landscapes as Temporalspatial Phenomena

In the introduction, I defined a landscape as a portion of the greater world around that can be taken in visually where human activity takes place. The temporalspatial nature of landscapes consists in how landscapes are drawn into and anchor the (interwoven) timespaces of people's activities as they carry on social practices. My consideration of the temporal-spatial character of landscapes begins by focusing on their status as visual object.

Landscapes are visually encountered in such activities as looking, gazing, observing, scrutinizing, staring, scanning, sizing up, checking out, and casting an eye over. The wider world around acquires the status of landscape only if the possibility exists of people engaging in one or more of these activities with regard to it. Since actions are moments of practices, it is in carrying out a practice that a person performs one of these activities with regard to a portion of the world around her. Hence, in examining landscapes as visually encounterable entities, we must consider the practices in which the wider world around is taken up as such. Of course, in almost any practice and activity a person is directed toward the world, cognizant of it in some way or other. In many activities and practices, moreover, people look at, scrutinize, and size up various entities and settings about them. That people are generally oriented toward entities and settings around them does not imply that they are encountering landscapes. The child who watches a DVD player while his parents wind their way through the horse farm countryside is not encountering a landscape, nor are his

Figure 4.4
Typical Bluegrass horse farm. Photograph by the author.

parents when they scrutinize a road sign, check the odometer, anxiously search for indications of the next roadside eatery, or look around the old-fashioned interior of the eatery. A landscape is a portion of the wider world around receding from the immediate setting of action that can be taken in—scrutinized, gazed at, and so on—as an expanse.

The wider world around thus figures as a landscape only in certain practices. More specifically, horse farm landscapes occur as such only in certain practices, for instance, those of touristry, city-county planning, historical preservation, fox hunting, and aesthetic appreciation. Horse-farm landscapes do not figure as such in other practices that are plied in this landscape, for instance, horse training, barn maintenance, building construction, sports, veterinary medicine, and children's play. Therefore, although encountering a Bluegrass horse landscape is hardly a specialized activity, it is an occasional one whose frequency probably correlates with other social marks such as occupation, education, class, and the like. The wealthy horse-farm owner and the poor Latino hired hand who trudges daily between the farm and one of the small hamlets that dot the horse-farm landscape out of sight of main roads and hilltop mansions encounter the world around them differently. The owner is more likely than the farm-hand regularly to encounter the farm's expanse as landscape.

In different practices, moreover, the places from which the wider world around is encountered as such are anchored in different subsets of the material entities that make up that world. Whereas the owner encounters the wider world as landscape at a second floor window, from a private road, on a hill on his property, and from on horseback, the tourist and historical preservationist encounter this along the main roads that pass through the countryside or from the private roads visited on a farm tour, while the fox hunter encounters them on horseback in the countryside and from under trees.

One way landscapes are involved in action is by being the objects of seeing activities (looking, gazing, etc.). Like other entities, they can also be involved in action by virtue of filling out the future and past of activity. This is an important way that landscapes are drawn into timespaces. When this occurs, a portion of the world around that can be taken in visually helps, as such, to constitute that to which someone reacts (or in the light of which she acts) or that toward which she comes in acting. For example, for the sake of seeing the landscape is the activity future of an horse-farm owner who is ascending a hill to overlook her property, just as it might be that of tourists who have finished lunch and are resuming their journey or of fox hunters who are finished with a kill (mostly coyotes, not foxes). Aspects of landscapes help make out the past of activity when, for example, an owner proposes to her family that some feature of the landscape be changed so as to enhance its appearance, a tourist takes a side road in search of a better scene (the present one is unsatisfactory), a fox hunter proposes that the ride stop for lunch in a particularly scenic spot, or a city planner advocates a particular positioning of a new road so as not to spoil the beauty of existing arrangements. Of course, it must not be forgotten that landscapes also occur in objective time. Not only do they and their features persist and change in objective time, but landscapes are encountered as landscapes, and form the futures or pasts of activities, for as long as the relevant activities are performed.

A landscape is encountered as such for only as long as the activities in which it is so encountered are performed. Landscapes, however, are not landscapes for only as long as they are encountered as such. Regardless of whether a landscape happens or happens not to be visually taken in as such during a given stretch of time, it can constitute a space of activity during that time. That is, regardless of whether or not it is taken in as such, a portion of the world around can be pertinent to and involved in activities and practices as an array of places and paths. When this occurs, landscapes are temporalspatial by virtue of anchoring spatialities. Again, this phenomenon must be distinguished from that of immediate settings anchoring places and paths through which activity proceeds. The car in which the tourist sits, like the hilltop copse under which the owner reclines and the roadside pullout where the city planner takes a rest, forms the immediate space, the array of paths and places closest to hand, though which these people's current and nascent activity proceeds. A landscape forms a space of activity when an array of places and paths that is distributed across a portion of the wider world around is relevant to what people do. Such is obviously the case in horse-farm supervision practices when the owner and his principal manager systematically move around the farm, inspecting various structures and watching the training of horses in different paddocks. It is also obviously the case in city-county planning practices when a planner moves through the landscape, noting as many features as possible that are pertinent to impending zoning decisions. Similar remarks apply to veterinary practices, fox hunting practices, and maintenance practices, indeed, to all practices that involve linked activities at, and movement between, different points in an expansive portion of the world that can be taken in visually: An array of places and paths distributed through this portion—though obviously not all the places and paths found there— is relevant to carrying out the practices involved. This is even true of tourist practices, since the roads tourists take are part of the landscape, and where tourists stop, the directions they look in and what they talk about are keyed to the distributions of places and paths in the landscapes they encounter.

Landscapes can also fill out the futures and pasts of activities in practices beyond those in which landscapes are visually encountered entities, for example, the practices of training, barn maintenance, building construction, religion, sports, veterinary medicine, and community organization. In construction practices, for instance, desired aesthetic effect or considerations of efficiency and organization vis-à-vis other buildings can teleologically order the construction of a building at a particular spot, just as consistency of appearance with neighboring farms can help motivate the construction of a barn with certain ornamental features. In religious practices, moreover, the beauty of the landscape can occasion thanks for God's generosity, just as in community organization practices efforts to

Figure 4.5
A Bluegrass country road. Photograph by the author.

embarrass the owner of some kitschy neon signs might be pursued for the sake of maintaining the traditional look of the landscape. The possibilities are endless. Indeed, the horse-farm landscape enjoys such significance for life in the Kentucky Bluegrass that aspects of it fill out futures and pasts in remarkably many practices there. It is worth adding that, insofar as the landscape is built, and thus built in particular practices, it is tied to particular teleological pasts and futures.

Landscapes, in sum, are thoroughly integrated into the timespaces of activity, as visual spectacles, as the contents of the pasts and futures of activity, and as spaces of activity, far-flung arrays of paths and places for human practices. In all these modes, the temporalspatiality of landscapes is tied to the practices in which these activities are performed.

Landscapes are also denizens of objective space-time. The objects composing them are arranged in three-dimensional space, and the events that befall these objects occur before and after other events. These facts point toward a further, extensive, and important area of investigation, namely, connections between objective space-time and the timespace of activity, in particular, those connections that work through landscapes. The depth of these connections is suggested by various phenomena, for example, the aforementioned fact that the space of activity, the array of places and paths through which a person proceeds, is anchored in geometrically arranged physical objects. This fact indicates that the space of activity is inherently linked to objective space: Whenever a person proceeds through the space of activity, he also deals with a linked objective space, just as whenever a person deals with objective space he also proceeds through some activity space or other. Another suggestive phenomenon in this regard is the fact that acting is an event that both occurs before and after events and is stretched out between a state of affairs toward which the actor comes and a state of affairs to which she goes back. It is a phenomenon of both objective and activity time. In the following I want briefly to explore one nexus of landscape-mediated connections between objective space-time and activity timespace.

Landscapes are not just present entities. Some present landscapes existed in the past, and many other present landscapes descended from past ones. In this context, pastness is a feature of the objective temporal sort. Hence, another way of putting the two just-mentioned facts about landscapes is that landscapes are historical entities, whose present forms are either relatively unchanged from or descendants of past forms. Relevant changes can include changes to entities that compose landscapes, to activities carried out in them, and to how landscapes are encountered.

As historical entities, landscapes are the objects of memory. Two types of memory are pertinent in the present context. Memory is, first, paraphrasing Patrick Baert's interpretation of G. H. Mead, the past for the present, that is, past states of affairs as objects of knowledge and recollection in practices.[31] Memory of this sort, as Gosden emphasizes, is an important component of practices: Carrying on most practices depends on knowledge and recollection of past states of affairs. This is just as true of tourist and aesthetic appreciation practices as it is of training, building maintenance, veterinary, historical preservation, and city-county planning ones. This first form of memory is also the source of possible teleological pasts. Many, though not all, states of affairs that motivate action are past states of affairs, and a necessary condition of a past state of affairs filling out the past of activity in a given practice is that it be the object of memory; past reactions to changes in land-use rules can motivate activity, for example, only if they are remembered. Conversely, it might be added, the fact that something fills out the past of activity, especially if it repeatedly does so, can have repercussions for memory *qua* knowledge and recollection of the past. For instance, repeatedly reacting to an assumed but in fact only imagined past aspect of the landscape often leads to that imagined past arrangement becoming an object of recollection and even being recorded for posterity.

The second form of memory is, again to paraphrase Baert's interpretation of Mead, the past in the present, that is, the persistence of the past into the present. It might be counterintuitive to label the persistence of the past a kind of memory. In defense of this characterization, for which I cannot here offer extended justification, notice that when someone says "I remember how to X," say, shoe a horse, this statement implies that the person learned how to shoe a horse in the past and still knows how to do so. Similarly, when someone says "I remember X," say, how many acres a particular farm covers or the sound of a filly, that statement implies that the speaker acquired knowledge of the figure or become acquainted with the sound in the past and still knows or is acquainted with it. In both sorts of case, memory consists in the persistence of the past, that is, something acquired in the past, into the present. (The sorts of connections between past and present that are required for or compatible with the existence of memory is a convoluted topic that will not be addressed here.) In any event, the feature of a practice that is analogous to these cases of memory-*cum*-persistence is the persistence of the determinations and orientations—the rules, ends, understandings—that organize the practice: The persistence of particular rules, ends, and understandings as organizing features of a practice is a type of memory, one that I would call *practice memory*.[32] This practice memory bears on landscapes insofar as landscapes are bound up with the organization of a practice, for example, as the object of or something referred to in rules, as something that figures in the content of ends, and as the object of understandings and projects. Landscapes are held in the memory of fox hunting practices, for instance, as the objects of persisting rules governing permitted entrance to, egress from, and paths across farms, in the preservation of landscapes being a long-standing end, in the repeated deployment of well-known pursuit stratagems, and in handed-down understandings of likely coyote hiding places.

Whereas the landscapes contained in the first type of memory are by definition in the past (though they might be past stages of present landscapes instead of landscapes that no longer exist), the landscapes held in the second form of memory can be past, present, or future. The intercalations of objective and activity timespaces that are effected in memories of the second sort are thus more diverse than those effected in memories of the first.

Both types of memory, finally, contribute to the identities of people participating in the practices involved by helping fill out the different statuses

that these individuals occupy. A person's identity as fox hunter, like the
identity of W. Fauntleroy Pursley as Master of the Hounds of the Iroquois
Hunt Club, is tied both to memories of past landscapes traversed in epic
hunts and to memories *qua* persisting fox-hunt practice-organizing ends,
understandings, and rules that pertain to landscapes. Rules that stipulate
that certain ceremonies be carried out at particular places in the landscape
make patent this dependence. Indeed, landscape memory is a principal
contributor to the identities of many, if not most, individuals and groups
in the Kentucky Bluegrass region. What I just wrote about the identities of
fox hunter and Master of the Hounds holds equally of the identities of the
vast preponderance of the varied residents of the Bluegrass.

III Conclusion

In this essay, I have argued that landscapes are not just spatial-temporal
phenomena, but temporalspatial ones as well. Their temporalspatial qualities consist in how they are drawn into or anchor the temporalspatial
dimensionality of human activity. Their temporalspatial qualities are at
once their contribution to humans proceeding in place. Timespace conceived of as activity timespace contrasts with space-time understood as an
objective matrix. Landscapes are phenomena of both: they are temporalspatial spatial and temporal entities. Many ways in which landscapes connect timespaces and space-times work through memory.

In section I, I wrote that two prominent features of the space-times
attributed to social life in contemporary thought are that they are conjunctions of time and space conceived of as separate phenomena and that
these separate phenomena are objective in character. A third feature of
such space-times is that they are multiple. This feature rises from two facts:
(1) that individual space-times are conceived of as the collections of temporal and spatial properties that attach to or arise from specific nexuses of
social processes or phenomena, and (2) that these collections are as numerous as are the social processes and phenomena considered. The account
offered in the present essay likewise affirms that timespaces are plural. In
one sense, in fact, timespaces are as numerous as are activities. This is a
misleading assertion, however, because, as discussed, the timespaces of activities and individual people necessarily exhibit considerable commonality and sharedness, features that derive from the inherent incorporation of
activities into practices. The claim that timespaces are as numerous as are
activities must be complemented by the thesis that particular timespaces
are the same or determined and delimited variations of one another.

Landscapes, too, are plural. I do not *just* mean that different landscapes are found around the globe. I do *not* mean, moreover, that landscapes are relative to particular activities or individuals, such that a given portion of the world is a different landscape to, for instance, anyone who encounters or lives through it. The just-mentioned commonality and sharedness defeat any such idea. Rather, I mean that visually encounterable geographical expanses contain up to as many landscapes as there are practices carried out on or toward it. Any visually encounterable portion of the horse-farm countryside surrounding Lexington, Kentucky, encompasses up to as many landscapes as there are practice nexuses propagating through it, including some touched on in the current essay: training practices, tourist practices, city-county planning practices, historical preservation practices, transportation practices, and fox hunting practices. In each of these, the world around is encountered and acted amid as a different array of places, paths, and regions. This means that members of different groups such as farm owners, managers, construction workers, trainers, groomers, tourists, planners, preservationists, and hunters, as well as members of such groups as Latinos and poor whites, live through different landscapes. Although these different groups and practices might exist and be carried out in the same portion of the world, the landscapes they live through or are performed amid vary. In addition, an individual person lives through and encounters as many different landscapes in a given portion of the world as there are practices he participates in there. Landscapes are relative, not to individuals or groups, but to practices.

Finally, a premise of this book is that landscapes are perennial objects of fascination. I believe that the temporalspatial character of landscapes helps explain this fact. The visually accessible world around houses human activity as a nexus of places and paths, and it is encountered visually in activities that take place at and along these places and paths. This world can also fill out the teleological past and future of human activity. As such, landscapes are central to, indeed, ineliminable from human existence in place. Landscapes also occur in objective timespace, but this fact is not nearly so central to human life as is their activity timespace character. This centrality helps explain their persistence as objects of interest and study.

Notes

1. See Schatzki, *The Timespace of Human Activity: On Performance, Society, and History as Indeterminate Teleological Events* (Lanham, MD: Lexington Books, 2010). The current essay presents a different version of ideas found in chapter 2 of that book.

2. Jeff Malpas, *Heidegger's Typology: Being, Place, World* (Cambridge, MA: MIT Press, 2006), p. 28.

3. See, for example, Carl O. Sauer, "The Morphology of Landscape," in *Land and Life: Selections from the Writings of Carl Ortwin Sauer*, ed. John Leighly (Berkeley: University of California Press, 1963 [1925]), pp. 315–350.

4. See, for example, Tim Ingold, *The Perception of the Environment: Essays in Livelihood, Dwelling, and Skill* (London: Routledge, 2000).

5. See, for example, Denis E. Cosgrove and Stephen Daniels, eds., *The Iconography of Landscape: Essays on the Symbolic Representation, Design, and Use of Past Environments* (Cambridge: Cambridge University Press, 1988).

6. Denis E. Cosgrove, *Social Formation and Symbolic Landscape* (Totowa, NJ: Barnes & Noble, 1984).

7. Karl Raitz, "Gentleman Farms in Kentucky's Inner Bluegrass: A Problem in Mapping," *Southeastern Geographer* 15, no. 15 (1975): 33–46.

8. Dennis Domer, "Inventing the Horse Farm," *Kentucky Humanities* (October 2005): 3–12.

9. See John Wright, Jr., *Lexington: Heart of the Bluegrass* (Lexington: Lexington Fayette County Historical Commission, 1982), chapters 5 and 6.

10. Besides the theorists discussed below, see David Harvey, *Justice, Nature, and the Geography of Difference* (Oxford: Blackwell, 1996) and Henri Lefebvre, *Rhythmanalysis: Space, Time, and Everyday Life*, trans. Stuart Elden and Gerald Moore (London: Continuum, 2004 [1992]).

11. Torsten Hägerstrand, "Space, Time, and Human Conditions," in *Dynamic Allocation of Urban Space*, ed. A. Karlqvist, L. Lundqvist, and F. Snickars (Lexington, MA: Lexington Books, 1975), pp. 3–14.

12. Don Parkes and Nigel Thrift, *Times, Spaces, and Places: A Chronogeographic Perspective* (Chichester: John Wiley, 1980).

13. Yi-Fu Tuan, *Space and Place: The Perspective of Experience* (Minneapolis: University of Minnesota Press, 1977).

14. Anne Buttimer, "Grasping the Dynamism of the Lifeworld," *Annals of the Association of American Geographers* 66 (1976): 277–292.

15. Parkes and Thrift, *Times, Spaces, and Places*, p. 32, fig. 1.

16. Ibid., p. 34.

17. Christopher Gosden, *Social Being and Time* (Oxford: Blackwell, 1994).

18. Ibid., p. 78.

19. Ibid., p. 82.

20. Ibid., p. 16.

21. Ibid., p. 82.

22. Ibid., p. 125.

23. Ibid., p. 122.

24. Ibid., p. 19.

25. Ibid., p. 187; see also p. 122.

26. Ibid., p. 78.

27. Martin Heidegger, *Being and Time*, trans. John Macquarie and Edward Robinson (Oxford: Blackwell, 1927/1962).

28. Strictly speaking, projection, thrownness, and being-amid are dimensions of existence, not activity. On my interpretation, however, being-in-the-world, which is the basic constitution of existence, is primarily acting in practical contexts. See T. R. Schatzki, "Living Out of the Past: Dilthey and Heidegger on Life and History," *Inquiry* 46 (2003): 301–323.

29. See T. R. Schatzki, *The Site of the Social: A Philosophical Exploration of the Constitution of Social Life and Change* (University Park, PA: Pennsylvania State University Press, 2002).

30. I wrote in the introduction that interwoven timespaces are a key feature of social life. The timespaces of different activities interweave by being common and shared and also by virtue of idiosyncratic elements being nonindependent. The interwoven timespaces that form infrastructures running through social life exist under the aegis of practices and their organizations.

31. Patrick Baert, *Time, Self, and Social Being* (Aldershot: Avebury, 1992).

32. Conceptions of memory such as this are pervasive in social theory. To take only one of many possible examples, Henri Lefebvre attributes memory to what he calls moments in everyday life. See Lefebvre, *Critique of Everyday Life*, volume II: *Foundations for a Sociology of the Everyday*, trans. John Moore (London: Verso, 2002). Moments are attempts, born of and within everyday life, to achieve the total realization of a previously impossible activity and thereby rise above the everyday in everyday life. Lefebvre attributes this memory to the moment, not to the individuals involved. What persists and is the content of the memory are the rules, rites, and principles that govern the activity involved.

5   The Edge(s) of Landscape: A Study in Liminology

Edward S. Casey

Where does a landscape begin—and where does it end? Which is to say: Where is its edge? We are tempted to think that landscapes just go on and on indefinitely—one vista giving way to another, one stretch of land blending into the next. And if this is the case, is not any attempt to determine, even to imagine, an edge, an act of human hubris? More pointedly: Does a landscape have any edge other than an arbitrary one? Think of a seascape opening up before your eager look: here, regaled before you, is one coherent and continuous vista, all the waters and currents merging and remerging. The perception of any one particular patch of water is like a willful cut into the blue deep: it is just what my glance happens to catch hold of, only to lose it again in the very next instant, releasing it into a neighboring patch, into which it seems to tuck itself effortlessly. Is there any effective edge here? Certainly none that lasts—none that we can count on.

Certain larger questions emerge: Does landscape (and, as a corollary, seascape) lend itself to quantification? Does it have a proper unit? How is its extent to be measured? And, threading through all this and acting as my particular focus in this essay, how are we to think of the edge of a given landscape or seascape? Assuming that it exists—something we cannot take for granted—is it a limit, a perimeter, a periphery? What is it, and how are we to think of it?

What follows is an essay on the edge (or edges) of land/sea/scape that is in turn an instance of an emerging discipline, *liminology*. A liminological study takes the understanding of something to its limit—to its *limen*, its threshold, its very edge.

I

In thinking of edges, there are two extremes to consider first: the Salient Edge and the Subtle Edge. The Salient Edge is perceptually obvious; it stands out, is unambiguous in its presentation, and is often marked as such. It is the kind of edge that announces itself *as an edge*. Examples would include window frames, the edges of tables, the contours of clothing. Such edges are undeniably present in ongoing perceptual experience: not only do we notice them easily, we cannot get around them without a certain amount of physical negotiation (e.g., walking around a table, going inside the house whose window frames we have noticed from outside, seeing the cut of clothing from a different angle). A Subtle Edge is something else; this kind of edge is ambiguous in its appearance: Is it an edge or not? we find ourselves wondering. It is so integral to a given phenomenon as to be barely, if at all, distinguishable from the phenomenon itself; and it is rarely marked as such. Instances include folds in clothing that are not simply pleats or seams, different parts of the green lawn of grass at which I am now looking, or stretches of the bright and cloudless sky at which I am staring. The subtlety is such that I cannot tell for sure that something is ending or not in a presumptive such edge: Does the fold represent a terminating of the cloth of which it is made or its continuation? This is difficult to determine—not just at first glance but with many subsequent glances. Leibniz, standing on the shore, posited *petites perceptions* whose subtlety matched that of the edges of the waves at which he was looking. Just as we cannot tell precisely where one wave begins and another ends, so we cannot know for sure where one such perception starts or stops, and where another begins. In both cases, the subtlety of the difference is such that we cannot track, much less name or number, the transition from one to the other.

Important and interesting as are these extremes, in the actual experience of landscape and seascape we are almost always somewhere in between. In this intermediate zone, the edges are neither starkly etched nor subdued to the point of indiscernibility. The exceptions stand out for their very rarity: the forest that comes to an abrupt halt for no apparent reason; the fog that swallows up every last edge in its embrace, allowing no single object to be discerned. For the most part, our experience of land- and seascape is quite different: We do make out particular objects or events, singly or in clusters. Moreover, we count on these distinctions for orientation in the perceptual world; without them, we would be quite lost. On the other hand, if everything in the surrounding landscape were perfectly distinct—if each was utterly itself in contrast with every other thing—we would be just as disoriented: For there would be no fading into the distance (and thus no depth) and no horizons, which are intrinsically indistinct. It would be as if we were in a brightly illuminated artificial studio, filled with plastic objects that have nothing to do with each other. Such a world would be as inhospitable, indeed as downright disorienting, as a world that obscured all its inhabitants—a "night," in Hegel's celebrated words, "in which all the cows are black." Notice that, either way, *les extrêmes se touchent*, since in both cases we have a situation in which all the ingredients are perceived as indifferent to each other's presence.

Fortunately (and doubtless for basic evolutionary reasons), we only rarely have to cope with such extremes. For the most part, once again, we find ourselves in a middle realm of partly differentiated objects and events—differentiated enough to allow us to recognize and identify them, yet not so clear and distinct as to rule out depth and horizons and other essentially indeterminate phenomena (e.g., the exact zenith of the sky, the precise contour of an expressive gesture made with outreached hands). We have to do with a commixture of such indeterminate phenomena—which exhibit "morphological" rather than "exact" essences in Husserl's nomenclature—along with other, much more definite entities and events. (I say "and events" to emphasize that we are not here dealing with the object-world alone but a world fairly bristling with a broad range of things of many ontological kinds, each of which possesses its own characteristic edges. Some of these edges are resolutely spatial, but many are temporal—and still others are spatiotemporal.)

The world we perceive comes, then, as a mixed picture. Far from being a defect or a shortcoming, this is as it should be—indeed, as it *has* to be. Integral to the being of the perceived world is the range of its composition, including both indeterminate and determinate features of things. And if this is so, it is true *a fortiori* of the specific landscapes and seascapes that populate this world—that are its most capacious place-holders and that constitute two of its most primal regions at the level of vision and action. For these two basic kinds of "scape" are in effect clusters of *places*, which provide the contents of the perceived world, exhibiting a deep display of all there is to see (as well as hear, feel, touch: modalities that are also always at play in the perception of other kinds of scape such as cityscapes). We sense these contents, we come to know them, as composing the place-worlds of ordinary (and sometimes extraordinary) perception. In such worlds, edges always figure. But how so—and in what particular ways?

II

Edges accrue to landscapes and seascapes in four distinct ways: as rims, gaps, borders, and boundaries. Let me say something about each of these.

A *rim* is an edge that is at once determinate and detachable; it is perceived *as such*, not only as the end of an object or event but as separate from it, or at least identifiable *in distinction from it*. Sometimes it is made from a different material than is the object or event of which it is the edge; but even if not, it is a part of it that is unequivocally *other*. Typically, a rim *surrounds* something, whether this is a thing or a nonthing (e.g., a hole, an empty can, in the earth), and it does so as closely fitting: It is invariably *next to* what it surrounds, as with the North Rim of the Grand Canyon. Aristotle's notion of place as an immediate, unmoved "surrounder" (*periechon*) would count as a rim as I describe it here.

Gaps come in many forms, for example, ditches, gulches, valleys, and moats. In each case, a gap serves to separate rather than surround. It differs from a rim by being *between* two things rather than tightly enclosing one thing or group of things. It is discontinuous with what it separates—spatially, temporally, and materially. A gap is an interval, a *diastéma* in the technical term of ancient Greek philosophers; but it is not necessarily something *intermediate* if this means something linking two existing things: A gap *qua* gap disconnects rather than unites. A gap is always more or less empty, and in this capacity it invites being filled, in fact or in imagination; once filled, however, it is no longer a gap but becomes an intervening connective space, a *metaxu* or "middle term" in Plato's suggestive terminology.

A *border* I take to be a humanly constructed entity, legal and/or cartographic, and as such it is historically and institutionally sanctioned; its concrete expression is often as a *borderline*: Hence the tendency to "trace" a border, to *delineate* it. The paradigm case of borders is that of international "dividing lines"—a revealing locution that signifies the function of most borders: not just to distinguish but to *keep apart*. What is kept apart varies from land and people (the most frequent cases in point) to animals and plants (as in wildlife "zones" or sections of botanical gardens). The emphasis is on continuity (there is rarely, if ever, a gap in a border) and consistency (i.e., of construction or representation). The effect is that of *impermeability*: not just the restriction of traffic or trespass but their exclusion wherever possible. Every border is constructed such that it is closed or subject to closure—and often at short notice. The relations between border, control, and surveillance are intimate; this is why "border inspections" are so common and expectable. It is also why there is rarely equality of traffic in both directions: At any given historical moment, one side of the border possesses more police or state power than the other, a point to which I shall return.

A *boundary*, in contrast with a border, is intrinsically permeable; it is porous by its very nature—filled with apertures and thus hospitable to the transmission of fluids, people, animals, and other substances. If borders in their closure ask to be transgressed—crossed in more or less defiant, more or less devious ways—boundaries are made for ease of two-way traffic. This is so both at a molecular level, where differences of air or water pressure determine the flow across a given boundary, and at more molar strata, where the passage of whole bodies is at stake. Although plants can grow over borders, they actively migrate across boundaries by dispersed pollination—as do animals in "animal corridors" that extend across natural boundaries (e.g., different grasslands or rivers). Human beings also move across boundaries, not just as migrants but as "im-migrants," where this last term implies moving *into* another region or nation that is open to their presence. The key idea is that the openings inherent in boundaries are built into them from the start—and thus are part of their very being or constitution rather than something forced upon them from without (as happens with a border fence that is cut open and trespassed "illegally," that is, without the express permission of the institutional authority that controls the border).

Although there are doubtless other ways of instantiating an edge, taken together these four forms of edge make up the infrastructure of the edge-world, its most characteristic configurations and its detailed shapefulness.

III

How do these four kinds of edge figure into landscapes? To begin with, two of them rarely figure at all, namely, borders and rims. Given their artificiality of origin and their externality of position respectively, neither is (normally) intrinsic to the perception of landscape. Borders are *imposed* on landscape—hence their indifference to local wildlife. At the U.S.–Mexico border at Tijuana, for example, the newly reinforced sheet metal wall that separates the two nations has been constructed—especially in its recently erected second tier—in such a way as to neglect its deleterious effects on the Tijuana Estuarine Reserve that is located immediately to the north, thereby undermining efforts of a decade and a half to restore this estuary and its abundant wildlife population.[1] Similarly, rims rarely stem from the

natural world itself (the North Rim is a notable exception) but are characteristically thrust upon it from without: as when a farmer plows around a
stand of trees in planting corn, the furrow becoming a rim for the stand
but not being related to it in any inherent way.

The situation is very different when it comes to gaps and boundaries.
Gaps often occur both in and around natural landscape areas—gaps that
are themselves natural in character. For example, a burned-out part of a
forest introduces a decisive gap into the forest: a "dead zone" that is, however, quickly reinhabited by plants and animals that come to populate it
in the wake of the fire.[2] Until full reforestation happens, however, there is
a gap in the fabric of the forest: It has been interrupted, both spatially and
temporally. Much more pervasive than gaps are boundaries in landscaped
areas. Consider only that virtually every edge of a forest that is not the
result of clear-cutting is a boundary. On that edge and through it are found
multiple plant outgrowths: often many species, mixed together in apparent
disarray (but in fact following an integral natural order). Across this edge
move equally diverse animal and insect and bird species—no respecters
of borderlines but beings who thrive in open-ended boundary situations.
Humans come and go, too: hunters and walkers, lovers and naturalists, and
even an occasional philosopher like Rousseau or Thoreau.

Call to mind the edges of virtually any forest or copse you may know,
and you will notice that it is comparatively uneven and unkempt. Only
the likes of timber jacks or border guards will attempt to cut the edge to
their specifications. At another level, surveyors and cartographers imagine
a perfectly regular edge at the level of representation even if none exists in
reality. (The analogue of such incursions in the case of seascapes is found in
meridians and parallels and in international date lines.) Both sorts of inter-
ventionist are trying to turn a boundary into a border—or, more rarely, a
gap into a rim (as when a road is built around a forest or an irrigation ditch
around a field). This is an all-too-human temptation—one that amounts
to reshaping a naturally given landscape by turning what is *natura naturans*
into *natura naturata*, something given into something created. The effect is
to exchange, in fact or in imagination, one form of edge for another. What
does this mean?

Two alternatives suggest themselves: Either we here witness a case of
metabolé eis allo genos ("transformation into another kind of thing") or else
we see an act of the sheer substitution of one kind of thing for another.
Which? I would suggest that both obtain—not at once but in sequence.
As one kind of edge (rough-hewn, indefinite, open) gives way to another
(pristine, proper, precise), often for purely utilitarian reasons, the very

being of the edge is altered. What starts as an instrumentalist enterprise ends by bringing about an ontological shift, a change in kind. There is no exact or predictable point where such a change happens; we can only say that it is engendered in the course of the work (forest work, map work, surveying work, border guard work).

The mere fact that edges, at least those edges that I am designating as "boundaries," permit such transformation by acts of substitution says something interesting about them. The fluidity of boundaries is such as to allow not just modifications in their surface properties but profound mutations in their being-status. This implies in turn that in the case of boundaries alterations in their secondary qualities, as well as in pragmatist manipulations of them, are far from superficial; they can affect the entire ontology of the things themselves.

It becomes clear that the situation is twofold. On the one hand, boundaried edges are not the kinds of things in which we can make a simple distinction between surface and depth: In their case, the depths are not just on the surface (as Wittgenstein is reputed to have said), they *are* the surface. On the other hand, far from being merely superficial features of human and animal and plant life-worlds, such edges are deeply inherent aspects of these worlds, part of their ontological furniture; thus, to change the character of an edge is to alter the being of the world in which it figures. This situation will obtain all the more conspicuously in the case of landscapes and seascapes, since these count as particular versions of very complex life-worlds—as their public faces. The way these faces are altered in real and imaginational modalities will affect not just their seen or felt presentations but the way they exist, their standing in the domain of objects and events.

IV

Boundaries *bound*, and in this capacity they not only enclose, they also ground. In the instance of landscape (and *pari passu* seascape), they provide something quite formative: a *double bound* for these special stretches of the life-world. Here we move from boundary as identifiable edge—in competition with borders, rims, and gaps—to boundary as material condition in the form of outer (or inner) limit. The effect is that of a double *framing* of a given landscape scene—from without and from within, from above and from below. Let me say more about this dual enframement.

The *upper bound* of a given landscape is double in turn: *horizon* and *sky*. If I look out into a long field, for example, I find the field itself effectively ending as it vanishes into a circumambient horizon, leading up to it and vanishing into it. This horizon, far from being a "horizon line," is an untraceable edge of the land itself: untraceable because it is not solid and continuous—as would be a rim set suddenly upon the outer edge of a landscape (as when one sees the wall at La Frontera from afar). The horizon is more of a band than a line: It is that peculiar part of the life-world that refuses to be an object. It encircles objects set in the landscape itself, acting as their ground of possibility: There are no objects except within the horizon that encompasses them even as they disappear into its embrace. (The same is true for events, which never happen without a temporal context acting as their historical horizon.) At the same time, the sky, looming just above the horizon, serves as a further circumambient boundary—now in an even more expansive format than the horizon itself provides. For the sky is more of a zone than a band: Where a band can be condensed into a line for various practical purposes (hence the temptation to reduce the horizon in this way), a zone resists confinement to either of these reductive spatialities. The sky is found not just above the end of land, as is the horizon, but stretches far over it in an audacious aura of cerulean space. It is still a boundary, but one that is not just occasionally or differentially permeable (as is the case with most finite boundaries such as skin): The sky presents itself as infinitely porous. In this capacity and in its overarching display, it is a boundary for all the more finite boundaries that configure a given landscape.

The *lower bound* of a landscape is constituted by the *Earth*. Under the same field at which I find myself looking lies the sullen but sustaining Earth, a vast layer of materiality composed of soil and stone that is, in its own way, as capacious as the sky. But where the sky is eminently visible, and the horizon coyly demi-visible, the Earth withdraws from sight at every remove: Only the outer surface of the topsoil gives itself to me as a manifest presence. It takes rare glimpses of its upturned depths—excavated earth, cliffs striated with sedimentary deposits—to sense what lies below the surface. In the case of the Earth, the depths are only rarely on the surface. Even if hugely hidden, the Earth nevertheless acts as a lower bound of the perception of landscape. It is a boundary that lies at our feet and under us at all times (it is felt, tacitly, even on city streets). As a material condition for sitting and standing, walking and moving in every way, indeed for living itself, it is an indispensable presence. As a visible and tangible lower bound, it acts as a telluric *a priori* for the perception of landscape.

Seascapes offer much the same double boundedness. There, too, horizon and sky frame from afar our vision of a water world that undergirds them while requiring them to fill out its full presence. In the case of seascapes, however, Earth retreats into murky depths that are far removed from ordinary sight. Its place is taken by the sea itself as the dominant medium of our ongoing perceptual engagement: Water replaces land in an extraordinary act of elemental substitution. Taken as the primary constituents of seascapes and landscapes respectively, water and land call for bounding, upper as well as lower. Without such double enframement, they would be all over the place, spilling out boundlessly, and thereby destroy the propriety of place that is essential to every land- and seascape. For these two scapes, considered as basic regions of the Earth, are composed of discrete places and themselves make up whole place-worlds.

The elemental boundaries to which I here point are in effect *parameters of place-worlds*. Horizon, sea, sky, and Earth act as upper and lower bounds of these worlds, which exhibit themselves to us primarily as landscapes and seascapes (alternately as cityscapes, gardenscapes, prisonscapes, warscapes). Land and sea set themselves out before us so as to be seen and felt at large—such is the root connotation of the suffix "-scape" itself—but they do not lay themselves out indefinitely. As elemental regions, they make up the particular place-worlds that give them coherence of presentation and signification. They are the delimiting boundaries of such worlds, and as such they are *sine qua non* in the experience of landscape and seascape construed as their proffered faces: that which we (and other animals and plants who inhabit the same worlds) face in the circumambience of the natural world and that which faces us (and other beings) in turn.

V

Two other kinds of basic boundary operate in the landscape world: external and internal. The former refers to the kind of boundary that rings *around* a landscape, the latter to those that go *through* it. Each merits further exploration. An *external* boundary is in effect a perimeter of a natural scene. In contrast with borders or rims—which may also surround such a scene but in ways that are almost always arbitrary and constructed to some significant degree—an external boundary is one that *belongs* to the scene itself and has evolved with it, even if at a differential rate of growth. Imagine a forest that abuts a savannah: At the edge of the forest, populated by pines and certain hardwood trees, is a ring of bushes that are not part of the savannah, yet are also not found in the interior of the forest. They exist equally at its outer edge; in many ways, they *are* its external edge. They mark it as such for any observer, and they are felt bodily by any animal that must make its way across them to get into the forest. They are dense in many places, and it is up to the ingenuity of the animal to find its way through. Perhaps most importantly, they are not detachable from the forest itself; they carry the forest to its own edge, establishing its own periphery. They also give to the same forest its characteristic outer shape, that by which it can be easily identified and located.

In contrast, an *internal* boundary is an edge or set of edges that forms an equally characteristic, even if often less salient, inner shape. To continue the previous example: Such boundaries would include inner pathways in the forest—those used by animals or humans—that structure it from within. Such pathways lack the precision of borders (they continually alter in width and viability), but they are crucial to the constitution of the forest by furnishing spaces for moving within it. They bring parts of the forest together at every juncture and, still more importantly, they give direction to all those who move through them: They are often the basis of orientation within the forest, and one might get lost without their guiding presence.[3] Such pathways contrast with another kind of internal boundary, that of the canopy of the forest as experienced from underneath. This canopy is a special kind of internal boundary that allows light and sound to constellate *from above*—from which position an animal or human being feels sheltered in basic ways. The Kaluli people of Papua New Guinea have developed the idea of "up over sounding" to express this peculiar experience of being bounded from the roof of a rain forest: not only by the nexus of trees but by the birds who sing so fervently in the midst of this nexus.[4] Some analogy, however faint, is experienced by anyone walking within a forest that is crowned by trees of a certain height.

Taken together, the internal and external boundaries of a landscape—and their analogues in a seascape (e.g., the shoreline and the meeting of diverse currents)—create a particular complexity that is integral to the material essence of being a sea- or landscape. Neither kind of scape comes as a simple block of space; each comes bounded from without and from within, both of these at once and in ever-varying combinations. Part of what is unique to landscape and seascape space is this second kind of double-boundedness, which disallows reduction to the simplicities and specificities of site and space.

The same internal/external doubling is essential to their being natural place-worlds: Such worlds are always bound from the outside as from the inside, the two together. When this double boundedness rejoins the first (i.e., upper and lower bounds), we witness a redoubled duplexity that makes for the uniqueness of each such place-world, no one of which ever replicates another—just as no landscape or seascape is ever exactly or fully repeated by any other.

VI

Other complexities ensue as we follow out the fate of the edge(s) of landscape. Here I shall single out one in particular: the *ecotone*, which is the technical term for the place where two different bioregions (or other naturally conditioned areas) meet—with the significant result that effects arise that could never have emerged in the two regions taken separately. An ecotone is formally defined as "the boundary between two natural communities where elements of both as well as transitional species intermingle in heightened richness."[5] The result of such intermingling is a "transitional zone" and, more particularly, an "edge effect" whereby an event of interpotentiation arises as the resources of one region cause those of the other to take a course not otherwise possible: a course of increased intensity (*tonus*, at the root of "ecotone," signifies "tension"). Instead of a mere summation of forces, there is an augmentation beyond the known and measurable forces of existing constituents: rather than $1 + 1 = 2$, we have a circumstance of $1 + 1 = 2 + n$. The ecotone is of particular significance for liminological studies of the sort I have been sketching in these pages. Let me trace out four major implications of the ecotone for such studies:

(i) *The power is in the edge.* Thanks to the ecotonal effect, the edge is "where most of the action is"—*not* the surface, as has been claimed by J. J. Gibson.[6] For the edge is where the most concerted activity is to be found, including activity that exceeds what we would predict on a simple summative paradigm. This means, more monumentally, that the endemic Western metaphysical privileging of centrist models of power and force here falls short—indeed, falls flat. These models have assumed that power accumulates in the central storehouses and monocentric structures, whether these belong to God, or the state, or the self. Margins are consigned to by-play and by-products. But Derrida has argued that it is in the margins of power that power itself resides.[7] So, too, the edges of landscape contain an unsuspected power, one of whose primary expressions is precisely the ecotone or the "ecotonal complex," as I prefer to call it.

(ii) *Every edge has power.* The first implication is not restricted to boundaries of landscapes and seascapes—my focus in this essay so far. It extends to *all* edges, including rims, gaps, and borders. At each of these, force accumulates, comes to expression, and brings itself to a point of power. The force takes many forms: for example, the North and South Rims of the Grand

Canyon as they have become a tourists' Mecca for viewing the grandeur below. The arroyos created by natural forces in arid regions of the same Southwest region to which the Grand Canyon belongs are gaps that bristle with destructive force when sudden showers fill them up. Borders are no exception to the ecotonal rule; indeed, they can be extremely effective places of power, as we see in the case of gated communities (the mechanical gates, to be opened only by those with the correct key or combination), the "corridors of power" (an expression that refers to a government's carefully crafted retention of legislative or judicial power), or at international borders such as the U.S.–Mexico border. Political forces collect at borders, to which they adhere with a special tenacity.

In the instance of La Frontera, the fearsome wall that has been constructed at this border since Operation Gatekeeper went into effect in the mid-1990s—the wall is fourteen feet high and made of thick sheet metal, with a concrete base that extends six feet into the ground—can be considered a political ecotone that concentrates state power in one stolid structure. With only minor exceptions, this structure retraces the geographical border that was established between the United States and Mexico in the wake of the War of 1848; but its continual reinforcement (most recently with stadium lights, high surveillance towers, and drone airplanes) is the unvarnished expression of the will of the U.S. government to keep unauthorized migrants from crossing into the country. At its juncture, two cultures, two economies, two languages, two peoples meet in a tightly regulated and highly supervised manner. The effect is the literal empowerment of those with superior military forces and the corresponding disempowerment of those who lack such forces. Nevertheless, the disempowered migrants possess a force of their own: that of transgression in the very face of military and technological prowess. As Nietzsche and Foucault have each insisted, the armed forces of the state (the "royal power," in Deleuze's terms) invite such subversive power (e.g., in the form of "nomadic" actions that confuse and disperse state power). If this analysis is correct, then the situation at La Frontera is not merely a display of one-way, hegemonic strength, but a duplex circumstance of active and reactive forces—all focused on the wall as a single structure whose very linearity embodies its status as a border in my sense of the term: as a borderline set in steel and etched in blood.[8] We are far from open landscape here—not in distance (at the end of the security wall is wild and very treacherous landscape) but in terms of the factors or units that count: Line has taken over from band or zone, border has replaced boundary.

(iii) *The eye moves to the edge.* Here I point to a seemingly innocuous phenomenon that is fraught with deeper significance: the fact that the human eye tends to move to the edge of things, seeking out the margins. This most often happens after the central phenomenon has been identified, allowing the eye to wander to the outer edge. (The same holds for the hand, which looks for the basic shape of what it handles: mostly at, and as, the edge.) This obtains notably in the perception of landscape and seascape vistas, which tempt the eye ever outward, farther and farther from the near-space in which they are at first ensconced and recognized. This is a literally extra-ordinary experience, taking the eye (or hand) out of the midst of everyday immersion in the tool-world or social world. It also contributes to the deconstruction of centrist paradigms of perception—that is, those that are mainly concerned with issues of precise identification and recognition of perceptual particulars and that concentrate on the main masses of these particulars rather than their edges.

The question of the origin of this lateralized looking is intriguing even if highly speculative: Was it a matter of learning to detect predators lurking at the edges of clear vision, hiding there so as to attack more effectively? The orbiting of the eyes and of the whole human head seems closely allied with such defensive and preventive attending to the edges of perceptual situations in forests and savannahs. Even apart from this intriguing hypothesis—which also helps to explain the unexpected importance of glancing in the human repertoire of looking[9]—the eye has good reason to gravitate to the edge of the visual field. For this is where such factors as the width and depth of that field are to be determined as well as where change and growth flourish: Darwin postulates that it is at the edges of primitive human settlements that the most innovative adaptations occurred. It is also where unanticipated actions are most likely to emerge. The action is thus for the most part at—and on, around, or near—the edge of a given experiential field. No wonder we look there so alertly in our eagerness to encounter the new and surprising where they arise.

(iv) *Energies accumulate at the edge.* Another basic reason why the eye moves to the edge is that it senses that this is where energies of several sorts accumulate and concentrate. I refer to optic energies that cluster around the defining outline of a visual object as well as to phototropic tendencies of plants; also at play are various physical and biological energies (i.e., kinetic and gravitational, organic and biotic). Such energies collect at the edges of visual fields as of life-worlds more generally, above all in ecotonal situations. As Florence R. Krall describes it:

In the natural world, edges where differences come together are the richest of habitats. Animals often choose these ecotones, where contrasting plant communities
meet, to raise their young where the greatest variety of cover and food can be found.
A doe will give birth to the fawn on the edge of a forest, where she can find shelter
as well as food in the open area beyond the trees.[10]

Animal and plant life here collude in the build-up of edge energies. In
such edgeful intensities, we witness what Gadamer calls *Seinszuwachs*, "the
augmentation of being."[11] Or rather we should say: the augmentation of
becoming. For once more it is not a matter of simple addition but of interpotentiation. The energies that seek and stay at the edge of things are
heightened in each other's presence. It is not unexpected that the eye and
the hand, indeed the entire organism, seek to track them and bring them
into our ken—not in order to foreclose them but to savor them and, if possible, to draw upon them directly.

Landscapes and seascapes embody and exemplify such energies at the
edge. Thanks to their holding powers (whereby they retain and preserve
these energies), they not only possess edges but also *exhibit* them—*energize*
them, turning them to dynamic biophysical uses that enliven the experience of such scapes and promote their exfoliation into further experiences of other vistas, other worlds containing other places: in short, other
place-worlds.

VII

I shall end with three extended remarks regarding the fate of landscape and
its edges.

(i) Landscape certainly still matters in contemporary national and global
culture—in fact, all the more so in view of the exponentially increasing siti-
fication of space: that is, its conversion into mere sites for building rather
than appreciating its inherently placial predicates and powers. At the level
of the plastic images promoted by news media and by popular entertain-
ment on television, cell phones, video, and DVD, we are presented with an
unremitting scene of *displacement*: in terms of the vast amounts of forced
migration happening today (it is estimated that fully 40% of all peoples on
Earth will soon be engaged in such migration, one example of which we
now witness at La Frontera) as well as in the literal sense of an active loss
of place or "dysplacement," as we can call it in analogy with dysphoria:
the diminution and dissolution of the experience of place itself, its effec-

tive interment under the site-centered consciousness fostered by shopping malls and online catalogs.

In the face of this crisis of placement, there are few viable options. One is to pursue a philosophy and politics of the "local absolute," in Deleuze and Guattari's version of the slogan to "live locally but think globally." This calls for a renewed engagement in the governance of one's city of choice, a civic commitment that brings one's own voice into consonance with the *vox populi* of fellow citizens—all the while realizing that the stakes are now much higher than they were in the nineteenth century when local government was more responsive to the requirements of the era. The ascendancy of transnational corporations, acting hand in hand with a surging privatization of social institutions, has meant that the flow of global capital is virtually unstanched—thereby reinforcing the hegemony of space over place. In this hegemony, the homogeneity and infinity of space as it was conceived in the seventeenth century are transmuted into the economic realm, with devastating consequences for those who live and work locally and who are in effect bypassed or co-opted by the flow of money itself. The result is a staggering increase in urban populations in every major continent, as wage-earners leave their home-places to find work in mega-cities such as Calcutta, Mexico City, Los Angeles, and Beijing. In the face of this loss of the place of one's origin and upbringing, it is quite tempting to call for a renewal of local consciousness.[12]

Another approach is to bring attention to the factor of landscape in people's lives. Landscape, along with seascape, is more difficult to leave behind than is one's village of origin, and it is not in direct competition with global capital—though it can be devastated through its commodification by capitalist interests. The clear-cutting of forests for timber, though still continuing, has been replaced by the leveling of land for the construction of suburban sites: tract homes and strip malls. Even if extensive areas of land are lost to commercial development, however, a vestige of landscape will always remain—just as a glimpse of seascape survives even the gentrification of choice coastal properties. Despite all the discouraging tendencies, *landscape and seascape remain.*

They remain as primary parameters of human (and other animal and plant) lives, providing not merely attractive vistas for looking or pleasant beaches for recreation but an abiding sense of what a place-world consists in—a place-world not undermined by the depredations of displacement/ dysplacement in the era of global capitalism. To experience such a world in its own natural setting is not just refreshing or a matter of sheer relief; it is to gain, or regain, a vision of what being-in-the-world construed as a nexus of places can be like. It is to be reminded of what a difference a place-world can make in the very face of the massive leveling-down we encounter everywhere in contemporary existence. Part of this same leveling is the attempt to "manufacture landscape"; but my argument has been that, as deeply immanent dimensions of human and animal experience, landscape cannot be built.[13]

(ii) Landscapes are not only crucial as countercultural presences that we need to heed, especially as unexploited natural resources vanish from the planet at an alarming rate (e.g., in the daily destruction of thousands of square acres of Amazon rain forests in Brazil). This is certainly true, but something still more basic is at stake in the impasse we currently confront, namely, that unmolested landscape and uncontaminated seascape are indispensable to life on the planet in another way. Quite apart from other species who thrive on healthy land and sea and would die without them, human beings, for all their pretensions to autonomy, *cannot do without the outreach they provide.* The issue for humans is not only that of physical survival but of the open and liberating views that land and sea bring with them at the level of experience and thought. If we were to try to do without these views, we would proceed at our own peril. The exemplary presence of open landscape and untamed seascape is essential to being on Earth in a human way. Without this presence, we would be confined to an inferno of artificial passages and airless corridors from which there is no escape: a disastrous environmental *huis clos.* We would be trapped breathlessly inside closed doors of our own devising.

In the end, these two primal kinds of scapement provide both *vistas* and *breathing spaces,* both of which are required for living on Earth with the range and scope human life calls for beyond its instrumentalist and materialist requirements. Vistas are necessary not just for the literal view of a pristine world but for the sense of expansive space—of the outlook that human beings require for their sense of being effective agents on Earth. By the same token, the breathing spaces that landscape and seascape afford are requisite to a fully embodied implacement on Earth: Not just the eye but the whole living body is here at stake—a body that feels itself able to move through the open-ended spaces that landscapes and seascapes furnish.

(iii) Indispensable to the realm of scapic life are the edges of land- and seascapes themselves. There would be no such scapes without the enlivening edges they bring with them. We cannot look at or move in them without an awareness of the farther bounds of our vision and motion.

These limitrophic edges are in effect visual and kinetic *a priori* structures of human life on this planet. Not only do they affect all that we see and feel, not only are they collectors of several forms of energy, they structure the very place-worlds we inhabit, giving to them their inherent delimitation and directionality. We have seen how this is so in the case of ecotonal complexes and of such elemental boundary phenomena as Earth, horizon, and sky regarded as lower and upper, outer and inner bounds of what we experience on a daily basis. But it is also true for many lesser phenomena of the place-world, including all the discrete edges we encounter in the undertakings of everyday life. There is no such life, no vision or movement, without the endings that edges introduce into that life, vision, and movement. The very freedom of outlook and outreach that matters so much to human beings would not itself be possible without the enclosures provided by edges—and to begin with the boundary edges that are so inherent to landscape and seascape.

Just as we cannot simply eliminate such edges from particular landscapes or seascapes if they are to be what they are—the scaping of land and sea lies largely in their edging—so these same edges are *sine qua non* as well for the place-worlds that are more and more at risk in late capitalism.[14] If these worlds are not to become wholly striated—regimented in such a way as to become reduced to sites—they have to be experienced in their edge-wiseness. For edges of the several sorts I have distinguished are essential to constituting places in their uniqueness, their idiolocality, much as the shape of our bodies is intrinsic to our personal identities. When places are concatenated into regions (as happens with every landscape and seascape), they participate in—indeed, they help to *create*—a smooth space that is the basis of every place-world.[15] In such open and receptive space, edges figure more as folds than as anything strictly linear. Boundaries in particular revert to their origins in "bounds," which are closely affine with folds. The bond between boundary, bound, and fold is intense, and all three give shape to the smooth spaces of new or renascent place-worlds.

From all this, we can discern a chain of nested indispensabilities in the concatenation of edges, landscapes, and place-worlds:

Edges > landscapes/seascapes > smoothly spaced place-worlds

Just as edges are requisite for land- and seascapes and their perception, so these two modes of scapement are, in turn, necessary for the constitution and experience of the basic place-worlds that are the ultimate modules of being-in-place. This first triadic chain is to be contrasted with another:

Lines > striated sites > abstract/homogeneous/infinite space

As lines (e.g., *qua* striations) are required for the very conception and construction of sites (e.g., in blueprints), so sites provide the basic units of abstract space. Sites represent the dark side, the deficient modes of landscape being and perception: their disappearance and undoing in the superfetation of constructed and projected entities. The effect is the predominance of striated and sited spaces amid an increasing dearth of robust place-worlds.

If place-worlds are to regain primacy in human experience, landscapes and seascapes must be reappreciated and revalorized. For this to happen, the edges of these smooth spaces have to be recognized in their incontrovertible importance. Such recognition will bring its own inexorable evidence; but this will happen only if we can find our way back to the very place where such evidence becomes once again accessible.

Notes

1. I give a more complete account of this situation in "Tijuana: Bordertown and Estuary," a chapter in *Up Against the Wall*, written with Mary Watkins (in preparation).

2. This is not to deny that certain gaps are humanmade, e.g., the celebrated "ha-ha" of British country estates that were meant to keep cattle contained within certain spaces; these structures were notable for the fact that they were disguised, so that views of the estate from afar would not be spoiled. See E. H. Gombrich, *Art and Illusion: A Study in the Psychology of Pictorial Representation* (London: Phaidon, 1968).

3. I give a more complete account of orientation in the place-world in "Becoming and Being Oriented by the Glance," chapter 3 in *The World at a Glance* (Bloomington: Indiana University Press, 2007).

4. For a remarkable account of "up over sounding" in Papua New Guinea, see Steven Feld, *Sound and Sentiment: Birds, Weeping, Poetics, and Song in Kaluli Expression* (Philadelphia: University of Pennsylvania Press, 1990).

5. Definition cited on the cover of Florence R. Krall, *Ecotone: Wayfaring on the Margins* (Albany: SUNY Press, 1994).

6. See J. J. Gibson, *The Ecological Approach to Visual Perception* (Hillsdale, NJ: Erlbaum, 1986), p. 23.

7. See Jacques Derrida, *Margins of Philosophy*, trans. A. Bass (Chicago: University of Chicago Press, 1985).

8. For a more detailed analysis of the circumstance at La Frontera, see the chapters on Nogales and Tijuana in *Up Against the Wall*.

9. See Casey, *The World at a Glance*, especially "Concluding Thoughts."

10. Krall, *Ecotone*, p. 4.

11. See Hans-Georg Gadamer, *Truth and Method*, trans. J. Weinsheimer and D. G. Marshall (New York: Continuum, 2005), p. 124.

12. For a penetrating study of these various displacements, see Mary Watkins and Helene Lorenz, *Toward Psychologies of Liberation* (New York: Palgrave Macmillan, 2008), especially chapter 11, "Communities of Resistance." One of the ironies in all this is that most of those who are forced to migrate—for political or economic reasons—come to live at the edges of the great urban centers: that is, in the *colonias* or *bidonvilles* (i.e., shantytowns) that have sprung up in the very shadow of these centers. These edge-cities are places of last resort, of desperation and misfortune. On this same phenomenon, see also Mike Davis, *Planet of Slums* (New York: Verso, 2006).

13. I refer to the recent film *Manufactured Landscapes*, which traces the effort to restructure whole landscapes in China and elsewhere.

14. I here adopt a position that resembles that of Jeff Malpas in his *Place and Experience: A Philosophical Topography* (Cambridge: Cambridge University Press, 2007): in effect, an argument for the transcendental status of edge as part of a larger commitment to the same such status for place itself (as is cogently argued by Malpas).

15. For the distinction between "striated" and "smooth" space, see Gilles Deleuze and Felix Guattari, *A Thousand Plateaus*, trans. B. Massumi (Minneapolis: University of Minnesota Press, 1987), chapters 12 and 15. For my own extension of these terms, see "Smooth Spaces and Rough-Edged Places: The Hidden History of Place," *Review of Metaphysics* 51, no. 2 (1997), as revised and included as an epilogue to Casey, *Getting Back into Place: Towards a Renewed Understanding of the Place-World* (Bloomington: Indiana University Press, 2009).

II Contexts for Landscape

6   Geographic Landscapes and Natural Disaster

J. Nicholas Entrikin

Nature does not complete things. She is chaotic. Man must finish, and he does so by making a garden and building a wall.

—Robert Frost

Introduction: Landscapes under Threat

As I was completing this essay, it was announced that one of the leading geographers of the twentieth century, Gilbert White, died at the age of ninety-four. White, a National Medal of Science recipient, had been a pioneer in what has been called environmental hazards research. His classic work in this area was the 1945 publication of his University of Chicago Ph.D. dissertation, *Human Adjustment to Floods*, in which he now famously noted that "Floods are 'acts of God,' but flood losses are largely acts of man."[1] White's work has been described as part of the University of Chicago intellectual heritage of American pragmatism, as practiced by one-time faculty member John Dewey. Dewey influenced many of the ecological traditions that flourished at the University of Chicago during the twentieth century. His influence on these traditions was most notable in their extrascientific emphases on the environment as a public good and on democratic community.[2]

One of the goals of White and his students was to bring the idea of hazard and natural disaster back into the realm of public discourse and out of the dark closet of technical expertise and management. In part this was achieved by connecting the study of natural hazard with the more general discourse of human–environment relations. As Kenneth Hewitt argues, the study of natural disaster had been put in intellectual exile on the "archipelago of isolated misfortunes."[3] He continues that, within such a perspective, "each disaster is an unplanned hole or rupture in the fabric of productive and orderly human relations with the habitat."[4] Within this perspective, natural disasters randomly disorganize space, annihilate places, and destroy landscapes. In these ways, they disrupt and threaten human communities.

From another point of view, physical geographers and other natural scientists characterize the geological and climatic events associated with natural disaster as simply dramatic and somewhat unusual processes of landscape change. Rather than being described as 'ruptures' or unique events, they are viewed as part of a continuum of possible events that continually give shape to and modify the Earth's surface. Such events may be unpredictable, but they are not random, and they often have beneficial consequences both for natural ecosystems and for future human projects. These benefits include such things as the deposition and replenishment of soil through flooding, the regeneration of vegetation through fire, or the creation of new land in volcanic eruption. From this perspective, natural events that are often calamitous in terms of their immediate human consequences are "normalized" as being part of a continuous process of landscape change.

Thus, natural disasters have at least two very different associations with the idea of landscape. In one sense they are a source of the destruction of landscapes, and in another they are dramatic moments of landscape change and renewal. These differences may be seen as being part of one basic geographic process in which places are continually being made, unmade, and remade in relation to human projects and in response to natural forces. Landscape, then, is the visible weave of the place-making process, and natural disaster is just one element, albeit calamitous in its human consequences, of this process.[5] Herder alluded to this process model in his comment on natural disaster, when those elements that make the Earth habitable to humans "periodically rouse up to claim their own."[6] For him, this process is simply part of humans making the Earth their home:

The formation of this our abode, and all the substances it can produce, must have already prepared us for the frailty and mutability of the history of man; and the more closely we inspect it, the more clearly do these unfold themselves to our perception.[7]

Such a process view would seem to point toward a single conception of landscape that draws together the natural and the social worlds. Indeed, this claim is sometimes made. It is, however, rarely sustained. Despite frequently made reductionist arguments, two quite distinct concepts of landscape coexist in geography. These have traditionally been labeled as the *cultural landscape* and the *natural landscape*. The natural landscape has been the most problematic in geography, in part because of its associations with a primordial or pristine natural environment. Human interference in the natural world and the fact that no part of terrestrial nature remains unaffected by human activity has led to frequent attempts to recast natural landscapes as cultural representations. These attempts are evident in disaster studies in which there has been increasing emphasis on human failings to properly adapt social projects to the basic cycles of the natural environment, and thus on the moral and technical failings associated with the making of cultural landscapes. The different epistemic goals associated with these two conceptions of landscape tend to keep them separate from one another, even though hope for their reconciliation is expressed, especially in public policy statements regarding landscape preservation and conservation.[8]

These two fundamental concepts of geographic landscape share some common areas of meaning, especially their holistic sense, but they have important differences as well. One such difference involves the temporal and spatial scales used to frame landscapes. The scientific space-time frame of natural landscape is incommensurable with the historical and geographic scales of cultural landscapes. Put another way, the physical space-time of natural history is of a different order than the place and period of human projects. In natural disaster the loss of cultural landscapes is immediate and disorienting. It disrupts human communities and destroys material traces of memory, both individual and collective. What is lost is the *place order*, an order that is both material and ideal.[9] The material aspect and the taken-for-granted quality of everyday cultural landscapes give this place order an appearance of being natural. It is only when threatened that its frailty as a human construct becomes evident, for example, when powerful natural forces threaten to transform cultural landscapes into natural landscapes.[10]

The natural landscape involves a much larger space-time frame, one rendered comprehensible from the scientific understanding of natural systems seen as wholes. Such landscapes provide an areal order to natural processes, an order of physical space-time that intersects with, but does not frame, the human place order. The natural history narratives of landscape reflect this scalar quality. Within such narratives the physical events that trigger natural disaster are normalized, and the adjustments that they make to natural systems, often occurring over long periods of time, are recounted as part of a process of ongoing change.

Core geographical concepts, such as place/space and landscape, do their conceptual labor at the border of nature and culture. Place is a thoroughly humanized concept in geography, whereas space is not. Landscape is used in both ways, as a reference to the humanly constructed landscape, as the visible "weave" of the rules of place, and as the space of nature. Through landscape one is able to see the relation of place to space, and the significance of making each comprehensible by giving them a sense of coherence and wholeness. It offers the promise of overcoming the culture–nature divide, but never completely fulfills this promise. Natural disaster presents a dramatic moment of exposure for this relationship. At its cataclysmic center, it is a sequence of events in which material landscapes that bear the meanings of human history are partially or completely erased by processes operating in physical time, and human places are, at least temporarily, transformed into natural spaces. The apparent "completed" quality of cultural landscapes is lost to seeming chaos at one scale, but at another it simply succumbs to a more powerful ordering force. Natural landscapes remain even as the place order disintegrates, gardens revert to weeds, and walls crumble to piles of rocks.

Lisbon to New Orleans

White's description of floods has a significant intellectual lineage. For example, Rousseau's 1756 epistle to Voltaire on the topic of Voltaire's 1755 poem on the Lisbon earthquake and tsunami expressed a similar belief, phrased in the vocabulary of natural evil:

Moreover, I believe that I have shown that, with the exception of death, which is scarcely to be counted as an evil except for the antechambers one is made to pass through to reach it, most of the physical evils we experience are likewise of our own making. Without leaving your chosen subject of Lisbon, you must acknowledge, for example, that it was not nature that piled up there twenty thousand houses of six or seven floors each; and that if the inhabitants of this great city had spread out more evenly and had lived in less massive buildings, the destruction would have been a lot less, and perhaps insignificant. . . . In my view, it's apparent over and over again that the sufferings nature imposes on us are less cruel than those we add on ourselves.[11]

The Lisbon disaster sent intellectual shock waves throughout Enlightenment Europe.[12] It stimulated not only Voltaire and Rousseau but also the young Immanuel Kant to address issues of tectonics, physical geography, and natural evil. The calamitous events of recent years—for example, the Indian Ocean tsunami of 2003, the 2005 United States Gulf Coast hurricane, and flood and the 2005 earthquake in Pakistan—have sent shock waves of a different sort throughout the world. Interpretations of these events have covered a quite broad and familiar range including divine retribution, but for the most part have been focused on issues of techno-logical deficiencies, vulnerable human settlement patterns, and inadequate government preparation. None of these events was entirely unexpected; each occurred in areas of the world where the environmental risk was known, but each was nonetheless devastating to human communities at the local, regional, and national scales, and in the case of the Indian Ocean tsunami, at the international scale.

With the possible exception of religious extremists, the shock created by these events is not about natural evil. In fact, much of the current writ-ing on natural disaster tends to downplay the role of the natural. This ten-dency is evident in phrases such as "unnatural disaster" used to refer to catastrophes linked to natural events, or in provocative statements such as that "there's no such thing as a natural disaster."[13] Such phrasing may well be an intentional overstatement, but it illustrates clearly the current direc-tion of disaster research toward emphases on human causes, social respon-sibility, social vulnerability, and the reduction of risk through planning.[14] In part this shift reflects the fact that distinguishing between natural and nonnatural disaster has become increasingly difficult in the heavily engi-neered modern world.[15]

Controversies surrounding the destruction of New Orleans in the after-math of Hurricane Katrina demonstrate this difficulty. The hurricane's gen-eration of sea-water surges contributed to the failure of poorly constructed levees flooding most of the city. This scenario had been foreseen by many. For example, the geographer Pierce Lewis wrote of the social and physical dilemmas facing the New Orleans community, highlighting the specific hazard that eventually flooded the city. He noted that the social ills of New Orleans might indeed be correctable through thoughtful, concerted action, but the physical threats, most notably flooding from the Mississippi river and hurricane-generated tidal surges, could not so easily be diminished. The prescient Lewis expressed skepticism about public action in relation to environmental hazards:

a good many residents take a relaxed attitude toward environmental hazards in general, assuming that they have always been under control and, therefore, that they will remain under control. Such insouciance may be justified when it comes to threats of river flooding. It is emphatically *not* justified when it comes to the matter of the hurricanes, and the murderous tidal surges that accompany them. . . . It is a great irony: the very levees that were built to protect life and property in southern Louisiana are potential agents of their destruction.[16]

Lewis's prediction has now become fact. The "evil" exposed in the after-math of Katrina is of a moral rather than a natural kind. Aspects of the heavily engineered, built environment failed, and a unique cultural landscape was destroyed. The previous loss of an extensive wetlands landscape, caused in part by the construction of levees to protect urban landscapes, is cited as being part of the cause of the calamity. Even though attitudes toward these wetlands had changed in recent years after almost two centuries of drainage and reclamation projects, this new attitude toward "nature in the city" came too late.[17] The place order, the visible material fragments of which were evidenced in the devastated landscape, collapsed. Natural processes of landscape change reclaimed the land.

Landscape as Peaceful Coexistence

In the not too distant past, such devastation would have been seen as a lost battle in the continuous war with nature. Harold Bloom describes this warlike relation between nature and society in ancient Greece in writing about the *Iliad* as a source of wisdom:

the world of peace is essentially a war between humans and nature, in which farmers rip out grain and fruit as so many spoils of battle. This helps explain why the *Iliad* need not bother to praise war, since reality is a constant contest anyway, in which nothing of value can be attained without despoiling or ruining someone or something else.[18]

For modern environmentalists, this "war" has entered a new phase. As the French historian of science Michel Serres writes, "In the days of the *Iliad* . . . the world wasn't considered fragile; on the contrary, it was threatening, and it easily triumphed over men. . . . Once victorious, the Earth is now a victim."[19] For the geographer Yi-Fu Tuan, the shift in battle lines is reflected in our understanding of landscape, even scenic natural landscape, which has historically referred to a "thoroughly humanized world": "Nature-wild nature-only began to draw appreciative glances when people no longer saw it as a threat. No longer a threat, wild nature could be incorporated into an aesthetic—the aesthetic of the sublime."[20] Early signs of this shift were evident in the eighteenth-century aesthetic theory of Edmund Burke in which the literal threat of nature was the source of the sublime.[21] For Immanuel Kant the sublime emerged from within the human subject.[22] According to Edward Casey the representation of this natural sublime in landscape was complex and vast, ranging "from the rugged to the reposeful, from the agitated to the tranquil, from the immense to the diminutive." He labels these two poles as the "apocalyptic" and the "contemplative."[23] The disconcerting mix of terror and awe, threat and joy that characterizes the sublime has been a significant part of the discourse of natural disaster.

Voltaire captured this sense of the apocalyptic and the chaotic consequences of natural events in his poetic description of the Lisbon earthquake and tsunami of 1755:

> Oh wretched man, earth-fated to be cursed;
> Abyss of plagues and miseries the worst! . . .
> Approach in crowds, and meditate awhile
> Yon shattered walls, and view each ruined pile,
> Women and children heaped up mountain high,
> Limbs crushed which under ponderous marble lie;
> Wretches unnumbered in the pangs of death,
> Who mangled, torn, and panting for their breath,
> Buried beneath their sinking ruins expire,
> And end their wretched lives in torments dire.[24]

The overwhelming scale of the social catastrophes of the twentieth and twenty-first centuries have led some to view this apocalyptic sublime as no longer rooted in the natural world.[25] The natural sublime, to the extent that it remains meaningful, has become more closely connected to the contemplative than to the apocalyptic. Strains of current ecocentric thought have moved naturally caused trauma in a direction more accurately characterized as erotic. For example, Michel Serres offers a description of his relation to the natural world, when he "tasted joy" during an earthquake (of significantly less destructive force than occurred in Lisbon!) in the San Francisco Bay area:

> All of a sudden the ground shakes off its gear: walls tremble, ready to collapse, roofs buckle, people fall, communications are interrupted, noise keeps you from hearing each other, the thin technological film tears, squealing and snapping like metal or crystal. . . . Who am I? A tremor of nothingness, living in a permanent earthquake. Yet for a moment of profound happiness, the spasmodic Earth comes to unite herself with my shaky body. Who am I, now, for several seconds? Earth herself. Both communing, in love she and I, doubly in distress, throbbing together, joined in a single aura.[26]

For Serres, unlike Frost, nature completes.

In modern thought, the cultural landscape has tended to be portrayed as either a thin wall of protection from the world of uncontrolled nature or an artifice masking an authentic, near-erotic relation of humans to the Earth. For Casey, landscape is "something situated at the intervening of earth and world."[27] Small wonder, then, that landscape has occupied a central position in the geographical project, one based on how humans make the Earth their home and how they shape the Earth into worlds. In the history of geographic thought, however, this hope of mediation has been more difficult to achieve in practice and, as I have already suggested, has been divided into two separate streams of thought. Occasionally, these two streams come together, but usually only at the level of policy and planning teams.

Landscape and Twentieth-Century Geographic Thought

J. B. Jackson refers to "landscape" as a word that on the surface seems "simple enough" as well as commonly used and understood, "and yet to each of us it seems to mean something different."[28] In the history of modern geographic thought, this variety has meant that landscape has been adapted to work within a mix of competing intellectual positions. The concept of landscape, similar to other core concepts in geography, moves easily from the language of everyday speech to the disciplinary language of academic specialists. Geographers have sought, with only moderate success, to offer a greater precision to their core concepts. The frequent outcome of such attempts is academic disputation over disciplinary directions.

Landscape studies in geography derive from nineteenth-century French and German geography, whose practitioners portrayed the "harmony" and "balance" between natural and cultural processes as the basis for understanding the impact associated with the changing social order of industrialization and urbanization. In North American geography, landscape offered a point of contention between two of the leading figures in the discipline, Carl Sauer and Richard Hartshorne. For Sauer, especially in his classic article "The Morphology of Landscape,"[29] the "landscape" concept was at the center of geography, the study of how cultural processes shaped human adaptation to the natural world. These so-called cultural landscapes, a name that Sauer borrowed from German geographers, became the signature concept for what has been referred to as the "Berkeley School" in American geography. Its goal in a very broad sense was to understand humans as geographic agents of change of their natural environment. Sauer sometimes phrased this interest as an examination of how "natural landscapes" are transformed into "cultural landscapes," starting with the basic interactions between humans and soil, vegetation, and the animal world. He eventually acknowledged the problematic qualities of "natural landscape."[30] The most notable of these was the difficulty of establishing a starting point for such studies. He came to see natural landscape instead as a useful fiction for advancing the understanding of human impact on the natural environment.

Although Sauer saw the cultural landscape as an essential part of a regional geography, his ideas have often been contrasted with the geographic tradition known as *chorology* or *chorography*, the study of areal differentiation, which put the "region" rather than "landscape" at the center of geographical study. Hartshorne, in *The Nature of Geography*, was dismissive of "landscape" as ambiguously applied by geographers and felt this lack of precision disqualified it as unifying concept for the scientific study of geography.[31] He noted that its proponents, such as Sauer, at times seemed to be using the concept to mean something equivalent to a region. He was especially critical of the separation of natural and cultural landscapes and the use of the former as a theoretical or instrumental concept for separating cultural from natural agents of change. The distinctive visual aspect of landscape, the "look of an area," was similarly criticized by Hartshorne because of its inherently subjective quality and the apparent lack of agreed-upon criteria for determining significance and selection.

These mid-twentieth-century disputes have largely disappeared in contemporary geographical thought with the gradual acceptance of a broader understanding of geographical "science" and a more complex idea of the geographic agent. There is currently much less concern for the "polluting" qualities of the subjective in geographic research. This expanded interest in the human subject involves as well a concern with the relation of the subject and the social milieu. Landscape in this view is a consequence of a complex relation between changing social conditions, human agency, and material conditions in which meaning is not purely subjective but is rather a socially mediated product. As Denis Cosgrove writes, "in recent years the ambiguities that so irritated Hartshorne have been actively exploited by geographers who positively value landscape's capacity to smudge the binaries of nature and culture, of reality and representation, of symbol and referent."[32] For Cosgrove, landscape extends rather than diminishes the chorological tradition:

While landscape obviously refers to the surface of the earth, or a part thereof, and thus to the chosen field of geographical enquiry, it incorporates far more than merely the visual and functional arrangement of natural and human phenomena which the discipline can identify, classify, map and analyse. Landscape shares but extends the idea of "area" or "region," both concepts which have been claimed as its geographical equivalents.[33]

Part of the overlap with the concept of region involves the sense of "wholeness" that is part of the meaning of each. Landscape, like region, implies a way of seeing things together in place. Casey suggests that such wholeness is in fact experiential: "the experience of landscape . . . is an experience of something that cannot be reduced to a finite set of discrete objects, much less to a single total object. . . . landscape is more scene than thing, more event than object, more place than site."[34] Whereas for Cosgrove landscape is something more than place because of its incorporation of the natural, for Casey, landscape is derivative of place in that there is no landscape without place:

Landscapes are, in the final analysis, placescapes; they are congeries of places in the fullest experiential and represented sense. *No landscape without place*: this much we may take to be certainly true. Not only is it difficult to imagine or remember an actual landscape devoid of places; it is not possible to come upon a landscape that does not contain them in significant fashion. . . . To be in a landscape is to be in the midst of places.[35]

This highly schematic story of the landscape concept in geography has overlooked other intellectual skirmishes associated with the desire among some to stake out topical areas in the study of human geography. These have included overlapping distinctions, all applicable in adjectival form in the discussion of landscape, such as ordinary (vernacular)/formal, material/symbolic, and social product/cultural text.[36] Landscape has been studied as forms of representation from painting to narrative and as a text to be read and interpreted.[37] Landscape's material quality has made it prominent in studies emphasizing the social relations of production.[38] Both its symbolic and material qualities have been drawn together in studies of social power in the creation of landscapes of dominance or liberation. This linkage has been traced historically to its roots as the areal extent of customary law and is a symbol of the body politic.[39]

Geographic landscapes have thus offered a broad conceptual cloth that geographers have used to weave into new or conforming styles of intellectual fashion. In general, however, these more recent developments have shifted the focus away from any consideration of the natural landscape except to the extent that the natural landscapes may be absorbed into the fabric of social relations. Concerns of harmony, balance, and the persistence of landscapes have given way to those of conflict and power in the transformation of landscapes, indeed in the contestation over whose identity is and should be reflected in landscape. It is work that reflects Pierre Bourdieu's observation that "Even the 'landscapes' or 'native soil' so dear to geographers are in fact inheritances, in other words, historical products of social determinants."[40] The modes of analysis of landscape between human and physical geography have largely diverged into separate research streams.

Landscape Ecology

At the same time as human geographers have adapted landscape to various social theories and theories of the subject, the concept has gained a second life within ecological science. Landscape ecology has taken as its object the landscape of natural processes. Its practitioners consider ecological change in terms of both natural and anthropogenic processes. As Burel and Baudry state: "Landscape is a level of organization of ecological systems that is higher than the ecosystem level. It is characterized essentially by its heterogeneity and its dynamics, partly governed by human activities. It exists independently of perception."[41]

As with all such attempts at definition it is not without controversy. As Turner notes in her review of the Burel and Baudry volume, such a definition locks into a particular sense of scale (e.g., "higher than"), in this case a notably hierarchical one that neglects the fact that scale is dependent on the type of system being described. The second issue is, not surprisingly, that of "independence from perception," a phrase suggesting that landscapes as natural systems are actual rather than mere representations. Ecological research has maintained a consistent link to holistic analysis, from its earliest roots in nineteenth-century biology to the present.[42] Holistic themes associated with the ecologists' emphasis on natural communities and their resistance to the reductionism prevalent in the modern biological sciences have become more muted over time but have never completely disappeared in debates over "ecosystems" and other core concepts. These issues are especially evident in discussions of the appropriate scale of analysis. Landscape ecology presents itself as an analysis that maintains a commitment to large-scale systems, such as habitats.

Despite its different origins and interests to those of the cultural landscape, landscape ecology shares some of the same conceptual ambiguities. The origins of landscape ecology are have been linked to the German geographer Carl Troll's use of aerial photography in ecological studies, and thus in its early use there is an idea of landscape as both "area" and "scene."[43] However, its meaning has gradually evolved toward one associated with concerns that are more strictly speaking "spatial" than "landscape" specific. Thus, definitions of landscape ecology refer frequently to the role of spatial structure in the functioning of organic communities. For example, in their text on landscape ecology, Forman and Godron[44] identify the basic components of such studies as involving spatial form, function, and flows. Even the more ecumenical formulations that encompass a greater role for human action translate this action into the vocabulary of space rather than place through their representation within geographic information systems.[45]

Landscape ecology has its origins in the study of natural systems but has had a close connection to policy and planning, and, thus, its practitioners have maintained a commitment to incorporate the human dimensions of natural systems.[46] One sees this quite clearly in the emphasis on land use change,[47] which is a troublesome component of most global climate change models. It is the natural scientist's goal to record and predict such change. However, land use involves a complicated set of factors involving not only questions of economic rationality but also of cultural ideals and values. The spatial modeling made possible through the use of geographic information systems adapts readily to social science research using rational choice theory but is relatively blind to all but the most basic of cultural themes. This gap reflects traditional divisions between social scientific and hermeneutic traditions in the human sciences. In contemporary ecological studies one finds many of the same intellectual dilemmas of nature and culture that have been part of the history of geographic thought for centuries. Policy studies concerning landscape preservation and conservation, especially prominent in Europe in part through the directives of the European Union, have attempted to reach across this divide through the formation of interdisciplinary teams, but with rather limited results.[48]

These classical intellectual dividing lines of geography have been challenged in recent research, especially in work that has examined the political significance of "natural" landscapes. In its renewed and current form, landscape study has become a favorite conceptual tool for those seeking to "rematerialize" the geographical expressions of culture and to emphasize the social production of landscapes, both natural and cultural. For example, the geographic disciples of Bruno Latour have explored so-called "hybrids," the blending of nature and culture in "things."[49] The goal of overcoming the dichotomies of the modernist project and exploring a "post-humanist" world has led to a consideration of nonhuman agency. This concentration on the processes of everyday practice seeks an intellectual position between the semiotics of landscape and the study of ecological processes of natural systems, emphasizing points of conjunction of the political and the material in a politics of nature. Natural disaster offers such a moment of conjunction.

Nature/Culture and Landscape Narrative

The historian Douglas Brinkley describes his sudden realization of the forces at work during the violent onset of Hurricane Katrina. After abandoning his home for the supposed safe haven of a high-rise building, he looked out the window to witness an unusual sight: "Just below me, the whitecapped Mississippi River was roaring backward—northward—due to Hurricane Katrina's wrath."[50] His characterization of Katrina as "a palpable monster, an alien beast" evokes the image of a force that not only destroyed much of the Gulf Coast but also appeared to disrupt the fundamental order of nature, such as the direction of river water flowing to the sea.[51] The historian narrator chooses a vocabulary that conveys the human experience of the event. The natural scientist describing the same climatic event and its landscape consequences employs a different vocabulary. Nature, in these descriptions, is neither angry nor monstrous, but rather is a set of ordered processes that act on the landscape in ways independent of human projects. The spatial and temporal boundaries of these two types of narrative description, cultural and natural history, differ fundamentally in that they depict the same series of events at two incommensurate scales, one of human experience and the other of physical systems. As Hewitt notes: "The power of scientific thought has derived especially from discovering scales and perspectives where phenomena seem to fall into elegant and parsimonious forms, regardless of how far these scales and perspectives diverge from the compass of everyday human experience."[52]

Presenting this difference as being primarily one of narrative scale might offer hope to some, especially environmental planners and policymakers, who seek an optimum middle point at which natural and cultural landscapes blend into one object of analysis as their scales merge. In fact, however, this difference in scale masks more fundamental ontological and epistemological differences. The cultural landscape is the visible weave of place order, a fully humanized world created by the complex web of projects associated with how humans make the Earth their home. The landscapes of the natural scientists are of a different kind. These areally bounded natural systems are neither always visible nor are they "objects" of human experience. The different narratives used to describe each are similar to the extent that they emplot landscapes as "wholes," but of different of orders and magnitudes. These orders intersect, but they are not reducible one to another.[53]

The oft-noted cultural or social production of natural landscapes in modern societies may be understood, then, as the application of the knowledge of these natural systems and their manipulation and use for human projects, rather than as the reduction of one landscape to the other. Examples of such projects range across a variety of seemingly "natural" landscapes, from gardens to ecological preserves and wilderness areas. This humanized place ordering of biological and physical components creates cultural landscapes rather than natural systems. Humans "complete" these cultural landscapes through the construction of a place order. Natural disaster dramatically exposes the contingency and fragility of this place order and its limits in relation to natural forces.

Conclusion

The landscape concept has offered geographers the hope of a seamless connective tissue between culture and nature. It is this promise that in part explains landscape's resilience and power within the geographical imagination. Like other core concepts within geography, landscape does its most significant intellectual labor at the border of nature and culture, but its uses, in the end, mirror rather than narrow this significant ontological and epistemological divide. Natural disaster studies highlight these differences.

Natural disaster and the human response to it also expose a point of potential synergistic contact between the discourses of the cultural and natural landscape. The coming together of these two modes of understanding landscape is not a conceptual or a theoretical synthesis, but rather a political and cultural act. It is a communal response similar to what John Dewey once described as the formation of a "public," a dynamic, relatively spontaneous, issue-specific form of collective action that is a central platform of his pragmatic conception of democratic community.[54] Gilbert White's focus on relating natural hazards research to questions of social planning and land use control was related to this Deweyan legacy. Similarly, White's intellectual descendants have remained committed to this philosophy in their expansion of the natural hazards research tradition into so-called sustainability science, a program based on the successful blending of scientific practice with democratic social institutions. Both recognize the value of connecting natural science to public discourse, but neither specifically focuses on the formation of the public and democratic community.

Such a focus is conceivable in relation to the complex aftermath of natural calamity, in which the intensity and broad collective sharing of the experience bring strong but fleeting grounds for communal solidarity. For example, the rebuilding of New Orleans is essentially a project involving the rebuilding of a place order in conjunction with the revival of community. However, the often invisible and taken-for-granted qualities of this order—for example, the implicit social rules of place that structure everyday interactions—are difficult to use as a guide for collective action.

The visible weave of place, the cultural landscape, thus moves to the forefront as an accessible, material source for the collective rebuilding of a meaningful place order. Similarly, landscape ecology also steps forward as a potentially valuable resource in this construction process, which may range from the renewal of streets and houses of residential neighborhoods to the moving of the Mississippi River and the reconstruction of coastal wetlands. Even in the most seemingly "natural" of these rehabilitation projects, knowledge of natural landscapes guides rather than determines the direction of the collective action. Such knowledge provides a potentially valuable tool for democratic experimentation with cultural landscapes that are the surface manifestations of potentially new forms of place and communal order. More than this, actual and imagined cultural landscapes have the latent capability of serving as the *lingua franca* of a public focused on community renewal.

Notes

1. Gilbert F. White, *Human Adjustments to Floods: A Geographical Approach to the Flood Problem in the United States* (Chicago: University of Chicago, 1945), p. 2.

2. See J. Ronald Engel, *Sacred Sands: The Struggle for Community in the Indiana Dunes* (Middletown: Wesleyan University Press, 1983); James Westcoat, "Common Themes in the Work of Gilbert White and John Dewey," *Annals of the Association of American Geographers* 82 (1992); Ben Minteer, *The Landscape of Reform: Civic Pragmatism and Environmental Thought in America* (Cambridge, MA: MIT Press, 2006).

3. Kenneth Hewitt, ed., *Interpretations of Calamity: From the Point of View of Human Ecology: The Risks and Hazards Series*, vol. I (Boston: Allen & Unwin, 1983), p. 12.

4. Ibid.

5. Robert Sack, *A Geographical Guide to the Real and the Good* (New York: Routledge, 2003).

6. Quoted in Clarence Glacken, *Traces on the Rhodian Shore: Nature and Culture in Western Thought from Ancient Times to the End of the Eighteenth Century* (Berkeley: University of California Press, 1967).

7. Ibid.

8. See, for example, Hannes Palang and Gary Fry, eds., *Landscape Interfaces: Cultural Heritage in Changing Landscapes* (Dordrecht: Kluwer, 2003).

9. Edward S. Casey, *Representing Place: Landscape Painting and Maps* (Minneapolis: University of Minnesota Press, 2002).

10. J. Nicholas Entrikin, "Place Destruction and Cultural Trauma," in *Culture, Society, and Democracy: The Interpretive Approach*, ed. Jeffrey C. Alexander and Isaac Reed (Boulder, CO: Paradigm Press, 2007), pp. 163–179.

11. See Voltaire, *Candide and Related Texts*, trans. David Wootton (Indianapolis: Hackett, 2000).

12. See Susan Neiman, *Evil in Modern Thought: An Alternative History of Philosophy* (Princeton: Princeton University Press, 2002), pp. 239–250; Glacken, *Traces on the Rhodian Shore*, pp. 517–537.

13. Janet Abramovitz, *Unnatural Disasters* (Washington, D.C.: Worldwatch Paper 158, 2001); Theodore Steinberg, *Acts of God: The Unnatural History of Natural Disaster in America* (Oxford: Oxford University Press, 2000); Neil Smith, "There's No Such Thing as Natural Disaster," in *Understanding Katrina: Perspectives from the Social Sciences*, Social Science Research Council, <http://understandingkatrina.ssrc.org/Smith>.

14. Susan Cutter and Christopher Emrich, "Moral Hazard, Social Catastrophe: The Changing Face of Vulnerability along the Hurricane Coasts," *Annals: American Academy Publications in the Social Sciences* 64 (2006): 102–112.

15. Theodore Steinberg, "What Is Natural Disaster?," *Literature and Medicine* 15 (1996): 33–47; 34.

16. Peirce Lewis, *New Orleans: The Making of an Urban Landscape*, 2nd ed. (Santa Fe: Center for American Places, 2003), pp. 162–163, 167–168.

17. Craig Colten, *An Unnatural Metropolis: Wresting New Orleans from Nature* (Baton Rouge: Louisiana State University Press, 2005), pp. 162–165.

18. Harold Bloom, *Where Shall Wisdom Be Found?* (New York: Riverhead Books, 2004), p. 74.

19. Michel Serres, *The Natural Contract*, trans. Elizabeth MacArthur and William Paulson (Ann Arbor: University of Michigan Press, 1995), p. 11.

20. Yi-Fu Tuan, "Foreword," in Kenneth Olwig, *Landscape, Nature, and the Body Politic: From Britain's Renaissance to America's New World* (Madison: University of Wisconsin Press, 2002), p. xix.

21. Edmund Burke, *A Philosophical Enquiry into the Origin of Our Ideas of the Sublime and Beautiful*, ed. James Boulton (Notre Dame: University of Notre Dame Press, 1759/1993).

22. Casey, *Representing Place*, p. 50.

23. Ibid., p. 45.

24. François Marie Arouet de Voltaire, "The Lisbon Earthquake: An Inquiry into the Maxim, 'Whatever Is, Is Right,'" in *Candide and Related Texts*, p. 99.

25. Gene Ray, "Reading the Lisbon Earthquake: Adorno, Lyotard, and the Contemporary Sublime," *Yale Journal of Criticism* 17 (2004): 1–18; Neiman, *Evil in Modern Thought*.

26. Serres, *The Natural Contract*, p. 124.

27. Casey, *Representing Place*, p. 272.

28. John Brinkerhoff Jackson, *Discovering the Vernacular Landscape* (New Haven: Yale University Press, 1984), p. 3.

29. Carl Sauer, "The Morphology of Landscape," in *Land and Life: A Selection from the Writings of Carl Ortwin Sauer*, ed. John Leighly (Berkeley: University of California Press, 1963), pp. 153–163.

30. Carl Sauer, "Now This Matter of Cultural Geography: Notes from Carl Sauer's Last Seminar at Berkeley," ed. James Parsons, in *Carl O. Sauer: A Tribute*, ed. Martin Kenzer (Corvallis: Oregon State University Press, 1987).

31. Richard Hartshorne, *The Nature of Geography: A Critical Survey of Current Thought in Light of the Past* (Lancaster, PA: Association of American Geographers, 1939), p. 169; J. Nicholas Entrikin and Stanley Brunn, eds., *Reflections on Richard Hartshorne's "The Nature of Geography"* (Washington, D.C.: Occasional Publications of the Association of American Geographers, 1989).

32. Denis Cosgrove, *Geographical Imagination and the Authority of Images*, 2005 Hettner-Lecture, Department of Geography, University of Heidelberg (Stuttgart: Franz Steiner Verlag, 2006), p. 31.

33. Denis Cosgrove, *Social Formation and Symbolic Landscape* (Totowa, NJ: Barnes and Noble, 1984), p. 13.

34. Casey, *Representing Place*, p. 45.

35. Ibid., pp. 271–272.

36. Donald Meinig, ed., *The Interpretation of Ordinary Landscapes* (New York: Oxford University Press, 1979).

37. See, for example, James Duncan, *The City as Text: Politics of Landscape Interpretation in the Kandyan Kingdom* (Cambridge: Cambridge University Press, 1990).

38. See, for example, Don Mitchell, *The Lie of the Land: Migrant Workers and the California Landscape* (Minneapolis: University of Minnesota Press, 1996).

39. Olwig, *Landscape, Nature, and the Body Politic*.

40. Pierre Bourdieu, *Language and Symbolic Power*, ed. John Thompson, trans. Gino Raymond and Matthew Adamson (Cambridge, MA: Harvard University Press, 1991), p. 287n4.

41. Françoise Burel and Jacques Baudry, *Landscape Ecology: Concepts, Methods, and Applications* (Enfield, NH: Science Publishers, 2003), p. 43, cited in Sandra Turner, "Review of *Landscape Ecology: Concepts, Methods, and Applications* by F. Burel and J. Baudry," *Landscape Ecology* 20 (2005): 1031-1033, at 1031.

42. Richard Forman, *Land Mosaics: The Ecology of Landscapes and Regions* (Cambridge: Cambridge University Press, 1995); Frank Golley, "Historical Origins of the Ecosystem Concept in Ecology," in *Ecosystem Concept in Ecology*, ed. E. Moran (Washington, D.C.: American Academy for the Advancement of Science Publications, 1983); Frank Golley, "Introducing Landscape Ecology," *Landscape Ecology* 1 (1987): 1–3; Robert McIntosh, *The Background of Ecology: Concept and Theory* (Cambridge: Cambridge University Press, 1985).

43. Golley, "Introducing Landscape Ecology," p. 1.

44. Richard Forman and Michael Godron, *Landscape Ecology* (New York: John Wiley, 1986).

45. Daniel Brown, Richard Aspinall, and David Bennett, "Landscape Models and Explanation in Landscape Ecology: A Space for Generative Landscape Science," *Professional Geographer* 58 (2006): 369–382.

46. Edward O. Wilson, "Foreword," in *Land Mosaics: The Ecology of Landscapes and Regions*, ed. Richard Foreman (Cambridge: Cambridge University Press, 1995).

47. Mattias Burgi, Anna Hersperger, and Nina Schneeberger, "Driving Forces of Landscape Change: Current and New Directions," *Landscape Ecology* 19 (2004): 857.

48. Hannes Palang and Gary Fry, eds., *Landscape Interfaces: Cultural Heritage in Changing Landscapes* (Dordrecht: Kluwer Academic, 2003); Hannes Palang, Helen Sooväli, Marc Antrop, and Guhild Setten, eds., *European Rural Landscapes: Persistence and Change in a Globalising Environment* (Dordrecht: Kluwer, 2004).

49. Bruno Latour, *We Have Never Been Modern*, trans. Catherine Porter (Cambridge, MA: Harvard University Press, 1993).

50. Douglas Brinkley, *The Great Deluge: Hurricane Katrina, New Orleans, and the Mississippi Gulf Coast* (New York: William Morrow, 2006), p. xiii.

51. Ibid., p. xiv.

52. Kenneth Hewitt, ed., *Interpretations of Calamity: From the Point of View of Human Ecology* (Boston: Allen & Unwin, 1983), p. 19.

53. Olwig, *Landscape, Nature, and the Body Politic*, p. 226; Robert Sack, *Homo Geographicus: A Framework for Action, Awareness, and Moral Concern* (Baltimore: Johns Hopkins University Press, 1997), p. 116.

54. John Dewey, *The Public and Its Problems* (Denver: Alan Swallow, 1927), pp. 3–36.

7   The Political Meaning of Landscape (Through the Lens of Hannah Arendt's *The Human Condition*)

Bernard Debarbieux
Translated from the French by Carlo Salzani

If political approaches take the lion's share in the analysis of territory and territoriality, they are proportionally less numerous in the case of landscape. Moreover, most political analyses of landscape, often inscribed within a historiographical project and cultural studies, have focused on the staging of monarchical and aristocratic power and on those landscapes that are emblematic of the national imagination.[1] On the other hand, the texts devoted to the contemporary political dimension of landscape in modern or hypermodern societies are certainly less numerous. This essay proposes an analysis of the contemporary status of landscape in European societies, which are experiencing major transformations in their collective and institutional territorialities.

For this analysis I will draw heavily on a work by Hannah Arendt, *The Human Condition*, written in 1958. Admittedly, this work does not deal with landscape—and only marginally with territoriality, by merely evoking indirectly, here and there, the national territories among the products of modernity. On the other hand, it proposes a reflection on the *vita activa* and the different forms of activities that characterize the human condition; with regard to these activities, it is possible to question the status of landscape. One of the advantages of this exercise—so I will attempt to show—lies in the fact that it enables one to emphasize the diverse meanings of landscape and to highlight the contemporary—notably political—stakes of its practices.

In *The Human Condition*, Arendt, skeptical of any abstract statement concerning *human nature*, strives to define *the human condition* as it is conditioned by our existence on Earth and our material environment: "The earth is the very quintessence of the human condition."[2] Her project aims more precisely to investigate "those general human capacities which grow out of the human condition";[3] in other words, men's (and women's) embeddedness within the terrestrial world, within a world of objects and interactions. If this project could be described as a philosophical anthropology,[4] it also emerges as a political philosophy of action. Indeed, Arendt proposes to divide human activities into three categories: *labor, work,* and *action. Labor* responds to the basic physiological needs of man—especially food. Labor satisfies those needs in an ever-ephemeral way and must necessarily be continuously renewed in order to ensure the survival of the individual and the species. Arendt links labor to the activity of the *animal laborans*: *work,* the product of the *homo faber,* which corresponds to the durable artificial objects that are transmitted from individual to individual, from generation to generation, and which together constitute humankind's cultural artifacts. Finally, *action* "goes on directly between men"[5] and relates them to each other through acts and words:

Speech and action reveal this unique distinctness [of man]. Through them, men distinguish themselves instead of being merely distinct; they are the modes in which human beings appear to each other, not indeed as physical objects, but *qua* men. This appearance, as distinguished from mere bodily existence, rests on initiative, but it is an initiative from which no human being can refrain and still be human.[6]

Thus, Arendt considers action simultaneously to be the source of the definition of the political identity of the subject and the modality through which men in society define what they have in common and what they place at the heart of the public space.

Arendt anchors her analysis of modernity in this ternary conception of human activity. According to her, modernity marks the triumph of *homo faber,* and then of the *animal laborans,* to the detriment of the political identity of the subject, which was essential in classic antiquity. She sees this triumph as the consequence of many factors, in particular the priority given in our modern civilization to economic production and to the constitution of nation-states and national societies.

Though apparently remote, at first sight, from the question of landscape, Arendt's proposition presents analytical advantages that allow apprehending the latter under the new status it was given in Western modernity. I will begin by presenting landscape in its status of *landscape-as-labor* and *landscape-as-work*; their complementarity and simultaneity are at the heart of the modern conception of landscape. I will then pursue the question of the complex status of landscape in contemporary societies and will identify *landscape-as-action* that, though not complying entirely with Arendt's historiographical perspective, appears to have emerged, in some peculiar circumstances, in recent decades.

I Modern Landscape: Labor, Work, and Political Instrumentation

In recent decades, academic works on landscape have often insisted, and rightly so, on the complexity of the notion of landscape: landscape is simultaneously material (matter) and representation, construction, and experience. I propose to consider it also as something that applies, differently according to the situation, to what Arendt calls the logics of labor and work. Two almost contemporary examples, taken from the eighteenth century, which constitutes a decisive turning point in this matter, will help to show this.

Jean-André Deluc (1727–1817) was a naturalist from Geneva, author of numerous works that stand out in the field of natural history in the mid-eighteenth century. He has been credited with the invention of the word "geology" and with the intuition that geological times are much longer than asserted in Genesis.[7] But he has been also considered a precursor to the human geography of the following century because of the attention he gave to the relations the alpine societies maintained with their natural environment.[8] In writings dedicated to this question, he contributed to the invention and diffusion of the idea that the Swiss mountain people showed a peculiar intelligence in their relations with the environment:

[this people] are certainly as fortunate as they are beautiful. And this means: a lot, since they are one of the most beautiful peoples of the world. But probably they are beautiful for the same reasons that make them happy. . . . How happy is man when he remains in the most natural state![9]

Deluc finds this same image of happiness in the harmony of some landscapes. In one of his letters to the Queen of England, he gives a description of the plain of Thun, in the alpine region of the Bern canton:

one could not imagine a more pleasant spectacle than that offered by this plain, both for the heart and the eye. Everything here reveals abundance. Not that precarious abundance resulting from the manufactures, but that incessantly deriving from the sky thanks to the sun and the rain, and that the earth concedes to men through abundant vegetation. An almost continuous orchard covers that soil, so good, so favoured by the influences of the air that the inhabitants do not fear to weaken the production of their gardens, fields or prairies with the shadow of trees.[10]

Deluc finds a moral and political explanation of this visual harmony: This letter, entitled *"Bonheur des pays qui ont gardé leurs communes* [happiness of the countries which have conserved their commons]," is intended as a defense and illustration of collective property at a time when private property, presented by the physiocrats as a condition of the prosperity of

Figure 7.1
Elisabeth Vigée-Lebrun, *Das Alphirtenfest in Unspunnen*, 1808. Oil on canvas, 84 ×
114 cm. Kunstmuseum, Bern.

peoples, was gaining ground. The celebration of the harmony of the landscape of Thun and the beauty of the residents of the area is thus indicative
both of aesthetic appraisal and of moral and political judgment.

At that same time, some painters were giving material form to this kind
of discourse. Elisabeth Vigée-Lebrun, in particular, after an 1804 trip to
that same canton of Bern with Germaine de Staël, painted one of the first
representations of the festival of Unspunnen. If the raison d'être of these
celebrations was principally political, Vigée-Lebrun's painting confers
upon them a communitarian signification: The mountain communities,
installed in a harmonious landscape, account through their gathering for
the social harmony that animated them.

Both Deluc's description of the Thun's plain and Vigée-Lebrun's painting of the Unspunnen festival are landscape representations, works in the
Arendtian sense. But these works share the same principal referent, peasant labor, or, more precisely, the product of peasant labor. They have in

common the fact of aiming at a realist representation of material land-scapes and of thereby contributing, together with a generation of travel-ers at the end of the eighteenth century, to the adoption of an objectivist attitude toward the Alps. However, this representation is anchored in a myth—that of the harmony of mountain societies—that was at the time being construed and which allows the perceived reality to be endowed with intelligibility. In this, these representations, textual and pictorial, are indeed symbolic.

Deluc's text and Vigée-Lubrun's painting are thus intended simulta-neously as works concerned with objectivity and as ideological interpre-tations of a preexisting reality that they aim to make intelligible. Aside from the myth of the free and egalitarian societies of the mountains, this trend of so construing the landscape representation constitutes a modality largely shared by a great part of the artistic, philosophical, and scientific production of the eighteenth and nineteenth centuries. The landscape rep-resentation—the work, textual or pictorial, scholarly or artistic—is subor-dinated to the vital activity—labor—whose products it makes visible. Note finally that this curiosity about the forms of adaptation of local societies to their natural environment, together with the propensity to identify the latter with local "characters," led to the production of representations that can be qualified as "territorial": the work puts together an environment, a landscape shaped by peasant labor, and cultural forms explaining a pecu-liar form of symbiosis, an idiosyncrasy.

Landscape by Brown: The Work in Itself, without Labor as Referent

Lancelot Brown (1716–1783) was one of the most famous landscape design-ers (*paysagistes*) of the eighteenth century. Almost contemporary with Deluc, he gained his fame thanks to some 180 different gardens and parks he designed and developed in England in the mid-eighteenth century. He is often presented as the inventor of a style—the "serpentine style"—gen-erally considered an inaugural form of the English garden. Like his prede-cessors in Italy, France, and the British islands, the landscapes he composed are extraneous to the forms stemming from peasant labor; unlike his pre-decessors, however, who worked on the scale of the enclosure of a private property, the developments realized by Brown integrate the surrounding country into the field of vision. The perspectives designed in his parks combine groves, lawns, and meadows within the space of the park, but also woods, villages, and clearings without, the limits of the private prop-erty being concealed from view in the form of ditches, the famous "ha-ha." Through the inclusion of the countryside into the composition of the landscape, villages and rural activities became the object of contemplation and composition.

However, the countryside in question is not the one Deluc describes and mythifies. It is a countryside where the peasants are involved in a double revolution: a revolution that first concerns land and economy and will lead, owing to the massive appropriation of land by a new generation of, to use the English term, "landlords," to a massive regrouping of lands—the "enclosure" movement—and to the adoption of a new mode of production; second, a revolution of the sensibility, insofar as this rural aristocracy elaborates new aesthetic codes that guide the appraisal of the inherited landscapes and of future developments. Consequently, the interventions of Lancelot Brown are not generally confined to the perimeter of the parks; they extend beyond the "ha-ha" and lead (for example) to the destruction of villages considered inelegant and to the modification in the appearance of fields and forests in the name of that landscape harmony which he seeks to establish around the property. As a side-effect, a part of the local peasantry was co-opted into the service of the nearby property or made to work in accordance with the expectations of the owner.

Brown's landscapes are works in the same way Vigée-Lebrun's *Fêtes d'Unspunnen* and Deluc's *Lettres* are. Yet as works, they are very different from the other two: Brown's landscapes are conceived for duration, unfolding on the surface of the Earth, unlike those of Vigée-Lebrun or Deluc, where only the referent, peasant labor and its products, unfolds in that fashion, and are works in themselves with no reference to labor. In a certain way, they are even a negation of the preexisting forms of labor. At best, labor, in the trivial sense of the word—that of the gardeners, of the peasants put in the service of the aristocratic property, and so on—is subordinated to them. It is never either their referent or the source of inspiration. What motivates the work in Brown and his clients (sponsors) is an ideal of nature as mere symbolic representation.

Political Readings

These first two examples are almost contemporaneous. This concomitance is indicative of the plurality of forms the attitude toward landscape always takes: Here we have seen the distance that could exist between two forms of landscape work in their reference to peasant labor, and the distance between two forms of representation.

To this double attitude we have to add another, more political or institutional. This third attitude is fundamentally bound to the ascendancy of dominant groups and political institutions explicitly or implicitly seeking mastery over the landscape as a modality of their territorialization.

Many academic books and papers of the last quarter of the century strive to emphasize how the landscape had become a social and political stake for the definition of dominant codes, "the discursive terrain across which the struggle between the different, often hostile, codes of meaning construction has been engaged."[11] Denis Cosgrove, in particular, has promoted a neo-Marxist interpretation of the definition of new landscape codes, especially for Brown's England.[12] Other works, at times by the same authors, have also insisted on the role of the modern states in the management of the resources and the iconography of the landscape.[13] These modern states, especially in Europe and North America, have construed their visibility and their legitimacy through landscapes emblematical of the territories on which they exercised their sovereignty. Landscape is seen as one of the numerous devices intended for the construction of a national territory and a corresponding national society, specifically through the manipulation of the appropriate symbology; this system is what Gottmann calls "iconography."[14] In other words, the *landscape* has been put in the service of the construction of *mindscapes*, which integrate landscape figures shared by the members of the same national community. These figures tended to become components of the national identity in two senses of the term: on the one hand, an expression of the singularity of the nation itself and of its territorial roots; on the other, a factor of the definition of the individuals composing the nation through the familiarity acquired with, and the attachment aroused by, those figures emblematic of a "we" under construction.

Social Body, Political Body, and "Earth's Body"

Many authors thus resorted to the double metaphor of the body in order to account for the whole or part of the triangular relation between state, nation, and landscape-territory. First, Marcel Gauchet, among others, suggests that the modern state is characterized by a massive investment of the territorial reference:

there is a transition from a power in extension to a power in depth, where the operation of the sovereign becomes to conduce in the interior of its limits the collective body in full correspondence with himself.[15]

Then Claude Raffestin sees in the process of territorialization, where the modern state has no monopoly, a *corps-à-corps*,[16] in other words, an adjustment of the social and political body to the body of the territory.[17] This is also the case, more important for us here, in the work of Kenneth Olwig, who showed that English and American landscapes were put in the service of the body politic.[18] He has shown very aptly, with the help of these

examples, that the modern nation-state produced a standardizing landscape illusion in order to mask the reality of territories divided in numerous regions with different laws and customs:

A consequence of this mindscaping is that landscape and country have come to be
perceived largely in scenic terms. The identification of country as a polity characterized by a socially constituted political landscape has become subordinated, in many
ways, to the idea of country as scenic physical landscape.[19]

Thus, he suggests that the way landscape becomes scenic and emblematic
of the nation-state implies a conception of landscape as something like the
outward face (*la face apparente*) of the social and political body.

If, on the one hand, in *The Human Condition* and her writings on the
nation-state, Arendt does not speak of landscape and hardly mentions territory, on the other, it seems possible to consider this appropriation and
manipulation of landscape symbols as part of what she calls the alienation
of the modern subject. With the increased importance of labor in industrial society, and the irruption of the public sphere in many areas that until
then had been reserved for the private domain—phenomena to which she
dedicates several pages—the institutionalization of landscape can be seen
as constituting a modality of the capacity, diminished in modernity, of
the individual to be an actor, to acquire his or her own identity through
action. In other words, the political institutionalization of landscape by
the modern states is not based on—but is rather the opposite of—a mobi-
lization of individuals as political actors in this process.

The modern age—or the "first modernity," as some call it—is thus characterized by three landscape trends: the production of scholarly and artistic
representations of landscape as it is shaped by, and sees itself as subordinated to, labor; the appearance of the idea of landscape-as-work with its
deployment first in private and then in public spaces, which requires that a
specific labor be subordinated to the production of the representation; the
subjection of certain representations of landscape to the needs of the territorial and cultural project of the modern nation-states, which is part of the
alienation of their relative individuals.

II   The Contemporary Landscape: Triumph of the Work and Emergence of the Society of *Empaysagement*

Compared to this organization of the representations, productions, and
instrumentalizations of landscape that characterize the first modernity, in
what degree does the actual situation—I agree to call it, with some authors,

the "second modernity," without questioning this terminology here—present reorientations or significant ruptures? This second section will address this question, first through the exposition of tendencies well identified in the spatiality of contemporary societies, and then by considering these tendencies together, which will allow for an explanation of the new value acquired by landscape.

Diversification of Contemporary Practices and Territorialities

We have today a body of observations focusing on the evolution of the spatiality of individual and collective practices in the second modernity. I want to highlight a few points in particular.

The explosion of individual mobility was facilitated not only by the relative drop in the costs of the means of transport, as well as the multiplication of those means, but also by the lessened capacity of states and communities to limit and control such mobility. This augmented mobility led to an individualization of life spaces, progressively made up of places more and more distant from each other and connected to each other through practices of motorized displacement. The result has been a great social diversification of spatial and territorial practices, and a lessened capacity of modern territories to serve simultaneously as containers and normative references for collective practices.

These new mobilities are strictly connected, in a relation of codetermination, to new logics of assemblage of the objects in space. In fact, the increased potential of mobility made possible a dissociation in the space of various practices, especially the well-known dissociation between place of residence and place of work. Urban planning thus tended to promote a functional specialization of places within the urban space, the logic of specialization having prevailed over the promotion of a general organization of those spaces. This paradigm also prevailed in architecture, in favor of the progressive autonomization of this art from city planning: In Françoise Choay's words, cities have tended to become groups of juxtaposed objects that no longer constitute a system; she sees in this trend "the death of the city" and the triumph of the "urban."[20] Similar manifestations have been observed in the irruption of objects that remain strange and extraneous to their environment: Great numbers of airports, nuclear plants, highways, high-tension lines, and rapid trains have come to punctuate or cross spaces to which they remain fundamentally extraneous, in the name of conceptions of space and of metrics independent from those of the places being punctuated or crossed.

The Weakening of Political Territorialities

The contemporary tendencies observed in the evolution of the practices and usages of the space have major political implications that are also identified by various authors. The circulation of people and information on macro-geographical scales helped to weaken the capacity of nation-states to regulate the processes of socialization and acculturation that ensure a certain form of homogeneity across the territory. The social sciences are on the verge of freeing themselves from the paradigm that presupposes a codetermination between nations, cultures, and territories—a paradigm through which they have long apprehended a collective spatial anchorage. By acknowledging the full scope of this evolution, the social sciences should be able to better explain intercultural relations, the heterogeneity of forms of territoriality, but also, for example, the strength of transnational movements.[21]

This evolution also constitutes a challenge for political institutions on a local and regional scale. Since political representation in Western democracies rests on the double network of electoral districts and collectivities (French and Italian regions, Austrian and German lands, Canadian provinces, American states and counties, etc.), any weakening of the coherence of the corresponding spatial systems burdens the capacity of the political representatives to have control over their territory and to present an image of it that takes part in the construction of the corresponding political bodies. This is notably the reason why in many countries, when considering the growing rupture of individuals' space of life, the municipal puzzle and the corresponding question of political representation have appeared obsolete. This is also why the absence of a network and of political representation at the scale of the urban area—the scale on which many of these spatial practices are constituted—has appeared to be a deficiency of our democracies.

The *Empaysagement*

The evolution of material and symbolic spatial practices, on the one hand, and the weakening of political territorialities, on the other, constitute, in my view, the two main motifs of the contemporary demand for landscape. This demand is considerable, as has been already acknowledged long ago. The term has invaded public debate and the question has become the object of numerous public policies. Landscape design (*paysagisme*) and landscape architecture as a profession have become important components of town planning and of rural development, especially in Europe. As for landscape consumption, it is, and has been for a long time, one of the main reasons for tourism.

This trivialization of the invocation of landscape and of landscape concerns in any form of intervention constitutes the visible face of what I propose here to call the *empaysagement* of our societies. This neologism[22] should not be understood as a synonymous with landscape design, or with *paysagement*,[23] where these terms refer to a growing social demand for landscape, and a growing technical ability to produce them, respectively. *Empaysagement* rather designates, on a more general level, a turning point in the way in which contemporary societies see themselves and see their material inscription through the intervention of landscape representation and landscape action.

The origin of this *empaysagement* of consciousness must be sought, on the one hand, in a desire, often backward-looking or nostalgic, to compensate for the evolution of our spatial practices and the endangerment of political territorialities; and, on the other, in a concern for reconstructing a political project with new territorial bases.

Landscape as Modality of Compensation

The geographical forms that result from the evolution of ordinary and professional practices of space (those of inhabitants, city planners, architects, developers) in the past decades have not generally been perceived as generating quality landscapes. Attempts at artistic reinterpretation of these new types of developments have been rare and little recognized compared with land art. So far, they have also been hardly adopted by Western societies. Under these conditions, interest in landscape has generally remained true to classical models of landscape aesthetic, especially in the case of the countryside. These models correspond, however, to modalities of life and production that are largely obsolete, and often put the emphasis on traditional agricultural practices that are in decline, if not already disappeared altogether. Consequently, attachment to this type of landscape can be seen as largely nostalgic or patrimonial, indeed schizophrenic, since the most praised landscapes are those that least correspond to the way of life of those who praise them.

This preoccupation is shared by numerous politicians for two kinds of reasons: On the one hand, they take it into consideration on account of the well-being and quality of life of their fellow citizens; on the other, they might see in it a symbolic instrument to court or restore the idea according to which traditional territorialities, which in the past had justified the modalities of political representation, retained a certain pertinence.

To illustrate the first point, we can take as an example the contemporary importance of landscape sensibility in Switzerland. It is well known—and the very old example of Deluc mentioned above was a remarkable illustration of this—that the Helvetian national identity owes much to the alpine myth and the alpine landscape. If contemporary Switzerland has seen a great evolution in its identity, its population and its elite remain strongly attached to the quality of the alpine landscape. The demand for landscape remains very strong among tourists, including Helvetians, to the point that it has been possible to try to assess their economic value. It is equally very strong among the urbanites and those living in suburbia. This demand reveals itself in the perpetuation of a policy of support for the mountain farmers that remains to this day one of the most expensive and ambitious in the world. Certainly nowhere else in the world has the idea of making mountain farmers into "nature gardeners" been so analyzed, worked on, and finally adopted by the majority of the professionals concerned.

To illustrate the second point, we can mention the effects of decentralization in France between 1980 and 2000. France, traditionally a centralized nation, committed itself since 1982–1983 to an ambitious policy of decentralization that transferred competences and responsibilities to its *communes*, its *départments*, and its *régions*, especially in the matter of urban planning and territorial development. The collectivities endowed with new political competences, confronted also with the necessity of acquiring a new form of legitimacy in the eyes of the citizens, invested very much in institutional communication and in the valorization of the territory entrusted to them. Heritage patrimony and landscape have been thus raised to emblematic status for these new-generation political entities. A similar process has concerned Spain and Italy owing to the introduction of their own policies of decentralization, and also the United Kingdom at the time of the devolution of autonomy to Scotland and Wales. In other words, in numerous European countries these collectivities have attempted to reinvent to their advantage the mechanisms through which the nation-states put emblematic landscapes in the service of the national imagination. It is possible to affirm, about this instrumentalization, that the landscapes thus evoked constitute potentially just as many fictions, that is, they are objects severed from the spatial practices of the people to which they are addressed; but they are very believable fictions, so strong seems to be the desire for landscape.

Landscape as Modality of Project

To this first group of political initiatives, largely placed in the hands of the political elite, we can counterpose a second group, which results much more from collective and participative interventions. At this stage, two examples, one from France, the other from Canada, can help elucidate the issue.

During the past thirty years, France, at the time when it put in place its institutional decentralization and during its deployment, created new levels of territorial organization: the regional natural parks since the 1970s, the *communautés de communes*[24] and the *pays*[25] since the late 1990s. These entities of different status were given the principal mission of conceiving and implementing territorial projects on their scale. Those who have followed the implementation of these policies have often been amazed by the importance these emergent territorial levels conferred upon the question of landscape. When local inhabitants and politicians asked what constituted the unity or the identity of these intermediary territories, the answers often invoked the surrounding landscape, especially in the rural areas. This invocation had many advantages: It bypassed the usual divisions anchored in sociopolitical customs; it satisfied the demand that we characterized above as nostalgic and schizophrenic; and finally, it allowed politicians and residents to address a resource long neglected, with its prospective valorization in projects of tourism or residential development. However, besides this convergence of interests, it also and foremost presented the advantage of building a consensus in terms of quality of life across very heterogeneous populations, which nevertheless shared in common the fact of living all or part of their lives in these places.

Another example, this time Canadian, of the concept of landscape-as-collective-project is provided by the role entrusted to a hill, the Mont-Royal, situated near the historical center of Montreal. The contrast that this relief presents with the Montreal plain quickly led city dwellers to identify it as a special place, to christen it non-officially as *la Montagne* ("the Mountain"), and, from the mid-nineteenth century, to develop in it very particular practices (especially of recreation) and institutions (cemeteries, public parks, and religious and academic institutions). During the twentieth century, this place, assigned to very particular usages, acquired the double status of urban icon, like the Eiffel Tower for Paris or the Empire State Building for New York, and emblematic place. A great many Montrealers, of extremely different origins and languages, have built with this place a familiar and affectionate relationship, which contrasts with the functional usage they maintain, like most of their contemporaries, with the majority of the city areas they nevertheless frequent every day. It is as if this singular place, whose singularity has been developed through decades of landscape-design (*paysagisme*), condensed all the expectations of landscape and anchorage in a shared space of a multicultural, hypermobile, and

Figure 7.2
Photograph posted on the Web page of the Quebec administration for cultural heritage, <http://www.cbcq.gouv.qc.ca/grand_dossiers/mont_royal/index.html>, during the official public conference (2002).

heterogeneous population. Moreover, considering its visibility from most areas of the urban agglomerate, "the Mountain" has become a landmark in function of which many urban projects have been conceived. This status of emblematic landscape has been recently acknowledged by the state of Quebec in its law on cultural heritage, after a large public conference and a strong appeal from residents and associations.[26]

The two examples above do not present exceptional traits; they could in fact be complemented by many other illustrations. Their interest lies in the fact that they attest to the emergence of landscape projects that link politicians, professionals, and residents in a reflection on what the landscape represents in what all of them think they have in common. They also testify to the capacity of landscape today to represent a point of commonality, at a time when cultural identities, especially in great cities like Montreal, and the individual spatial practices show—indeed, exalt—diversity and heterogeneity.

Further Remarks on *The Human Condition*

Once presented in the variety of its forms and motivations, this revival of landscape in the sphere of the political deserves to be analyzed along Arendt's typology of the *vita activa*. From this vantage point, the present situation, if compared to that in which Deluc, Brown, and Vigée-Lebrun were actors and witnesses, and if compared also to that of a nineteenth

Figure 7.3
Photograph posted on the Web page of the Quebec administration for cultural heritage, <http://www.cbcq.gouv.qc.ca/grand_dossiers/mont_royal/index.html>, during the official public conference (2002).

century marked by the burgeoning interest of the nation-states in this object, shows interesting reversals.

Today, labor, in the sense understood by Arendt, plays a very marginal role in the shaping of the materiality on which the landscape, or what is recognized as such, is construed. The everyday life and the trivial acts of most of our contemporaries no longer "make" the landscape: They usually combine places and objects the arrangement of which is not generally acknowledged as presenting the character of landscape.

In contrast, more than ever, a landscape is a work: the work of landscape professionals in the precincts of gardens, parks, or cemeteries, even more in residential estates or recreation parks, for the management of which the expertise of landscape architects is required; the work of farmers when they are compared to "gardeners of nature," thus reducing the productive dimension of their activity; the work also of the landscapes themselves, conserved as national heritage. The landscape-as-work triumphs on every scale and in every place, thereby creating large numbers of employment opportunities in the service of its conception, realization, and maintenance. However, since it remains the business of specialists, this type of landscape continues to be part of a process of alienation. This is the principal argument, besides the concept of alienation, of a much earlier book, which posed the problem, especially regarding its effect on home owners: "In fact, the elimination of effective participation in landscape-making has been so complete, with total house and streetscape designs and the breadth and minuteness of hyperplanning controls, that the suburban house owner cannot modify his place in anything other than trivial cosmetic ways."[27]

For landscape-as-action, the contemporary diagnosis requires a more delicate formulation. The interest of the nineteenth-century nation-state in landscape was described above in terms of alienation. The revival of objectives and modalities of that instrumentalization of landscape by political collectivities endowed with new competences, for example in France, Spain, or Scotland, is certainly a matter of the same form of alienation. In contrast, the same surely cannot be said about territorial projects and landscape projects when both expressions designate a convergence of social expectations and a true collective participation in their elaboration. This revival of landscape concerns, within the frame of new political and democratic practices, provides an illustration of what can be called *landscape-as-action*, the term "action" being evidently understood in the sense Arendt confers upon it: Action is conceived—I want to emphasize this one last time—as the source of the definition of the political identity of the subject and the modality through which men and women in society define what they have in common and what they place at the heart of the public space. Arendt also insists strongly on the role of objects, understood as works, in the definition of the "public" and the "common" that men and women furnish themselves in order to live together:

the term "public" signifies the world itself, in so far as it is common to all of us. . . . This world, however, is not identical with the earth or with nature, as the limited space for the movement of men and the general condition of organic life. It is related, rather, to the human artefact, the fabrication of human hands, as well as to affairs which go on among those who inhabit the man-made world together. To live together in the world means essentially that a world of things is between those who have it in common, as a table is located between those who sit around it; the world, like every in-between, relates and separates men at the same time.[28]

The landscape can become such an object—a "work"—and be directed at the construction of a "common"—an "action"—and this all the more so since the spatial practices of individuals tend, through their diversity, not to have much in "common" anymore.

Further Remarks on the Metaphor of the Body

Finally, by way of developing matters a little further, I will pursue again the metaphor of the body, which constituted a moment of this essay. I suggested above, by referring to authors in whom this idea appears, that landscape could also be conceived as the territorializing representation of an adjustment between two types of body: the Earth's body as it shows itself from a certain perspective, and the social body when it embraces a political project. Landscape was thus conceived as the visible, spectacularized form of these two bodies entering into a correspondence.

Nevertheless, the arguments developed above push the metaphor to a certain analogy: an analogy between the body of landscape and the human body. Our modern societies—the fact is known and well documented by numerous works—have developed a great attention to and a real know-how of the mastery of the human body. Cloning, genetic therapies, but first and foremost, as far as this essay is concerned, the consumption of cosmetics, aesthetic surgery, the recourse to prothesis, the conservation of corpses, and voluntary scarification constitute as many laboratories and hopes of societies more and more concerned with the appearance of individuals and the modalities of exposition in public space.

What kind of parallel, what kind of analogy can we reasonably construe between this concern with the mastery of the body and (what we called) the *empaysagement* that would help analyze both concepts? In both cases, what is expressed is a preoccupation with the control of forms taken by living systems (the organism in one case, territory in the other, in a common perspective of illusory resistance against processes considered degenerative); an imaginary of the production of ideal forms (conservation of anterior forms, actualization of ideal forms); a narcissistic concern, individual and collective, for the exhibition (*mise en scène*) of the self or of the "us"; and, incidentally, the entrance of both into the economic and political spheres.

Posing the question in these terms, by way of starting point, at the end of this essay, I merely want to suggest that the question of landscape in our contemporary societies leads us well beyond its political nature. Here as well, as for many other objects, the political question joins the anthropological question.

Notes

1. See especially Simon Schama, *Landscape and Memory* (New York: Alfred A. Knopf, 1995) and François Walter, *Les figures paysagères de la nation* (Paris: EHESS, 2004).

2. Hannah Arendt, *The Human Condition*, 2nd ed. (Chicago: University of Chicago Press, 1998), p. 2.

3. Ibid., p. 6.

4. See Paul Ricoeur's introduction to one of the French editions of *The Human Condition*, *Condition de l'Homme moderne* (Paris: Pocket, 1983).

5. Arendt, *The Human Condition*, p. 7.

6. Ibid., p. 176.

7. See Gabriel Gohau, *Une histoire de la géologie* (Points Seuil, 1990) and Martin Rudwick, "Minerals, Strata, and Fossils," in *Cultures of Natural History*, ed. N. Jardine, J. A. Secord, and E. C. Sparry (Cambridge: Cambridge University Press, 1996), pp. 266–286.

8. Claude Reichler, *La découverte des Alpes et la question du paysage* (Lausanne: Georg, 2002).

9. J. A. Deluc, *Lettres physiques et morales sur l'histoire de la terre et de l'homme, adressées à la Reine de la Grande-Bretagne* (Paris: Duchesne, 1779–1780).

10. Ibid.

11. Denis E. Cosgrove and Stephen Daniels, "Spectacle and Text: Landscape Metaphors in Cultural Geography," in *Place/Culture/Representation*, ed. James S. Duncan and David Ley (London and New York: Routledge, 1993), p. 59.

12. See Denis E. Cosgrove, *Social Formation and Symbolic Landscape* (London: Croom Helm, 1984).

13. See Schama, *Landscape and Memory*; Walter, *Les figures paysagères de la nation*; Cosgrove and Daniels, "Spectacle and Text."

14. Jean Gottmann, *La Politique des Etats et leur géographie* (Paris: Armand Colin, 1952).

15. Marcel Gauchet, "Les lettres sur l'histoire de France d'Augustin Thierry," in *Les Lieux de Mémoire*, vol. 2: *La Nation*, ed. Pierre Nora (Paris: Gallimard, 1992), p. 287.

16. [The French "corps à corps" is untranslatable in English; literally it means "hand-to-hand."—Tr.]

17. Claude Raffestin, "Écogénèse territoriale et territorialité," in *Espaces, jeux et enjeux*, ed. F. Auriac and R. Brunet (Paris: Fayard-Fondation Diderot, 1986), pp. 175–185.

18. Kenneth Robert Olwig, *Landscape, Nature, and the Body Politic* (Madison: University of Wisconsin Press, 2002).

19. Ibid., p. xxxii.

20. F. Choay, "Le règne de l'urbain et la mort de la ville," in *La Ville: Art et architecture en Europe, 1870–1993* (Paris: Éditions du center Georges Pompidou, 1994).

21. Arjun Appadurai, *Modernity at Large: Cultural Dimensions of Globalization* (Minneapolis: University of Minnesota Press, 1996).

22. The term originated in a discussion with Claude Raffestin on this topic.

23. The term *paysagement* was proposed by Augustin Berque in "De paysage en outre-pays," *Revue le Débat* 65 (1991): 4–13, to designate the contemporary concern to combine the sensory (those of the experience) and rational (those of science and technology) approaches to landscape.

24. This is an new institutional level created in 2000 for improving the coherence of municipal policies (especially in planning) for contiguous *communes*.

25. This is another level of organization, larger than the previous one, created in 1999, which requires a set of adjacent *communes* (between 6 and 20) to adopt common development and environmental strategies.

26. It is interesting that among the tools utilized for this consultation was a Web page that displayed a map of the city along with many photos showing Mont-Royal as it is seen from many points in the city: <http://www.cbcq.gouv.qc.ca/grand_dossiers/mont_royal/index.html>. For a history of the place and the relationship the Montrealers have built with it, see Debarbieux, "The Mountain in the City: Social Uses and Transformations of a Natural Landform in Urban Space," *Ecumene* 5 (1998): 399–431, and also Bernard Debarbieux and Charles Perraton, "Le parc, la norme et l'usage: Le parc du Mont-Royal ou l'expression de la pluralité des cultures à Montréal," *Géographie et Cultures* 26 (1998): 109–127.

27. Edward Relph, *Rational Landscape and Humanistic Geography* (London: Croom Helm, 1981), p. 99.

28. Arendt, *The Human Condition*, p. 52.

8 Entry and Distance: Sublimity in Landscape

Andrew Benjamin

I

Stefano Bricarelli's 1914 photograph *Nell'alta valle della Dora Riparia*, a photograph recently exhibited and which is owned by the Fondazione Torino Musei, an image therefore that is as much a historical document as an artwork, stages the concerns of landscape.[1] Moreover, the photograph recalls, intentionally or not, aspects of the sublime that occupy landscape painting from the eighteenth century. However, rather than simply accept the sublime as a given, it will be repositioned in terms of a relationship between distance and representation. Indeed, the conjecture is that as a structure of thought, the sublime, at least as it appears in the work of Edmund Burke, concerns the interplay between distance, immediacy, and representation. Nonetheless, the conventions of sublimity are present within the photograph. The mountains bear a slight covering of both mist and cloud. They hover in the distance between full presence and a form of vanishing. Scale, which is provided by the positioning of the human figures in relation to the mountains, works to reinforce a form of sublimity.

Prior to a consideration of the sublime, a consideration that demands, as will be argued, a reworking of its terminology, there is the more pedestrian question of entry into the scene. The entry is not immediately visual. Rather, it concerns the manner in which the scene within the image is being entered. To this it should be added that the question of its being constructed as landscape—the possibility that landscape may only exist as such because of that entry—must play an important role in any analysis of the photographic image. Allowed for by this possibility is a conception of presence that is not mere construction but a form of production.

In the photograph there is a path marking the valley floor. Two women are beside it. One wears a hat. The other carries a parasol. They are *en route*. They are walking. Hence they occupy a place. (The quality of that place

Figure 8.1
Stefano Bricarelli, *Nell'alta valle della Dora Riparia* ("in the high valley of the Dora Riparia"—Dora Riparia is in the Valle di Susa, west of Turin), 1914. Photograph (silver gelatine bromide print). Fondazione Torino Musei, Archivio Fotografico, Fondo Stefano Bricarelli, Turin, Italy.

and thus the name to be deployed in order to identify it remains, as has been noted, an open question.) The woman wearing a hat is carrying a bag or a basket. Whether it contains provisions or merely personal items is not the issue. What matters is that they are present. While human presence may be a further element brought to an original setting, and therefore there is a process in which that form of presence comes into consideration, what is present brings with it a transformational quality. Human presence does not exist *in simpliciter*. It becomes the mark—a mark that is integral to the construction of the image under consideration—of the overdetermined. Human presence in this setting—the context of artwork—resists a logic of addition in which the presence of the human would then be no more than the addition of a further singular element. Were that logic to have been followed, then the setting—the "landscape"—would itself be defined in terms of self-completing singularity to which an addition had been made. Moving from the logic of addition means that human presence constructs, while present, an original form of distancing[2]—a distancing that occurs because of the impossibility of creating a founding synthesis. The elements—mountains, path, human, parasol, bag, and so on—are held together only because they are held apart; as such they construct a plural event.[3] Furthermore, implicit within this differing sense of addition is the creation of a space between what is given and what accompanies the given. Entry into the valley brings with it, therefore, an ineliminable distancing, underscoring the recognition that the place in question is defined by an original spacing and therefore, precisely because of a founding irreducibility, is an event of plurality. (This is an initial description of the contents of the photograph; the situation becomes more complex when the question of the image is introduced.)

Spacing, therefore, does more than refer to the place the walkers enter. The situation has a different quality, for what is at work within that space is a form of production. Spaces, while given, are also produced. (Production is signaled by the move from space to spacing; the latter is the continuity of produced space.) Spacing and distancing, as they open up within, though also as the image, begin to define the relationship between the walkers and place. The necessity of distancing is demanded by the impossibility of their assimilation. One cannot be the other. In place they are distanced. (It might be that "landscape," if the term can be given an adequate description, is the name of this specific distancing.)

The photograph contains its own sense of direction. The path moves. The background is created. Further along the path there is another group of walkers. The path leads to the organized presence of buildings. Though ordered, they can barely be discerned. Moreover, they are dwarfed by the mountains. The walkers are at a distance from the buildings to which they appear to be walking. The distance between the walkers inscribes a sense of time. The space between them can be measured as much by the distance to be traveled as by the time it would take to catch up with them. Equally, time figures as the step. The woman carrying the bag has just taken a step. Her left leg is beginning to leave the ground; pressure would be on her right leg. She leans slightly to the right. Within the photograph, she is moving. The raised foot is the moment—the moment that will vanish after the photograph, not in the afterlife of the photograph but within the sense of continuity that delimits the work as a photograph and thus as an image. The image brings differing senses of time into play. One form of discontinuity creates the work's life by constructing an afterlife. However, the afterlife of the image is its having been constructed. Within that afterlife the step continues as the moment. The step in the image is already complete, though not completed.

Even though it is essential to continue detailing the contents of the photograph, what has to bear on any description is the recognition of the work as an image and not just the presentation of content. The further element that needs to be noted, therefore, is that the location of any concern with landscape is its positioning within the relationship between the image and a conception of the external. In other words, both description and the specific quality of the image need to define the setting in which any claim about landscape, even the attribution of the name "landscape," would need to figure. And yet, even the image cannot be attributed an abstract generality in which the particularity of both medium and content did not figure. In this instance, the specific image, Stefano Bricarelli's 1914 photograph *Nell'alta valle della Dora Riparia*, makes a particular demand. It has a twofold presence. The interplay of scale and distance, in the first instance and clouds and presentation in the second, open up, as has already been indicated, the image's link to the sublime. The demand does not preclude other ways of approaching the photograph. Nonetheless, the scale of the mountains and therefore the position of the walkers, coupled with the presence of the clouds, open up an almost inevitable link to Northern Romantic art on the one hand and the more general question of sublimity on the other.

The question of the sublime's own identity, an identity beyond any straightforward reduction to a form of textual presence, is the question that any image stages. Images are not experiences in any direct sense, and yet the question of their being experienced is one for which there needs to be an account. The contention here is that part of the significance of the sublime is that once reworked it provides the basis for a philosophical account of that specific form of an experience.

II

In *A Philosophical Enquiry into the Origin of Our Ideas of the Sublime and the Beautiful*, Burke argues that the presentation of sublimity is more successful in literature than in painting. Painting's limit is defined in the following terms:

If I make a drawing of a place or a temple, or a landscape I present a very clear idea of those objects; but then (allowing for the effect of imitation which is something) my picture can affect at most only as the palace, temple or landscape would have affected in the reality. On the other hand, the most lively and spirited verbal description I can give, raises a very obscure and imperfect idea of such objects; but then it is in my power to raise a stronger emotion by the description than I could do by the best painting.[4]

What is initially of importance about the way the limit is established is its location within the relationship between the "landscape" and "reality." The limit of painting lies in the way this particular connection is understood. When the artistic presentation and thus the process of representation become "clear," then the presentational force is restricted. This restriction is the result of what can be described as the presentation's commensurability with externality. Restriction is constructed by an identification of the artwork with the literal, and thus with the supposition of what could be described as a possible literality.

What this introduces into the argument is twofold. In the first instance it concerns a relationship between immediacy as a way of defining a connection between a painting and externality. Immediacy is announced within the *Enquiry* in terms of "clarity." In the second instance "obscurity" and thus the possibility of sublimity occur because of distance. (Distance is as much temporal as it is spatial.) This means that the move from painting to words (accepting, initially, Burke's understanding of these terms), or from clarity to obscurity, must be understood as modalities of distancing. Hence, if painting is to have a subliminal presence, then there needs to be a type of "obscurity" and thus a distancing. This becomes clearer when Burke turns to a consideration of the relationship between sublimity and color. In this regard he argues that: "An immense mountain covered with a shining green turf, is nothing in this respect [the sublime] to one dark and gloomy: the cloudy sky is more grand than the blue; and night more solemn and sublime than the day."[5] Painting, as opposed to literature, may be limited. And yet, precisely because the clarity of an image can undo the ground of any possible sublimity, it is also the case that painting is able to deploy a strategy allowing a form of presentation in which clarity and immediacy will have given way to distance. Distance, it can be argued, is a key term in order to account for the specificity of the Burkean sublime. The importance of distance is its temporal nature. Before noting Burke's actual formulation it should be stated in advance that the force of distance is as much its capacity to inscribe the spatial into the temporal as it is its capacity to underscore the temporal nature of spatial relations. In sum, distance allows for the move from space as a given to space as an activity. With the occurrence of the latter, space becomes spacing. In other words, space as a given dimension of an artwork cedes its place to spacing as integral to the workful, thus active, nature of the work.

In one of the initial presentations of the sublime in the *Enquiry* Burke introduces a timed sense of distance. He does this after having argued that the one "source of the sublime" may be that which is "analogous to terror."[6] It is essential to note Burke's formulation. What is implicated in the sublime is not terror per se but a relation given within the structure of an analogy. The argument continues in the following terms: "When danger or pain press too near they are incapable of giving any delight and are simply terrible; but certain distances and with certain modifications, they may be, and they are, as we every day experience."[7] Of the many elements that are central to this passage, two are integral to the argument being developed in this context. The first is the possibility that "danger" and "pain" can be too close. It is not just that they "are simply terrible," as significant as the effect is on the subject. The subject *is* terrified. In other words, the subject is commensurate with terror. Arguing that the subject *is* terrified is to define the being of the subject in terms of that terror. (The *"is"* both defines and maintains identity.) An identification of this kind marks the closure of any possible space. What is closed off from the start therefore is the space in which the experience that is the sublime will occur. Equally, this identification marks a temporal as well as a spatial simultaneity. The interplay of space and time in terms of simultaneity and identification reveals the other significant element in this passage. The sublime as a possibility only arises because of distance and modification. The role of analogy within the argument—analogy arising in the move from pure terror to its comparable situation—allows for that which terrifies to become, through a form of modification, an object for a subject and thus able to be experienced. The emergence of the object occurs within and as the opening of the subject–object relation. Within that opening the subject is no longer commensurate with being terrified. Hence, not only is there a change in the nature of the subject, such a change is accompanied by a concomitant change or modification in the quality of the object that accompanies the sublime. (The latter only ever exists within the structure of experience.)

The sublime involves a distancing in which relations are held open and thus forms of closure or immediacy resisted. This gives the sublime an additional quality. In the writings of Burke the sublime is a physiological state. Equally, it is the demand engendered by a specific object, and thus it involves a subject–object relation. Within the context of a painting—and in this instance, painting can stand for the produced image—that which is opposed to the sublime can be defined in terms of immediacy. The relation between the interior and the exterior in being immediate can be expressed negatively as the impossibility of distance and thus the refusal of a founding event of plurality. Immediacy on the level of the image, as has been noted, is clarity. On the other hand, the immediacy of feeling that can be equated with the state of being terrified can only become the sublime thought of terror through the process of distancing. Within this formulation, there is both the immediacy of identity as well as its undoing. In the case of clarity, the immediacy occurs within a mimetic relation. Sublimity occurs not by breaching the mimetic relation but by introducing elements that render immediacy impossible. As a consequence, time and distance becomes the defining element. What is excluded is a link between presentation—the appearance of the image and the image as appearance— and any argument concerning the literal.

This interpretation of the sublime provides a way of understanding the impossibility of immediacy and the literal, on the one hand, and the continuity of distance, understood as the activity of distancing and thus spacing, on the other. There is, however, an important move in which the sublime stages a series of concerns that cannot be equated with the sublime, where the latter is taken as no more than an end in itself. Once this occurs, the sublime twists free of its historical location. Indeed, as has been suggested, the sublime can be reworked. This occurs once the refusal of both "clarity" and immediacy are repositioned so that what they stage is a refusal of the literal. If the literal is understood as the identification of the object with itself, so that its self-presentation and thus interpretation involve the presentation of a self-completing and thus self-identical object engendering a singular and unequivocal experience, then the sublime becomes a way of marking the productive distancing of this conception of the object and the mode of experience that it will have necessitated. What this means is that the sublime cannot be reduced to arguments concerning presentation's limits or impossibility.[8] This is not to argue that all objects figure within the sublime. Rather, it is to claim that the textual presentation of the sublime is another moment in which the philosophical distances itself from the literal and thus from the self-identical. The literal would no longer be either the point of departure or the assumed point of completion. Reworked so that its concerns broaden, the sublime opens beyond itself. What the sublime allows for is the staging of a point of origination that already has an inherently plural quality. (This is the setup referred to earlier as a plural event.)

III

Stefano Bricarelli's 1914 photograph *Nell'alta valle della Dora Riparia* is an image. The valley is present within a photograph. The landscape in question therefore only exists within the image (leaving open, at this stage, the question as to whether there could be a landscape that was not an image). What emerges as problematic in any discussion of the image is the place of experience within it. What sublimity opens up is the necessity to account for the experience that delimits it. Although there are significant differences between the ways Kant and Burke characterize the sublime, what draws their positions together is the positioning of the sublime in relation to experience rather than its being the assumed quality of an object. To the extent that this connection is maintained, the question that has to be addressed concerns the relationship between sublimity and the image. In other words, if the sublime is an experience, what is it to experience an image? Again, it is essential to be precise. If the image is not sublime per se, but rather what the image stages is an event the experience of which is sublime, then would there be any force in the argument that the sublime as an experience is a way of approaching images? Responding to these questions necessitates recognizing that in the case of the image under consideration, and in the sublime, what has already emerged are two different senses of distance. In the context of the photograph the first occurs with the entry into the setting that is then photographed. The second, as has been noted, occurs with the introduction of the sublime. The relationship between object and experience that characterizes the sublime is one in which time and distance work to eschew the reduction of either the object or the experience to the structure of immediacy and, with it, the literal, thereby allowing the image to be repositioned as a plural event.

Spacing and distancing are already at work in the presentation of landscape, thereby indicating that not only does experience have a setting, but that setting involves active relations and therefore spacing rather than mere spatiality. The setting, to deploy the formulation noted above, is a holding together that is also a holding apart, the working of the work. To the extent that the setting is construed in such a way, experience is from the start delimited by an already present conception of relation, the latter as generative of spacing, in which the related—thus the setting—cannot be reduced to its constituent parts. If that setting were to be defined, then its quality would be such that there cannot be a singular experience that is identical with the setting itself. Neither the experience nor the setting can be singular. Both admit to a founding plurality. The impossibility of singularity is the impossibility of the literal. That impossibility is not the impossibility of any statement; it is rather the impossibility of any statement or experience having a completing finality. (Plurality is ontological, not merely interpretive.) As such, there is a genuine affinity between statements and thus the work of philosophical thought and the setting itself. Moreover, once any form of possible literality and immediacy is distanced, then the standard opposition between thought (the term staging the interconnection between philosophy and language) and the image needs to be reconsidered.

Apart from the historical register of any image, what then marks the specificity of landscape? The force of the question stems from the following considerations. What has emerged thus far is the argument that the incursion of the human into a setting—an incursion underscored by an inherent unmasterability—creates a series of relations that preclude their incorporation into a simple logic of addition. Moreover, the presentation of the sublime, within the writings of Burke, though there is a plausible generalizability here, can be reworked so that one of the sublime's defining elements becomes the form of distancing that will allow for a presentation that cannot be reduced to a setup responding to the exigencies of representation—an exigency depending on the presence of a singular event to be represented and thus demanding the exactitude of a one-to-one relationship, a relationship, which, if only as an aspiration, defines representation. This is the structure of immediacy.

There is a range of questions raised by landscape, but the most demanding, and the one consistent with the argument as adumbrated thus far, relates to the specificity of landscape. The question to be addressed concerns the possibility of landscape existing independently of its construction. (The history of landscape is after all part of the history of images.) Although the question of the image is insistent, it needs to be linked to distancing. Indeed, the suggestion that landscape is the interplay of cohering and distancing provides the way into this latter consideration.

Stefano Bricarelli's photograph involves the concerns of landscape for the precise reason that it stages the relationship between the contents of the image and a concern with the image itself. The leg of the woman within photograph, the leg that is beginning to be lifted from the ground, dramatizes the distinction between the afterlife of the image and the continuity of the setting. The image continues with its presentation. The continuity of that which is other than the image would always have to remain a conjecture. Any attempt to capture it, and thus to present its continuous progress, would necessitate recourse to a further image. Her movement has been arrested. It is, of course, that very cessation that allows for the complex of relations at work within the setting and which is staged as a moment—though a moment that contains the infinite of any image—to be noted. If there is a direct conclusion to be drawn from this position it is that the truth of landscape—and here truth would mean as much the complex of relations that its construction necessitates as the role of experience within (thus also of) that landscape—only emerges within an image. In other words, the truth of landscape is the impossibility that it—landscape as a totality—is ever given to be experienced as such. Hence, it is equally as impossible that there is an experience that totalizes and thus encapsulates whatever it is that the "landscape" is taken to be.

Does this mean, however, that landscape cannot be differentiated from other images? To address this question it is essential to distinguish between the situation that both defines and locates any image, namely, an ineliminable reference to generic concerns—for example, a portrait refers of necessity to the history of portraiture of which it forms a part—and what could be described as a more general argument concerning the relationship between the ontology of images and the project of interpretation. In regard to the latter, although the particularity of the medium is fundamental to that account insofar as materiality generates and sustains meaning, it is also the case that the attribution of meaning—the project of interpenetration—is held open by work. The afterlife of an image—and it is the ontology of the image that occasions this life—is inextricably bound up with the impossibility of interpretation's having a completing finality.[9] The interpretation of images has then to note that presence, while at the same time being able to make substantive and defensible interpretive claims. These formal claims have a particular determination within landscape.

Images are viewed, and as such they are experienced. However, landscape—be it the result of photography, sketch, or painting—already involves experience. There is a relation to the land, the experience of which becomes, in ways that can be neither determined nor predicted in advance, the work—work as the site of material presence. At the same time, and with equal importance, there is the actual incorporation of the subject of experience into the work. Landscape attests as much to the ineliminability of experience within the realm of images as it does to the already present inscription of the experiencing subject. Any philosophical account of landscape, therefore, has to involve an account of experience. Experience's involvement is an already present form of inscription. However, that account cannot be naive: it has to be positioned as much in terms set by the formal quality of the image, as it is in relation to the necessity that any account of experience within the realm of the artwork—the actual creation of the artwork—is from the start the construction of an image. What this means, therefore, is that if landscape becomes the way in which the question of experience has its most exacting form of presence within an artwork, then there has to be an account of how that experience is manifest.

What is experience in art? What occurs with the reference to the sublime is, of course, the location of experience as an already present quality of the work. This sets the measure in relation to which it becomes possible to return to the image under consideration.

IV

In the photograph, her head seems to be turned; its slight inclination indicates the possibility of a conversation. Walking as an experience would then no longer exert as strong a hold. To the extent that conversation, mingled with looking, takes over, the body's concerns would diminish. Or is her gaze steadfast? Absorbed by what she sees, she and her companions walk in silence, having given themselves over to sight, allowing sight to absorb the possible words that might have been uttered—as though the valley, clouds, and mountains rendered words, if only momentarily, redundant. The woman whose head remains covered by the parasol, and who can only ever be the subject of speculation, is already positioned within a dialogue (be it successful or not, actual or potential).

Looking at the image—its being viewed—can begin with the couple walking. The narrowing road, the scale of the mountains position them. There is, of course, a productive reciprocity at work here. What, however, is being looked at? The direct answer is the complex of relations that the image presents. However, the question can be clarified: If the two women walking become the focus of the question, then what matters is their presence as experiencing subjects. What are they experiencing? And if the looking is underscored and thus the presence of the image as that which is seen is central, then what is being staged is seeing that which is being seen. This particular act of photography—an act, as has already been noted, that is formally indebted to the history of landscape painting—involves a form of positioning. The camera is the external element that creates their presence within the frame. Any viewer of the image takes on that position. If what is being seen involves nature as potentially intimidating, it cannot be separated from the specific sense of vulnerably and exposure that the presence of the two women indicates. As their description takes on greater detail, the question of what the viewer sees does not just become more nuanced, as significant as this question is. Detail brings to the fore the insistence of that other question: Who is the viewer?

The question of the viewer provides an opening. However, the space opened cannot be occupied by a sense of agency defined in relation to either neutrality or singularity. The viewer as position and as positioned is from the start overdetermined. The presence of the viewer within the image—again, within it while being part of it—and the presence of the image's viewer continue to structure the question of experience. Precisely because it involves two related elements, that structuring can be described as the "doubling of experience." The object of experience is doubled, as is the experiencing subject. The doubling in question is, once again, positioned beyond the logic of addition. The original event—an event of complex relations—involves elements, as has already been indicated, that refuse a founding singularity. Subject and object continue to have a plurality that is insistent from the start. The work maintains the quality of a plural event.

The supposition advanced earlier—that landscape is the name for a setting defined by spacing and distancing—can now be clarified. The description that is fundamental to landscape inheres within the complex doubling of experience. Landscape demands the insistent presence of experience. Even if the experiencing subject does not figure in the work as such, landscape reports to experience while being, at the same time, the report of experience. This is not to deny that any one landscape refers by definition to this history of landscape. However, beyond simple appearance, that referentiality forms part of the presentation of that which is essential to landscape. Moreover, the essential stands in opposition to the reduction of landscape to its literal presence, a move that could only have been made if referentiality were conflated with the essential and thus with the appearance of landscape. Here the essential necessitates the affirmation of landscape as the exemplary instance of the presence of the constituting interplay of spacing and distancing, a setup that continues to sustain the constitutive doubling of experience. Approaching landscape through a reworking of the sublime draws these elements together. Sublimity, in the way it has been formulated here, becomes a mode of thought in which both subject and object, while present, demand forms of presentation in which being present is neither to have been represented nor does it attest to a failure to present. If what is at stake were abstraction, then representation could be understood as distanced to the extent that perspectival space no longer has a determining effect on presentation; in the case of landscape, however, the presentation of experience's doubled presence continues to present both human and geographical figures within a spacing and a distancing whose recall is the continuous presentation—presentation as production—of encounters that can only ever continue to be worked out. The continuity in question has a form of necessity that is derived from the move from a conception of the work as a series of already given or determined spatial relations to one in which relationality is present as the continuity of activity. Landscape has specificity within art because of the way it works as art.

Notes

1. Stefano Bricarelli (1889–1989) was a photographer based in Turin.

2. For a more sustained development of the relationship between distancing and space understood as occurring within the continuity of its construction, see "Spacing and Distancing," in my *Art, Mimesis, and the Avant-Garde* (London: Routledge, 1991), pp. 43–61.

3. For a detailed discussion of this term, see my *The Plural Event* (London: Routledge, 1993).

4. Edmund Burke, *A Philosophical Enquiry into the Origin of Our Ideas of the Sublime and Beautiful*, ed. James T. Boulton (Notre Dame: University of Notre Dame Press, 1993), p. 60.

5. Ibid., pp. 81–82.

6. Ibid., p. 39.

7. Ibid., p. 40.

8. In other words, the conception of the sublime that is being presented here is not compatible with the reworking of the sublime in the writings of Jean-François Lyotard. Lyotard's conception cannot be separated from a problematic of loss and impossibility as opposed to the affirmation of the incomplete and a founding event of plurality. In regard to this aspect of Lyotard's work, see his writings on the avant-garde and on Barnett Newman in his *L'inhumain: Causeries sur le temps* (Paris: Galilée, 1988).

9. I have presented this position in "The Matter of a Materialist Philosophy of Art: Bataille's Manet," in my *Style and Time: Essays on the Politics of Appearance* (Chicago: Northwestern University Press, 2006), pp. 124–138, as well as in my *Disclosing Spaces: On Painting* (Manchester: Clinamen Press, 2004).

9   Reinterpreting the Picturesque in the Experience of Landscape

Isis Brook

Introduction

The picturesque is usually interpreted as an admiration of "picture-like," and thus inauthentic, nature. The design of inauthentic landscapes and even the way we think of land as landscape is attributed to this maligned aesthetic tradition. In contrast, this chapter sets out an interpretation of the picturesque that is more in accord with the contemporary love of wildness. I briefly cover some garden history in order to contextualize the discussion and proceed by reassessing the picturesque through the eighteenth-century works of Price and Watelet. I identify six themes in their work (variety, intricacy, engagement, time, chance, and transition) and show that, far from forcing a "picture-like" stereotype on nature, the picturesque guided the way for a new appreciation of wildness—one that resonates with contemporary environmental philosophy.

There is undoubtedly a current interest in and love of wild nature expressed in the form of protecting pristine wilderness or traditional rural landscapes. The rise of the appreciation for wild landscapes in the wild was well charted by Nicholson, and we are often struck by the now almost unthinkable worldview that saw mountains and dark forests as frightful wastelands that were best ignored and hidden from view or used as evidence of the biblical Fall or Flood, the idea behind the latter being that God conjured up these abominations in response to human sin.[1]

We often look directly to the concept of the sublime characterized by the dramatic impact of mountains for the source of this sea change in attitudes to nature, but I would like to focus on the often overlooked, because misunderstood, picturesque in garden design. The picturesque is often characterized both as informally rustic and as following the rules of composition in landscape paintings.

The suggestion that we track the love of wild nature through garden styles and traditions seems immediately problematic, as what could be more unnatural than a garden? It has exactly the mix of natural entities, that is, plants, and their constraint or artificial arrangement that is the mark of the unnatural. A piece of architecture is an artifact with no direct pretensions to be nature. A naturalistic style of gardening, by contrast, seems the very essence of the inauthentic; it cannot help but fail to inspire a love of real, wild nature. I am not suggesting that this task will be easy, just that there are aspects and undercurrents here that are worth bringing out.

A Brief Historical Sketch

The earliest record of garden layouts comes from Egyptian tombs from around 2000 B.C.E. Their typical forms have been confirmed, in terms of what was actually on the ground, by archeological evidence.[2] A typical design would be a walled area with a central rectangular fish pond with flowering lotus, surrounded by fig trees and edged with flower beds. All is symmetrical and there are tall shade trees. This basic pattern crosses many cultures and many centuries. The Persians created elaborate gardens along these lines, and the garden as a *hortus conclusus*—an enclosed space—continued for centuries.

What is being excluded from such gardens varies across the types of nature to be excluded. The Egyptian enclosed garden creates a formalized and ordered place, where the extremes of heat and cold, drought and flood are managed by design. In the English context, the garden is a clearing in the vegetation, a sun trap where overshadowing vegetation is controlled. A crucial motif of the *hortus conclusus* is thus the exclusion of raw nature.

This exclusion of nature is furthered by the ordering of what is inside the wall. Running through centuries of garden design is the straight axis and the symmetrical arrangement of planting areas and plants themselves. To us it appears that order and a horizontal axis reigns supreme, but these early gardens were also about order and a vertical axis that connected the labor of humans to their God. It was the vertical axis relationship that was important to them, not their relationship to the world outside the garden wall.[3] In the early botanical gardens we see an attempt to re-create the Garden of Eden, which would, of course, have been an ordered world.[4]

Breaking Down the Wall

For a brief tour of the important shifts in this garden story I will focus on the various garden technologies that begin to break down the wall. These technologies take away from the garden its role of excluding nature and point to a deep shift in cultural responses to nature.

An early, postmedieval development was called a *mount*. This small constructed hillock would allow those enjoying the garden to view the world beyond its enclosure. Often such hills were *mounted* by a spiral walk, and the summit graced with a summer house arranged for the best views. For example, at Hampton Court, this provided a view of the Thames.

At the same time as the development of the mount, walls were being pierced with window-type openings to allow for views beyond the garden. Possibly the most innovative pierced wall, because the gap reached to the ground, was a *saut de loup* ("wolf's jump"). In French formal gardens, this was a means of ending a broad walk with a gap in the wall; the grills of early versions of this form of opening were able to be dispensed with by introducing a ditch and embankment to prevent animals passing into the garden. In a text by A. J. Dezallier d'Argenville of 1709 this is called an "Ah Ah."[5] This is, of course, the precursor to the revolutionary innovation that changed the English landscape on an immense scale, the ha-ha. Instead of a gap in the wall, the ha-ha, by extending the ditch horizontally, dispenses with the wall entirely. Nature is now so redeemed that it can be enjoyed, not as something glimpsed from the safety of the garden, but as the backdrop to the garden. In fact, the visual illusion of the ha-ha is that the two, garden and nature, have become a seamless whole. The illusion, however, only works because at the same time as the wall is dissolving the garden within it has been changing.

These contemporaneous changes could be seen as a way of bringing nature into the garden. Before the break with formal garden styles and the move to the more informal, there was already a trend for setting aside part of a garden for small areas of woodland or informal planting. These were called wildernesses (which of course sounds hopelessly naive today), and indeed they were often planted with trees in straight rows or with the informality contained within hedges and traversed by straight paths. But there was something there, some stirring of a precursor to feelings we currently have for nature. An early reference to this practice is in Francis Bacon's essay "On Gardening," published in 1625, where he advised having a heath or wilderness of six acres within the garden.[6] This was a managed area, but it was managed to look like a flowery heath.

The ha-ha, as we saw earlier, was a way of blending the garden with the land around it, and this was spoken of as the garden blending seamlessly with nature. One of the earliest proponents of the style of gardening that the ha-ha facilitates was Stephen Switzer. In his *Iconografia Rustica* (1718), Switzer suggests that opening out the garden allows for enjoying "the extensive charms of nature."[7] The garden around the house is further simplified and "naturalized" by getting rid of formal structures and introducing serpentine paths.

I should point out that these are, in some senses, small steps; there is both a disjunction between what Switzer said and what his patrons allowed and, along with other writings such as Shaftsbury's, we need to be careful about imposing a contemporary understanding of what they meant by "nature." In the early eighteenth century, this could just as well be taken as meaning the beauty of geometrical forms. We need to proceed in small steps rather than make grand causal claims, but now at least the steps can take an irregular and not a straight path.

Moreover, another way of looking at the ha-ha is not as an opening of the garden to nature but as taking the gardening mentality of shaping land to specific, art-determined, aesthetic ends and applying it to nature. In that guise the English landscape garden becomes not a newfound appreciation of nature but a new opportunity for even greater domination.

From this observation a familiar story begins to emerge. What this is leading to is the idea of landscapes as scenic, as Italian art-inspired tableaux and the prominence of English estates shaped to the aesthetic of the landscape paintings of Claude Lorrain and Poussin. This is a well-trodden path and one that leads directly to contemporary critiques, such as Allen Carlson's "Landscape Scenery Model" of incorrect aesthetic appreciation of nature. Here the prime suspect in distorting our relationship to nature is the picturesque, which he describes as "a mode of appreciation by which the natural world is divided into scenes, each aiming at an ideal dictated by art, especially, landscape painting."[8] However, what I will now do is look in detail at the idea of the picturesque and see if there isn't something, or indeed a number of things, going on there that could redeem this maligned aesthetic notion.

The Picturesque

What I aim to do is to give expression to some of the now less heard, early spokespersons for the picturesque and see if what they have to say about the appreciation of local natural settings as they occur, rather than as artificially shaped to an artistic ideal, seems to chime with contemporary voices in environmental philosophy.

First we need to look in some detail at the commonplace but in fact rather strange definition of the picturesque as being "like a picture." The construction of the word and the way it was used, both in the eighteenth century and since, certainly suggests that interpretation, but it is strange nonetheless. I want to argue that this definition is either meaningless or tautological. A landscape is not and indeed cannot be like *any* picture; pictures come in many styles and with many subjects, so the definition "like a picture" is obviously useless, as it means almost nothing. We could extract from it a more focused meaning that goes something like "a scene or landscape that has the qualities sought by particular landscape painters such that it appears a fitting subject for a landscape painting of that style." But what does "style" mean here? If it means "picturesque," we have a tautology, not an explanation. The problematic circularity of the "like a picture" definition is identified by Uvedale Price in 1794[9] and discussed very clearly in his objection to Gilpin's definition. He endorses Gilpin's observations but points out that a definition has to be able to divide some things from others, and as many things, here he quotes Gilpin, "please from some quality of being illustrated in painting,"[10] such a definition does nothing to explain what specifically is the quality of the picturesque. Gilpin's travels are to particular types of places and show an appreciation of particular types of things and not others, so it is necessary to examine those types so that a descriptive definition of the picturesque can emerge such as we have for the beautiful and the sublime. Here Price is clearing the way for sharpening up the definition, but he doesn't merely make the obvious point that not all paintings or subjects of painting are picturesque and so "being a fitting subject for a painting" does not make something picturesque. He has much to say about the role of art in developing our appreciation of landscape. However, he also begins to unravel the idea that our appreciation of landscape is wholly driven by our appreciation of landscape painting. Although the weight of historical scholarship on the picturesque is against such a claim,[11] I think it is worth contemplating an alternative. Perhaps we have been so blinded by the cultural interpretation of our taste being driven by art that we forget that at some point someone had to think that there was something about nature that was worth painting. In chapter 3 of *On the Picturesque* Price presents an alternative origin of the term:

The Italian pittoresco is, I imagine, of earlier date than either the English or the French word, the latter of which, pittoresque, is clearly taken from it, having no analogy to its own tongue. Pittoresco is derived, not like picturesque, from the thing painted, but from the painter; and this difference is not wholly immaterial. The English word refers to the performance, and the objects most suited to it: the Italian and French words have a reference to the turn of mind common to painters; who, from the constant habit of examining all the peculiar effects and combinations, as well as the general appearance of nature, are struck with numberless circumstances, even where they are incapable of being represented, to which an unpractised eye pays little or no attention. The English word naturally draws the reader's mind towards pictures; and from that partial and confined view of the subject, what is in truth only an illustration of picturesqueness, becomes the foundation of it.[12]

Nature is then packaged, commodified, and sold as an ideal that can become a scene that nature either lives up to or not. Of course, the inspiration for painters such as Claude and Poussin was nature as allegorical setting, not nature itself. The early English landscape gardens of Kent and Bridgeman and later those of Lancelot "Capability" Brown were allegorical landscapes; they move out into "nature" as poetic setting, as can be seen by the classical temples that they placed as focal points to the scene.[13]

There is certainly evidence in the writings and actions of landscape designers and landowners of the time of exactly this kind of idealized picture making, where ancient trees are felled and even villages moved to create exactly the right vistas at just the right points to be viewed and enjoyed by the trained eye—trained, that is, in reading the landscape as allegory. In one sense this is the picturesque in full swing, and it has a great deal to do with the emulation of particular styles of painting and a great deal to do with control. But it is not, I contend, the whole picture. To find some redemptive element in the picturesque as a way in to nature I again return to the writings of Uvedale Price.

Although we often see the picturesque aligned with the break with formality (and of course it does reject the formal), it is better seen as a rejection of a particular type of contrived informality best exemplified by the landscapes of Lancelot "Capability" Brown and his imitators. Price and Richard Payne Knight, though they differ in some quite fundamental aspects,[14] both abhor the style and prevalence of the Brownian landscape. Their criticisms of this are in accord and attack Brown for being formulaic, boring, and *unnatural*. Price equates Brown and his imitators to quack physicians with a single cure for all ills:

in both arts the quacks are alike—they have no principles, but only a few nostrums, which they apply indiscriminately to all situations, and all constitutions. Clumps and Belts, pills and drops, are distributed with equal skill. . . . The best improver or physician is he who leaves most to nature—who watches and takes advantage of those indications which she points out when left to exert her own powers; but which, when once destroyed or suppressed by an empiric of either kind, present themselves no more.[15]

The popularity of Brown's style for a brief but wealthy period in English history meant that many large estates were taking on the same appearance, which, though it purported to connect to nature in its serpentine paths and "naturalistic" clumps, bore no relationship to its geographical location. Thus, not only was each estate rendered bland and boring as an individual landscape, but they were all bland and boring in the same way. Copying pictures is not the way to a picturesque landscape, but what is? At the heart of the picturesque is a love of wild nature in a small compass, and it is this impulse that, I think, might have contributed to our current sensibilities and certainly has still more to say. Before mounting my defense of the picturesque as an engaged love of nature-as-experienced, I want to outline two further technologies that would seem to suggest that such a defense is impossible. These are the viewing station and the Claude glass.

The Stationary View

The term "viewing station" is used to refer to both an identified spot from which one would view a particular scene and a small building placed on such a spot. Contemporary readers of early guides to the English Lake District might be surprised to see how these books sought to shape and manipulate readers' experience by identifying precisely where one should stand in order to see prescribed views. Compared to the twentieth-century guides of Alfred Wainwright, who charts the whole passage of a walk, these instructions appear rather stilted and closer to the instructions for an amateur landscape artist—which, of course, they were. The buildings are an elaboration of the same idea, as well as a convenience, since they would not only obviously mark the place for the prescribed view but could also shelter the amateur artist while they sketched the perfectly proportioned section of landscape that made a picturesque scene.

These little buildings already seem rather remote from the themes that I want to claim are also central to the picturesque, but the technology impinges even more on any attempt to see the picturesque as not just an art-directed and distanced view of nature. Consider the example of Claife Station above Windermere. This mock Gothic building (built in the 1790s) was equipped with different colored glass in each of its windows so that the view could be "enhanced" in a way that simulated the atmosphere of each of the seasons: green for spring, yellow for summer, orange for autumn, and blue for winter.[16] Other viewing stations, such as one built in 1708 at the Falls of Clyde in New Lanark, Scotland, were equipped with mirrors arranged to reflect the scene. Here the viewer, or amateur artist, would be able to stand with her back to the actual landscape and see its reflection in the mirror and thus have it contained and easier to reproduce in her sketch book.

Viewing stations described in eighteenth-century guidebooks and marked on maps are evidence of the growing popularity of wilder

landscapes at the time. However, their prescriptive nature and the introduction of buildings to these sites seems to militate against claims for the
picturesque as evidencing any kind of authentic engagement with nature.
Even so, we need to remember that the idea that these local landscapes had
aesthetic qualities was relatively new and that it is therefore reasonable
to suppose that people might have needed some direction in how to see
qualities they were unaccustomed to tuning in to.

Through a Glass Darkly?

The mirrors of viewing stations find their way into the backpack of the
tourist in search of picturesque scenes in the form of the Claude glass. This
portable optical instrument was a hand-sized convex mirror tinted gray or
sepia. When held to reflect the scene behind the shoulder of the traveler it
could reduce the chosen panorama to picture-like dimensions and coloration. The mirror's tinting was not just to make the scene look like an old
painting in the style of Claude Lorrain but to compress the tonal values
and help strip out detail so that the forms and unifying lines of the scene
were easier to discriminate and thus reproduce in sketches and watercolors.
Gilpin was a keen user and recommender of the Claude glass as a way
to assist the recording of picturesque scenes, and these instruments were
widely used by travelers following his recommended journeys. What this
looks like is exactly the shaping of wildness to art-determined ends rather
than an appreciation of what is there. Lars Kiel Bertelsen's treatment of
the subject is a standard view. He describes the Claude glass as a sample of
"positivistic hardware" (as if the term "positivistic" can be used as unprob-
lematically descriptive) and goes on to describe the Claude glass thus:

The glass instantaneously positions the operator—for what else should we call the
one who handles it?—in a virtual space between the two backs of the case: between
the matt black velvet and the ice-cold curved mirror that sends an enfolded slightly
distorted perspectivistic projection of the surroundings into the operator's eyes,
allowing him/her to read the world like a text.[17]

However, I am not sure we need to read even this piece of technology in
quite this way. Gilpin is always quick to emphasize that his focus is on
observation and on assisting people in their observation of nature.[18] This
suggests that there might be more to the interaction between natural landscapes and the traveler/tourist with his sketchbook and Claude glass than
might be obvious to a contemporary reader. As Francesca Orestano points
out, the early ridicule of Gilpin (in the figure of Dr. Syntax in a satirical
novel by Combe) meant that his work was never fairly assessed. Orestano

draws attention to the fact that sketching, as opposed to painting in oils, demanded very little in the way of tools or direct tuition; this meant that it became a means by which the burgeoning middle class, and particularly women, could engage with landscapes and thus "acquire a point of view, maybe even a voice."[19] Gilpin's simple rules about what makes a good picture and his prescriptions about where to find views worth sketching seem terribly restrictive to the modern eye and sensibility used to engaging with nature. Even so, it is arguable that his guidebooks gave many people who lacked the education of the Grand Tour and access to painting masters the license to look at nature and the confidence to record it in a way that would be deemed acceptable to others.

One of the things we need to remember about any sketching activity is that the drive to represent, even within the confines of a system, leads to closer observation of what is there. Hence, the eighteenth-century enthusiast of the picturesque would have spent more time actually taking in the places she visited than a modern traveler equipped with a camera. And if we ever wonder why the pictures we take fail to capture the real majesty or charm of a place we experienced, this surely has much to do with the indiscriminate nature of the camera lens, which captures all the detail rather than conveying the weight or delicacy of the forms that impress upon the human observer the nature of the place he is stopping to contemplate. I am not for one moment suggesting that the image in the Claude glass should be exalted as an authentic capturing of the real place; I am just suggesting that stopping to draw leads to a more engaged looking and perhaps a justification to spend more time closely observing a particular place.

The moral of these brief comments regarding the technologies that suggest most starkly that the picturesque should be understood as an art-led, inauthentic engagement with nature is this: Even in regard to these technologies, there is more going on than many commentators (who, arguably, overtheorize what is going on) have recognized. But if this is the case even in regard to technologies that might be regarded as "Exhibit A" for the prosecution of the picturesque (i.e., as an art-led, inauthentic engagement with nature), then it might be reasonable to think that a more general consideration of the picturesque could reveal that it has done more to inform our contemporary love of nature than has hitherto been recognized.

The Appreciation of Wildness as Evidenced in Six Picturesque Themes

How exactly does this idea of an appreciation of wild nature come through in writings on the picturesque proper? I would like to identify and explore six themes, all of which, I maintain, are linked to our current affection for, enjoyment of, and impulse to protect nature.

The first, drawn directly from Uvedale Price, is the idea of *variety* as pleasing.[20] It is a characteristic of nature, in the eyes of this Herefordshire landowner, that it is varied and that variety is something to treasure, not to obliterate through inappropriate, style-driven management of the land. Pleasing variety as shown in the changing variety of plants and shapes and forms encountered while walking an "unimproved" country lane is not the only type of variety. The idea of variety as a good in itself of course finds contemporary resonance with ideas of biodiversity. But, lest we mistake Price for wanting the equivalent of a botanical garden or zoo remember that in his anti-Brownian polemic we saw that he admires the natural variety that makes one place different from another. Nature in Herefordshire is not like nature in Lancashire, and the garden style that tries to emulate the same form everywhere (particularly one imported from another country entirely) is destroying what Pope, in 1731, had called the *genius loci*[21] and what we have now come to call local distinctiveness.[22] I am not claiming that Price, if alive today, would have been taking part in the antiglobalization movement, just that his attack on Brown has resonance with the anti-McDonaldization idea. For Price it was each place itself that was the source of rich aesthetic experience. For example, the way a path turned or the way sheep, just through use of a sheltered spot, hollowed out spaces in the banks of a track and revealed the gnarled tree roots. To enjoy and cherish such things was the appreciation of place rather than the hankering for another place. This feeling for *genius loci* and rejection of formulated landscape ideals perhaps has much to say to us today about cherishing nearby nature rather than only hankering for wilderness on a grand "untouched" scale.

The next, connected, theme is that of *intricacy*. Again it is Price who brings this out explicitly. The term suggests a density of detail, but Price adds a specific meaning when he describes intricacy as "that disposition of objects, which, by a partial concealment, excites and enriches curiosity."[23] Variety and intricacy work together, but for Price intricacy is what stimulates our curiosity and imagination. On a country lane it is this that makes the gnarled tree roots fascinating and drives us on to see what is around the next bend, hidden from view. I might be stretching the point here, but this notion of intricacy does seem to point also to an enjoyment of and a desire to know the specifics of nature: to enjoy *this* particular clump of primroses, to want to find out more about *this* particular woodland. We need to remember that the period of the picturesque is also that of Enlightenment empiricism. The rejection of a poetic/emblematic landscape, the new enjoyment and appreciation of a landscape for itself, and our being intrigued by it and wanting to understand its intricacies, all fits well with that wider cultural shift. Currently we can see a similar understanding of nature emerging in something like understanding local ecology, not necessarily from a reductive scientific understanding, but something more akin to an informed amateur naturalism or the resurgence in interest in Goethean observation and in understanding nature through his idea of a delicate empiricism.[24]

My third theme, *engagement*, is developed more fully in the writings of French essayist Claude-Henri Watelet. In his 1774 *Essay on Gardens* he discusses the problem of likening the work of laying out a garden to that of an architect designing a building. He makes the point that with a building we enjoy taking it in at a glance, admiring particularly its organization of vertical space. But that mentality applied to the garden has given us the formal structures of straight paths and symmetrical patterns, which do not entice the viewer to even venture out into the garden itself, as Watelet says:

while an immense parterre or endless allées may astonish, this pleasure lasts but a few moments. One questions the purpose of walking across such great expanses when a single glance has already explored them. . . . But even if one were to undertake this tedious task, this walk that nothing encourages him to hasten or slow down, he would no doubt be like a man who moved his legs without going anywhere.[25]

For Watelet the garden must be planned out in the place itself, utilizing its natural irregularities and pleasing views, not indoors at a draftsman's table, and not to point to this or that fable or myth but to be itself. The land then becomes something to explore. And note that for Watelet exploration is driven by the land itself; it speeds us or slows us according to what is happening in the land. And what are the fruits of this kind of engagement? For Watelet they are psychological, such as peace for the soul, respite from the tiring concerns of society. His accounts of gardens in the essay are given as *perambulations*; they record not just the scenes but the movement through landscapes and the thoughts and feelings such engagements bring out. For example:

The last rays of the sun sometimes find me considering in silence the tender concerns of the swallow for its young, or the cunning tricks of the kite attempting to capture its prey. The moon is already up, and I am still sitting. This is an added pleasure. The whispering water, the sound of the leaves in the breeze, the beauty of the sky, all immerse me in a sweet reverie. The whole of nature speaks to my soul as I wander listening.[26]

I don't feel I need say much to bring out the contemporary feel of this. The engagement calls to mind Arnold Berleant's work on the role of engagement in environmental aesthetics;[27] the multisensory account chimes with aspects of eco-phenomenology;[28] and the soul-healing notion of nature contemplation hints at what is later developed in ecopsychology.[29]

My fourth theme is *time*. This is obviously connected to movement; if the form of nature appreciation becomes the walk, rather than the picture or isolated scene, it has to take place over time. The shaping of the landscape by the passage of people or animals over time crops up in Price as he eulogizes over the twisting path "shaped by the mere tread of passengers and animals, as unconstrained as the footsteps that formed it."[30] We are properly carried through the wilder landscape not on the planned paths of the "improver" (a term used for landscape designers such as Brown), whether they be straight or serpentine, but by the paths that emerge through long-term interaction and engagement.

The most obvious aspect of time in the picturesque is the enjoyment of the action of nature over time on the works of humans. The classical temple that had meant one thing, once weathered and decayed, now tells a new story, part of which is evident in the ruin itself and requires no prior learning. Here nature as entropic of human order brings about unplanned changes that render what was once simple and smooth—the epitome of the beautiful—into the epitome of the picturesque. Price gives a wonderful time-paced account of this process:

Observe the process by which Time, the great author of such changes, converts a beautiful object into a picturesque one: First, by means of weather stains, partial incrustations, mosses, &c. it at the same time takes off from the uniformity of the surface, and of the colour; that is, gives a degree of roughness, and variety of tint. Next, the various accidents of weather loosen the stones themselves; they tumble in irregular masses upon what the perhaps smooth turf or pavement, or nicely-trimmed walks and shrubberies—now mixed and overgrown with wild plants and creepers, that crawl over, and shoot among the fallen ruins. Sedums, wall-flowers, and other vegetables that bear drought, find nourishment in the decayed cement from which the stones have been detached; birds convey their foods into the chinks, and yew, elder, and other berried plants project from the sides; while the ivy mantles over other parts, and crowns the top. The even, regular lines of the doors and windows are broken, and through their ivy-fringed openings is displayed, in a more broken and picturesque manner. . . .[31]

His account in this passage also ushers in my fifth theme, that of *chance*. What is admired in the variety, intricacy, and developments through the passage of time is that the changes are wrought by chance. Yes, we can create the appearance of a decaying ruin, and of course this was done once it became a popular aesthetic. However, the value that Price and other writers were finding was not in decaying ruins per se but in them as emblematic of nature at work; nature indifferent to human likes and dislikes and just doing its own thing. In the English context of a moist temperate climate, this was verdant growth wherever and however it happened to find a place. Although Price and others talked of creating this effect, it was very much by letting it happen or rather not stopping it, so that the "effect" was what would be there if we were mere participants in rather than conquerors of the land for which we had responsibilities. This opening oneself to chance encounters or developments—going with the flow—and enjoying the surprise of what the other has to offer is seen today as psychologically healthy. And, of course, the idea of letting nature *be* became the clarion call of the contemporary environmental movement.

My sixth theme, *transition*, brings us up to date with recent work in environmental philosophy; even here we can find useful ideas and precursors in the picturesque. The Brownian design was much criticized by Price, Knight, and later garden designers because it took the green sward—the smooth expanse of grass—right up to the house, having dispensed with the fripperies of intricate parterres and flowering plants. Price does not advise that the roughness and unplanned nature of the picturesque should rule everywhere, despite some early criticisms that suggest he did;[32] Price felt that certain comforts of the home necessitated some order, such as smooth driveways and decorative embellishments close to the house in the garden proper.[33] Hence, rather than writing the informal garden over the wider landscape he makes a nice distinction between the human environment close to the house as the garden and that which is beyond the garden to be enjoyed for its picturesque qualities. The picturesque can then be seen as a transition between the human realm and the very wild realm of nature further afield as sublime. Indeed Edmund Burke, writing in 1757, saw it functioning in exactly this way.[34] Here the picturesque can be seen as a mixing and juxtaposing of the sublime and the beautiful, such that the smoothness of the beautiful is ruffled with a rustic patina of nature–human relations and the quasi threatening disorder of the sublime (untouched wild nature) is toned down to a charming irregularity. Gilpin also brings the two together by describing the picturesque as "Beauty lying in the lap of horrour."[35]

What the picturesque allows is the transition to be made from one realm to the other without seeing wilderness or wild places as somehow there for us to tone down and shape to our sensibilities, but as places for us to experience as they are. Also we can still value the particular qualities that an ordered garden can bring where human design has the upper hand. The transition zone is where both humans and nature have a hand, but neither is tyrant; deer roam, sheep graze, trees might be coppiced, but this is a more direct working with what nature affords and an enjoyment of its bounty. The idea of the landscape of utility can also be found in Watelet. He develops the idea of the embellished farm where the function of the mill, arable fields, and dairy are not contrived but useful, and yet nothing is developed to such a scale that they do not delight the person passing through them with their appositeness to the land and their variety. Here the picturesque is the landscape that can arise with the human working in and with nature as a participant. This strikes a chord not just with a Leopoldian style land ethic[36] but also with recent concerns about the wilderness discourse of early environmentalism leaving no place for a healthy and nature-respecting, but nevertheless human, mode of life.[37] The picturesque can help us make aesthetic sense of those mixed communities such as the urban park or sensitively farmed land, as well as help us bridge the gap between our love of order and love of extreme wildness.

Conclusion

I have sought to show that the picturesque, interpreted in this way, has many resonances with understandings of human–nature relationships in contemporary environmental philosophy. There is much to poke fun at with its later interpretations and, particularly, what I would call its decayed form with its fake ruins and rustic hovels. Indeed, as mentioned above, there were even satirical novels produced at the time.[38] However, my aim was simply to suggest that we take a closer look before consigning it to the history book of bad design ideas or corrupting influences on our understanding of the natural world. There was something deeper going on there, which I maintain has aided and abetted other cultural ideas to help us see the natural world as both pleasing to us and as a kind of agency with which we can and indeed must engage.

The implication of this reinterpretation is that environmental philosophers can look to an aesthetic notion other than the sublime to explain and further inspire our love of wild nature. Moreover, if we think of the sublime as inspiring the love of and drive to protect wilderness landscapes, then the picturesque serves a similar role for the more local landscapes. In this way, sensitively farmed country and city refuges, such as parkland, and even the carefully but not over tended back yard or garden, can be seen not as poor cousins of wilderness but aesthetic places that inspire a love of nature in their own right. The six themes I have drawn out of the picturesque can be used to explore our relationship to nearby nature, and I suspect they can do much to honor and help direct our feeling for local nature and endorse our care for nature in a small compass. The aspiration to preserve wilderness is not thereby undermined; rather, wilderness takes its place as one type of nature that requires care and respect, but not the only type.

Acknowledgments

An earlier, shorter version of this essay was published as "Wildness in the English Garden Tradition: A Reassessment of the Picturesque from Environmental Philosophy," *Ethics and the Environment* 13, no. 1 (2008): 105–120.

Notes

1. M. H. Nicolson, *Mountain Gloom and Mountain Glory* (New York: W. W. Norton, 1959/1963), pp. 196–198.

2. H. E. Winlock, *Excavations at Deir el Bahri 1911–31* (New York: Macmillan, 1942).

3. R. Aben and S. deWit, *The Enclosed Garden* (Rotterdam: 010 Publishers, 1999).

4. Thomas Heyd, "Thinking through Botanic Gardens," *Environmental Values* 15, no. 2 (1996): 197–212.

5. A. J. Dezallier d'Argenville, *La Theorie et la Pratique du Jardinage* (1709), quoted in Jane Fearnly-Whittingstall, *The Garden: An English Love Affair* (London: Weidenfeld Nicolson, 2002), p. 123.

6. Francis Bacon, "On Gardening" (1625), quoted in Ralph Dutton, *The English Garden*, 2nd ed. (London: Batsford, 1950), p. 49.

7. Stephen Switzer, *Iconographia Rustica* (1718), quoted in Charles Quest-Ritson, *The English Garden: A Social History* (London: Penguin, 2001), p. 112.

8. Allen Carlson, *Aesthetics and the Environment* (London: Routledge, 2000), p. 45.

9. Uvedale Price, *On the Picturesque* (Edinburgh: Caldwell, Lloyd & Co., 1794/1842).

10. William Gilpin, *Three Essays* (London: R. Blamire, 1792), quoted in Price, *On the Picturesque*, p. 78.

11. See John Dixon-Hunt, *Gardens and the Picturesque* (Cambridge, MA: MIT Press, 1992) and Dabney Townsend, "The Picturesque," *Journal of Art Criticism* 55, no. 4 (1997): 365–376.

12. Price, *On the Picturesque*, p. 80.

13. Dixon-Hunt, *Gardens and the Picturesque*, pp. 50–75.

14. Stephanie Ross, *What Gardens Mean* (Chicago: University of Chicago Press, 1998), pp. 121–154.

15. Price, *On the Picturesque*, p. 187.

16. Mark Haywood, "Claife Station: Looking at the World through Colored Glasses," paper given at the Romantic Spectacle Conference, July 2006, Roehampton.

17. Lars Kiel Bertelsen, "The Claude Glass: A Modern Metaphor between Word and Image,' *Word and Image* 20, no. 3 (2004): 182–190, p. 182.

18. Francesca Orestano, "The Revd William Gilpin and the Picturesque; Or, Who's Afraid of Doctor Syntax?," *Journal of Garden History* 31, no. 2 (2003): 163–179, p. 171.

19. Ibid.

20. Price, *On the Picturesque*, p. 69.

21. Alexander Pope, "Epistle to Lord Burlington" (1731), quoted in Penelope Hobhouse, *The Story of Gardening* (London: Dorling Kindersley, 2002), p. 207.

22. Sue Clifford and Angela King, eds., *Local Distinctiveness: Place, Particularity, and Identity* (London: Common Ground, 1993).

23. Price, *On the Picturesque*, p. 69.

24. J. W. von Goethe, "Maxims and Reflections," in *Scientific Studies*, ed. and trans. Douglas Miller (New York: Suhrkamp Publishers, 1988), p. 307.

25. Claude-Henri Watelet, *Essay on Gardens: A Chapter in the French Picturesque*, ed. and trans. S. Danon (Philadelphia: University of Pennsylvania Press, 1774/2003), p. 51.

26. Ibid., p. 59.

27. Arnold Berleant, *The Aesthetics of Environment* (Philadelphia: Temple University Press, 1992).

28. See Isis Brook, "Can Merleau-Ponty's Notion of 'Flesh' Inform or Even Transform Environmental Thinking?," *Environmental Values* 14, no. 3(2005): 353–362, and Charles Brown and Ted Toadvine, eds., *Eco-phenomenology: Back to the Earth Itself* (New York: SUNY Press, 2003).

29. Deborah Winter and Sue Koger, *The Psychology of Environmental Problems* (Hillsdale, NJ: Lawrence Erlbaum, 2003).

30. Price, *On the Picturesque*, p. 71.

31. Ibid., p. 82.

32. H. Repton, "Letter to Uvedale Price, Esq.," in Price, *On the Picturesque*, pp. 411–416.

33. Price, *On the Picturesque*, p. 297.

34. Edmund Burke, *A Philosophical Enquiry into the Sublime and the Beautiful* (Notre Dame: University of Notre Dame Press, 1757/1993).

35. W. Gilpin, *Northern Tour to the Lakes, etc. Made in 1772* (1786), quoted in C. Hussey, *The Picturesque* (London: Frank Cass and Co., 1927/1983), p. 22.

36. Aldo Leopold, *A Sand County Almanac: And Sketches Here and There* (Oxford: Oxford University Press, 1949/1989).

37. William Cronon, "The Trouble with Wilderness; Or, Getting Back to the Wrong Nature," in *Uncommon Ground*, ed. W. Cronon (New York: W. W. Norton, 1995), p. 69–90.

38. William Combe, *Tour of Doctor Syntax in Search of the Picturesque* (London: Routledge, 1812/1878).

10   Garden, City, or Wilderness? Landscape and Destiny in the Christian Imagination

Philip Sheldrake

Thomas Traherne, the evocative seventeenth-century English poet and religious writer, was inspired by the city of Hereford and its surrounding countryside. He delighted in ordinary landscape transfigured into a source of spiritual vision and into a gateway to heaven.

Your enjoyment of the world is never right till every morning you awake in heaven, see yourself in your Father's palace and look upon the skies and the earth and the air as celestial joys.[1]

The corn was orient and immortal wheat, which never should be reaped, nor was ever sown. I thought it had stood from everlasting to everlasting. The dust and the stones of the street were as precious as gold. The gates were at first the end of the world. The green trees when I saw them first through one of the gates transported and ravished me.[2]

The purpose of this essay is to explore some aspects of the important role of landscape in the Christian religious imagination. Throughout human history, features such as forests, fields, mountains, gardens, and cities have been both geographic realities where social practices were enacted and also imaginary realities—powerful symbols that evoked fear or desire.[3] Thus, "landscape" is an ambiguous concept. While based on physical phenomena, it expresses more than these. In reality, landscape portrays the material world mediated through human experience. This implies that landscape is irreducibly *historical*. Simon Schama, in his monumental work *Landscape and Memory*, is also clear that "Landscapes are culture before they are nature; constructs of the imagination projected onto wood and water and rock."[4] In other words, landscape has provided the physical features upon which human beings draw imaginatively in order to shape distinctive identities and to express worldviews. Inevitably, worldviews reflect the dominant values of a given time. Therefore, "landscape" is unavoidably associated with issues of power.

Landscape in Christian Thought

Landscapes of various kinds, real or imagined, have played an important role in Christian thought from the Bible to the present. In a Christian way of understanding the world, humans are capable by means of the imagination of discerning transcendent truths through material existence, including nature. Indeed, historically, Christian writers from the patristic period to the Puritans regularly expressed a sense that the natural world is the second book of divine revelation alongside the written scriptures. In this context, Christianity has presented an artful representation of landscapes in terms of its fundamental concerns. In particular, certain landscapes have been used to portray ideas about the ultimate destiny of human existence—that is, paradise or heaven.[5]

In classic Christian artistic representation and writing, three types of landscape stand out in relation to human destiny. First, there is the familiar natural image of the paradise garden. Then there is the humanly constructed landscape of the city. These two landscapes are sometimes contrasted with each other and sometimes combined. However, such landscapes are ambiguous. While the idyllic Garden of Eden (Genesis 2:8–3:24) was a "place" of original blessing and an image of the hope of paradise restored, it is also is a symbol of "the Fall," a loss of innocence and of human disobedience to a benevolent creator. In the case of cities, the Bible portrays Cain who murdered his brother Abel as the founder of the first human city (Enoch). Thus, the city is first of all an archetype of human pride and violence and symbol of humanity's refusal of God's gift of paradise, Eden (Genesis 4:17). However, if the Bible begins in a garden, it ends in a mythic city (Revelation 21), the New Jerusalem let down from heaven. This becomes over time an archetypal image of heaven.

Finally, a third type of landscape in Christian thought, marginal wilderness, functions in rather different ways. "Wilderness" in Christian literature embraces forests, mountains, remote islands, and the ocean as well as deserts. Wilderness landscapes usually appear in Christian mystical or monastic literature where they are both places of encounter with the divine and places of struggle with the forces of evil. It is worth noting briefly at this point that such wild landscapes also point to a tension in Christian thought concerning the overall placed nature, or otherwise, of the sacred. For such marginal landscapes also underline a sense that the divine is most powerfully encountered on the edges of "culture." Wilderness becomes the archetypal liminal space—a boundary between the contingent everyday world and "the other world," thought of in terms of infinity and eternity.

Implicit in this is a sense that displacement and perpetual movement are an inherent aspect of true encounters with a God who is ultimately indefinable and unknowable.

The Bible and the longer Christian tradition are concerned with the desire for "place." Particularly in the Jewish scriptures this preoccupation is formulated in terms of "land" and landscape. Landscape is always a particular patch freighted with social and historical meaning. In this sense, Christian thought has prioritized the notion of "place" over the abstractions of "space." Place is always tangible, specific, and relational. It therefore has a moral content. The American scholar Walter Brueggemann notes that a critical point about biblical approaches to landscape is an intimate connection between landscape and a sense of place. The Jewish God (and by extension the Christian understanding of God) is a God of place. Thus landscapes as much as historical events are the medium for divine self-revelation and human response.[6]

In the Jewish scriptures, the God of place is most obviously associated with the King David or Jerusalem tradition of theology. Here, a covenant between God and the people of Israel assured the Jewish people of a landscape of their own, the "promised land." Thus, the David–Jerusalem tradition was grounded in the settled experience of the land and the building of a temple in Jerusalem as a cultic center. The land was a possession forever (albeit solely by divine gift) and the power of the king of Israel was linked to the dwelling of God's power in some special way on Mount Zion. A God who cannot finally be named or be contained in a single landscape is nevertheless made known by continual acts of self-placement (see, e.g., 2 Samuel and 1 Kings).

Given the central significance of "land" in Jewish theology, it may seem strange that New Testament texts make little direct reference to it. However, the Christian scriptures were to a large extent the product of the Jewish urban diaspora throughout the Roman world. They also reflect an atmosphere of apocalyptic, intense future-directed expectations. The "promised land" becomes largely symbolic and the focus moves to the impending overthrow of all earthly conditions as a prelude to the final establishment of the Kingdom of God.

The Christian situation was also complicated by a powerful belief that divine revelation was focused not on a particular place but on a person, Jesus Christ. Although the Holy Land and traditional Jewish sacred places continued to have some importance, this was primarily as places where Jesus, the source of meaning for Christians, lived and died. So landscape became a spatial expression of his life and teachings. In the dialogue with a Samaritan woman in the Gospel of John 4:4–42, Jesus is described as proclaiming that worship of God will no longer be tied to particular places ("the hour is coming when you will worship the Father neither on this mountain nor in Jerusalem," 4:21). Worship of God "in spirit and truth" is not relativized, but the importance of sacred place and landscape is.

It is also clear from the foundational Christian texts that there was one urgent concern for Christians in the earliest period. This was to move out from the local landscape into the entire inhabited world. Indeed, the Book of Acts 1:8 suggests that Jesus explicitly exhorted his disciples to leave the city of Jerusalem to go to the ends of the earth in pursuit of their mission to preach the Kingdom of God. For Christians, God was increasingly to be encountered in whatever place they found themselves. The experience of "being in transit," of journey, became a central metaphor for encounter with and response to God. Indeed Christians became known as people "of the way" (e.g., Acts 24:14). For the early followers, significant conversion experiences often occur "on the way" in situations of displacement or transition, for example, the disciples on the road to Emmaus (Luke 24) or the conversion of Saul on the road to Damascus (Acts 9). In a sense, it seems that the marginal ground *between* fixed places is where God is frequently encountered.

Evoking Paradise: From Garden to City

Christianity has sometimes been accused of an antiurban bias. Certainly the Bible gets off to a tricky start. The Book of Genesis seems deeply gloomy about cities. Cain, symbol of human pride and violence, is portrayed as the founder of the first city, Enoch—an alternative to God's Garden (Genesis 4:17). Later, the people of Babel seek to replace the authority of God (Genesis 11:1–9) and Sodom and Gomorrah become classic symbols of corruption (Genesis 19). In the light of these texts, the modern French Protestant thinker, Jacques Ellul, suggests that "the city" stands for a refusal of God's gift and humanity's desire to shape life autonomously. Thus "God has cursed, has condemned the city instead of giving us a law for it."[7]

Yet, there are other positive biblical images of the city in the David–Jerusalem tradition, for example in the Book of Psalms. God is enthroned in the sanctuary of Zion (Psalm 9), the city becomes a living reminder of God's power and faithfulness (Psalm 48), and is described as the house of God (Psalm 122). In the Jerusalem tradition the city is intended to express the peace of God. Those who live in the city are required to share God's peace with one another (Psalm 122:6–9). Turning to the New Testament, in the gospels Jerusalem is the focal point and climax of Jesus' mission. The cities of the Roman Empire become the center of Christian mission in the Book of Acts, particularly in the strategy of the Apostle Paul. Christianity rapidly became an urban religion.[8] Most striking of all, on the very last page of the New Testament (Revelation 21), a new holy city of Jerusalem, perfectly harmonious and peaceful, is made the image of the final establishment of God's kingdom.

Nevertheless, in early Christianity paradise, both as landscape and as a state of harmony with God, was initially imaged predominantly as a garden. For example, the earliest late third- and fourth-century monastic texts, as well as other Christian writings, while frequently associated with desert wilderness, also continued to portray monastic life in terms of a Garden of Eden restored. The garden and wilderness in one sense both stood over against "the city" as a symbol of this-worldly power. The imagery of early monasticism often portrays a return to a pre-Fall paradise state. One of the strongest symbols of this restoration and anticipation was the ability for humans and wild animals to live at peace with each other within the monastic enclosure, which is often as verdant and fruitful as a paradise garden. A classic example appears in "The Life of St. Onophrius," the Egyptian hermit.[9] The Syriac theologian and poet St. Ephrem (306–373 c.e.), in his *Hymn of Paradise* (9:5–6), also writes of a garden full of greenness, flowers, fruits, and fragrance.[10] The Irish monastic journey of St. Brendan (to which we will return later), following the pre-Christian voyage tales, describes the islands of the West as verdant, fruitful, and in a state of perpetual springtime.

Other medieval monastic texts describe paradise in terms of a garden or as naturally fruitful. European monastic life during the Middle Ages was predominantly agrarian. Settlements were typically built in obscure places where the restoration of untamed landscape to proper order or "civilization" was an important element of the monastic life. In this way, monastic enclosure anticipated the reversal of the fall from grace in the Book of Genesis and the restoration of biblical paradise. Otfrid, a ninth-century German monk suggested that "There, lilies and roses always bloom for you, smell sweet and never wither, their fragrance never ceases to breathe eternal bliss into the soul." The twelfth-century German monastic text, *Elucidation,* describes the new creation of paradise as a fragrant pleasant garden without thorns. The everyday world of grinding labor and struggle against the natural elements is replaced by a harmonious reflection of the classic monastic cloister garden.[11]

In the hundred years between 1150 and 1250 western and central Europe underwent a major cultural shift caused by a revival of cities, which increased roughly eightfold. This resulted in the creation of new and increasingly dominant urban classes of wealthy merchants and skilled artisans and had a serious impact on social and religious perspectives. This included an increased optimism about material existence, a renewed sense that the sacred could be vividly represented by the physical world, including built environments and an inevitable relationship between religious symbolism and new frameworks of social power. The notion of "heaven" lost some of its philosophical abstraction and became more and more associated with a wider world view. In religious writing heaven shifted increasingly from the re-creation of the Garden of Eden of the Book of Genesis to the New Jerusalem of the Book of Revelation—from nature to culture.

Medieval Urban Visions

Interestingly, the heavenly city was often imaged in terms of actual human cities, and conversely, some cities, particularly in Italy, promoted design elements that reflected the symbolism of the Book of Revelation. New religious images were inspired by the recently flourishing cities of walls, towers, cathedrals, busy market places, public squares, workshops, and wealthy merchants' houses. For example, the thirteenth-century Franciscan friar and poet, Giacomo de Verona, in the elegant Italian of his text "On Heavenly Jerusalem," describes heaven in terms of the avenues and piazzas of a beautiful city. His writing clearly reflects his significant knowledge of urban architecture and especially his own city of Verona.[12]

One of the most evident consequences of the new urbanism was the development of the great Gothic cathedrals. In the city cathedral, paradise was in a conscious way symbolically evoked and also brought down to Earth. To enter the cathedral was to be transported into a transcendent realm by the vast spaces, a flooding of light through the dematerialization of walls with glass and by increasingly elaborate liturgies. For Abbot Suger of St. Denis in Paris, often credited with the formal birth of French Gothic, church buildings were the gateway to heaven and had to be more impressive than all other buildings. The architecture of the cathedrals acted as a kind of symbolic landscape, a microcosm in stone and artwork of the whole cosmos. This was a utopian space where an idealized heavenly harmony was portrayed in the here and now.[13]

However, the social symbolism of medieval cathedrals was also ambiguous. We cannot ignore the fact that while the architecture of cathedrals portrayed divine–human unity, it also manifested the divisions of the social order. Within the building, the space was demarcated:

some parts were reserved for clergy alone, and in the laity's space, subdivisions reflected ranks and distinctions, and substantiated a hierarchical order with seats given over to the powerful who did not wish to stand and could afford particular proximity to the holy.[14]

It has also been noted that representations of heaven in the art of cathedrals tended to reproduce rather than subvert social separations—for example, of the peasantry from the aristocracy or monarchy. Thus, on the west front of Chartres above the great door,

elongated figures of "saints" thinned out of the world to reach a God above, and stout, stocky figures of this-worldly artisans and peasants supporting with the sweat of their brows that other "leisure class" who have all the time and energy for liturgies and mystical contemplation, point to a conception of spirituality indelibly sculptured in the cathedrals of our collective unconscious.[15]

At its best, cathedral design promoted something more than a two-dimensional, static, urban "map." It portrayed a third and a fourth dimension—movement through space on both vertical and horizontal planes and human transformation *through time*. Cathedrals were repositories for the cumulative memory and constantly renewed aspirations of the community. In his outline of an urban aesthetic, the American philosopher Arnold Berleant suggests that in the premodern city the cathedral (and other great churches) acted as a guide to an "urban ecology" that contrasts with the monotony of the modern city, "thus helping transform it from a place where one's humanity is constantly threatened into a place where it is continually achieved and enlarged."[16]

The City as Sacred Landscape

Medieval notions of "the sacred" in the city were not restricted to ritual sites (cathedrals). There was a clear sense that the city as built environment embraced a wider sacred landscape of the streets. Even today, street corners in predominantly Catholic countries frequently retain medieval examples of religious plaques and statues. For example, the rich collection of street shrines in the *città vecchia* of the Italian city of Bari, ranging in age from the twelfth century to the present, has been the subject of scholarly writing.[17]

The sense that the city as a whole was a sacred landscape was reinforced by processions and blessings. In medieval cities the Christian Eucharist was a *public drama*, not only in the many churches but also the feast-day pageants, mystery plays, and street processions, for example on the feast of

Corpus Christi. Processions, before Lent and on Rogation Days (days of prayer in early summer to protect crops) and ceremonies to mark out the boundaries of each parish (known in England as "beating the bounds") together symbolized a continual purification of the city from the spirit of evil.[18] Medieval citizens sometimes made the heavenly Jerusalem of the Book of Revelation 21 a model for urban planning. Thus the Statutes of Florence of 1339 emphasized the existence of the sacred number of twelve gates even though, in fact, the city had by then extended to fifteen gates. The 1334 Statutes of Imola also describe that city entirely in terms of the sacred number twelve from the Book of Revelation—twelve chapels, three each in four city quarters.[19]

Later in the Middle Ages, the development of the great Italian urban piazzas owed much to the new religious orders such as Franciscans and Dominicans and their preaching churches. These buildings opened onto great spaces where crowds gathered to listen to sermons (for example, the piazzas outside Santa Croce or Santissima Annunziata in Florence). The colonnaded piazza offered a vision of the city, metaphorically (it engendered a concept of public space for intermingling) and practically (it opened up new urban vistas).

Italy also defended the ideal that city life, with its organized citizenry living in concord, could be just as much a way to God as monastic life. A literary genre of poems, the *laudes civitatis*, articulated a utopian ideal of civic life. The *laudes* depict the human city as a place where, like the Heavenly City, many and diverse people are able to live together in peace. The *laudes* further portrayed cities as renowned for the quality of communal life in which every citizen found a particular place contributing to building up the whole. The city itself was idealized as sacred with a number of key spiritual qualities.[20]

Mingling Garden and City

The medieval shift of landscape imagery from paradise garden to heavenly city was not totally exclusive. A number of texts actually mingle the two landscape images. Thus, the visionary material associated with the twelfth-century English Cistercian monk Gunthelm suggests two versions of paradise. The first is a walled city, but inside its walls, the city turns out to be a garden with plants, trees, birds, and fragrant flowers. Thus paradise is a city when seen from the outside but a garden when seen from within. Other late medieval portrayals of heaven also mingle the city with natural landscapes. For example, Gerardesca of Pisa (1210–1269) envisaged heaven as an Italian hilltop city state where God dwelt with the angels and major saints (the Virgin Mary and Apostles), surrounded by castles on nearby hill-tops for the saints of second degree and minor forts for the remainder of the blessed. However, the central walled city was accessible to everyone. The whole of this paradise landscape was surrounded by a celestial park and open fields.

A hundred years later, Renaissance landscape imagery of heaven also mingled cities with gardens. Although Italians of the Renaissance period had a profound interest in cities and civic life, there was also a significant recovery of an idealized view of the countryside. This was provoked in part by a philosophical appreciation of the natural world and in part by the practical reality that late medieval cities had relatively few public gardens or parks within their walls. A striking artistic example of this trend is the mid-fourteenth-century Mantova chapel in the famous church of Santa Maria Novella in Florence. There, a wall painting portraying the righteous in heaven mingles the images of a city of crystal and gold with that of a paradise garden.

Paradise as Industrious City

The second great European and North American urban expansion took place during the Industrial Revolution during the course of the nineteenth century. Interestingly, the rapid growth of industrial cities provoked a renewal of paradise imagery in some quarters, not least in North America. A number of portrayals of heaven in Protestant literature drew on urban imagery. However, they did so in a way that was different from the Middle Ages. It was no longer so much a question of focusing on visualizations of landscape, because from its beginnings a great deal of Protestantism tended to be ambivalent toward the material world and to downgrade physical mediations of the sacred. Heaven was now described as an *active* place, modeled on the productivity of the new industrial cities. So, the morally righteous do not find in heaven a place of eternal *rest*, for that would be lazy and frivolous (so no paradise gardens are mentioned), but lead industrious and busy lives of decent work and public service. This is especially striking in the book *Physical Theory of Another Life* by the American Scott Isaac Taylor in the 1830s. William Clark Wyatt, a late nineteenth-century New York pastor, also suggested that "Heaven will be a busy hive, a center of industry."[21]

Le Corbusier, de Certeau, and the Modern City

The twentieth-century city is a long way from the compact medieval city landscape whose footprint remained essentially local rather than global.

The Swiss architect Le Corbusier had a powerful influence on European urban design during the mid-twentieth century. Le Corbusier was inspired by aspects of Christian symbolism and by the writings of the Jesuit priest-paleontologist Pierre Teilhard de Chardin.[22] However, fundamentally, he believed in a kind of mystical utopianism rather than in conventional Christianity. Le Corbusier was also a Platonist who sought to create an ideal world through the perfection of design and planning. In his vision, the architect became a version of Plato's all-powerful philosopher-king. His matter–spirit dualism was also influenced by the philosophy of Descartes and Pascal as well as by gnosticism. Le Corbusier's approach underpinned a division between public and private life. In this, he reflected the closely related tendencies of Enlightenment rationalism to prioritize an individualistic interior self and to ignore the fact that "the self" is a product of human *interaction*.[23] The outer, public world was of dubious worth. Consequently, Le Corbusier's city designs made it difficult for people to congregate casually in public space. He was highly influential in modernist city planning, especially in its tendency to create sterile public space.[24]

Le Corbusier's "radiant city" had no churches because all human desires could be met and realized in this quasi-paradise environment. In this spirit, Le Corbusier called the skyscrapers of Manhattan "new white cathedrals." They engineered a kind of euphoria and not only embodied transcendence in their sublime height but offered a finalized, "total vision" of reality symbolized by panoramic vistas.

An interesting critical commentator on the nature of the twentieth-century urban is the seminal French cultural theorist, religious thinker and maverick Jesuit priest Michel de Certeau (1925–1986).[25] Especially in his essay for architects, "Ghosts in the City," it seems probable that one of de Certeau's targets was Le Corbusier.[26] Le Corbusier stood for two aspects of modernist planning that de Certeau abhorred: a tendency to erase the past and to subordinate the realities of people's lives to abstract concepts of "space."

In "Walking in the City" de Certeau offers a striking contrast to Le Corbusier's reading of Manhattan. Standing on top of the World Trade Center, he wrote of the almost erotic pleasure and temptation of "seeing the whole," of looking down upon the city and of thereby totalizing it. There we are (or were) lifted out of Manhattan's grasp—becoming *voyeurs*, not walkers. We then read the city as a simple text. But this is really an illusion. As de Certeau puts it, "The fiction of this kind of knowledge is related to a lust to be a viewpoint and nothing more."[27] De Certeau compares this way of seeing to the aloofness of the urban planner. Meanwhile the ordinary practitioners of the city live down below, promoting "the microbe-like, singular and plural practices which an urbanistic system was supposed to control or suppress."[28] These everyday practices by ordinary people are what make the city *lived* space.

De Certeau's attacks on modernist planning for destroying history were not mere nostalgia. On the contrary, de Certeau was a professional historian and philosopher of history who strongly emphasized the power of narrative to shape environments and to transform them. Indeed, the city landscape created by architecture or planning must enable people to "narrate" the city as a means of creative living.[29] Stories take ownership of spaces, define boundaries, and create bridges between individuals. Similarly, making space for narrative is a vital factor in creating the city as community rather than just a collection of buildings and spaces.[30] De Certeau's understanding of narrative embraced the *history* of "place" because without respect for the past a city would become dysfunctional and dangerous.

De Certeau's rejection of definitive urban utopias and his promotion of a fluid, mobile city forever "on the way" in the life and practices of its citizens, parallels in some ways St. Augustine's *City of God* on pilgrimage toward the Kingdom of God until the end of time. For de Certeau, like St. Augustine, the contemporary city landscape is a virtual reality that anticipates a visionary future; hence his opposition to all forms of secularized salvation, especially when realized through the social engineering of highly regulated city planning.

Wilderness Landscapes

A third type of landscape employed in the Christian imagination is the "wilderness." As a landscape without boundaries, wilderness is a more ambiguous symbol of human destiny. From earliest times, two wilderness themes stand out—displacement and social marginality. After Christianity became the established religion of the Roman Empire in the fourth century C.E. under Constantine, successive generations of men and women withdrew from the cities in the context of a growing sense that Christianity had compromised itself with the values of "worldly" power. As single hermits, or in new monastic settlements, they ringed the cities of the Christianized world from the days of St. Anthony of Egypt onward.[31]

Early monasticism was therefore essentially concerned with changing places, literally and metaphorically. In moving away from the *polis* (city) to the *eremos* (desert), the ascetic wanderer was not in some simple way rejecting culture for nature—after all, the desert more obviously signified wildness, danger, and suffering rather than the beauty or romantic harmony of a paradise garden. Rather, the monastic ascetics, by means of discipline and struggle, sought to reconfigure a disordered world into an earthly paradise that also anticipated the final arrival of the Kingdom of God. The desert or wilderness in its various forms has exercised a peculiar fascination throughout Christian history. This is especially true of the fourth-century originators of the monastic movement in Syria, Palestine, and Egypt.

Christian monasticism . . . originated in the kingdom of the scorpion and the hyena: a world of rock and heat. Several centuries later the biographers of holy men in north-west Europe also depicted their subjects as seekers after landscapes and environments which were correspondingly forbidding.[32]

Why was physical wilderness chosen for monastic settlements? In one sense it was a dramatic contrast with "the city" understood as a symbol of a life focused on this-worldly values. Equally, there have been many attempts to describe a special association between religious experience and "the desert," whether literal or figurative. The theme of the desert is common to many monastic texts. It is, as we have already seen, both a paradise and at the same time a place of trial where ascetics encounter and overcome inner and outer demons.[33] However, "wilderness" is also frontier territory. Living on this kind of physical boundary symbolized a state of liminality—of existing between two worlds, the material and the spiritual, the disordered and the reordered.

The ascetic desert was originally associated with a theology of death and rebirth. It was to become the tomb before the tomb. It is recorded in Athanasius' life of Anthony of Egypt that he began his life in the desert by literally sleeping in a tomb among the bones of the dead. What more powerful symbol could there be of a loss of conventional human needs and values?[34] However, the underlying point is that through struggle, physical deprivation, and submission both to God and to the realities of an empty landscape, the monk enters into a new world and new life.

To move to the desert was metaphorically speaking to journey both toward a holy place and away from the place of sin. To strive for moral perfection involved a topographical displacement. So the attainment of a state of holiness was understood also in terms of a movement in space. The early ascetics in Syria, Palestine, and Egypt, from the late third century c.e. onwards, deliberately sought out the empty spaces of the wilderness as the context for spiritual transformation. One element seems to have been a desire to be freed from an identity provided by normal social ties. Monastic disengagement from the start was a social and political statement as well as a religious one.[35]

Egyptian monks did not live as close to the ordinary world as Syrian ascetics normally did. These differences were partly geographical. The traditional agrarian culture of the Nile valued a regulated life. Combined with the harsh realities of the Egyptian desert, this necessitated a spirit of cooperation for survival. Thus we see the gradual development of monastic villages. Syrian wilderness was never deep desert in the same way and was not so starkly separated from human habitation. Consequently the ascetics remained visible challenges near where other people lived. In their geographical isolation, the Egyptians tended to recreate the format of village community and became the *oikumene* (settlement) in the *eremos* (desert). The Syrians, while living closer to ordinary settlements, adopted more eccentric lifestyles, such as Simeon Stylites living atop a roadside pillar near Antioch.[36]

In later centuries, the Celtic form of monasticism especially in Ireland but also in Wales and Scotland was also characterized by the existence of numerous hermits living in wild and isolated places. It is interesting to note that in these countries quite a number of traditional Christian sites are commemorated in modern place names by the various local words for "desert." Thus in Scotland it is Dysart, in Wales it is Dysserth or Dyserth, and in Ireland it is Diseart.

The great Celtic saints regularly found their special "deserts" on the borderlands of normal settlement patterns. The British Isles are full of caves, Roman ruins, islands, and coastal headlands with Celtic Christian associations and remains. For example, St. Cedd chose as his home the present-day village of Lastingham on the edge of the North Yorkshire Moors. Lastingham was on the border between the rich agricultural settlements of the vale of Pickering and the wilderness of the high moors. This, according to Bede, was remote and more suited to robbers.

Cedd chose a site for the monastery among the high and remote hills, which seemed more suitable for the dens of robbers and haunts of wild beasts than for human habitation. His purpose in this was to fulfil the prophecy of Isaiah: "in the habitation of dragons, where each lay, shall be grass, with reeds and rushes," so that the fruits of good works might spring up where formerly lived only wild beasts, or men who lived like wild beasts.[37]

However, Lastingham also relates to the Celtic Christian fascination for the spiritual quality of boundary places.

There are also close ties particularly in the Irish Christian tradition between the wilderness and the ocean. Earlier pre-Christian legends probably played a part, but it is likely that the Irish ascetics who crossed the wilderness of the sea in search of paradise had also been encouraged by their regular monastic readings of the Old Testament. Adomnan's *Life of Columba* speaks of the monks who "have recently gone out desiring to find a desert place in the sea that cannot be crossed."[38] In the Irish tradition, the ultimate point of spiritual wandering was to "seek the place of the resurrection." This was the place where the particular wanderer would settle and spend the remaining years doing penance and waiting for death. It is significant that this special, appointed place was not determined by tribe or culture but was attributed to divine inspiration alone. This acted as a symbolic counterpoise to the Irish attachment to clan and inherited landscape. The impulse was to cast oneself upon the mercy of God symbolized by the uncontrolled and unpredictable elements of sea and wind.[39]

One source of wandering asceticism stems from the pre-Christian voyage tradition. The earlier journeys to the Land of Promise and rebirth elide eventually with Christian ideals. There is a great tradition of Irish voyage tales, the *echtra* ("outing") or the *immrama* ("rowing about"), where the interest is in the journey itself and not merely on its end point or purpose. The most famous is the Voyage of Bran (on which it is likely that the St. Brendan Voyage is modeled), dating probably from the seventh century. Bran journeyed into the ocean from somewhere in the West of Ireland after hearing a song of the delights of the other world.[40] In the pre-Christian tradition the world of the dead was simply a happier replica of this world. The soul was immortal and could travel far from its native land to mysterious and legendary islands. Among the names given to this world were: Island of Women, Land of the Living, Land of Youth, Land of Promise, Land of Joy. This land had no tempests and no excess heat or cold. There were no dangerous animals. The Land of Eternal Youth was unvisited by death or disease and was in an eternal springtime, where fruit and flowers grew without labor.

It was not difficult to connect these traditional motifs with Christian ideas of eternal life. The tendency of pre-Christian legends to locate such a land in the West probably relates to the direction of the setting sun. Far in the West was the divine land where the Sun God rested. There is a close relationship between elements found in the voyage of Bran and that of St. Brendan. The famous *Navigatio Brendani* probably dates from the ninth century even though the hero-saint lived in the sixth century. It has a simple plot that blends pre-Christian journey traditions, folk lore, Christian legend, a strong narrative, poetry, and monastic imagery.[41] Brendan encounters mysterious hermit monks living on the *insula deliciosa*. Brendan's voyage is accompanied by many sensuous delights: a wonderful fragrance, shining light, singing birds, and marvelous foods. However, the purpose was to seek "the Land of Promise of the saints."[42]

Conclusion: Forever on the Way

In some respects, Christianity inherited from the Jewish scriptures not only some elements of the David–Jerusalem theology of place but also the theology of the Moses tradition based on the narrative of the Book of Exodus— particularly the forty years of wandering in the wilderness. This theological perspective suggested that the faithfulness of the people of Israel to God's promise (later transposed into Christian terms) implied being constantly in transit, spiritually if not actually, because they were to find their place in God alone. According to the logic of Christian understandings of a transcendent, unbounded, and ultimately indefinable God, the divine could never appropriately be described in relation to one place or imaged by only one landscape.

For Christianity, the ultimate destiny of humanity is, like God, essentially ineffable—that is, beyond place, beyond knowing, and beyond any image. "Heaven" is not to be thought of as a "place" or landscape that exists in the way that England or the planet Earth can be said to exist. Rather, the notion expresses a destiny that is more akin to a state of existence or being. Because in this sense the nature of human destiny is indefinable, the metaphors for it in Christian literature are not limited to landscapes or place but also include references to sight (light, darkness, or a cloud of unknowing in different texts), sound (music or a paradoxical singing silence), taste (the heavenly banquet), or fragrant smell. Fundamentally, there is a persistent tension in Christian thought between a sense of contingent place-identity and placelessness, between a localized and temporal material existence and a process of being drawn beyond these boundaries into what is complete or universal, conceived as the all-embracing life of God.

At its most profound level, the landscape metaphor of wilderness, including its variant of ocean journeying, also embraces this quest for transcendence and boundlessness. This is graphically expressed by the notion of human life as a continual journey. For example, the Irish monastic writer Columbanus (c. 543–615) employed the notions of "road" and "journey" as his favored metaphors for human life. To live was to be on a roadway that led ultimately to eternity. "Therefore let this principle abide with us, that on the road we so live as travelers, as pilgrims, as guests of the world."[43] Other major Christian figures also found the notion of life as a journey particularly apt. In the thirteenth century Francis of Assisi wrote in his *Later Rule*: "As pilgrims and strangers in this world who serve the Lord in poverty and humility, let them [the friars] go begging for alms with full trust."[44] Later in the sixteenth century the *Constitutions* or rule of the Jesuit Order written by Ignatius Loyola explicitly promoted an ethos of mobility.

While this related to the Order's missionary ethos, it also embraced a broader spiritual principle. "One should attend to the first characteristic of our Institute . . . this is to travel' (*Constitutions*, para. 626).[45] Another early Jesuit, Jeronimo Nadal, Loyola's assistant, linked mobility to a kind of universalism—"the world is our house." "They [Jesuits] consider that they are in their most peaceful and pleasant house when they are constantly on the move."[46]

If this-worldly existence in Christian terms may appropriately be portrayed as a road, a journey, or a pilgrimage toward the eternal reality called God, the notions of "heaven" or eternity have more generally been conceived as states of eternal rest, finality, completion, and changeless certainty. Yet even here, Christian thought is ambiguous. For a Christian writer like Augustine, human destiny must always be thought of as perpetually expanding and dynamic, for the divine reality is always more than we can grasp. "Just as love grows, the search for the one who has been found [God] also increases" (Homily on Psalm 104). In this sense, "heaven" too may be thought of in terms of persistent growth—a perpetual journey—toward further revelation and enlightenment that is never complete. The fourth-century Christian philosopher and theologian, Gregory of Nyssa, also argues that the human desire for God necessarily involves perpetual movement beyond what may be finally grasped or defined. In his *Life of Moses* he represents the human journey in terms of an ascent up a mountain, a parallel of Moses encountering God on Mount Sinai. Because possible visions of God are deficient in relation to what God fully is, the journey is toward ever deeper darkness.[47] Therefore, Gregory of Nyssa has God assert: "The place with me is so great that the one running in it is never able to cease from his progress" (Book 2.242).

This truly is the vision of God: never to be satisfied in the desire to see him. But one must always, by looking at what he can see, rekindle his desire to see more. Thus, no limit would interrupt growth in the ascent to God, since no limit to the Good can be found nor is the increasing desire for the Good brought to an end because it is satisfied. (Book 2.239)

For Gregory, God may be experienced but never finally known; and so the human journey is a never-ending progress toward perfection that is never finally concluded.

Christian religious language has maintained a paradoxical tension between definition and unknowing, between affirmation by means of images and denial that any image, or imaging in general, captures the reality of the divine. Thus, while Christianity has persistently employed landscape images for human destiny, it has at the same time carefully affirmed that God and the nature of "heaven" remain elusive and beyond the capacity of human imagination finally to express.

Notes

1. Thomas Traherne, *Centuries of Meditation*, I. 27 and 28 (London: Mowbray, 1975).

2. Traherne, *Centuries of Meditation*, III. 3.

3. See, for example, Jacques Le Goff, *The Medieval Imagination* (Chicago: University of Chicago Press, 1988), pp. 12–13.

4. Simon Schama, *Landscape and Memory* (London: HarperCollins, 1995), p. 61.

5. Three of the best works on the relationship between conceptions of paradise or heaven and landscapes are: C. McDannell and B. Lang, *Heaven: A History* (New Haven: Yale University Press, 1988); J. Burton Russell, *A History of Heaven: A Singing Silence* (Princeton: Princeton University Press, 1997), and A. McGrath, *A Brief History of Heaven* (Oxford: Blackwell, 2003).

6. W. Brueggemann, *The Land: Place as Gift, Promise, and Challenge in Biblical Faith* (Philadelphia: Fortress Press, 1977), p. 5.

7. J. Ellul, *The Meaning of the City* (Grand Rapids: Eerdmans, 1970), p. 16.

8. See, for example, Wayne Meeks, "St. Paul of the Cities," in *Civitas: Religious Interpretations of the City*, ed. Peter S. Hawkins (Atlanta: Scholars Press, 1986), pp. 15–23.

9. See, for example, the experience of monastic space as paradise restored in "The Life of St. Onophrius," in *Journeying into God: Seven Early Monastic Lives*, ed. T. Vivian (Minneapolis: Fortress Press, 1996).

10. For Ephrem's hymns, see K. McVey, ed., *Ephrem the Syrian: Hymns* (New York: Paulist Press, 1989).

11. Both Otfrid and *Elucidation* are quoted in McDannell and Lang, *Heaven*, pp. 70–72.

12. See McDannell and Lang, *Heaven*, pp. 69–80.

13. For a study of the medieval cathedral as a spiritual "text," see my "Reading Cathedrals as Spiritual Texts," *Studies in Spirituality* 11 (2001): 187–204.

14. Brigette Bedos-Rozak, "Form as Social Process," in *Artistic Integration in Gothic Buildings*, ed. Virginia Chieffo Raguin, Kathryn Brush, and Peter Draper (Toronto: University of Toronto Press, 1995), especially pp. 243–244.

15. Aloysius Pieris, "Spirituality and Liberation," *Month* (April 1983): 120.

16. See A. Berleant, *The Aesthetics of Environment* (Philadelphia: Temple University Press, 1992), p. 62.

17. See N. Cortone and N. Lavermicocca, *Santi di strada: Le edicole religiose della città vecchia di Bari*, 5 vols. (Bari: Edizione BA Graphis, 2001–2003).

18. See P. Ackroyd, *The Life of Thomas More* (London: Random House, 1999), p. 111.

19. C. Frugoni, *A Distant City: Images of Urban Experience in the Medieval World* (Princeton: Princeton University Press, 1991), p. 27.

20. See P. Raedts, "The Medieval City as a Holy Place," in *Omnes Circumadstantes: Contributions toward a History of the Role of the People in the Liturgy*, eds. C. Caspers and M. Schneiders (Kampen: Uitgeversmaatschappij J.H. Kok, 1990), pp. 144–154.

21. See McDannell and Lang, *Heaven*, pp. 280ff.

22. See F. Samuel, *Le Corbusier: Architect and Feminist* (Chichester: Wiley, 2004), p. 100.

23. For sharp criticisms of the kind of Cartesian "rhetoric of interiority" that imbued Le Corbusier, see W. A. Davis, *Inwardness and Existence: Subjectivity in/and Hegel, Heidegger, Marx, and Freud* (Madison: University of Wisconsin Press, 1989).

24. For a detailed study of Le Corbusier's theories of self and society, see S. Richards, *Le Corbusier and the Concept of the Self* (New Haven: Yale University Press, 2003).

25. Michel de Certeau's thinking about cities is to be found especially in "Walking in the City" and "Spatial Stories," in *The Practice of Everyday Life* (Berkeley: University of California Press, 1988); Part 1: Living, especially "Ghosts in the City," in *The Practice of Everyday Life*, vol. 2: *Living and Cooking* (Minneapolis: University of Minnesota Press, 1998); "The Imaginary of the City" and other isolated comments in *Culture in the Plural* (Minneapolis: University of Minnesota Press, 2001).

26. See comments in I. Buchanan, *Michel de Certeau: Cultural Theorist* (London: Sage Publications, 2000), chap. 1, especially p. 20.

27. De Certeau, "Walking in the City," p. 92.

28. Ibid., p. 96.

29. De Certeau, *The Practice of Everyday Life*, p. 115.

30. Ibid., pp. 122–130.

31. See P. Brown, *The Making of Late Antiquity* (Cambridge, MA: Harvard University Press, new edition 1993), chap. 1: "A Debate on The Holy."

32. R. Morris, *Churches in the Landscape* (London: Dent, 1989), p. 104.

33. A. Louth, in *The Wilderness of God* (London: DLT, 1991), provides a recent attempt to describe the special qualities of the religion of the desert. The essay "The Wilderness in the Medieval West" by J. Le Goff in *The Medieval Imagination* (London/ Chicago: University of Chicago Press, 1988) has some illuminating remarks on the understanding of "desert" in Western monasticism, including the Celtic tradition.

34. R. C. Gregg, ed., *Athanasius: The Life of Anthony* (New York: Paulist Press, 1980), paragraph 8, pp. 37–39.

35. See Brown, *The Making of Late Antiquity*, chap. 4: "From the Heavens to the Desert: Anthony and Pachomius."

36. On the geographics of monastic "style," see P. Brown, *Society and the Holy in Late Antiquity* (Berkeley: University of California Press, 1989), pp. 110–114.

37. Bede, *Ecclesiastical History*, Book III, chapter 23, trans. L. Sherley-Price (London: Penguin Classics, 1990), p. 181.

38. A. O. Anderson and M. O. Anderson, eds., *Adomnan's Life of Columba* (Oxford: Clarendon Press, 1991), pp. 166–167.

39. On Celtic *peregrinatio* see E. G. Bowen, *Saints, Seaways, and Settlements* (Cardiff: University of Wales Press, 1977), chap. 3: "The Saints and the Seaways."

40. N. Chadwick, *The Celts* (London: Penguin, 1971), pp. 280–282.

41. See J. Anderson, "The Voyage of Brendan, an Irish Monastic Expedition to Discover the Wonders of God's World," *American Benedictine Review* 43 (1992): 262–282.

42. See K. Hughes, *Early Christian Ireland: Introduction to the Sources* (London: Hodder & Stoughton, 1972), p. 212.

43. G. S. M. Walker, ed., *Sancti Columbani Opera* (Dublin: Dublin Institute for Advanced Studies, 1970), Sermon VIII, 2; p. 97, ll. 11–13.

44. *Later Rule*, chap. 6.2 in R. Armstrong and I. Brady, eds., *Francis and Clare: Complete Works* (New York: Paulist Press, 1982).

45. See G. E. Ganss, ed., *The Constitutions of the Society of Jesus* (St. Louis: The Institute of Jesuit Sources, 1970).

46. *Monumenta Historica Societatis Jesu, Monumenta Nadal, V,* nos. 195 and 773 (Rome: Institutum Historicum Societatis Iesu, 1905).

47. See E. Ferguson and A. J. Malherbe, eds., *Gregory of Nyssa: The Life of Moses* (New York: Paulist Press, 1978).

III Studies in Landscape

11 "All foreground without distance": The Rise of Landscape in Late Medieval Painting

Reinhard Steiner
Translated from the German by Robert Savage

I

In Ambrogio Lorenzetti's frescoes of Good and Bad Government in the Palazzo Pubblico in Siena, "landscape," understood as a genre of painting, bursts onto the scene of early modern art with a maturity that is as astonishing as it is unexpected. On the eastern wall, on which the positive consequences of good government are depicted, a vast surface area is taken up by representations of the well-ordered city and a thriving landscape. They are separated in the painting by an almost diaphanous partition, which makes city and countryside appear, not so much as alternatives, as the inseparable halves of human existence in the world. In thus being literally placed side by side, both *topoi* explicate and delimit each other: The city as a public interior space is juxtaposed, in ideal-typical fashion, with the landscape as a natural exterior space, from which the gaze is directed out into the world at large. From here, it is but a small step to the topographical landscape of the fifteenth century and the so-called world landscape of the early sixteenth century. In the history of the pictorial imagination, however, a quantum leap separates Lorenzetti's vision from the *topocosmos* of the Middle Ages. This *epoché* will be sketched in what follows.

In his celebrated *Civilization of the Renaissance in Italy*, Jacob Burckhardt coined the wonderfully apt and memorable phrase "all foreground without distance." Introduced in the chapter on the discovery of beauty in landscape, it reads in context:

By the year 1200, at the height of the Middle Ages, a genuine, hearty enjoyment of the external world was again in existence, and found lively expression in the minstrelsy of different nations, which gives evidence of the sympathy felt with all the simple phenomena of nature—spring with its flowers, the green fields and the woods. But it is *all foreground without distance*, particularly when we realize that the crusaders, who traveled so far and saw so much, are barely recognizable as such in their poems. Even epic poetry, which describes armor and costumes so fully, does not attempt more than a sketch of outward nature; and the great Wolfram von Eschenbach scarcely anywhere gives us an adequate picture of the scene on which his heroes move. From these poems we would never guess that their noble authors in all countries inhabited or visited lofty castles commanding distant prospects. Even in the Latin poems of the wandering clerics, we find no traces of a distant view—of true landscape—but what lies near is sometimes described with a glow and splendor that none of the knightly minstrels can surpass.[1]

Still more evidently than to poetry and the epic, the two cases cited by Burckhardt, the phrase "all foreground without distance" applies to the visual conventions used to represent nature and landscape in the pictorial arts of the (late) Middle Ages: no horizon to give a sense of depth and breadth, no proportional relation between things near and far, no modulation of light—can one even speak of landscape when faced with this world of things without atmosphere? The answer seems obvious. Just as an infinite, homogeneous space, one that precedes the concrete arrangement of things and allows them to appear more or less in focus, enlarged or reduced in scale, depending on the viewpoint and in accordance with their position, their relative distance and proximity, could not be imagined in *pre*perspectival painting (i.e., before around 1420), so there could exist neither distance as a *relatum* nor its visual equivalent, a horizon to invest the picture with the illusion of depth. But if there is no horizon in the distance, there can, so it would seem, be no landscape either. With that, the discovery of perspective becomes the sole criterion for the development of landscape painting, inasmuch as the shift from "aggregate space" to "systematic space," to borrow Panofsky's terms,[2] for the first time implies the relational interconnection of things *within* the space of nature. It will be shown that there is no such clean break in history, and that the conquest of distance in art's field of possibilities proceeds instead by way of detours that emerge from aesthetic experience, and so also, one might say, from the aesthetic articulation of the embedded experience of landscape and of place. At the same time, the role of distance and nearness in such placed experience, at least as evident in late medieval art, and so also their role in the experience of landscape itself (if that term can indeed be used here) will also be exhibited.

II

As far as the concrete experience of the world is concerned, Burckhardt's phrase does not imply that the medieval world was smaller than his own, or that it appeared smaller to its contemporaries. With the view that everyone in the Middle Ages believed the Earth to be a disc having been disproved some time ago,[3] one could now almost believe the opposite to have been the case. It is unnecessary to recall that the crusaders, maritime traders, and missionaries who ventured as far afield as India and China brought back with them a vastly expanded *horizon*,[4] in the experiential sense of the term. For on the other hand, it would appear that distance and the experience of distance remained closely bound to the hand-eye field of one's own body and were not calculated with abstract units of measurement. That is why, according to Arno Borst, "almost all units of measurement" are referred back

to the man who is working in a given space. That begins with the cubit and the yard, the length of the human forearm, and the fathom, the human armspan. "Foot" and "pace" directly recall the wanderer's path; the mile, consisting of a thousand double paces, was the commonest unit of length. The day's journey is no different.[5]

Much the same holds true for measurements of area and time. In other words, distance *as such* was not and could not be an intentional object of representation and thought, since it could not be grasped and seen within the experiential horizon of one's own reach. If someone was "far away" or "in the distance," then this was understood to be a particular and localizable place that the traveler perceived as nearby. Whatever lay beyond the horizon of the hand–eye perceptual field did not just withdraw from (com) prehension, it was alien as well, and generally a source of anxiety.[6]

In this "patchiness"[7] of a space or world made up of innumerable nearby locales and locations, even what was far off and alien was tailored to what was close at hand, visible, and graspable—not just inner-worldly distance, but also distant places of an other-worldly kind such as paradise or hell. Not just the visions of the hereafter of a Tundal attest to this, but also the topography of hell, purgatory, and paradise in Dante's *Divine Comedy*, which was not depicted as a more or less relational spatial continuum until the fifteenth century. Until then, even the path to the beyond is vividly and concretely represented by a bridge, which the departed are shown crossing.[8] Elsewhere, too, the treatment of space in visions of the underworld is highly distinctive. As Aron Gurevich writes, there is

a symbolic "topography" of visions, dividing left and right, east and west. In order to reach hell it is necessary to go towards the north; the gaze of sinners awaiting punishment is also turned in that direction. But are we dealing here with space in a real sense? One should rather suppose that the topographical terminology is applied to non-spatial phenomena: fears and hopes are expressed in similar "geometricized" images. For "north" in the visions is not a part of the world, but the concentration of the soul's despairs, just as "east" is the embodiment of the expectations of salvation. The space of the visions is above all the exteriorization of the "mental space" of medieval men.[9]

Not just the hereafter was subjected, in the medieval imagination, to a symbolic interpretation and mode of representation. Although it is perhaps unsurprising that the cartography to be found in representations and visions of the hereafter is purely symbolic, only in travel narratives, with their peculiar mix of projection and factual report, can the extent to which sensuous perception was preformed by knowledge derived from literature be fully recognized. Authors were *auctoritates*, and "collective information handed down from literature was considered to be at least as important and reliable as the individual's direct observation of nature."[10] The high, and at times superior, claim to plausibility that emanated from literary knowledge exerted considerable influence, not least on the genre of travel narrative. The accounts of John of Plano Carpini[11] and William of Rubruk, both from the mid-thirteenth century, as well as those of Marco Polo[12] and the Franciscan monk Oderico da Pordenone,[13] both dictated by the travelers to their scribes in the first third of the fourteenth century, stick fairly close to the facts when it comes to depicting what the travelers had experienced themselves; only on rare occasions are their reports contaminated by details drawn from fable or hearsay. What is astonishing is not the considerable popularity that these reports enjoyed, but what that popularity rested on. In Marco Polo's narrative, for example, precisely the passages based on firsthand experience—his description of customs or his lists of figures—seemed so fantastically exaggerated as to defy belief. And while Oderico's portrayal of his voyage to India and China was a popular success, it became still more popular through an author "who had himself never been to South and East Asia"[14] and who presumably never ventured outside Central Europe. John of Mandeville,[15] who was probably born in England and who died in Lithuania in 1372, nonetheless composed perhaps the most famous and widely read late medieval travel narrative, and this despite the fact that his information was drawn solely from travel literature.[16] In his text, first published in 1356, realistic pieces of information were interwoven with purely fictional details about distant realms to create a literary amalgam in which truth and invention could no longer be distinguished, since the author chose not to reveal his sources. The book owed its unparalleled success to the author's rhetorical skill in generating the appearance of an unconditional love of truth; indeed, his occasional admissions not to have this detail or that from firsthand observation served only to demonstrate the seriousness of his intentions. At any rate, it is certain that he was considered more trustworthy than the comparatively prosaic Marco Polo, just as it is certain that his book, along with the partly legendary events and characters still to be found in the later illustrated editions of the fifteenth century, did not just pander to the demands of a public eager for sensation, but still corresponded to a worldview for which the faraway epitomized all that was alien and unimaginable.

III

These few references may suffice to give a rough idea of the coordinates that, in the imaginary world of representation and the spatial world of sensual perception, were occupied by the forms of intuition "proximity" and "distance." As late as the thirteenth and fourteenth centuries, the visual order was still so exclusively oriented toward things present and near at hand that even what was in reality remote was represented in terms of its graspability and accessibility. It seems as though the assumption that the *obiecta visus*—whether they be qualities or material things—could only be perceived through (spiritual) "species sensibiles in medio,"[17] since an *actio in distans* or action at a distance was considered to be impossible, prevailed until well into the fourteenth century, even though William of Ockham had long since demonstrated action at a distance in perception. As difficult as it may be to prove the influence of philosophical disputes on the fine arts, which, after all, were not practiced by artists in the modern sense of the term, the correspondences are undeniably striking.[18]

The test case is provided by those paintings that reduce phenomena that are perceptible only from a distance—very large objects, or objects that cannot be seen in their entirety from close up, such as mountains or cities—to the dimensions of things near at hand and capable of being taken in at a single glance. By being grasped as nearby objects, they are not so much depicted as symbolically intimated. That this was not necessarily the sign of second-rate craftsmanship but could, at least to an extent, be the result of methodical deliberation, may be inferred from a remark in Cennino Cennini's "libro dell'arte."[19] The painter who wants to represent a mountain is advised to place a rock on his drawing table and to depict it accurately in every detail. As simple as the instruction may sound, it aptly conveys the thinking of the time: Only things that are nearby are representable, because only they can be sensuously experienced as a whole, being both visible *and* graspable. For all their individual differences, many of the mountains in the planimetric pictorial arts of the late Middle Ages—whether in Giotto, in Simone Martini, or in less significant painters of the Trecento—look like enlarged and stylized rocks. Much the same can be said of representations of the city. It, too, is a macro-phenomenon that can only be transformed into a representable, clearly visible whole through recourse to techniques of abbreviation or *pars pro toto*.

Whereas the macro-phenomena of mountains and cities lose their proportions through the process of abbreviation, which turns them into palpable things, as it were, thereby also forfeiting what, to modern eyes, would seem to be their proper function, that of disclosing an atmosphere in which milieu and situation are able to unfold, the same gaze has the opposite effect when directed at an individual, graspable thing. From Frederick II's book on falconry, for example, to the herbariums of Manfredus de Monte Imperiali,[20] the microscopically exact study of nature sets out to capture the *individuality* of small, palpable objects. As Otto Pächt has shown, however, such attention to detail serves predominantly empirical and natural-historical purposes.[21] It leads neither directly nor indirectly to a painterly, relational spatialization of individual things in a uniform landscape, still less to a modern aesthetic view of the natural world. In short, landscape is not yet an optical field *sui generis*. Even in Giotto, for instance in the *Dream of Joachim* in the Arena chapel in Padua, one can still see that, despite more attention being paid to the depiction of the milieu, accurately and recognizably represented plants remain particular, individual objects rather than parts of a natural locale. Here, too, we find an accumulation of things that, whether near or far, are all reproduced in the same close-up view, without metrical proportion in relation to their milieu and devoid of atmospheric nuance.

Was there such a thing as landscape per se, and, if so, what was understood by that? One could answer the question in summary, if also overly schematic, fashion by setting out from a strict art-historical classification of genres. Landscape painting, seen in this way, would be an autonomous domain in which landscape, rather than functioning simply as a backdrop, is shown as a continuum that connects foreground and background and is represented for its own sake, that is, ideally in the absence of human figures and action. From this viewpoint, landscape cannot be said to have existed until well into the sixteenth century.[22] A cursory glace at the history of ideas can confirm and document that the word, the phenomenon, and their significance entered into different, specific constellations over time. In German, the word "landscape" (*Landschaft*) has existed for around a thousand years, although it initially had a political and geographical meaning: "In Old High German it means a province or region, and is more or less identical to *regio* in Latin."[23] In a ninth-century translation of the gospel text of Matthew 3, 4, for example, the passage "omnis regio circa

Jordanem" is rendered: "all the landscape around Jordan" (*al thiu lantscaf umbi Jordanem*); but only since the Renaissance is the concept likewise used for the artistic representation of a region, and thus extended to the content and depiction of the landscape. In 1518 in Basel, there is a reference, in a set of instructions on making an altarpiece, to "the landscape gold- or silver-plated and glazed." In 1521 we find the word "landscape painter" being applied to Joachim Patinier in Dürer's diary of his journey to Italy.[24] The Italian word *paese* seems to have come into use around the same time as a term for painted or drawn landscape, not just for (political) territory. Leonardo da Vinci, for instance, sees only "tristissimi paesi" in the work of Sandro Botticelli, who is criticized for paying insufficient attention to the study of landscape. Botticelli, according to Leonardo, was of the erroneous opinion that "by merely throwing a sponge soaked in a variety of colors at a wall there would be left on the wall a stain in which could be seen a beautiful landscape."[25]

The geographical meaning of *regio*, or the cartographical meaning that understood landscape in the sense of a political territory, continued to exist for a long time alongside this theoretically ill-defined term for an artistic genre. It was not until the Romantic period that an emotionally charged concept of landscape, strongly determined by freedom from purpose, was finally established, such as is still predominantly in use today.[26] It would nonetheless be wrong to conclude, conversely, that nature did not exist as an aesthetically experienced phenomenon prior to the emergence of an "aesthetic landscape."[27] The ancient pastorals or the biblical verses on Paradise contradict this view, as do poetic depictions of the "locus amoenus."[28] For instance, in canto 28 of the *Purgatorio* in Dante's *Divine Comedy*, or in certain passages of the *Carmina Burana* (c. 1230), such as the following:

Murmurs of a gentle breeze
blew up from the meridian;
the place was gay with greenery
from emerald to viridian:
somewhere, hidden in the grass,
a little stream went splashing,
chatting merrily to itself,
now dithering, now dashing.[29]

Such sensitive and detailed descriptions may be rhetorical *topoi* that conjure up the image of an idyll that is painted, not for its own sake, but in order to provide the framework for a mythological scenario in which—as in the above-cited excerpt from *Carmina Burana*—Phyllis and Flora are free to pursue their amorous fantasies. A sense of breadth and depth, which might have infused the intimacy of the grassy seat with the atmosphere of landscape, may also be lacking; for all that, the depictions are undoubtedly aesthetic.

The situation is hardly any different in painting. With the exception of a few examples motivated by considerations of content—Giotto's *Miracle of the Spring* from the St. Francis Cycle in the Upper Church in Assisi, for example, in which the humorous bisection of a mule allows us to imagine the scene as a detail from a larger contiguous landscape—landscape space is confined to a delimited *space*, such as the *locus amoenus*, or is overwhelmingly determined in functional terms, as is the case in monumental painting. One need only think of the two earliest large-format secular frescoes to have been preserved intact, those by Duccio and Simone Martini in the Sala del Mappamondo of the Palazzo Pubblico in Siena.

The first, uncovered in 1977 and dated to 1314, is located directly below Simone's painting. According to recent scholarship, it is to be regarded as a "ritratto topografico."[30] It shows the surrender of the Castle of Giuncarico to Siena in March 1314, and, like other contemporary examples such as Duccio's *The Temptation of Christ* (Frick Collection), it can only be adequately understood from a particular interpretative viewpoint. The disproportion between the near life-size human figures and the castle in the fresco is especially striking. Despite a painstaking attention to detail in many parts and a treatment of light that, at first glance, gives the impression of consistency, there is no uniform scale. Bellosi therefore refers to "due vocaboli separati di una stessa storia"; rather than speaking of a separation, it would be more meaningful to speak of a mixture in which reality and allegory are optically united in an *allegoreality*,[31] a phenomenon also to be found in Ambrogio Lorenzetti. There can be no question here of landscape, in which the milieu and figures vary, according to the parameters of proximity and distance, in relation to a horizon that sets the scale.

The case is more complicated when it comes to Simone Martini's fresco, which depicts, with a hitherto unprecedented monumentality, the Sienesian commander Guidoriccio da Fogliano in front of the besieged town of Montemassi. The fresco was painted in 1330–1331, measures approximately ten meters in length and three and a half meters in height, and is likewise to be found in the so-called Sala del Mappamondo in the Palazzo Pubblico in Siena. Of the four mural paintings originally commissioned by the council of Siena to document its important conquests, Simone's fresco of the siege of Montemassi is the only one to have survived. Until the uncovering of Duccio's Giuncarico picture, the opinion of Uta Feldges-Henning, according to which Simone's fresco was a prototype in the history

Figure 11.1
Simone Martini (1284–1344), *Equestrian Portrait of Guidoriccio da Fogliano*, 1328–1330. Fresco, Palazzo Pubblico, Sala del Mappamondo, Siena, Italy.

Figure 11.2
Ambrogio Lorenzetti (c. 1290–c. 1348), *Effects of Good Government in the City and Countryside* (right side), 1338–1339. Fresco, Palazzo Pubblico, Sala dei Nove, Siena, Italy.

Figure 11.3
Duccio di Buoninsegna (c. 1255–1319), *Altarpiece—Maestà* (The Temptation of Christ on the Mountain), 1308–1311. Tempera on poplar panel. The Frick Collection, New York, USA.

of the Italian city-states that registered the political intention to represent the city's dominions within the council chamber, could still claim a measure of plausibility. To judge by the historical implications of the 1977 discovery, however, the representations would seem also, or perhaps in the first place, to have the status of *legal titles*, comparable to deeds of property. Indeed, according to Max Seidel they document a political conflict that can be identified quite precisely: the conflict between the legal claim to dominion asserted by the city over the countryside, the *contado*, on the one hand, and the rights of ownership enjoyed by the feudal aristocracy, on the other, which rested on imperial privileges.[32]

In terms of the content, what we see is the representation of a political territory, more precisely, the fortress of Montemassi conquered by the commander Guidoriccio. One can scarcely speak of landscape here, notwithstanding the enormous dimensions of the painting, above all the lateral extension of the terrain, which the movement indicated by the profile of rider and steed only accentuates. What is new in this particular case is that we know which locale is being represented. If the contemporary source of the chronicler Agnolo di Tura del Grasso is to be believed, a kind of topographical portrait seems to have been intended. It is stated there that the Nine of Siena commissioned Master Simone to paint Montemassi and Sassoforte in the Palazzo "a l'esemplo come erano"—literally, "following the example of how they were."[33] There is evidence that a year after completing the Montemassi fresco (1331), Simone Martini traveled to the region of Maremme, to Arcidosso, Castel del Piano, and Scanzano, whose forts he subsequently painted in the Palazzo Pubblico. For all that, the term *l'esemplo* is not clear enough to ascertain beyond all doubt that Simone Martini was sent to inspect the forts in his capacity as a *painter*, just as it is anything but certain that the sentence cited above is meant to designate the direct imitation of external appearances. *A l'esemplo* could simply mean that a convincing, that is, "exemplary" model of the conquered city was required. Presumably the city did not escape visible injury while under siege, particularly when one considers that an enormous catapult can be seen in the fort[34] lying opposite Montemassi, painted in the colors of Siena, which no doubt could and did cause a great deal of damage.

To put it precisely: The beleaguered city, the Sienese encampment with its strategic fort, and the victorious commander Guidoriccio constituted the painting's real representational object. Perhaps the profile of the terrain even played a certain role. Signs of a new conception concerned, not least, with reproducing a particular geographical formation are the "bisected" mountains at the margins of the picture, but also the tips of the standards and pennants of a further encampment to be seen *behind* the mountains, as well as the paling fence crossed by the lower border of the picture. All these indicate that the terrain does not just possess—or is not just meant to possess—lateral extension, but also spatial depth. Yet despite a vague similarity with the real form of the landscape,[35] any experience of distance is contradicted, in the overall impression, by the linear schematism of the craggy contour, uniformly rising toward the right-hand side of the picture, as well as by the disproportion between mountains, encampment, and commander. The horizon is so close as to seem within reach; what is more, it is not a virtual border that could be pushed back, but is identical with the contour of the terrain itself. The deepening of space is not a categorical feature, and hence one that precedes and foregrounds everything in the picture, including the hills, but is staged as an extended locality, a local extension.

A veritable paradigm change is heralded by the works of another Sienese painter, Ambrogio Lorenzetti, to whom I referred at the start of this essay. There are only two places where this can still be verified: first, in the partially destroyed frescos of the San Francesco monastery in Siena, which, as the literary account of Lorenzo Ghiberti confirms, depict a thunderstorm or burst of rain, atmospheric phenomena which essentially pertain to natural landscape;[36] and second, in the frescoes of Good and Bad Government in the Sala dei Nove (or the Sala della Pace) in the Palazzo Pubblico in Siena.

In their characteristic amalgam of allegorical statement and "realistic" attention to detail,[37] these latter frescoes are likewise to be reckoned to the aforementioned conceptual figure of "allegoreality" much in vogue at the time. Yet although the guiding intention of the entire ensemble may be allegorical,[38] the representation of the effects of good government on the city and the *contado* differs significantly from the earlier examples in terms of its painterly imagination. In this instance, Burckhardt's phrase "all foreground without distance" no longer holds unreservedly true, despite the fact that the conditions for landscape painting postulated at the beginning of this essay, particularly those of perspective, are by no means satisfied.

Before examining the "landscape" of the Buon Governo more closely, it is necessary to clarify the role played by the allegorical figure of Securitas, since it seems at first glance to discredit any claim to modernity raised by the panorama. In contrast to the central image, which is unmistakably staged as an allegorical program through the differences in scale of the figures alone, the winged allegorical figures Securitas and Timor in the side walls, depicting the effects of good and bad government, soar above the sphere of earthly affairs. With the help of scrolled texts, they present the principal themes of what is happening in the scenes below. That of

Securitas announces that "everyone can journey freely and without fear and till his field so long as the commune has this lady as its ruler, because she wards off evil-doers." She is thus the personification of the authority entrusted with protecting *utilitas*, and hence the benefits to the community arising from rural or agricultural labor. Securitas accordingly makes the *contado* her domain, her possession, her political territory. But Securitas is also the patron saint of travelers, and thus of a kind of relationship with the countryside which sanctions (free) movement instead of mere use. In his description of the fresco in the Sala della Pace, Bernadino of Siena even claimed to have seen men bathing.[39] A dynamic element, travel, and with it the idea of breadth and distance, has thus crept almost unnoticed into the representation of a particular and delimited region.

There is a remarkable correspondence here to the material and phenomenal presence of Lorenzetti's innovative picture. The fresco on the wall with the "effeti" of good government—that on the opposite wall showing bad government and its consequences crams the allegory *and* the effects of bad government onto a single wall, and so fails to overwhelm the eye in the same way—is so big that it cannot be surveyed in its entirety by a stationary viewer; one has to walk up and down it not just to inspect the details, but to get a sense of its breadth as well. Even if this effect was not consciously planned, it is nonetheless far more in keeping with the *corporeal* experience of a real landscape space than any *locus amoenus*, precisely because its actual extension on the wall plausibly models a situation in which the hand–eye field is surpassed. In addition, there are several details of the internal composition of the *contado* that corroborate the assumption of a conscious intention on Lorenzetti's part.

In this panoramic view of city and country, there emerges an extraordinarily detailed and broad depiction of disparate natural milieus that are not exhausted in the additive concatenation of individual sections of scenery. The initial impression is instead that of a spatial continuum in which foreground and background are no less smoothly interconnected than the adjacent urban and rural milieus. The forms of the mountains or hills differ markedly from their Byzantine-influenced counterparts in Duccio or from Giotto's magnified rocks.[40] The jagged, sharp-edged, bare, and sheer mountain forms of yesteryear have made way for gently undulating hills and vales, in parts stripped of vegetation, in parts lush with pasturage— almost ideal prototypes for Tuscan tourism brochures. It would nonetheless be inappropriate to speak of an untimely naturalism. The perspective on the farms is not entirely consistent, while the trees are often too large in relation to their surroundings, the hills all too monotonous.

Something else is decisive when it comes to judging the painting's novelty. The fresco is split roughly in the middle by a city wall, which is shown in considerably foreshortened perspective. On the left, we are afforded a glimpse into the densely built, bustling city, while on the right, the panorama of the *contado* offers itself to the gaze. Closer inspection reveals that the masterfully foreshortened city wall does not just have a symbolic and thematic function, but serves also to separate two different kinds of perspective. The city is seen from quite low down, as one can tell from the fact that the rooftops are higher in the foreground; the *contado*, by contrast, appears in a kind of bird's-eye perspective, optically supported by the road, which makes a steep descent right behind the city gate. As John White has convincingly argued,[41] the effect is quite intentional, although the primary aim is not to ensure the strict separation of city and country; the wall would be simply too decorative for such a purpose. Rather, the fresco is fitted out with a perspective that is all its own and whose point of departure lies in the town center—a perspective with lateral extension, so to speak. Seen from the piazza with its disproportionately large dancers, there is a diminution in scale not just of the figures toward the city gate, but also, and still more evidently, of the figures and animals located toward the right-hand edge of the picture, in the *contado*; the ground level increasingly sinks away, until things can barely be identified and seem to disappear behind the frame. The minor inconsistencies do nothing to detract from the optical coherence, which encompasses and integrates both halves of the picture.

The distribution and direction of light in the fresco provides further visual confirmation of this. Light and shadow—brightly lit and dark sections of the houses, for instance—are generated by a light immanent to the picture, which decreases in intensity as its distance from the town center increases. On the other hand, the perception of depth evoked by the hilly landscape seems more indebted to actual visual experience than to any perspective of meaning immanent to the picture, even though the landscape is situated at the top of the painting. Whereas the hills in the foreground are covered with vegetation and feature surfaces of an intense brown and brownish green, the growth further away (or rather, further to the top) becomes ever more scanty and the coloration correspondingly brighter, interspersed only here and there with trees and bushes. An illogical but for that reason all the more emphatic sign of an intentional effect of distance is provided by an abbreviated and captioned representation of the harbor town of Talamone, which is shown *behind* a comparatively high mountain in the middle of the right-hand third of the picture, thereby perhaps attesting to the fact that Talamone cannot be seen even from the most elevated point in Siena.

Notwithstanding all the reservations one could have in relation to the horizon, for instance, which lies far too high up, one can thus recognize, in the representation of the *contado*, a turn of the painterly imagination away from the immediate hand–eye field and toward a standpoint that can only be imagined or adopted under particular conditions of perception. Such conditions, however, presuppose a new attitude to landscape, one most vividly portrayed in Francesco Petrarch's account of his epochal ascent—whether real or fictional[42]—of Mont Vedoux. This attitude, reduced to the essential aspects of Petrarch's celebrated account, will be summarized by way of conclusion.

IV

In a letter to Francesco Dionigi in Paris, dated April 26, 1336, Petrarch reports on his ascent of Mont Vedoux in Provence, from which he claims to have just returned. He sets out his motives at the beginning of the letter: "Today, led solely by a desire to view the great heights of it, I climbed the highest mountain of the region which is appropriately called Windy Mountain."[43] The neuralgic points that mark the event in its peculiarity are to be found already in the opening lines: first, the "cupiditas videndi," the desire to see, which at the time was still subordinated to the sin of *curiositas*;[44] second, and more important for our argument, the object of such desire, the remarkable height of the place to be visited, "insignem loci altitudinem." The latter is unprecendented, for the following reasons: Mountains, like the sea, were places of dread owing to the dangers thought to lie in wait there for the traveler.[45] Moreover, height as such had to a certain extent been taboo since antiquity, insofar as it was associated with the presumptuous wish to delve into the "arcana naturae" and the "arcana coeli" and to view the world from above.[46] Petrarch's first break with tradition thus lies in his curiosity to see the unusual height of the mountain with his own eyes, a break that he himself will later experience as painful. To justify the undertaking, he notes that on the previous day, he had read in Livy's *History of Rome*—by chance, naturally—about Philip of Macedon's mountain-climbing exploits, adding that he, being a young man, should be allowed to do what no one begrudges an elderly king. For all his efforts at self-legitimation, however, Petrarch is quite aware of his forbidden curiosity. Having justified his longing to reach the summit, during the ascent, as a goal of human pilgrimage, he finally arrives at his destination:

First of all, moved by a certain unaccustomed quality of the air and by the unrestricted spectacle, I stood there as in a trance. I looked back. Clouds were beneath me. And suddenly what I had heard and read about Athos and Olympos became less incredible to me when I looked out from this mountain of lesser fame.[47]

No sooner has Petrarch reached the summit of the real mountain than he starts to demythologize. Olympos and Athos are no longer holy mountains, unapproachable and divine; they have nothing more to offer than the Windy Mountain. He feels literally on top of the world, looks back over the course of his life so far and is recalled only gradually to the here and now. He sees the mountains, the gulf of Marseilles and the Rhône lying before him, and slowly comes to his senses: "While I was admiring such things, at times thinking about earthly things and at times, following the example of my body, raising my mind to loftier things, it occurred to me to look into the *Book of Confessions* of Saint Augustine."[48] The perusal of his favorite author becomes a humbling experience when he chances upon the following passage: "*And they go to admire the summits of mountains and the vast billows of the sea and the broadest rivers and the expanses of the ocean and the revolutions of the stars and they overlook themselves.*"[49] Petrarch once again feels dazed, but this time because Augustine has opened his eyes to his all too earthly curiosity. He has now seen enough of the mountain, and turns his inner eye upon himself as he makes his way back down to the plain. Whereas just moments before, in his euphoria at his commanding view, the Alps had "seemed very close to me although separated by a great distance,"[50] during the descent he constantly turns around to gaze up at the summit, which now strikes him as "scarcely a cubit high in comparison with [the] loftiness of human meditation."[51]

Despite Petrarch's rueful introspection and his retrospective diminution of the mighty mountain to a tiny corporeal unit of measurement, his climb, after so innocuous a beginning, has become an irreversible frontier crossing. The view from on high can no longer be erased, the violation of the taboo only mitigated through confession. While the concern for salvation is once again given the last word over curiosity, the astonishment and pleasure felt by Petrarch at the sight of nature are so overwhelming as to compel him to commit the experience to paper on the evening of the same day. The *contemplatio coeli*—actually a theoretical vision—with which Petrarch had justified his ascent has become a sensuous, indeed aesthetic view of nature, or at least the preparation for such a view. Petrarch has not just cast his gaze upon the directly graspable things of nature, upon what is discrete and close to hand. Karlheinz Stierle goes so far as to recognize in Petrarch's account "the essence of the new aesthetic experience of a landscape opened to a far-off horizon and losing itself in the distance. The new aesthetic experience is an experience of the horizontal depth of space, which stands opposed to the vertical depth of space."[52] What is true of the imaginative conquest of the "horizontal depth in space" in the epistolary medium in Petrarch is likewise true, albeit with a slight time lag, in the medium of painting. Through the geometrical means of perspective, landscape opened up to a distant horizon finally becomes a genre of painting in its own right—at times, notably in the eighteenth and nineteenth centuries, even the most important, because the most sublime and sacral, form in which nature can appear. The historical reasons for this are contained *in nuce* in Petrarch's mountain-climbing expedition, which proved influential in two respects: It removed the taboo from high-altitude regions previously held to be sacred, while at the same time laying the foundation stone for a resacralization of the distant zones of landscape, since "the distant zone of landscape conveys something of the privileged status which the most high has always enjoyed in the two-dimensionality of sacred images."[53] In other words, and put simply, landscape in the modern sense of the term only arises when and where the perception and presentation of empirical distance are concretized in the horizon. And only from this point can Walter Benjamin's definition of the aura, as "the unique appearance of a distance, however close it may be," be understood as the aesthetic remythologization of an appearance that has spatialized the numinous.

V

The recapitulation of the central sentences in Petrarch's literary depiction of his ascent of Mont Vedoux was intended to show the break that separates the old view of the world or landscape from the new. The view from above, which distances itself from the particular things of nearby nature, is essential to this depiction. By choosing an elevated standpoint, Petrarch perceives nature in its expansiveness and looks out into a concrete distance dotted with nameable and individual places. This new way of seeing is as foreign to that of Gottfried of Strasbourg, who allows his Tristan to climb a mountain only to describe the scene in the most arid, general, and formulaic of terms, as it is to that of Nicholas of Cusa, for whom the view from the top of a tower provides an appropriate locale for philosophical speculation solely in a metaphorical sense. It would appear that Lorezetti's painted landscape, which stands before our eyes in comparable isolation to Petrarch's account, was seen by painters for almost a century afterward as an inimitable *coup d'oeil*. The view from above with which Petrarch and

Lorenzetti imagined the breadth and distance of landscape is epochal, in the literal sense of the term: The field that bound together hand and eye is henceforth irrevocably *di-vided*, viewed apart. Now the eye abstracts from things, astounded by the proximity of remote phenomena and by the relativity of distance; it gains an overview. In the resulting "flight" of space and place, lands and landscapes that had previously been conceived topocentrically, so to speak, are seen as excerpts—and thereby metaphors—of the world. The early modern landscape, and the aesthetic encounter with place that it may be said to embody, thus arises through a division into a functional landscape of the hand and an aesthetic landscape of the eye, or, put differently, through the inversion of medieval landscape: as "all distance without foreground."

Notes

1. J. Burckhardt, *The Civilization of the Renaissance in Italy*, trans. S. G. C. Middlemore and I. Gordon (New York: American Library, 1960), p. 219. Translation modified and emphasis added.

2. E. Panofsky, *Perspective as Symbolic Form*, trans. C. Wood (New York: Zone Books, 1991).

3. A. Koschorke, *Die Geschichte des Horizonts. Grenze und Grenzüberschreitung in literarischen Landschaftsbilder* (Frankfurt am Main, Suhrkamp, 1990), p. 23.

4. Ibid., p. 7: "The horizon . . . is not an object within the empirical realm that can be treated aesthetically in various ways, but a line in relation to which the empirical order first constitutes itself. It is not integrated into the field of perception, but organizes that field. Neither factually given, in the strict sense of the term, nor invisible, it marks the border and the transition by means of which a totality of experiences is defined and simultaneously referred to its determinate negation, to the fact that it could potentially exist otherwise or not exist at all."

5. A. Borst, *Lebensformen des Mittelalters* (Frankfurt am Main: Ullstein, 1979), pp. 144–145.

6. J. Delumeau, *Angst im Abendland*, vol. 1 (Reinbek bei Hamburg: Rowohlt, 1965), pp. 63 ff.

7. A. Gurevich, *Categories of Medieval Culture*, trans. G. L. Campbell (London: Routledge & Kegan Paul, 1985), pp. 25–39.

8. See, among others, P. Dinzelbacher and H. Kleinschmidt, "Seelenbrücke und Brückenbau im mittelalterlichen England," *Numen* 31 (1984): 242–287; P. Dinzelbacher, *Mittelalterliche Visionsliteratur. Eine Anthologie* (Darmstadt: Wiss. Buchges, 1989), p. 41.

9. A. Gurevich, *Medieval Popular Culture*, trans. J. Bak and P. Hollingsworth (Cambridge: Cambridge University Press, 1988), p. 132. Translation modified.

10. Gerhardt, "Gab es im Mittelalter Fabelwesen?" *Wirkendes Wort* 38 (1988): 159.

11. John de Plano Carpini, *Kunde von den Mongolen, 1245–1247*, trans. F. Schmieder (Sigmaringen: Thorbecke Verlag, 1997).

12. Marco Polo, *The Travels of Marco Polo*, trans. T. Waugh (London: Sidgwick & Jackson, 1984).

13. Oderico da Pordenone, *Die Reise des seligen Odorich von Pordenone nach Indien und China* (1314/18–1330), trans. F. Reichert (Heidelberg: Manutius-Verlag, 1987).

14. F. Reichert, "Einleitung," in *Die Reise*, p. 15.

15. *Von seltsamen Ländern und wunderlichen Völkern. Ein Reisebuch von 1356*, ed. and trans. G. Grümmer (Leipzig: Brockhaus, 1986).

16. Ibid., pp. 13–14.

17. A. Maier, "Das Problem der 'species sensibiles in medio' und die neue Naturphilosophie des 14. Jahrhunderts," in A. Maier, *Ausgehendes Mittelalter: Gesammelte Aufsätze zur Geistesgeschichte des 14. Jahrhunderts*, vol. 2 (Rome: Edizioni di storia e letteratura, 1967), pp. 149ff.

18. Regarding the fact that fine artists of the Trecento were by no means innocent of theory, see J. Larner, "The Artist and the Intellectuals in Fourteenth Century Italy," *History* 54, no. 180 (1969): 13ff.

19. Cennino Cennini, *Das Cennino Cennini Handbüchlein der Kunst*, ed. W. Verkade (Strasbourg: Heitz, 1916). M. J. Friedländer draws attention to this passage in his *Essays über die Landschaftsmalerei und andere Bildgattungen* (Den Haag: Stols, Cassirer, 1947), pp. 9–23.

20. *Liber de herbis et plantis* (Salerno: c. 1350).

21. O. Pächt, "Early Italian Nature Studies and the Early Calendar Landscape," *Journal of the Warburg and Courtauld Institutes* 13 (1950): 13ff. In this respect, too, there are astonishing similarities to questions and tendencies in contemporary philosophy, including the philosophy of Ockham, whom K. Flasch characterizes as a "naive realist." K. Flasch, *Das philosophische Denken im Mittelalter von Augustin bis Macchiavelli* (Stuttgart: Reclam, 1986), p. 454.

22. R. Fechner, *Natur als Landschaft. Zur Entstehung der ästhetischen Landschaft* (Frankfurt am Main: Lang, 1986); J. Ritter, "Landschaft. Zur Funktion des Ästhetischen in der modernen Gesellschaft," in *Subjektivität. Sechs Aufsätze* (Frankfurt am Main: Suhrkamp, 1974), pp. 141ff.

23. This and the following quotations are to be found in C. Troll, "Die geographische Landschaft und ihre Erforschung," in *Studium Generale* 3 (1950): 163–164; R. Grünter, "Landschaft. Bemerkungen zur Wort- und Bedeutungsgeschichte," in *Landschaft und Raum in der Erzählkunst*, ed. A. Ritter (Darmstadt: Wissenschaftliche Buchgesellschaft, 1975), pp. 192ff.

24. A. Dürer, *Schriften, Tagebücher, Briefe*, ed. M. Steck (Stuttgart: Kohlhammer, 1961), p. 73.

25. M. Kemp, ed., *Leonardo on Painting* (New Haven: Yale University Press, 2001), p. 201.

26. See the anthology of W. Busch, *Landschaftsmalerei* (Berlin: Reimer,1997).

27. In this sense, J. Ritter's influential thesis (in "Landschaft. Zur Funktion des Ästhetischen in der modernen Gesellschaft," pp. 150–151) is to be qualified as "aestheticist." For Ritter, landscape is "nature which is aesthetically present when viewed by a sensitive and receptive observer. The fields which fringe the city, the river as 'border,' 'trade route' and 'problem for bridge-builders,' the mountains and steppes of shepherds and caravans (or oil prospectors)—none of these are as such already 'landscape.' They first become this when man turns toward them with no practical goal in mind, in the 'free' pleasure of contemplation, in order to be himself in nature."

28. See, among others, E. R. Curtius, "Rhetorische Naturschilderung im Mittelalter," in *Landschaft und Raum in der Erzählkunst*, ed. A. Ritter (Darmstadt: Wissenschaftliche Buchgesellschaft, 1975), pp. 70ff.

29. *Selections from the Carmina Burana*, trans. D. Parlett (Harmondsworth: Penguin, 1986), p. 98.

30. M. Seidel, "'Castrum pingatur in palatio.' 1. Ricerche storiche e iconografiche sui castelli dipinti nel Palazzo Pubblico di Siena," *Prospettiva* 28 (1982): 17ff.; L. Bellosi, "'Castrum pingatur in palatio.' 2. Duccio e Simone Martini pittori di castelli senesi 'a l'esemplo come erano,'" *Prospettiva* 28 (1982): 41ff.

31. The concept is to be found in P. Czerwinski, "Per visibilia ad invisibilia: Texte und Bilder vor dem Zeitalter von Kunst und Literatur," *Internationales Archiv für Sozialgeschichte der deutschen Literatur* 25 (2000): 1ff.

32. M. Seidel, "Castrum pingatur in palatio."

33. U. Feldges-Henning, *Landschaft als topographisches Porträt. Der Wiederbeginn der europäischen Landschaftsmalerei in Siena* (Bern: Benteli,1980), p. 30, incautiously translates "*l'esemplo come erano*" as "imitation as they were."

34. This fort was apparently made of wood and was constructed especially for the siege.

35. U. Feldges-Henning reproduces a photograph alongside the fresco to demonstrate this.

36. M. Seidel, "Wiedergefundene Fragmente eines Hauptwerks von Ambrogio Lorenzetti," *Pantheon* 36 (1978): 119ff.

37. See H. Belting, "Das Bild als Text. Wandmalerei und Literatur im Zeitalter Dantes," in *Malerei und Stadtkultur in der Dantezeit. Die Argumentation der Bilder*, ed. H. Belting and D. Blume (Munich: Hirmer, 1989), pp. 23ff.

38. The scholarship on this is copious, but it cannot be discussed in the present context, and such a discussion is, in any case, not needed.

39. Cited in I. Origo, *Der Heilige der Toskana. Leben und Zeit des Bernadino von Siena* (Munich: Beck, 1989), pp. 130ff.

40. On this point I must disagree with M. Baxandall, for whom precisely the form of the mountains betrays a backward-looking kind of historicism. M. Baxandall, "Kunst, Gesellschaft, und das Bougier-Prinzip," *Freibeuter* 33 (1987): 23.

41. J. White, *The Birth and Rebirth of Pictorial Space* (London: Faber & Faber, 1972), pp. 93ff.

42. In W. Busch, ed., *Landschaftsmalerei* (see n. 25 above), Petrarch's account functions as the sole medieval source, pp. 58ff.

43. F. Petrarca, *Rerum familiarium I–VIII*, trans. A. Bernado (Albany, NY: SUNY Press, 1975), p. 172.

44. See the still important interpretation of H. Blumenberg, *Der Prozess der theoretischen Neugierde* (Frankfurt am Main: Suhrkamp, 1973), pp. 142ff.

45. J. Delumeau, *Angst im Abendland*; A. Borst, "Alpine Mentalität und europäischer Horizont im Mittelalter," in A. Borst, *Barbaren, Ketzer, und Artisten. Welten des Mittelalters* (Munich: Piper, 1988), pp. 471ff.; J. Wozniakowski, *Die Wildnis. Zur Deutungsgechichte des Berges in der europäischen Neuzeit* (Frankfurt am Main: Suhrkamp, 1987), pp. 71ff.

46. C. Ginzburg, "Hoch und niedrig. Erkenntnisverbote im 16. und 17. Jahrhundert," *Freibeuter* 10 (1981): 9 ff.

47. Petrarca, *Rerum familiarium I–VIII*, pp. 175–176.

48. Ibid., pp. 177–178.

49. Ibid., p. 178.

50. Ibid., p. 176 ("iuxta michi vise sunt, cum tamen mango distent intervallo").

51. Ibid., p. 179.

52. K. Stierle, *Petrarcas Landschaft. Zur Geschichte ästhetischer Landschaftserfahrung* (Krefeld: Scherpe, 1979), p. 26.

53. A. Koschorke, *Die Geschichte des Horizonts*, p. 53. Koschorke goes on to observe that "distance and sky, which converge in the horizon, [take up] the same place in the paintings which, in the fourteenth century, was almost always occupied by the gold foundation or an illuminated color foundation." The gold foundation, which can be understood as the imageless placeholder of transcendence and immateriality in the image, is thus replaced by phenomena from the world of appearances.

12   Landscapes of Class in Contemporary Chinese Film: From *Yellow Earth* to *Still Life*

Stephanie Hemelryk Donald

Few would dispute the connection between the delineation of modernity at the turn of the century and the development of the modern metropolis.
—Frisby (2001), p. 159

In David Frisby's work on cityscapes of modernity, he asserts the theme of twentieth-century European sociology, that the modern is an urban phenomenon, and that the landscape of modernity is therefore a cityscape. Frisby, and most others, were looking at European and American cities for their inspiration. Now, at the end of the last century and in the present era, the development of Chinese modernity in the Reform period is the focus of the world's attention. This is not to say that modernity has not been underway in China for at least 150 years; rather, China's global visibility is now such that the frenzy of accelerated modernization is sometimes mistaken for a sudden onslaught of modernity per se. In this essay I will suggest that, while the urbanization of China is indeed the big story of China's physical infrastructure, nonetheless the slow burn of development has been having an impact on the Chinese landscape, rural and urban, for a very long time. The landscaping of China is partly about modernization, a little about modernity (depending on how liberal one is with that definition), but mostly about a longer narrative of continuous and traumatic pressure inflicted by the people on the motherland. The struggle between beauty and pragmatism is acknowledged in films about the poor, and manifested through the class aspirations of the new rich. It is then the signs of struggle that articulate the Chinese landscape as a work of destruction and reconstruction in constant progress.

Living in the Chinese Landscape: "We'll Just Keep Running"

In his expansive discussion of Chinese development and its impact on the human and physical environment, Peter Kessler recalls the many visitors to

China who have bemoaned the lack of landscape, recording only "a peasant, a field, a road, a village" as they travel by train across the northern
provinces.[1] Kessler's point is that Chinese history might also be thought
of as an endlessly repetitive story of power taken, lost, and resumed, but
with no sense of momentum or shift as the years and the regimes pass by.
His points are provocative, but nonetheless observant and evocative, as
understanding the physical and historical landscapes of China does indeed
require a specific way of looking and thinking about change and continuity. The reader of Kessler's book, the China scholar, or the visitor, must
come to grips with the temporal scale of Chinese history and, by extrapo-
lation, with the spatial nuance and sweep of Chinese land. Traveling by
train across the north and down the coastal provinces reveals "peasant,
field, road, village" and, one might also argue, "mega-city suburb, concrete
town, scrubland." Traveling further to the south one will encounter all of
the above but also (although perhaps not out of the train window) mountains with swirling mist at their foot, immediately recalling and verifying
water and ink (*shuimo*) landscape paintings that might in any other tradition be fanciful, but here are a more or less absolute rendering of place.
North or south, the landscape is not, however, unchanging, nor has it been
so in the past. As I hope to show in the following discussion, the landscape
of China has been shaped by its people, its politics, and its climatic conditions at a rate that is not necessarily commensurate with its historical
patterning, but which is nonetheless sensitive to movements within and
across such seasonal adjustments. One might summarize these in terms of
the regular fluctuations of dynastic power, the slow but profound emergence of modernity (an urban phenomenon from the 1860s through to the
present), and both the revolutionary and reform-era high-velocity shifts in
farming, industry, and urbanization. All these have continued over many
years, and some have had a direct impact on the spatial formation and re-
formation of the landscape over generations. The most obvious contemporary example is the high levels of urbanization since the 1980s. The growth
of towns is a direct outcome of Reform policy, supported by decentral-
ized planning initiatives that have actively encouraged provincial areas to
engage in high-density production and capitalization of their major asset,
people. The people, particularly rural people whose livelihood as farmers
continues to be comparatively poor, have responded in waves of urban
migration and return, causing population stress for both the new provincial cities and the metropolitan centers of Shanghai and Beijing. The "peasant, field, road, village" must increasingly be understood as extensions of
urban environments and ecosystems shattered by overfarming on the one

hand and a lack of year-round pastoral care on the other. The land is no longer enough.

Yet we should recall that this is not only a story of the last thirty years of reform management and economics. The environmental historian Mark Elvin has argued that governments in the old kingdoms that used to comprise the current geopolitical reality of China long made environmental impact a tool of influence and a rationale for harmony among people and the land. He quotes a gazetteer of the early nineteenth century writing of events of previous centuries in the far southwest: "They cut channels in the sides of hill and drew water from the springs. They constructed dikes and built dams to hold water. . . . Thus when the weather turned to drought, they had water to provide for irrigation. . . . All the wasteland among the forests was fully developed." He goes on to justify this in terms wider than agricultural survival:

The commandery of Lian used long ago to be described as a place of disease due to pestilential vapours, on account of its deep valleys and dense woods. The population was sparse, and the aethers of the Bright and Dark forces not healthy. . . . It was always overcast with rain, and there were floods in its streams and torrents. . . . At the present time, the forests are sparse and the torrents widened out. The light from the sky above shines down; the population is dense and every day more forests are opened up. . . . It is a long time since Lian and Lingshan were affected by disease due to pestilential vapors.[2]

Elvin's work traces a history of environmental change that is closely associated with legitimation of governance and order in the centralizing networks of power represented by imperial rule. Elvin's argument demonstrates that, in the circles of government at least, discourses of modernization were contesting those of belief and superstition. While the appreciation of landscape, management of the elements, and the cultivation of agricultural land were all necessary and easily demonstrable components of good government, they were also easily related to the Gods and to supernatural intervention. Thus, arguments over the sources of quality in an emerging "Chinese" geopolitical sphere could be thrashed out over land, landscape, and the "placing" of power.

The current rhetoric of harmonization, the "harmonious society" of the current Party state, is concerned to claim that the whole nation—rich and poor—can move forward together to solve the problems of change and modernization. Contemporary history does not claim that it has achieved improvements in land-use. Where Elvin's gazetteers welcomed the attention to shaping land for human habitation, now it is painfully obvious that intense human occupation is proving harmful to the Chinese landscape.

Social and economic harmonization is still given as the answer to all modern ills, however, and this anthropomorphic present and future is manifest in the fashion for lifestyle enclaves.[3] Spindly trees, brooks, and grassy golf courses are the centerpieces to these places of sanctuary for those seeking a lifestyle landscape. Yet even there, the clear-sighted are aware of the precariousness of the perfect place in a ruined ecology. In recent conversations in one such up-market development outside the Sichuanese city, Chengdu, residents commented that they had moved out of the city to get away from pollution, but did not think that they would ever have moved far enough for safety. They were determined to stay in China but were uncertain of just how far from the centers of human activity they would need to go. "We'll just keep running," said one woman somewhat ruefully.

Landscapes of Class

Those residents were self-identifying members of the new middle class. A small but influential sector of the population, they could afford to make choices, albeit constrained ones, to decide how far and where they might run away from the unmanaged effects of change.[4] Their choice reflects the degree to which social positioning affects relationships between people and landscape, particularly in the creation of micro-landscapes designed to mitigate the disasters of overpopulation and industrialization, and perhaps even to the extent of allowing one the luxury of "seeing" landscape at all. For many peasants in the same area, lifestyle developments entail the loss of their fruit farms, and cause enforced relocations to the city from which the new occupants are escaping. The power of class is evident in the spatial formations of change and mobility. Class is not a new word in Chinese politics, but it is a newly articulated notion[5] that allows the concept of "harmonious society" to hinge on the elaboration of the success of the middle-income (actually high–income, but the harmonious term *"zhong = middle"* is preferred) consumer and the wealthy to a wider population. The actual likelihood of that extension is doubtful in the immediate future, especially given the environmental problems of modernity, which hit the poorest hardest and first.

    The emergence of a class discourse in China is associated with two moments of Party history. The first, in 1949, was the victory of the CCP and the establishment of the People's Republic of China. At that point, what Apter and Saich[6] have called the "exegetical bonding" of identity to Maoist-Marxist-Leninist orderings of peasant, worker, landlord, and intellectual classes (to name a few in a more complex system) was set to be nationalized beyond the imaginations of the CCP strongholds of Yan'an (in Shaanxi) and the Party faithful in Shanghai and Jiangsu. The second iteration is much more recent, and has grown from the post 1978 Reform era (reforms, it should be noted, that were planned at least fifteen years earlier by Deng Xiaoping), and the appearance of new social stratifications, haves and have-nots, and—most recently—new structures of taste and feeling in people's approach to their priorities and lifestyle choices. *Class* is again speakable and semantically necessary, because it cannot be endlessly denied or written off as a revolutionary error when it is working its way through society with such bravado at the present time. Nor can it be completely understood as a top-down articulation of social or political management—although that is, of course, still part of the picture—but must be approached as a complex phenomenon stemming from Reform economics, personal wealth creation, and an awareness of global and domestic contingencies and conditions of life. Class is now apparent and observable, not solely as a political category based on the organization of production, but as a mode of being in a society newly oriented to money as the most important marker of success, and aspiration as a core value in everyday life.

The apparent ubiquity of the middle-class idea (*zhongchan jieji*) in China is, however, predominantly an urban phenomenon and is mostly associated with larger cities. This is not to say that rural and small-town folk do not have aspirations, nor that some of them do not succeed in achieving wealth and self-betterment, but that the prevailing trend is for urbanites to feel morally and financially superior to subprovincial and rural conationals. It has indeed been argued that the middle class is not a new grouping at all, but merely another descriptor for long-term high-level financial success and political privilege. In this account the Chinese version of the "new rich"—a categorization that was used to sum up the success of Asian capitalism in the early 1990s[7]—includes those with leadership ambitions in key sectors of government, the economy, and cultural provision. The scope of the category of the Chinese middle class is somewhat more porous than that, especially given that it is not merely the possibilities for conspicuous consumption[8] but also the taste for "quality" of life that characterizes the new urban so-called élites. They are indeed determinedly pursuing the tasteful consumption of cultural goods, but they are also articulating a desire to achieve the best possible lifestyle for themselves and their children according to quite varied levels of income, means, and social relations. So, class is something more than *origin* and *production*, and is very much associated with how people envisage their place in the national landscape, in both symbolic and actual terms.

The idea of "landscapes of class" pulls together the two themes of contemporary Chinese social change—environment and the stratification of a modern society. Social stratification is increasingly discussed in sociological literature but is also becoming important to debates on culture. The rural–urban divide remains the most remarked division, but there are increasing subtleties in the ways in which class is remarked. A recent piece on cinema characterized the "complicated and intriguing codes" of filming certain bodies as "classed" portraits,[9] while Chew has used the present phenomenon of class discourse to interrogate the sartorial slips between provincialism and style in the "global cultural hierarchy."[10] The relation between class and the environment remains relatively unexplored. In the remainder of this discussion I would like to suggest that two of the key texts of Reform-era cinema, Chen Kaige's *Huang Tudi (Yellow Earth)*, 1984, and Jia Zhangke's *Sanxia Haoren (Still Life*, literally *Good People of the Three Gorges)*, 2006, can be viewed as landscapes of class, book-ending the Reform era from the early 1980s to the present.[11] While the films actively focus on class differences, between soldier and peasant in *Yellow Earth*, and between impoverished migrant and successful entrepreneurs in *Still Life*, they do so in specific and significant landscapes. These spatial articulations of a shared idea of China illustrate the atemporal relation between historical seasons (revolution, reform, modernity) and the manipulation of the natural world, within which human mobility is symptomatic of both without claiming ascendancy on either. Meanwhile, China itself appears as an idea that is supported by the assertion of national, political power. In both films, Mao Zedong is a continuing immanence in the mountains, a presence behind the appropriation of rural hinterlands for infrastructure projects to support the urban drift, while also central to the dictum of maintaining certain iconic spots of "national landscape" in the visual lexicon of Chinese society and politics.

The two texts emanate from what have been seen as competing discourses of post-Mao cinema,[12] but are nonetheless and likewise linked across the seasons of film style by their regional choices of location, their concern with the contrast between privileged and nonprivileged perspectives on major social change, and their subtle reference to Mao's influence in historicizing China's landscapes to the cause of revolutionary, and now Reform, dynamics and development. It is also relevant that Jia has stated admiration for *Yellow Earth* as one of the few 1980s "fifth generation" titles that he appreciates.[13] These films are connected, then, by the sensibility of directors at certain moments in their artistic development, by the imaginary of Chinese modernity and the continuing influence of Mao, and by the topographical laylines of the major hinterlands of Chinese modern history.

Yellow Earth, a landmark film set in northern Shaanxi, was made by Chen and filmed by Zhang Yimou, both at the beginning of their now famous careers. A soldier visits a peasant community to listen to their songs, learn about their lives, and spread the word of revolution. It is the 1930s, and peasant hardship is extreme. The narrative enunciates this suffering by juxtaposing the warmth of human interaction with stark and barren landscape shots that visually overwhelm the protagonists and literally render futile their hopes for a better future. The film was noted at its release for its use of space and its relation of the apparent endlessness of the Shaanxi landscape to the timelessness of the peasant condition. A small family of a father and two children eke out a living on tough ground, which is hard at the best of times, frozen in winter, and often in drought. Their songs are of grief and toil, and the sound of their singing is harsh and aching, binding those that sing to the landscape, which echoes and fosters the timbre of their voices. Thus, the idea of "borrowing" these bitter songs and reappropriating them for optimistic lyrics on new China would require that the landscape itself is somehow changed, or made gentle. This, the film is sure, cannot happen.

In *Still Life*, the setting is contemporary. Jia is a filmmaker from Shanxi who has done a great deal to correct the need for films that essay the provincial urban landscape of small towns (*Unknown Pleasures*, *Platform*, and *Xiao Wu*), and the relatively modest but potentially divisive aspirations of their people.[14] In his most recent film (from 2006), *The World*, Jia follows a family of Shanxi migrants into a Beijing theme park, and narrates the painful contingencies of the underclass of migrants in the capital. The argument of that film is that, although migrants are utterly necessary to the everyday workings of Beijing's international, reform economy model, they have little or no access to either the "real world" or to the reality of a middle-income success story, and are more likely to die in an undercompensated industrial accident than to achieve the modern life for which they made the trek to the metropolis. In *Still Life*, Jia visits the classic landscapes of China's hinterland and makes them central to his narrative of China's modernization. Here, his key characters are again from Shanxi. One is a coal miner (San Ming—who also appears in minor roles as a character in *The World* and *Platform*), a quiet man whose reasonableness is apparent but whose quiet stoicism makes him a subject rather than an agent of the change around him. The other major character is a nurse (Shen Hong), also visiting the area from Shanxi to find her husband. Indeed both are coming south to find their spouses. San Ming is seeking his estranged wife, simply because he wants to see her and, especially, his daughter, after a sixteen-year absence. Hong wants to tell her husband, who has all but deserted her while making a fortune in construction and destruction in the Three Gorges Dam project, that she is leaving him for someone else and moving to Shanghai. Thus the narrative of the film is centered on movement between and across the key sites of Chinese history, development, and outlook. Between Shanxi, Sichuan, and the idea of Shanghai, *Still Life* traverses the scope of China. The film requires an understanding of the present as premised on the past, as much as the face of reform (Shanghai) is dependent on the ravages of development in China's West and on the movement of peoples from the northwest to populate (and indeed depopulate) that development.

The film's action is set in Sichuan in a small town, Fengjie, on the Yangtze. The town is being progressively flooded as the dam project moves forward. Many people in the town are sojourners, coming to work on the destruction sites. As a result the small town has become a minor hub of inner China cosmopolitanism, as people move through and learn about each other's origins in other parts of China's national landscape. The foreignness of the northern visitors is pointed out in a sequence when a landlord is initially unable to understand San Ming's dialect, and is reiterated by San Ming's own inadequacy in comprehending the daily realities of this somewhat chaotic site of transformation.

The film opens on a ferry, which has traveled on tributaries and thus down the Yangtze River to Fengjie. The first scene is one of Jia's signature long takes as the camera travels around the boat showing us the chatter and excitement of "ordinary people" as they travel for work, or to see the Gorges as they are depicted in the images and poems of Chinese culture—iconic symbols in the national imagination. These sights will of course soon be unrecognizably changed by the flooding project and become icons of modern developmental brutalism. Much of the old town of Fengjie is already underwater, but there are still levels of habitation in use, although also due for immersion, once the job of demolition is complete on each level. Above the rising waters, a new town has sprung up, although many of the original residents have already left or are leaving, seeking out new lives and means of livelihood in other provinces, Liaoning, Guangdong, or even Shanxi—where the little ferry has come from. In one poignant scene a young girl of sixteen years asks Shen Hong if they need maids where she comes from. Shen Hong does not answer the question directly, although by saying that she comes from Shanxi, she does in fact respond in the negative: Maids are only linked to the biggest cities and major domains of migration, namely, in the south and on the eastern seaboard. But, for a moment, we are reminded of the young girl, Cuiqiao, in *Yellow Earth*, fruitlessly asking the errant soldier if he will take her with him when he returns to base camp in the south. North to south, south to east, the girls seek to travel to catch up with contemporary China, but in both cases their mobility is held back by their class position. Even if the young Sichuanese does make it to Shanghai as a maid (*dagongmei*), she will be very fortunate to earn enough or to have the right kind of employers to take her much further up the ladder toward a middle-income existence. Cuiqiao does not even make it safely across the Yellow River.

Meanwhile, in Fengjie, older residents argue with local officials over compensation for their flooded homes, or with factory bosses over conditions of work. As are the lives of those who inhabit it, this landscape is precarious. The rugged beauty of the Kuimen (Kui Gate), the famous rounded hills that frame the river entry to Fengjie's part of the river, is still apparent, but it is scarred by the rising concrete of the new town in the foreground, and by the ugly bridges necessitated by the dam. As the night draws in and colored lights are turned on for the evening, a successful entrepreneur waves his arm toward the bridge and its garish lighting scheme, boasting to business colleagues that he has realized what originally was envisioned by Mao, the recapture of a national landscape for modernity.

The landscapes in the two films, one in Shaanxi in the northwest and Fengjie in Sichuan in the west, are linked by their regional proximity, as much as they are separated by provincial differences. The national narrative, as encapsulated by the Shaanxi plains of revolutionary history, and the Sichuan gorges of modern development, is in the west of China, not on the booming eastern seaboard of Shanghai and Beijing. Likewise, the class disparities of the whole of China, which are the main talking point of politicians and social activists in China's centers of influence, are seen clearly at these points of origin and sojourn. In this context, the approved narrative of the urban middle class seems both a distorted version of change and a vision of social harmony that is as doubtful as the Kuimen bridge's spanning of the once beautiful gate.

Despite the travesties of environmental development and social ordering, and notwithstanding the views of a filmmaker like Jia, Andrew Nathan has recently commented (in response to a much earlier "post-Tiananmen" discussion on the regime's health), "there is much . . . evidence . . . to suggest that . . . the regime as a whole continues to enjoy high levels of acceptance."[15] This acceptance is presumably based on a promise of further future development, in creating a national landscape of class that includes the interests of farmers and workers. The trouble is, just as Jia (and this critic) wonders in horror at the lights over Kuimen, so the peasants are reviled as unable to grasp the credentials of middle-income taste. In China the rural working class is no longer simply *nongmin* (peasants)—always an ambiguous term in terms of benefit in any case and always considered in need of improvement—but is now quite openly spoken of as those without sufficient quality (*suzhi*) to be classed at all.

Meanwhile, in urban areas, especially in the many small towns and cities that characterize China's development, but also in the large metropoles and the planned megacities, there are only those who are poor, richer than before (*bi qian fu*), or doing very well indeed (*xiaokang, xingui*). Thus, likewise, there is no real benefit to being "working class" in political discourse in China today; there is only aspiration, and aspiration is based on middle-class market access, however that occurs. Indeed, Elizabeth Perry has pointed out that to be *gongmin* (worker) is actually dangerous if you espouse aspiration in the wrong way.[16] Those who set up labor movements or lead other forms of political activity are more likely to be punished by death than, for instance, students who do not have worker credentials or those who run carefully balanced NGOs, which urge certain types of reform—environmental, property ownership, and so on—but do not directly challenge the state by appeals to working class solidarity (or sheer numbers).

These class issues are fundamental to understanding the dynamics of *Still Life*, where the main character and those he meets in the waterside town of Fengjie are excluded from the middle-class hopes, aesthetics, and lifestyle of the people who are "running away" from the smog of Chengdu traffic. Even within the ranks of the relatively dispossessed, there are gradations of "quality." San Ming is variously mocked even on arrival "off the boat" from Shanxi by those who are similarly poor, but who at least are local and already fluent in the habits of migration. Of course, within the oeuvre of Jia's work we know that there is a San Ming who has been to Beijing, but there is no certainty that this is the same man merely because it is the same actor, or that any character is more than a cipher of the era, endlessly starting anew in different parts of the country. Nonetheless, and perhaps in contradiction to the disappearance of formal working-class consciousness, San Ming does find a certain camaraderie, perhaps what we could describe as latent or resurgent class recognition, with others in similar conditions. In particular, he finds his way to an unlikely friendship with a younger man. In this extremely tenuous society, where everyone is always about to leave the flood zone and move somewhere else, and where hopes are based on the ability to survive or even to capitalize on traumatic upheavals, their friendship is based on atemporal fragments and competing nostalgias of the Reform era. This is captured in a sequence where they compare their mobile ring-tones. Both tunes are nostalgic; San Ming's is an old-style ballad of good will to good men, *haoren*, while the young man uses a contemporary sentimental ballad for the waters of the Yangtze. This hopeful relationship culminates in the young man's death in an industrial accident, when the sound of his doleful, tinny ringtone in the rubble indicates to San Ming where he lies.

The unevenness of modernity is also key to the tragic central relationships in *Yellow Earth*, both within and across class structures. In the respective moral structure of the two films and periods, the peasant is now the migrant worker, while the revolutionary can be equated with the entrepreneurial new rich in *Still Life*. In *Yellow Earth* privileged access to the revolutionary future is represented by a 1930s educated soldier/cultural worker who, collecting songs for redeployment with upbeat lyrics, is helping to create a symbolic language and aesthetics of new China, through which peasant culture will be filtered and managed. Through *Still Life* and *The World*, we are reminded that the labor of the migrant workers is used to create symbols of reform—from the bizarre bridge lights at Kuimen to the sophisticated skyscrapers of Shanghai.

Landscapes of the Nation

In 1979, three years after the death of Mao and the humiliation of the Gang of Four, John K. Fairbank observed: "This rural industrialization bears the stamp of Chairman Mao. . . . Tarnished or not, his monument is in the countryside."[17] In 1997, in an earlier paper on Mao and landscape in *Yellow Earth*, I noted that the landscapes of Shaanxi had been symbolically occupied by Mao by virtue of the Yan'an base histories—which orient revolutionary history as a whole—and the subsequent memorializing of the man and the mountain in a 1959 painting by Shi Lu, *Fighting in Northern Shaanxi*:

Mao's size, a tenth of the height of the painting, bestows it with a heightened reality, a revolutionary romanticism. . . . It may be titled *Fighting in Northern Shaanxi*, but for Mao [in this aspect] the battle is retrospective. He is not [depicted as] the young fighter of the mid-1930s. He is already victorious, the national figurehead who declared Liberation . . . in 1949. . . . The legitimacy of the new regime is [contained and commissioned through this picture]. . . . [T]he political legitimacy of Mao's Liberation is fixed by the provision of a national landscape.[18]

Fairbank's note[19] that the national landscape of China's hinterland was also the monument to Mao suggests that the painting was prescient of the enormous effects that the man and his regime would wreak in the provinces. Chen's *Yellow Earth* comments directly on the gap between peasant immiseration and the revolutionary rhetoric of liberation and the "national landscape." The peasant father in the film bears an uncanny resemblance also to "Father"; Luo Zhangli's 1980 portrait of the essential peasant man, still the face of poverty four years after Mao's death, and thus the film also refers us to the historical atemporalities that frame the classed experiences of the present.

In another symptom of atemporality, Chen's film treats the Shaanxi landscape with extreme, almost fetishistic, respect. While evacuating its revolutionary credentials he nonetheless returns the landscape to the category of a repository of Chineseness for the urban imagination to savor and eschew, which the revolutionary histories also encourage. In 1984, *Yellow Earth* was a surprising essay on a betrayed people in a landscape under siege from the rising political waves of the 1930s. The mountainous and barren ranges of Shaanxi are shown to be home to peasants who are mired in superstitions, and whose class cannot be transcended by the hopes and trust proffered by the men who walk from the south. Now, and in relation to the massive dislocation of peasants and to the rapid urbanization of China's provinces since 1984, the unequal power of the culturally privileged, the politically competent, and the economically effective with the poverty and relative powerlessness of those who work the land, seems to be the film's retrospective contribution to debates in China about seeking harmony, about land grabs, and about the price of development in terms of the environment.

In Jia's film too, the landscape is as much a class player and a national icon as are the people who inhabit it. Nearly thirty years apart, the films speak to the end of one era and the start of another. They also bracket, or describe, a provincial axis of modern China—from Shanxi to Sichuan—which places Beijing beyond consciousness altogether—except in the presumed person of final arbitrary political control—and which positions Shanghai as the preferred destination for the "classy" and the beautiful (such as the second, female protagonist in the film, Shen Hong), but not a place that is yet available or imaginable to the majority of the population. In *Still Life* we are told that peasant migrants escaping from the rising waters of the Three Gorges go east and south, but mainly to Guangzhou, the nearest, biggest urban destination for making a new life and some money. This is an accurate summary of how people move in China today.

It is common to meet, say, hairdressers, who have moved from Sichuan to Guangzhou, and then perhaps, have finally been taken up by an entrepreneur who moves to Shanghai to make more money with his "creative team." There are, however, other people who cannot move, who do not have transferable skills from land to city, or who are too old or too timid to start again. These are the ones who are without sufficient "quality" to make their way in new China, and who are most in need of succor in a promised harmonious society. They are rather like Cuiqiao trying to cross the river at the end of *Yellow Earth*: They must either swim against the current of capital accumulation and precarious livelihoods, or sink.

The idea of a shared national landscape is necessary to the idea of a unified China. However, while the class of habitation affects what level of power one has on the construction of the landscape, the unexpected cosmopolitanism of migrancy creates dialogues that both destabilize and confirm the nation. This is delicately narrated in *Still Life*. San Ming is sitting with other workers from the demolition sites, trying to find a way to communicate, if you like, to articulate their shared Chineseness in such a way that transcends the differences of provincial cultures and language. A banknote—a 10 yuan note—is produced, when a Sichuan man asks if San Ming noticed the Kaimen when he passed through the Gorges on the boat on his way south. San Ming doesn't know what his workmate is talking about, so he is shown the image of the famous mountainous river pass on the back of the note—an image he must have handled almost every day of his adult life without knowing where it was or what it might ever have to do with his own destiny. He then reaches into his own wad and pulls out a 50 yuan note, which shows a similar iconic scene from the national landscape—a mountainous pass in Shanxi "Hukou Falls," both images as iconic as the mountain in *Fighting in Northern Shaanxi*. As the men look at the images and flip the notes to and fro, the face of Mao—visible on the other side of both notes, of course—goes unremarked. Both men compliment the other on the beauty of their own province, and the Sichuan man agrees to look out for the sight when he moves north for more work. When San Ming checks out Kaimen, the shot opens with a close-up of Mao's face on the banknote, before he turns it over to compare the sight of the Kuimen with the banknote's depiction of it.

In a later conversation the same men are sharing farewells as San Ming prepares to return home. They ask him about possible well-paid work in the Shanxi region and he tells them that coal mining will bring them about five times what they earn as a daily wage on demolition sites. Anyone with familiarity with contemporary China hears that conversation with huge foreboding. China's mining industry is extremely dangerous; safety regimes are regularly flouted and many hundreds if not thousands of men die every year in accidents. The two scenes therefore bring together— as does *Yellow Earth*, in a different way—the new inequalities and immiser- ation of China's second industrial revolution, or the Reform era that we are witnessing today, with the romance of a shared national landscape and a Chineseness that transcends the obvious barriers of language, culture, and experience in different provinces.

Still Life is also a film about beauty, and it offers both a description of the consolidation of the power of urban middle class in appropriating beauty to the national narrative of cohesion and a critique of the loss of beauty through the loss of place (through the double destruction of both natural environments and human habitations and communities).

The film is closely concerned with the images on the national currency, and what might become of them as actual environments. When the entre- preneur proudly points out the lights of the bridge, it is an awful sight in both senses of the word. The magic of what is now a memory of unspoiled beauty is rendered garish and semiurban by the bridge itself, the wrecked buildings around it, and the pollution of light. It is perhaps not fanciful to suggest that this incorporation of the landscape into the national dis- course of self-improvement, enforced quality, and accelerated modern- ization is on a continuum with the blandishments of the new versions of classy beauty that are under construction in the lifestyle magazines in Shanghai.[20] Entrepreneurial, state-managed bridge lighting is supposed to harmonize the national landscape with the national economy and the aspirational tastes of the middle class with the loyalty of the working poor to the fruits of their labors.

With the exception of Jia's *Still Life*, in contemporary urban film aes- thetics there seems to be muted concern for the possible beauties of the Chinese landscape, and much more attention paid to the scruffiness, dilap- idation, and filth inherent in the rapid urbanization and industrialization of China. Characters inhabit concrete prefabricated blocks, pink-tiled, landscaped, gated communities, or bleak tenements where the developer has used the standard latrine-like white tiling on the outside, while inside there is nothing but thin paint. But, if the landscape is an achieved visual- ization of national meaning, this is precisely why there is little actual dif- ference between a mountain and a demolition site in *Still Life*, or benighted spots along the Suzhou river, or in a provincial beauty parlor as in other films of the past few years. All these spaces and views are clues to how land, class, and modernization move hand in hand in describing the current contingencies of the national soul.

Conclusion

The Chinese landscape is prey to the issue of moral quality (*suzhi*), which captures and defines the urban worker and the peasant, the new middle class and the failed migrant. It is urban and peri-urban, modern and ancient. It has an air of quality or degradation, both determined by class aspiration or despair. For everything here is fully human. Quality defines the landscape as much as it defines or refuses people. The legitimation of quality might be figured as the ability to encompass new China by not only surviving the new economy, but also by demonstrating a class-based capacity to evoke or embody cultural memory and the financial luck to define and meet contemporary standards of beauty, cleanliness, and safety. Quality is the ubiquitous stumbling block for those with hardly any power at all, the migrant, the landless, and the unskilled. The "new" filmic landscapes of urbanized trauma are stunningly affective—in that the concretized urban views and miniatures in city films suggest displaced and reinvented sensibilities of the moral landscape of the eighteenth century, in which miasmas of disease can be overwhelmed by large scale engineering works and ever larger populations. The moral landscape of China is laid out in the desolation of abandoned towns on the Three Gorges. The rural and semirural landscapes of Shanxi, Shaanxi, and Sichuan resonate in *Still Life* and *Yellow Earth* as spatial and temporal constitutions of the nation, of how and by whom it is occupied and managed. To rephrase Frisby: Few would dispute the connection between the delineation of the Chinese nation at the turn of the twenty-first century and the development of the denuded rural and urban landscapes of the Reform era.

Acknowledgments

This essay is developed from work on a project funded by the Australian Research Council on middle-class discourse and taste structures in China: Donald, S.H. and Y. Zheng: The Cultivation of Middle-Class Taste: Reading, Tourism, and Education Choices in Urban China, 2006–2008.

Notes

1. P. Kessler, *Oracle Bones: A Journey between China and the West* (London: John Murray Publishers, 2007), p. 3.

2. M. Elvin, *The Retreat of the Elephants: An Environmental History of China* (New Haven: Yale University Press, 2005), p. 29.

3. On the connection between class and lifestyle enclaves, see sociological case studies in Mexico, Hong Kong, and China: L. F. Cabrales Barajas and E. Canosa Zamora, "Residential Segregation and Urban Fragmentation: Closed Neighborhoods in Guadalajara," *Espiral* 7 (2001): 223–253; T. W. Chan and T. L. Liu et al., "A Comparative Analysis of Social Mobility in Hong Kong," *European Sociological Review* 11 (1995): 135–155; L. Tomba, "Creating an Urban Middle Class: Social Engineering in Beijing," *China Journal* 82 (2004): 1–26.

4. Andrew Walder's arguments on elite mobility in the workplace might also apply to actual movement and relocation for lifestyle—see A. G. Walder, "Privatization and Elite Mobility: Rural China 1970–1996," Asia Pacific Research Center Working Paper (Stanford: Stanford University, 2002), p. 40. For class complexity see also A. Y. So, "The Changing Pattern of Classes and Class Conflict in China," *Journal of Contemporary Asia* 33 (2003): 363–376; J. Wang, "Bourgeois Bohemians in China? Neo-tribes and the Urban Imaginary," *China Quarterly* 183 (2005): 532–548; J. Wang, "Youth Culture, Music, and Cell Phone Branding in China," *Global Media and Communication* 1 (2005): 185–201; A. G. Walder, "Social Dimensions of China's Economic Transition: Organization, Stratification, and Social Mobility," Asia Pacific Research Center Working Paper (Stanford: Stanford University, 2003): p. 40; S. Wang, D. Davis et al., "The Uneven Distribution of Cultural Capital: Book Reading in Urban China," *Modern China* 32 (2006): 315–348.

5. Y. J. Bian et al., "Occupation, Class, and Social Networks in China," *Social Forces* 8 (2005): 1443–1468.

6. D. Apter and T. Saich, *Revolutionary Discourse in Mao's Republic* (Cambridge, MA: Harvard University Press, 1998), p. 416.

7. D. S. G. Goodman, ed., *The New Rich in China: Future Rulers, Present Lives* (London: Routledge, 2008).

8. Wang, "Youth Culture, Music and Cell Phone Branding in China"; S. Wang and Z. Zhang, "The New Retail Economy of Shanghai," *Growth and Change* 36 (2005): 41–73.

9. V. Jaffee, "'Every Man a Star': The Ambivalent Cult of Amateur Art in New Chinese Documentaries," in *From Underground to Independent: Alternative Film Culture in Contemporary China*, ed. Y. J. Zhang and P.G. Pickowicz (Lanham, MD: Rowman & Littlefield, 2006), p. 87.

10. M. Chew, "The Dual Consequences of Dual Localization: How Exposed Short Stockings Subvert and Sustain Global Cultural Hierarchy," *Positions—East Asia Cultures Critique* 11 (2003): 479–509.

11. Jaffee is also discussing Jia Zhangke—although not from the perspective of landscape.

12. Y. J. Zhang, "My Camera Doesn't Lie? Truth, Subjectivity, and Audience in Chinese Independent Film and Video," in *From Underground to Independent*, pp. 23–45.

13. S. Teo, "Cinema with an Accent: An Interview with Jia Zhangke, Director of *Platform*," *Senses of Cinema* 15 (2001), <http://archive.sensesofcinema.com/contents/01/15/zhangke_interview.html>, accessed August 10, 2010.

14. For a series of informative essays on this filmmaker, see Zhang Zhen, ed., *The Urban Generation: Chinese Cinema and Society at the Turn of the Twenty-First Century* (Durham: Duke University Press, 2007).

15. A. Nathan, "Authoritarian Resilience," *Journal of Democracy* 14 (2003): 6–17 (p. 13), quoted in E. J. Perry, "Studying Chinese Politics: Farewell to Revolution?" *China Journal* 57 (2007): 7. The full quote from Nathan is: "There is much other evidence from both quantitative and qualitative studies to suggest that expressions of dissatisfaction, including widely reported worker and peasant demonstrations, are usually directed at lower-level authorities, while the regime as a whole continues to enjoy high levels of acceptance."

16. E. J. Perry, *Patrolling the Revolution: Worker Militias, Citizenship, and the Modern Chinese State* (Lanham, MD: Rowman & Littlefield, 2006.

17. J. K. Fairbank, *The United States and China*, 4th ed. (Cambridge, MA: Harvard University Press, 1983), p. 449, quoted in E. J. Perry, "Studying Chinese Politics," p. 5.

18. S. Donald, "Landscape and Agency: *Yellow Earth* and the Demon Lover," *Theory, Culture, and Society* 14, 1 (1997): 97–112, p. 105.

19. Fairbank, *The United States and China*, p. 360.

20. S. Donald and Y. Zheng, "A Taste of Class: Manuals for Becoming Woman," in *Positions—East Asia Cultures Critique* 17, no. 3 (2009): 489–521.

13 Searching for a Place in the World: The Landscape of Ford's *The Searchers*

Ross Gibson

Every now and then I delve into my files to puzzle over an essay by Fereydoun Hoveyda called "Sunspots," published in *Cahiers du cinema* in 1960.[1] Each time, I marvel at how it's beautiful and strange, possibly meaningless, possibly brilliant. Mostly, it describes the *dynamics*—the sense of shifty placement—that one feels when attending the cinema. A vivid lens for scrutinizing contemporary spatiotemporal consciousness, "Sunspots" shows how cinema has defined how we know modern time, how memory and desire give qualities to every known space, and, through both space and time, how cinema has shaped our encounter with place and with landscape.

Using image-ideas not customary in conventional European aesthetics, Hoveyda explains that cinema works best when it captures and channels an ever-unfolding force that runs through the represented spaces and temporal rhythms of a film and also through the audience in the dark room. When a film really works, he explains, energy pulses coherently in space, in time, and in people so that the animus of a scene flares through all the components of an individual shot and then arcs like electricity from shot to shot, from moment to moment, from screen to audience and back again. The rhythms and melody-lines (visual as well as sonic) all generate a charge that carries, excites, and transforms every part of the film. Characters, objects, spaces, luminance, time-patterns, and viewers all get altered as the dynamics play out. The result is pantheistic, somehow. When a film lights up like this, a charge is harnessed, swirling around us and through us. In front of the cinema screen, we are sometimes bathed and buffeted by a force that's vital like the sun. Hence the name: "Sunspots."

When I first encountered Hoveyda's essay as a postgraduate philosophy student during the 1980s, I thought: "maybe it's a con, a parlor game staged by one of the *Cahiers du cinema* insiders under cover of an extravagant *nom de plume*." But I thought too that it had a palpable sincerity, that it was propelled by an ardent intellect and an avid emotion, that it fizzed with a yearning for the power that courses through movies. I sensed how the author revered radiance and really wanted to *know* kinetic urgency, to understand the dynamics that define cinema. I remember thinking, "maybe it's some kind of mystical text, a Sufi thing perhaps, a sparkling mystery designed to riddle some realization slowly out from my bewilderment." That thought passed through me momentarily until, youngster that I was, I let some other notion take me elsewhere.

Even so, I've kept coming back to "Sunspots." And I've learned a little about Hoveyda (1924–2006): how he was indeed a *Cahiers* editor, but not one with a *nom de plume*; how it's probably true that a mystical charge is the main topic of his essay (whether this charge is "Sufi" at all, I'm not qualified to say); how he was the son of a diplomat and eventually became a celebrated philosopher, metaphysician, and historian. In the secular domain, he was appointed Iranian Ambassador to the United Nations; and his older brother Amir Abbas Hoveyda was Prime Minister in the Shah's regime prior to being executed in 1979 during the fundamentalist ructions. When he wrote "Sunspots," the younger Hoveyda was living in Paris, studying aesthetics and developing an enduring friendship and professional partnership with the great neo-realist director, Roberto Rossellini.

As for the elemental energies that Hoveyda brought so lucidly into focus, they've always been in cinema. When the Lumière brothers set up their first films in the 1890s, viewers flocked to the screenings when they heard, among the chattered reports, some amazing accounts of trees! Maxim Gorky, for example, was disturbed by the way some kind of ghost-power seemed to shiver the leaves.[2] Framed aloft in the dark, the trees appeared to be oddly alive. For Gorky, cinema offered life in spectral form. He saw not an intensification or clarification, but a leached trace of natural vitality. It worried him. However, it galvanized him too; the vivacity of his writing betrays him. All the things moving on the screen were like kindred creatures signaling to the human beings in the darkened room, as if the screen were transmitting a fellow-feeling that jumped out of the trees, across the auditorium, into the audience, and back again. In such a world, all things with movement in them might be considered siblings somehow. If city-folk had lost the ability to sense such animism, this cinematograph might bring them back to the mysteries. Perhaps cinema, which Gorky called "the kingdom of shadows," was too savage for him. Or too pagan. But he couldn't stop himself confessing how engaging it was.

At cinema's inception, many people felt they had access to a quickened world, one they'd lost but could recognize as kindred to them as soon as they saw it jittering above and through them. No longer, when observing pictures, were viewers simply assaying objects or locations awaiting annexation. Rather, witnesses to this new art were encountering a world flaring out against darkness, a world that was protean, spirited, and wondrous, perhaps even sacred and not entirely tractable. From its earliest moments, cinema offered an entry point to a mentality different from the objectivity that has governed Western reality for several centuries. Not affirmative of a stable, nominalist world, cinema came as a cult for shape-shifters. Right from the start, it was animated by that radiant energy which Hoveyda would later evoke so well in his metaphor of the transformative sunspot.

In recent times, the practice of ecology has helped us understand how an interconnecting energy might weave through space and time so that the definitions of what is inert and what is alive must undergo extensive redefinition. Many cultures give spirit-names to an animating force that binds places, things, and rhythms into the lively world. Hoveyda hinted at spiritualism when, like an astrophysicist priest, he suggested that the cinema screen in the auditorium resembles the sun in deep space, its energy boiling on the surface and surging into the dark ambit, altering everything that has light in it or on it.

The director Robert Bresson regarded cinema similarly. Filmmaking is a process of binding "persons to each other and to objects by looks," he asserted in his gnostic *Notes on the Cinematographer*. When a film is working well for Bresson, the world portrayed seems alive and radiant because every element of the film "clings" to "knots" of "force" and "security" that get generated all the time the celluloid is running through the projector. A powerful resonance is produced, as if the filmstrip combines with the projector to form a fusion-reactor: "an image [can be] transformed by contact with other images as is a color by contact with other colors." Bresson declared that there can be "no art without transformation." He made a note to himself: "Your images will release their phosphorous only in aggregating."[3]

I've tarried a while with Hoveyda and Bresson because they can help my fundamental idea: A film can generate of *sense of self* that is an energetic *sense of place*. Like some phosphorescent transformer fusing space and light and sound and time, a film can build up a luminous charge. Thus the cinema screen is no mere lodgement for the things represented on it; rather it is an energy field connecting the viewer to the cosmos, making a dynamic place where the viewer gets meshed into all the represented scenes of the film. Everything activated on and by the screen gets transformed so that each thing represented there can be known as no longer a self-contained object but a sensate and interconnected part of a flowing system of energy sizzling in space and time. It's a fact: The screen pulses with light and movement. Energy. And this energy moves through the viewer and goes back to the world.

Irradiated thus, consciousness can alter and expand radically during a movie. I mean *all consciousness*—of the entire represented world, not just the viewer. The screen receives and generates energy over time. This energy affects everything it plays upon, everything represented on the screen and everything in the auditorium and beyond. Such is the allure of cinema: It engrosses us in its force field; it helps us feel a volatile but coherent world surging through our nervous systems; it alters us at the core and at the edges of what we think to be ourselves.

This brings me, at last, to my exemplary place-making artifact, John Ford's Western, *The Searchers* (1956). Taking Hoveyda's ideas, sensing how they resonate with some other practical philosophies of place that I've been reading lately (for instance, the writing of David Mowaljarlai and Bernard Cache[4]), I want to assay the extraordinary power in the opening minutes of Ford's masterpiece, to understand the way it remakes, or *replaces* me, every time I become part of it.

The Searchers starts by marking an edge: The lights go down and in the darkness we get a symphonic blast from an orchestra, a couple of frames ahead of the Warner Bros. logo. The noise and the logo set a boundary in time and space: "For this session, your film consciousness starts here and now." Next come the credits, and a song, intoning "what makes a man to wander?" You're being eased out of the workaday world that you brought into the auditorium. The song lulls and lets you loosen your focus, lets you wander just a little until the credits have done the business and the lyrics tail out: "RIDE AWAY . . . RIDE away . . . ride away." Then blackness. Followed by a single white title on black: "TEXAS 1868." And blackness returning, as the title fades off. Fleetingly you realize that the sequence has taken on the rhythm of a person blinking.

Then, continuing that rhythm, a patch of whiteness intrudes on the blackness, and in the next blink you understand that you are seeing a door being unlatched like an opening eye. You are seeing from inside a dark room that looks out on to a landscape that's so bright and stark you can't help but keep blinking.

In the door frame, there's a woman, silhouetted like a dark pupil, who looks out from the room's eye. Then comes a tracking drift forward toward the door and across the threshold, out to the liminal porch, while the woman moves as if she's being pulled by some motive stronger than the combined propulsion of her own walking and the implied push of the dollied camera. A startling play of forces contend at the door frame: Wind ruffles her clothing; light pours in toward you; she stutter-steps forward; the camera half-follows, half-shoves her out to the porch until she and you sense that the landscape is holding her now, more than equaling the power of the camera, momentarily. Indeed the camera seems to acknowledge this—it stops its push forward, with the effect that after all this blinking, pulsing, breathy buffeting, pushing and pulling, after the mess of all this organic effort—everything pauses in a tense, elastic balance. She stops, and the camera stops as if it has surrendered her will, while she halts and looks out and the wind plays all over her edges, as if to signal that this stillness is not stoppage but just a moment in which restless movement changes rather than ceases.

Let's stop the film for a moment. For we need to take stock of everything that's been implied in this initial shot.

After examining this sequence countless times over the years, I now understand that just about everything that will come in *The Searchers* has already been presaged in the first shot. The whole film is given to us, not as a set of themes or meanings, but as a system of power-surges back and forth between the incursive and the incumbent, between place and space, the built and the given, the imposed and the impounded. Ford will spend the rest of the film teasing all this out as meaning. But in his first camera setup, he gives us the entire movie as a retinue of contending *sensations*. He gives us an overwhelming sense of a place as a dynamic system.

When running the film in a dark lecture-hall, I often call out to the room, asking students to ask themselves, "Who or what is looking right now? Who or what is listening right now?" Also I ask, "What forces are shaping the scene right now, what's making everything tend in a particular direction?" At first I have to badger the class, repeating the questions several times over. For it takes everyone a while to sense what we're looking for: We're trying to divine a kind of organized, shape-shifting spirit moving through the film and through ourselves.

"Who or what is looking right now?" "Who or what is listening right now?" "What forces are shaping the scene right now? What's making everything tend in a particular direction?" Let's go back and put these questions to the first shot of *The Searchers*.

Recall how I kept talking about *the camera* following and looking? Well, that was me avoiding the most unsettling issue, which is: The camera is really just a device serving something else that's doing the looking. Yes, it's you—the viewer, served by the camera—doing the looking. But it's something else too. Already the film has turned you into something other than yourself. It's a sensation that's both unsettling and thrilling. By the end of the first shot, the viewer is you and something more than you. You sense it before you know it.

Who or what is looking and listening?

We'll get to an answer before too long. But first let's just keep the question ticking in the background while I set *The Searchers* running again.

The second shot of the film is a tight reverse-view. It lets me look at the woman and at the windowed wall of the cabin (this wall-eyed, wind-eyed cabin) behind her. On the steps of the porch, the camera is still attached to the cabin, I surmise, and the landscape is at my back, feeling ominously present behind me. So, from these steps on the porch, the camera looks at her looking. She is still buffeted by the wind and by the light and she holds on to a stanchion while she raises her left hand in a balancing gesture that also affords her some shade. She's awash in all kinds of energy. And some of it is tamped inside her, ready to pour out. You can see that.

Who or what is looking *right now*? Well, it's no human character that we've met. It's the film itself, possibly. But that's too glib. In this shot offered from the steps, the looking thing—the conscious thing—is rhythmically related to whatever was looking in the first shot. I feel this relationship because of a continuity that flows across the edit from the first shot to the second. This continuity, which has been sustained by the music and the wind, tells me that the entity looking is the same in each shot, despite the radically different perspectives availed by the camera. This entity is extensive; it is large and contains multitudes.

Then comes the third shot, from a new place on the porch. Looking out toward the sunlight, we get a full view of a landscape with a horseman approaching in the middle distance. We see how the wind keeps agitating. We see the wind working on a blanket slung across a tethering rail that marks the edge of the cabin in the lower foreground.

With the next camera-shift, looking back to the cabin, from the steps again, we see people start to come out of the front room, as if drawn out by the landscape but also as if willfully disgorged by the cabin. Something palpable pushes out from the cabin and through you as you feel yourself placed between the forces defining the cabin and the forces defining the landscape. These contending dynamics move you and move through you. As this feeling registers, three more people ooze out from the cabin. A dog comes out too, onto the porch. Then another person. It is as if the cabin has chosen to produce all these emissaries in response to the stimulus of the landscape and the horseman. The dog starts barking. You realize that you are *listening* (and thus placing yourself aurally) while you are *looking*, and because sound is so much more surrounding and immersive than perspectival vision, you realize that the soundtrack has been "dispersing" you all over the scenes from the first instant the film commenced.

Still on the porch, but from an entirely new camera setup now, you get a mid-shot view of the dog. Then with the sound of the dog still barking, you get a view that might be from the perspective of the dog, but it might also be from any or all of the human characters who have been spirited out of the cabin. And from this camera vantage, you see that John Wayne has brought his outrider character, Ethan, to the steps of the porch.

You see looks and handshakes exchanged. You hear choppy noises of greeting and waiting. All this is perceived from camera setups on the porch and from a "hearing place" that is nowhere pinned down, that is everywhere.

Then there's a wide shot, from out in the landscape, looking back to the cabin from the "wild" side of the tethering-rail. You feel this cut like something shocking, thrilling, and threatening. It's a major development. For the first time, you are clearly detached from the cabin, and it feels hugely significant, panicky in its importance. This sense of panic flickers half-formed in you, before the camera bumps you back to the more comforting porch-step position and frames a close view of the cabin. You thank the film for this return of sanctuary. Oddly, you feel you have come back to yourself.

Next, from the porch steps, you see and *feel* a sequence that's flat-out astonishing. As the woman keeps her eyes on Ethan, she backs into the cabin, through the door and into its interior. Ethan moves forward, as if drawn by powers stronger than him. And everyone else, including the dog, does the same. Ineluctably, it seems, the cabin takes everyone into itself.

To show this ingestion, the camera has rebounded, with a hard cut, back out into the country. From out on the wild edge of the landscape, out where you've just had that sudden feeling of disturbing detachment, you see the cabin reclaim its settlers and you feel how keen you are to be drawn back in there too. You feel it like an organic flex in yourself, as if you're craving to be part of the cabin, as if you have rights and responsibilities over everything in the cabin. Now that this intruder Ethan has come into the world and now that the film has buffeted your edges, you feel a need to find yourself again. And you realize, with a shock that is vertiginous and *organic*—you realize that you have become the cabin!

The cabin is yourself. All the camera setups and edits have built and braced you so. And it's a living thing, this cabin. It's the eye of this desert world. It is the sensate center. It is pulsing, blinking, looking, listening, remembering. The cabin has worldly compulsions coursing through it. It is no inert object. It is assertive. It is a being in a large system of needing and wanting. You know this because you have felt what it feels, and you have felt your need for it. You have experienced a spirit-possession of sorts. You have been mildly inculcated to an animistic realm, a world where every thing is live and conscious. (Remember Gorky's astonishment in front of the shivering trees.)

Question: Who or what is looking, listening, breathing, feeling? Answer: For the first three minutes or so, it's the cabin. It's you as the cabin, as this conscious space. This realization finishes the film's prelude.

Next there's a lengthy interior sequence where you understand ever more clearly that if the cabin walls could speak they would tell of a painful and only partially acknowledged yearning between Ethan and the woman. Only three characters know this completely: the woman, Ethan, and the cabin. How achingly the cabin knows it. How nobly the cabin keeps its knowledge. Indeed, how nobly the cabin does its myriad different keeping tasks. It keeps coolness and shaded ease safe against the hot glare of the landscape; it keeps a spectrum of colors in balance—blues against reds—as it arrays a comforting space for all these folks surviving not only the abrasions of the landscape but also (we glean this knowledge from conversations) the recent depredations of the Civil War. The cabin keeps domestic stillness counterpoised against natural wildness and political malfeasance. The cabin knows everything that has passed among this tiny, vulnerable colony. And you are beginning to know this too, because you have been allowed to be the cabin. You don't know it *cerebrally* so much as *nervously*, as a series of blinking, pulsing emotions, anxieties, and affections all infused within the cabin. You feel a real affection—self-love I suppose it is—for the timber and stone, for the table, the stove, for the spaces of conviviality that the cabin offers to all the desiring characters who are sluicing around inside it. You feel the cabin's organic completeness, its sensitivity.

This is why you will feel something like a nervous collapse at the first narrative turning-point, a few minutes later, when the cabin and most of its humans are destroyed by the Comanche raid.

Inveterate *Searchers* watcher that I am, each time I witness the raid, I feel the desecration of the cabin with an electrical distress that takes charge of me and commands my allegiance, for a while, to the berserker vengeance of Ethan. The nervous shock I feel when the cabin gets destroyed impels me into the film, compels me to ride alongside Ethan in shock and with my blood up, accompanying the mad revenger until I come to my senses anew and realize finally, sixty minutes later, that he is insane and inhuman and I have to find or *make* another consciousness that can lead me to another morality—not Comanche and not Ethan—that might guide me through the tragedy of this stolen country. Over the duration of the entire film I experience an ethical flow from naive affection, to blood-simple revenge, to analytical reflection, to personal conjecture and conviction.

This is the greatness of *The Searchers*: It is an active and activating system of urges all organized toward the creation of an ethical system that is not clearly modeled at the start. The film just propels me toward this unguided place. There is no point of moral stasis (other than Ford's overwhelming affirmation of the basic goodness of generous love, perhaps) pinning the film down, treatise-like. I am not propelled toward one unarguable standpoint. Rather, the film puts me in motion, tipping me into its moral turbulence and setting my passions in contention with my reason. Over a couple of hours, the film lets me know space and time that are neither "Western" nor "indigenous," that are both animistic and objective, that are ancient and entirely contemporary and always under construction. The film makes a moral landscape that is restless but coherent.

All the transformations that the film works on you push you toward new knowledge. But it's a knowledge that looms in your sentiments before it registers in your intellect. Only afterward as the end-credits roll, when you're enthralled, puzzled, and reflective, only then can you bring some of these sensations into cognition. This is not to say the film is "savage" or "primitive" particularly, but it is certainly not Cartesian.

This brings me back to the philosophies of place that I've been reading while getting ready to display my *Searchers* mania in public like this.

Perhaps the most "visionary" of these philosophies comes from David Mowaljarlai, an indigenous Australian elder who spent the final twenty years of his life creating a spiritual system—pragmatic, ethical, ecological—that he was determined to communicate to nonindigenous Australians. This system was based on ritual knowledge stored in his country in the northwest of the continent and it was enlivened by his bold decision to share portions of this knowledge more broadly than they had ever been transmitted before. Reasoning that the colonial invasions had brought so much fundamental change that the indigenous systems needed to react by changing too, Mowajarlai asserted that the country has psychic, social, geological, and botanical life all synthesized into a vitality that can guide a person to sensible actions—strictly, literally sensible. In the writings and interviews he left as a deliberate legacy, Mowaljarlai describes how he can feel the presence (or not), the valence (or not), the direction (or dissipation) of this vitality, and how he can act in communion with it. It's an erotics of country, a system of compulsions, sacred but also mundane and practical. Mowaljarlai can find spots in space and moments in time where the urgency in country is intensified, where this force signals through to the inhabitants most emphatically. He says he can sense the land's animus "swinging" around him.[5] He can attune to it through cultural work, through ritual tale-telling and remembering, making events and structures that frame and intensify the force—marking the ground, lodging painted figures in caves, determining sightlines to other sacred zones, bouncing sound off cliff-faces. In other words, he arranges a *mise en scène* of country and from that *mise en scène* he gets cues for action, taking direction from the scene, on the understanding that countless ancestors have already fashioned it into a kind of energy-generator and view-finder.

Mowaljarlai and Hoveyda would have understood portions of each other's beliefs. Ditto Bernard Cache when he describes how architecture is best understood as "a cinema of things," a system of frames and folds that channel the continuous flow of time and space through each other, integrating all the materials, surfaces, sheets of light, vaults of air, and volumes of sound that are ready to resonate in any environment.[6]

Amplifying Cache's provocations, Elizabeth Grosz has suggested that architecture is place-making, and place-making is truly the primary art because it establishes frames that concentrate nature's dynamics—the sill of a door that makes a floor distinct from the ground, the soffit that emphasizes the shelter of a roof against a wall, the frame forming a window, a directional cairn of stones that's been set down to show how to bring a river to you when you make tracks through a savannah. Grosz describes architecture as a place-making process whereby one renders space *lively* by harnessing and organizing the tendencies that are abroad in the territory that is being constructed.[7] Place-making does for space what social history and personal memory do for time—providing gravitas and momentum. It's close to Hoveyda's vision of cinema's irradiated universe.

So, to sum up and to lead you back to the film: The pulse detected by Mowaljarlai, Cache, and Grosz accords with the liveliness you feel when you are the cabin in *The Searchers*.

Dylan Thomas once wrote of his yearning to catch "the force that through the green fuse drives the flower."[8] This feels *almost* right for what John Ford marshals in *The Searchers*, except that we need a metaphor with more heat in it, more blood. For the cabin represents passion, even gore. The cabin stands for colonialism and the clash of incursive and indigenous consciousness; it hosts domestic peace but it also shelters the hunter who has come home steeped in a carrion smell and unspeakable memories. In the cabin, femininity contends with masculinity and desire pushes against repression, passion disturbs reason, conciliation vies with vengeance. All these forces give a restive vitality to the cabin, make it a world animated with desire and history.

Ten minutes into *The Searchers*, because of the way the cabin has moved through you and made you as you've felt the flowing construction of the film, and because the cabin is the first creature killed in the film, you know in your nerves the drama of America, founded as it is on violence and landgrabbing, maintained as it is in blood, burned as it is by all the flaring energy that drives it, inside and out, across all its spaces all through modern time. You understand that this is what *The Searchers* lets you feel: America and its place in the world, America and its place in and as yourself.

The cabin is you and the cabin is America. The nineteenth century. The twentieth century. The twenty-first. The beast itself, through all these times. America pulsing, America breathing, wanting, vulnerable as it is vital, mad as it is visionary. America in 1956, and before then, and forever after. This made place, America. Always poised to be dismembered and dismantled even as it gets created, even as it remakes and replaces everyone who encounters it. Movie-made America. Remaking the entire world in its own image even as it makes its own place in the world.

Acknowledgments

A different, animated version of this essay first appeared in issue 8 of the splendid online journal, *Rouge*: <http://www.rouge.com.au>. I thank the editors for prompting me to work on these ideas and for giving the piece its first airing.

Notes

1. See *Cahiers du cinéma: 1960–1968—New Wave, New Cinema, Re-evaluating Hollywood*, ed. Jim Hillier (Cambridge, MA: Harvard University Press, 1986).

2. Maxim Gorky, "Newspaper Review of the Lumière Program at the Nizhni-Novgorod Fair, *Nizhegorodski listok*, July 4, 1896," anthologized in *In the Kingdom of Shadows: A Companion to Early Cinema*, ed. Colin Harding and Simon Popple (London: Cygnus Arts, 1996), pp. 5–6.

3. Robert Bresson, *Notes on the Cinematographer* (London: Quartet, 1975/1986), pp. 12, 25, 9, and 82, respectively.

4. See David Mowaljarlai and Jutta Malnic, *Yorro Yorro: Everything Standing Up Alive* (Broome: Magabala Books, 1993); Bernard Cache, *Earth Moves: The Furnishing of Territories* (Cambridge, MA: MIT Press, 1995).

5. See David Mowaljarlai, "Aboriginal Law," ABC (Australian Broadcasting Corporation) radio feature, <http://www.abc.net.au/rn/talks/8.30/lawrpt/lstories/lr311001 .htm>.

6. See particularly Cache, "Oscillation," in *Earth Moves*, p. 29, and chap. 9.

7. See Elizabeth Grosz, "Chaos, Territory, Art, Deleuze, and the Framing of the Earth," *IDEA Journal* 6 (2005): 15–25.

8. Dylan Thomas, "The Force That through the Green Fuse Drives the Flower" (1934), *Collected Poems 1934–1952* (London: Dent, 1966).

14   Framing the Landscape: The Anglo-Florentine View

Katie Campbell

Between the unification of Italy in 1860 and the onset of the Second World War in 1939 an extraordinary collection of British and American Romantics settled in the hills around Florence, creating one of the most famous expatriate communities of the modern world. Few of them bothered to learn the language, fewer still had friends among the local population; what they were drawn to was an *idea* of Florence, an idea that was largely embodied in the landscape.

Celebrated in Western art and literature since classical times, the landscape surrounding Florence was familiar to educated English visitors long before they even set foot on Italian soil. From Pliny's *letters* through Dante's *Divine Comedy*, from Elizabeth Barrett Browning's poetry to John Ruskin's criticism, from Fra Angelico's frescoes to Joseph Turner's landscape paintings, Tuscany's ancient, domestic, patch-worked slopes were a virtual emblem of pastoral harmony. Virgil's *Georgics*—a four-part poem on Italian rural life—was a staple of the British classical education; indeed Roland Barthes suggests that the very name *Virgil* evokes "an era of bygone, calm, leisurely, even decadent studies: English preparatory schools, Latin verses, desks, lamps, tiny pencil annotations."[1] Quick to find Virgilian precedents in their lives, the Anglo-Florentines saw in the Tuscan hills an image of Virgil's Arcadia.

The Irish poet Seamus Heaney, in an essay entitled "The Sense of Place," distinguishes two ways in which place is known: one is "lived, illiterate and unconscious," and the other is "learned, literate and conscious."[2] The Anglo-Florentines were initially drawn by a "learned" idea of Florence, but what they acquired, over time, was a "lived" appreciation. With its rich cultural heritage it is virtually impossible for visitors to approach Florence without preconceived ideas; even today almost every experience the tourist has of the city is s mediated by some painting they've seen or some text they've read. In the early nineteenth century when the writer Frances

Trollope first entered the city, she reported feeling that she was "about to enter bodily into the presence of Dante, Petrarch and Boccaccio."[3] At the end of the nineteenth century Lady Paget was unable to describe her gardens without reference to famous artists, extolling the "Perugino sky," the grass walks "fit for Fra Angelico's angels to tread," and the rose bower "like an Alma Tadema."[4] In the early twentieth century the art historian Bernard Berenson would gaze at the outline of a distant hill, murmuring: "Look, a Corot."[5] So widespread was this attitude that E. M. Forster mocks it in his 1908 novel *Room with a View* where the pretentious Mr Eager spends a hillside picnic attempting to find the exact spot from which a particular painter painted a particular view five hundred years before, while the more sympathetic members of the party succumb to Tuscany's charms with appropriately rustic activities.

It is not by chance that Forster set his novel of sensual and intellectual enlightenment in Florence; for the literate English reader, the city had long been associated with empowerment, self-discovery, and, indeed, rebirth. Hailed as the cradle of capitalism and republicanism, Florence basked in the glow of the Renaissance well into the eighteenth century when it was a favorite among English gentlemen on the Grand Tour, many of whom preferred this industrious northern city to the southern cities of Rome and Naples with their heavy Catholic influence.

In 1820 when Shelley urged his cousin join him in Florence, he famously described the city as a "paradise of exiles, refuge of pariahs." In the mid-eighteenth century the ruling House of Lorraine had granted Tuscany religious freedom in an attempt to entice Protestant and Jewish merchants to settle there; half a century later, during his brief reign as Emperor of the Italian peninsula, Napoleon guaranteed sexual tolerance when he refused to criminalize homosexuality. Supplementing these liberal attitudes, the climate was benign and the lodgings were cheap, ensuring that for much of the nineteenth century Florence was a mecca for English rogues and revolutionaries. After unification, however, a more sober type of expatriate was drawn to the region. Fleeing the social, aesthetic, and economic turmoil of the Industrial Revolution these Anglo-Florentines sought the lifestyle, art, and architecture of what the novelist known as Ouida called "a statelier and freer time than ours."[6]

Although Florence was their focus, they moved out of the city, choosing to inhabit the rural villas in the surrounding hills. As Harold Acton described it, "these representatives of Albion took root among the vineyards and became a part of the landscape."[7] Indeed it was through landscape, with all the ambiguities of the word, that the Anglo-Florentines

integrated with their chosen homeland, exploring the countryside, reno-
vating ancient dwellings, designing elegant gardens, and working the land.

With their country house tradition and Romantic regard for rural life,
it is hardly surprising that the English should be attracted to the hilltop
villas. For many, the idea of Florence encompassed the surrounding countryside as much as the city itself, not least because English chroniclers had
long depicted Florence as the focal point in a vast vista of hills, fields, and
river. Gentlemen on the Grand Tour favored panoramic views of the city
painted from the hill towns of Fiesole and San Domenico in the north
and Bellosguardo and San Miniato in the south, while local artists quickly
catered to the popular taste. Giuseppe Maria Terreni's 1789 *View of Florence
from Bellosguardo* (Florence, Gallery of Modern Art, Pitti Palace), Thomas
Harley Cromeck's 1845 *View from Bellosguardo* (Florence, collection of the
Cassa di Risparmio di Firenze), and John Brett's 1862 *Florence from Bellosguardo* (London, Tate Britain) demonstrate the consistency of viewpoint
through the centuries.

Similarly, English writers tended to describe the city in terms of its rural
setting. In 1824 William Hazlitt evoked a "scene of enchantment, a city
planted in a garden."[8] Fifty years later Henry James described the city as
deposited among the hills "like an egg in a nest."[9]

The villas themselves were of particular interest, often featuring promi-
nently in descriptions of the city; Shelley writing to his wife explained:
"As we approached Florence the country became cultivated to a very high
degree, the plain was filled with the most beautiful villas, and, as far as
they eye could reach, the mountains were covered with them."[10] Edith
Wharton, quoting an old chronicler, claimed: "the country houses were
more splendid than those in the town, and stood so close-set among their
olive orchards and vineyards that the traveler thought himself in Florence
three leagues before reaching the city."[11] Though today the approach from
the north is blighted by the airport and its attendant industrial wasteland,
as late as 1907 the architect George Elgood extolled "the villa-sprinkled
landscape and the far-reaching purple mountains."[12]

Though *villa* nowadays is often taken to mean simply the dwelling,
the Italians use it to embody the whole of a rural estate: house, gardens,
attached farms, and working fields. English commentators had long been
struck by the way Italian villas harmonized with the landscape. Acton
observed that Tuscan buildings seem to grow from the landscape "as if in
sympathy with the hills and local vegetation."[13] Wharton was impressed
by the early architects' ability to integrate house, surrounding gardens, and
the wider countryside: "the architect looked forth from the terrace of his

villa, and saw that . . . the enclosing landscape was naturally included: the two formed a part of the same composition."[14]

The Italian villa was first established in classical times during the expansion of the Roman Empire. Though villa life deteriorated in the Middle Ages when rural Italy was overrun by conquering barbarians, it was revived in fifteenth-century Florence as the ruling Medici family attempted to emulate the ancients. Where the early Roman villa had been a working agricultural estate, the Renaissance villa was primarily a rural retreat designed specifically for leisure and contemplation.

The protracted struggle for independence in the eighteenth and early nineteenth centuries undermined villa life once again, but in 1861, when the disparate duchies, city-states, and principalities that made up the Italian peninsula finally united into a single nation, Tuscany's hills were littered with abandoned properties whose aristocratic owners had been impoverished by decades of political turmoil. As James wryly observed, the villas were so numerous "you can have a tower and a garden, a chapel and an expanse of thirty windows, for five hundred dollars a year." He added, rather poignantly: "Their extraordinary largeness and massiveness are a satire on their present fate. They were not built with such a thickness of wall and depth of embrasure, such a solidity of staircase and superfluity of stone, simply to afford an economical winter residence to English and American families."[15]

Certainly, from their lofty hilltop villas Anglo-Florentines could imagine themselves a part of the early Renaissance metropolis with its cosmopolitan charm and naive art, a far cry from the industrial city that was expanding before them. In 1865, when Florence was named temporary capital of the newly unified Italy, the city undertook a massive renovation program, sweeping away the ancient market place and the picturesquely squalid ghetto, replacing narrow, winding streets with the straight, wide, tree-lined avenues that epitomized late nineteenth-century urban modernity. Most profound of all in this process of transformation, however, was the demolition of the medieval city wall. Though fiercely resisted by the foreign community, the destruction of the wall encouraged new relationships between the city and surrounding countryside; as Grazia Sica suggests, "the distinction between inside and outside was lost allowing a new history to begin."[16]

In the early 1860s before the renovations, Sir John Temple Leader, Janet Ross, Vernon Lee, and Lady Paget, all prominent Anglo-Florentines, lived within the city walls; by 1890 all had moved to the surrounding countryside, which unification had finally freed of the revolutionaries—if not the bandits—who had inhabited it for centuries. Temple Leader reforested the hillside below his medieval castle; Ross restored the olive groves and farmed for a living; Lee researched Baroque gardens from her modest villa, while Paget renovated the medieval tour of Bellosguardo and created a pre-Raphaelite garden surround.

At the turn of the twentieth century the art dealer Sir Arthur Acton purchased the sixteenth-century villa La Pietra, a mile from the city gate, and created a magnificent baroque-style garden to house his sculpture collection. At about the same time the American art critic Bernard Berenson purchased the modest farmhouse of I Tatti, which he expanded and embellished with gardens. Soon after, a young English widow, Lady Sybil Cutting, settled in the nearby village of Fiesole in the fifteenth-century Villa Medici, famed as the birthplace of the humanists, and previously owned by an earlier artist/art-dealer William Spence. A generation later, Cutting's daughter Iris married the Marchese Antonio Origo, an illegitimate Catholic aristocrat, with whom she purchased La Foce, a 3,500 acre estate in the Val d'Orcia, south of Florence.

This remarkably literate and literary community displayed a powerful compulsion to record their experience, as though to justify their unconventional lifestyle to distant family and friends. The typical Anglo-Florentine scenario entails falling in love with Tuscan culture, discovering a neglected villa, restoring it to Renaissance splendor despite incompetent workers and interfering bureaucrats. Some created gardens despite the quaint but ineffectual methods of the local gardeners; others restored agricultural land or picturesque countryside, combining peasant practice with modern science; still others spent their days touring the countryside, observing aspects of Tuscan history and culture. These modern Virgils inserted themselves into the rural panorama, duly recording the daily spectacle and seasonal rituals for publication. Indeed, so common was this practice that Mabel Luhan averred: "It is perhaps foolish to write here of these things that everybody in the whole world has already written about," before adding her own account to the record.[17]

Against the backdrop of their restored villas, furnished with renaissance art and antiques, the Anglo-Florentines created historicized identities, casting themselves as modern humanists in their pursuit of art and scholarship. Those who did not deal in paintings and sculpture created an impressive array of critical studies on Italian history, culture, politics, artists, poets, and palaces. Luhan, an acute observer of the community, observed: "Everyone played with the past in Florence. It was the material of their day."[18] A generation later Harold Acton reiterated this idea,

asserting, "all serious people under forty came to Florence to apply themselves to some period of the past."[19] While art and architecture provided an
obvious link with the past, a subtle but more profound link was provided
by the landscape itself.

Anne Spirn claims that landscapes "record a collective, cultural past,
even a past beyond individual experience or human memory. They trans-
mit memories from one generation to another."[20] Despite the clear associations with the Renaissance and the classical world, many Anglo-Florentines
were drawn to the region's earlier inhabitants, the Etruscans. Considered
the most ancient and civilized of Italy's indigenous tribes, these mysterious people had long captured the English imagination; in *Paradise Lost*
Milton had evoked "Etruscan shadows" haunting the woods around Florence, while Bryon, in *Childe Harold*, had described Florence as "the Etruscan Athens."

In 1865, when William Spence found the remnants of an Etruscan wall
on his property, he put up a plaque to commemorate the event; fifty years
later Origo noted that the sunny hillside would have seemed tame without "the great stone blocks" of that ancient wall.[21] Visiting the Etruscan
necropolis at Cornato was a favorite outing for the expatriates; in her 1878
diary, Lady Paget gushes: "Some of the tombs were so fresh they brought
one quite near that strange and mysterious people in whom love of life and
its luxuries and pleasures seems so blended with a longing for the hereafter."[22] In *Those Barren Leaves*, his 1925 *roman à clef* about the Anglo-Florentine community, Aldous Huxley ridicules this fascination, having his
protagonists rhapsodize over an indecipherable inscription on an Etruscan
tumulus. At the same time, however, an equally eminent writer, D. H. Lawrence, spent his dying days writing a peon to the joyful, natural civilization
of the ancient Etruscans, in stark contrast to his own rational, industrial
world. Though Lawrence's *Etruscan Places* is clearly a dying man's fantasy
of a life-affirming culture, its immediate success demonstrates the potency
of the Etruscan myth in the English imagination of the time.

By mythologizing their setting, the Anglo-Florentines completed their
retreat from modern life. They were escaping not only their homelands,
but the historical present; from their charmed lives in their lofty villas
they could ignore the social unrest, food shortages, labor strikes, and tax
increases that were erupting around them. Describing an evening at I Tatti
just before the First World War, one enchanted visitor recalled: "how hand-
some all those young people were . . . all the beauty and wit seemed to be
gathered there."[23]

After the First World War others adopted this elegiac tone, presenting villa life as a bulwark against the horrors of the present world. A 1928 guide written by an American designer describes Italy's villas as "a joy to the eye and a balm to the soul," attributing to them "a peace that passes understanding," and observing that "since the shadow of the great war ceased to darken the face of the earth, a general desire for beauty has led to the enlargement of existing gardens and the creation of new ones throughout the Italian peninsula."[24]

Given this attitude it is hardly surprising that once again, through the censorship, xenophobia, and increasing Fascist atrocities of the 1920s and 1930s, the Anglo-Florentines managed to remained detached, hidden away in their rural villas. Acton admits: "As foreigners we kept aloof. My father continued to improve the gardens and his collection of paintings, undisturbed."[25] Origo emphasizes how villa life cushioned its inhabitants while admitting that "even in our secluded life at La Foce it became impossible not to observe, read, listen and speculate."[26] As the new war approached, the Anglo-Florentines continued to find comfort in their fantasy of the past, as Acton reveals: "From the terraces of La Pietra one could enjoy the illusion of being far from Fascism. Looking directly across the valley to the Villa Palmieri, one could contemplate the site of Boccaccio's 1348 novel *Decameron*, a serene refuge from another kind of plague."[27]

Even in the heat of the Second World War, Acton admitted: "It is hard to connect war with so tranquil a site, and I like to think that some of our men were able to rest here between the endless slogging of that obstinate, bitter campaign. The benign spirit of the place must have refreshed them. One young English lieutenant would sit out in the garden all day, as in a dream, before he went over the Futa to meet his death."[28]

In *The Poetics of Space*, the French philosopher Gaston Bachelard expounded the theory that the self is shaped by the dwellings it inhabits[29]— a view that Winston Churchill succinctly expressed with the observation "first we shape our buildings, thereafter they shape us." Indeed the Anglo-Florentines identified themselves so closely with their villas that Huxley derides their attitude in *Those Barren Leaves*. In a portrait based on Sybil Cutting, his protagonist, an ambitious English intellectual determined to emulate the glories of the Renaissance, buys a crumbling villa. In so doing she feels she is purchasing the history of the nation: "Everything it contained [was] her property and her secret. She had bought its arts, its music, its melodious language, its literature, its wine and cooking, the beauty of its men and the virility of its Fascists."[30]

Though her medieval Torre de Bellosguardo could boast such illustrious Renaissance owners as the Capponi banking dynasty and the Medici architect Michelozzo Michelozzi, Lady Paget was most proud of its earliest owner, one Guido Cavalcanti, whose main claim to fame was his friendship with Dante. In her memoirs she frequently speculated that Dante must have sat in her loggia and surveyed the same scene as she, nearly seven hundred years later. Soon after purchasing the villa she began to dress in homemade pre-Raphaelite gowns and she persisted in referring to the city as "the Florence of Dante," though at that very moment it was being brutally modernized.[31]

Similarly, Janet Ross asserted that her thirteenth-century fortress, Poggio Gherardo, featured in Boccaccio's *Decameron*. Though her brooding, castellated dwelling is a far cry from the elegant palace described in the novel, the Anglo-Florentine community happily colluded in her fantasy, as it reinforced their spiritual link with the past.[32]

Sir John Temple Leader's medieval castle of Vincigliata provided a more authentic link to the Middle Ages, as historical record indicates that it had been sacked by the English mercenary John Hawkwood. After writing a biography of the Essex-born mercenary, Temple Leader purchased the ruin and set about restoring it, creating an eccentric Victorian version of a medieval Tuscan castle, complete with a dragon pulley that owes more to gothic fantasy than any local tradition.

Much more impressive, however, was Temple Leader's transformation of the countryside around his hilltop castle. Texts such as the *Decameron* indicate that in the fourteenth century the hills north of the city had been a sylvan refuge—the memory of whose shady pools still lingered in such local place names as La Fonte, La Fontanella, and Il Vivaio. During the Renaissance the countryside was turned into a wasteland by the numerous quarries that sprang up to supply the stone for the city's building boom— a phenomenon that is illustrated in Benozzo Gozzoli's famous 1460 *Procession of the Magi* (Florence, Palazzo Medici-Riccardi), which shows vestiges of forest amid the lunar facades of dozens of quarries. Determined to restore the landscape to its pre-Renaissance splendor, Temple Leader purchased many local quarries, some of which he flooded to create picturesque pools; he also acquired several dozen farms and villas to rejuvenate the fields that lay neglected around them. Most dramatically, however, he bought up and reforested the barren slopes, planting cypresses in the rocky crevices, filling the fertile areas with indigenous trees, shrubs, and wildflowers and gradually shaping the landscape to resemble that depicted in medieval paintings.

Iris Origo felt a similar compulsion to restore the land, purchasing a vast tract of the Val d'Orcia that had been left to ruin since the rural depopulation of the Middle Ages. Her first impression of the barren estate is presented in anthropomorphic terms: "the vast, lonely, uncompromising landscape fascinated and compelled us." She goes on to describe her urge "to arrest the erosion of those steep ridges, to turn this barren clay into wheat fields, to rebuild these farms and see prosperity to their inhabitants, to restore the greenness of these mutilated woods."[33] Although she makes no reference to the recent war, this passage was written in 1924 and her image of mutilation inevitably suggests its victims.

Although Raymond Williams famously suggested that "a working country is hardly ever a landscape," it was precisely the working country that appealed to the Anglo-Florentines.[34] Indeed it was through working the landscape that they felt most connected with the past. Janet Ross kept her grape vines carefully draped between pear trees in the manner described by Virgil. She proudly asserted "the best commentary on the Georgics is still agriculture in action in Tuscany."[35] A generation later Origo delightedly records that her tenant farmers' rogation rites are similar to those described by Virgil.[36]

Even for those Anglo-Florentines who simply observed, the landscape was a source of constant fascination, particularly the *vendemmia* or grape harvest. Undertaken during the balmy days of autumn, this was the most picturesque of the annual festivals, and few were unmoved by its pagan charms. The essayist Vernon Lee expresses the elegiac attitude of her peers, extolling: "For how many thousands of years has the procession wound through that valley? Surely long before Christ was born; in the days of Pales and Vertumnus, who knows of what gentle gods of the fields, before the days of Rome or Etruria."[37] Joseph Lucas, who rented most of his land to professional farmers, insisted on cultivating a small vineyard: "the very word conjures up visions of . . . Arcadian delights."[38] Acton expresses a similar attitude, claiming: "To enter Tuscany in September is to enter Arcadia."[39]

The olive harvest, conducted in the bitter cold of early January, was less celebrated but no less important. Acton describes the groves around La Pietra with characteristic reverence: "the olives, pruned like chalices, were centuries old, increasing in fertility with age."[40] Though he is clearly oblivious to such practicalities, the olive trees were traditionally pruned in a cup shape to enable the sun to penetrate evenly.

Origo was unusual in her ability to see beyond the picturesque rural scenes to empathize with the hardships involved in the primitive lifestyle.

Meticulously recording the customs, superstitions, and practices of the local farmers, she notes that in the early days the ancient stone olive press was turned by sweating men, naked to the waist, working through the night by oil lamp, before adding: "Now, in a white tiled room, electric presses do the work in one tenth of the time. One can hardly deplore the change, yet it is perhaps at least worth while to record it."[41] And record it she did, depicting the disappearing peasant lifestyle in several autobiographies.

Though many were equally fascinated by peasant life, few had such genuine sympathy for the local people. Until the Second World War agricultural estates in Tuscany were run on a profit-sharing scheme that had its origins in the Middle Ages. Described as *mezzadria* or "half-and-half," the landowner would decide what was to be grown, supply and maintain the agricultural buildings, and provide half the capital for livestock, seed, fertilizer, and machinery. The tenant farmers, or *contadini*, would provide the labor, and all profits would be shared equally.

Contadini were a major feature of villa life; indeed the unchanged appearance of the Tuscan landscape through the centuries is largely the result of their guardianship. When properties were passed through families or sold to foreigners, the *contadini* generally moved with the land from owner to owner, continuing to manage the land in the traditional manner. Ross's grand-niece Kinta Beevor describes an idyllic childhood learning "the dance of the seasons" from the local *contadini* who taught her to harvest wild garlic, mushrooms, chestnuts, and truffles, one harvest following another, "domestic and wild crops alternating . . . so that the wise could dry or conserve enough to last until the following year."[42]

Despite the ubiquitous presence of the *contadini*, however, many Anglo-Florentines had an ambivalent relationship with these peasants on whom they were so dependent. Luhan reveals a common paranoia when she speculates that her gardener's wife, the "black-browed Rosita," belonged to a secret society "whose members steal things from their *padrone* and send them away to sell."[43] Paget condemned all *contadini* as "short-sighted and childish."[44] Georgina Graham, who wrested an English-style flower garden from the recalcitrant Tuscan soil, warned, "the bedrock of the Tuscan character is suspicion."[45] Origo, more ecumenically, damned the *contadini* as "illiterate, stubborn, suspicious and rooted, like countrymen all the world over."[46]

Acton revealed an uncharacteristic affection for his *contadini*, praising their wit, courtesy, and "picturesque fluency of expression."[47] Lucas too describes his treasured Enrico as "the last of his race," from "a clean and honest family of ancient lineage."[48] Such amiability, however, reveals that even the friendliest Anglo-Florentines tended to perceive the local people with more amusement than empathy, viewing them as part of a picturesque spectacle. Origo reveals a similar attitude toward the Florentine nobility, asserting: "the Rucellai, Pazzi, Strozzi, Gondi . . . had been interwoven into the long tapestry of Florentine history. . . . Their ancestors had been priors under the Commune, merchant princes in the Renaissance, or liberal country gentlemen in the nineteenth century. For centuries they had ruled and administered their city and cultivated their lands, and some were still proud to belong to the great charitable Confraternity of the Misericordia, founded in the thirteenth century."[49]

Mario Praz traces this attitude to the tradition of the Grand Tour, claiming it tainted the Anglo–Italian relationship by encouraging the English to see Italians not as equals but as features in the spectacle. "For centuries we Italians have gone abroad to work, and the English to enjoy themselves. And you expect the people to whose country you go for enjoyment to be picturesque and educational just as the Drunken Helots were for the Spartans. . . . For the English, rather than expanding their ideas, the Grand Tour became a dangerous isolating factor."[50]

Though they may have been isolated from and indifferent to the local people, the Anglo-Florentines were enchanted by the landscape, a fascination that was played out in the passion for touring; Luhan reports: "I visited every nook and corner of that landscape. . . . Everybody did. One was always 'visiting.'"[51] Origo recalls: "the sight of a cypress avenue leading to a fine villa or the mere mention of its existence in a guidebook, was to my mother irresistible," before describing how the astonished owners would emerge from their villas as Lady Cutting, swathed in a dust coat, emerged from her chauffer-driven Lancia, loftily asserting: "I know you won't mind us glancing round for a moment."[52] So common was this attitude that when irate owners confronted Sir George Sitwell trespassing in their grounds, his manservant had only to explain that his master was "an English Signore" and the owners would retreat with apologies.[53]

Though the Anglo-Florentines' arrogance is staggering, one must not underestimate the commitment and indeed the courage of these intrepid tourists. As well as bad roads, unreliable trains, erratic horse-drawn vehicles, and the absence of edible food or potable water, brigands lingered in rural Italy long after unification. In the 1890s when Lady Paget returned from the city to her villa at night she took the precaution of carrying a revolver, "for the surroundings of Florence are no longer safe to walk about after dark as they were of yore."[54] As late as 1912 a guidebook to Italian gardens reassures readers wishing to visit Caprarola, "This road used to be dangerous, the Ciminian Forest having for centuries past borne an evil reputation, but now the excursion is an absolutely safe one."[55] The spread of the automobile in the early twentieth century made touring easier though the early cars were erratic and uncomfortable, especially before the invention of the windscreen.

But it was through gardening that most Anglo-Florentines really connected with the land. Though Italy had a distinguished horticultural heritage, by the late nineteenth century most of the grand Renaissance gardens had succumbed to neglect, and few Italians had any interest at all in garden making. Taking their inspiration from the classical texts of Pliny and Virgil, from the Renaissance art of Fra Angelico, Benozzi Gozzoli, Ghirlandaio, Botticini, and Mantegna, from the fiction of Boccaccio, Petrarch, and Dante, the Anglo-Florentines imported their national art-form and created gardens around their restored villas. Their passion for horticulture bemused the local people. Some were horrified at their desire to cloak the architecture in vines and climbing roses—not least because they could harbor noxious insects. Others were appalled at their love of flowers, which in nineteenth-century Florence were cultivated only for export and funerals. Still others were intrigued at their penchant for afternoon picnics, strenuous hikes, and dining outdoors under vine-draped pergolas.

The venerable grand dames Paget and Ross caused consternation by insisting on working the land alongside their hired help; Ross oversaw the harvest at Poggio Gherardo well into her eighties, and Paget's diaries record that she would rise at dawn and go straight to the garden: "I lop off the branches myself, dig and do all the other things, . . . painting, digging, making roads, furnishing. I don't think there is anything I have not turned my hand to. I have even broken stones."[56] She also expected her aristocratic guests to help, noting of Lord Lamington, the Governor of Queensland: "Wallace is excellent, simple and true; he weeded a great many baskets of groundsel."[57]

Leaving aside such considerations as exercise, aesthetic pleasure, and financial reward, for the women of the community gardening was a way of proclaiming their modernity. From her first horticultural publication, *Gardening for Ladies*, published in 1843, Jane Loudon had promoted the novel idea that women should work physically in the garden: "no lady is likely to become fond of gardening who does not do a great deal with her own hands," she suggests before going on to instruct her readers in how to dig without unsexing themselves.[58] Gertrude Jekyll, on whom Loudon's mantle fell, also engaged in the physical activity of gardening; indeed she was so busy working in the garden that her portraitist, William Nicholson, was reduced to painting her muddy work boots while waiting to complete his portrait of Miss Jekyll (*Miss Jekyll's Gardening Boots*, 1920, London, Tate Gallery).

But gardening also had other ends. For those members of the community who dealt, discreetly, in art, a garden provided an appropriate backdrop against which to display their wares. The gardens at Arthur Acton's La Pietra, Bernard Berenson's I Tatti, and William Spence's Villa Medici all proclaimed their owners' scholarship and taste. Indeed La Pietra contained over a hundred sculptures, and though social protocol prohibited him from advertising his works for sale, Luhan reported the local gossip: "They say, my dear, you can buy anything in his villa if you want it."[59]

Another renowned, if aloof, Anglo-Florentine, Sir George Sitwell, turned to gardening to recover from a nervous breakdown in his native Derbyshire. Having spent several decades touring the Italian peninsula in search of old gardens, in 1909 he produced a slim volume, *On the Making of Gardens*. Marrying a morbid *fin de siècle* aestheticism with genuine scholarship, Sitwell celebrates the "fluteless Pans, headless nymphs and armless Apollos," "the faint, sweet fragrance of decay," and the general "air of neglect, desolation and solitude" of Italy's old gardens.[60] Similarly, in one of her final essays, Vernon Lee describes the defaced effigy of a roadside Madonna that has weathered to resemble the limestone of the local hillsides, having thus acquired "a certain divineness of beauty and pathos; becoming, as she does, not merely one with nature, but consubstantial with so many antique gods similarly dealt with by the elements."[61]

This elegiac air permeates the writing of the Anglo-Florentine community. Whether they are describing the local countryside or the decaying gardens, they ooze what Mary McCarthy describes as a "sickly love" for their adopted city. Indeed McCarthy accused the Anglo-Florentines of expropriating the living city and transforming it into a shrine to the past, blocking modernization by turning its romantic history into "an incubus on its present population."[62]

Ironically, this community she excoriates had been virtually expunged from Florentine consciousness even before it physically expired. In 1931 in an attempt to prove Italian horticultural supremacy, the Fascist government hosted a grand exhibition on Italian Gardens at the Palazzo Vecchio in central Florence. Although the Anglo-Florentines had initiated the study of Italian horticulture, restored neglected villas, evolved a modern Renaissance garden style, and rejuvenated Tuscany's fields and forests, their contribution was utterly ignored in the exhibition.

In "The Sense of Place," Heaney explores the richness that a cultural heritage can add to a site, asserting that "our sense of place is enhanced, our sense of ourselves as inhabitants not just of a geographical country but of a country of the mind is cemented."[63] It is this union of physical topography and literary idea that creates the *genius loci*, the spirit of a place. In the Florentine hills in the late nineteenth century the hyper-intellectual, hyper-educated, hyper-imaginative Anglo-Florentine expatriates imbued the landscape with a spirit so powerful that it seduced many of them to commit their lives to the region, stranded in that uneasy limbo of expatriation. Unlike exiles they had not been banished; unlike immigrants they had not forsaken their homeland to embrace a new culture. Nonetheless, in the Tuscan landscape they found a consolation so profound it kept many of them there through the upheaval of two world wars and the postwar threat of a Communist takeover.

Notes

1. Richard Leeman, *Cy Twombly: A Monograph* (London: Thames & Hudson, 2004), p. 90.

2. Seamus Heaney, "The Sense of Place," lecture given in the Ulster Museum, January, 1977, published in Seamus Heaney, *Preoccupations: Selected Prose 1968–1978* (London: Faber, 1980), p. 131.

3. Frances Trollope, *A Visit to Italy* (London: Richard Bentley, 1842), p. 94.

4. Lady Walburga Paget, *In My Tower* (London: Hutchinson, 1923), pp. 297, 330, 328.

5. Iris Origo, *Images and Shadows* (London: John Murray, 1970), p. 132.

6. Ouida, *Friendship* (London: John Murray, 1914), p. 86.

7. Harold Acton, *Memoirs of an Aesthete* (London: Methuen, 1948), p. 9.

8. William Hazlitt, *The Complete Works of William Hazlitt*, vol. 10 (London: Dent, 1932), p. 211.

9. Henry James, *Letters*, vol. I (Cambridge, MA: Harvard University Press, 1974), p. 150.

10. Laura Raison, *Tuscany: An Anthology* (London: Cadogan, 1983), p. 13.

11. Edith Wharton, *Italian Villas and Their Gardens* (New York: Century, 1904), p. 19.

12. George Elgood, *Italian Gardens* (London: Longman, 1907), p. 107.

13. Harold Acton, *Tuscan Villas* (London: Thames and Hudson, 1970), p. 133.

14. Wharton, *Italian Villas and Their Gardens*, p. 7.

15. Henry James, *Italian Hours* (Boston: Houghton, 1909), p. 124.

16. Grazia Gobbi Sica, "Florence between the 19th and 20th Centuries," in *Of Queen's Gardens: The Myth of Florence in the Pre-Raphaelite Milieu and in American Culture*, ed. Margherita Ciacci and Grazia Gobbi Sica (Livorno, Italy: Sillabe, 2004), p. 47.

17. Mabel Dodge Luhan, *European Experiences* (New York: Harcourt, Brace, 1935), p. 136.

18. Ibid., p. 101.

19. Acton, *Memoirs*, p. 148.

20. Anne Whiston Spirn, *The Language of Landscape* (New Haven: Yale University Press, 1998), p. 62.

21. Iris Origo, *Images and Shadows* (London: John Murray, 1970), p. 116.

22. Walburga Paget, *The Linings of Life* (London: Hurst & Blackett, 1923), p. 262.

23. Sylvia Sprigge, *Berenson: A Biography* (London: Allen & Unwin, 1960), p. 200.

24. Rose Nichols, *Italian Pleasure Gardens* (New York: Dodd, Mead & Co., New York, 1928), pp. vii, 229.

25. Acton, *Memoirs*, p. 110.

26. Origo, *Images*, p. 225.

27. Acton, *Memoirs*, p. 388.

28. Ibid., p. 8.

29. Gaston Bachelard, *The Poetics of Space*, trans. Maria Jolas (Boston: Beacon Press, 1958/1976).

30. Aldous Huxley, *Those Barren Leaves* (London: Chatto & Windus, 1928/2005), p. 22.

31. Paget, *The Linings of Life*, p. 136.

32. Though modern scholars believe Boccaccio invented an idealized country retreat, the palace he described suggests the Villa Palmieri. Closer to Florence, more graceful than Poggi, and sited beside the Mensola stream, which is mentioned by name in the novel, the villa had a more plausible claim as Boccaccio's inspiration, a fact not lost on its British owner, Lady Crawford, who adopted the nickname, "Lady Boccaccio," which must have been a constant source of irritation to the competitive Ross.

33. Origo, *Images*, p. 201.

34. Raymond Williams, *The Country and the City* (London: Chatto & Windus, 1973), p. 120.

35. Janet Ross, *Italian Sketches* (London: Kegan Paul, 1887), p. 112.

36. Origo, *Images*, p. 208.

37. Vernon Lee, *Genius Loci* (London: John Lane, 1908), p. 27.

38. Joseph Lucas, *Our Villa in Italy* (London: Unwin, 1913), p. 32.

39. Acton, *Memoirs*, p. 12.

40. Ibid.

41. Origo, *Images*, p. 211.

42. Kinta Beevor, *A Tuscan Childhood* (London: Viking, 1993), p. 33.

43. Luhan, *European Experiences*, p. 144.

44. Paget, *Tower*, p. 184.

45. Georgina Graham, *In a Tuscan Garden* (London: John Lane, 1902), p. 18.

46. Origo, *Images*, p. 204.

47. Acton, *Memoirs*, p. 12.

48. Lucas, *Our Villa in Italy*, p. 144.

49. Origo, *Images,* p. 159.

50. A. Cane, ed., *Mario Praz, Belleza e bissarria, Saggi scelti* (Milan: Mondadori, 2002), pp. 323–324.

51. Luhan, *European Experiences*, p. 137.

52. Origo, *Images*, p. 95.

53. Sir George Sitwell, *On the Making of Gardens* (London: Duckworth 1909), p. xvii.

54. Paget, *My Tower*, p. 395.

55. Aubrey Le Blond, *The Old Gardens of Italy* (London: John Lane, 1912), p. 138.

56. Paget, *My Tower*, p. 59.

57. Ibid.

58. Jane Loudon, *Gardening for Ladies* (London: John Murray, 1843), p. 6.

59. Luhan, *European Experiences*, p. 104.

60. Sir George Sitwell, *On the Making of Gardens* (London: Duckworth, 1909) pp. 8, 11.

61. Lee, *Genius Loci*, p. 22.

62. Mary McCarthy, *The Stones of Florence* (London: Harcourt, Brace, 1959), p. 22.

63. Heaney, *Preoccupations*, p. 132.

15 This Green Unpleasant Land: Landscape and Contemporary Britain

Michael Rosenthal

Holiday brochures would lead anyone contemplating a visit to Britain to expect to find it a place of stone walls and red telephone boxes, of which practically none remains.[1] She could anticipate arriving in a country that might be "small" but which still boasted "an astounding collection of busy cities, towns rife with history, quaint villages, looming castle, cathedrals, mansions and abbeys. Add to this wild moors and mountains, stark beaches and tranquil lakes, and you've got a wish list a mile long already."[2] Among the enticing trips on offer would be one to "Oxford, Stratford and the Cotswolds," where the tourist might visit "Christchurch College, where Harry Potter scenes were filmed and where Albert Einstein studied"; or the Cotswolds themselves: "a charming blend of cottages with honey colored walls and thatched roofs, market towns with crooked half-timbered houses lining the High Street, and ancient stone crosses, all set in the gently rolling hills, 'wolds,' that are so typically English in character."[3]

One would hardly expect a holiday brochure to mention the characteristic heroin addiction in some of those very same market towns; that all may not be tradition, however, and salubrity is evident from one description of London as "a city that exhilarates and intimidates, stimulates and irritates in equal measure . . . a cosmopolitan mix of Third and First Worlds, chauffeurs and beggars, the stubbornly traditional and the proudly avant garde," which perhaps supplies some reassurance that graduates do not lose all their critical faculties once they enter employment.[4] Indeed, after dark, central London, like most British cities, can become an urban jungle somewhere beyond the wilder imaginings of William Hogarth.

The kind of national iconography—Big Ben, Cotswold Cottages—used to present Britain to foreigners has increasingly less fit with actualities. Yet, national imagery—*if* an image of nation is actually possible during a period when many Scots foresee an end to the union and when the population is becoming increasingly polymorphous—is insistently presented as the landscape of southern England (as against the North, or even Wales).[5] There is a paradox in something itself inherently unstable embodying the concept of nation in a troubled, postindustrial, and multicultural nation. England is an urban or suburban place. The countryside, always subject to transformation, is adapting still as farming practices change (many farmers are selling up to anonymous proprietors who cultivate the land through contractors), indigenous populations of charming market towns or villages are driven away by impossibly inflated house prices, and country pubs struggle to survive.

In 2005 the BBC collaborated with Tate Britain in launching a book, an exhibition, a television series, and much else under the umbrella title *A Picture of Britain*. "Between them," stated the foreword to the book, "Tate Britain and the BBC have created something which reaches out to everyone who lives in or visits Britain and who wishes to enjoy and understand the nation's physical and emotional character through its landscape."[6] That American "reaches out" signals that this mighty cultural event might not be altogether in the disinterested Reithian tradition. David Dimbleby, presenter of the television series, and whose name headlined the book, explained that the project was predicated on the *aperçu* that it "took the vision of artists and writers, particularly over the last three hundred years, to lead people toward an understanding of its [Britain's] natural beauty, to see things they had never really looked at, and so come to realize that the British landscape was to be cherished."[7]

It helps here to know who David Dimbleby is. Dimbleby, now in his early seventies, is a scion of British televisual aristocracy. His father, Richard, commentated on Churchill's funeral, and bequeathed Dimbleby Junior the role of televisual narrator of great state occasions. He is prominent as chair of the BBC television program, *Question Time*, where panelists, always including senior politicians, engage in debate among themselves and with the audience in what can seem the last properly democratic forum in Britain. Dimbleby projects an affable persona, but there is another side to him. In 1993 he had taken over as sole proprietor of the Dimbleby Newspaper Group, which, in April 2001 he had sold on for a reputed £8 million. He had not been a worker-friendly employer. He admitted to paying his staff "peanuts" and to feeling no embarrassment "at paying miserable wages," although he claimed as mitigation that people received an excellent journalistic training in lieu of a decent income.[8] The papers were printed by Dimbleby Printers Ltd., "an associated company"; a dispute between them and the "National Graphical Association . . . over redundancies led to a strike in August 1983. David Dimbleby dismissed the striking printers" and contracted for the printing with a nonunionized firm.[9] At the time, the Thatcher government was carrying on a full-scale assault on Trades Union rights (culminating in the Battle of Orgreave of May 29, 1984, when mounted police in full riot gear would attack striking miners), and in this context it is little surprise that the National Union of Journalists viewed the establishment figure of Dimbleby as an enemy.[10]

The significance of that class position will become clearer as this essay proceeds, although we can begin to explore the issue by investigating what *A Picture of Britain* as book and as a broadcast program had to say both about the paintings of John Constable, and, in particular, *The Hay Wain*, and the association of each with "Constable's Country." That latter term was first used by Constable himself, in an 1832 letter to David Lucas, who was mezzotinting some of his landscapes:

In the coach yesterday coming from Suffolk, were two gentlemen and myself all strangers to each other. In passing through the valley about Dedham one of them remarked to me—on my saying it was beautifull—"Yes Sir—this is *Constable's* country!" I then told him who I was lest he should spoil it.[11]

The "lest he should spoil it" probably reveals Constable's awareness that his reputation was such that there was a real possibility that the gentleman might have followed his gratifying recognition of the unique association of one artist with one terrain with some animadversions directed against the artist's personality.

The region in question lies on the borders of the eastern English counties of Essex and Suffolk. Bounded to the east by the port of Manningtree, which lies on the estuary of the river Stour, it can be said to occupy both banks of that river perhaps upstream as far as the village of Nayland, where Constable's aunt commissioned from him an altarpiece for the church. The greater concentration of Constable's landscape subjects lay between his native village of East Bergholt in Suffolk, Flatford, where his family operated the mill, and the villages of Stratford-St.-Mary, Langham, and Dedham in Essex, where his father managed the watermill.[12] Such has the fame of this circumscribed area developed that Flatford Mill is now a long-established and very popular tourist destination that "struggles to cope" with the environmental impact of "200,000 visitors a year." And, whereas twenty years ago it was impossible to see the landscape of *The Hay Wain* for trees, the National Trust, which owns the whole property, has opened up that view for the benefit of those visitors.[13] The complex history of the development of this iconic landscape has been brilliantly detailed by Stephen Daniels.[14] From him we learn how Constable had become the quintessentially "English" painter by the 1860s, and how "by the turn of the century" *The Hay Wain* was "well on its way to becoming a national icon."[15]

So it is no surprise that David Dimbleby should have written that "*The Hay Wain* remains the most popular of all English landscape paintings" or have observed in the broadcast that because "of this picture they come here in their thousands and stand and look and see it through his eyes."[16] Evocative though that alogical assertion is, it is significant that tourists come to inspect the places Constable painted. Interestingly, they tend to stick to the area around Flatford Mill. Such views across the Stour Valley as may be prospected from the road connecting Flatford with the village of East Bergholt, and which formed the subjects of *Dedham Vale, Morning* (1811, private collection) or *View of Dedham* (1814, Boston, Museum of Fine Arts) are hardly visited, even though the oak tree prominent in the middle distance of the former is still recognizable. At Flatford, Dimbleby was filmed talking to the gang which was clearing the view through which the distant meadow is prospected in *The Hay Wain*, one of whom in remarking "it is an English thing" may not have been making obvious sense but did raise the association of Constable's paintings with some notional "Englishness."

By late January 2006 the British national press was carrying stories of a hot dispute carrying on in the villages of Great and Little Horkesley, north of the town of Colchester, on the Essex-Suffolk borders. A local firm, Bunting & Sons, was planning to transform redundant greenhouses into "an outstanding Heritage and Conservation Centre." Among other things it would supply a visitor center and a fine art "outstation gallery" that "will display the works of John Constable and other great artists of the region." It was planned, too, to have a garden center, a Suffolk Punch breeding center "to help save from extinction East Anglia's only breed of heavy horse," an "authentic Chinese Garden," and a restaurant and leisure/function areas.[17]

The proposal generated outrage. Commuters, established farmers, local small businessmen, the two local MPs, and esteemed local author Ronald Blythe were united in opposition.[18] It was estimated that the proposed center would attract some 760,000 visitors per annum.[19] Allowing for a day's closure at Christmas, this would still mean some forty-one busloads every day, except that people would come by car—something that would have real implications for traffic on the local roads and lanes, particularly as one would imagine that visitor numbers during the summer holiday season would be disproportionately greater than those who came during the winter months. The potential environmental damage would be colossal.

As Will Pavry, Chairman of the Stour Valley Action group, formed to fight these proposals, put it: "This is simply commercial exploitation of the site which has nothing to do with Heritage or the celebration of the English countryside."[20] The national press was pretty much of this view, too: in the *Financial Times* the proposal was labeled a "theme park," and Caroline McGhie noted how there was to be "a restaurant and café with 1,125 covers," and how 80 percent of the turnover was to come from retail sales. As one journalist wrote: "What if you could bottle 'essence of Constable's countryside,' slickly repackage it and sell it to the punters? Now, that would really bring them in."[21] There was a damning leader in *Country Life.*[22]

The proposal came because Bunting & Sons, prominent as nurserymen in Colchester since 1820, had discovered that tomato production under glass was no longer viable. The firm was justifiably proud of a long and innovative history which had over the years involved unique contacts with the Far East, and, more recently, what they had described as their "pioneering work on biological control," an environmentally impeccable system of pest control. This, however, was all in the past, the cessation of tomato production the last gasp of the firm's horticultural endeavors. Alternative productive uses for this plant had been explored but found lacking. The firm was now the owner of a gastropub, serving traditional English food made from their own produce, a conference and meeting center, and a boutique winery it cost £4 to visit. Horkesley Park would be a major expansion of its interests in leisure and retail.[23] And it was trailed as a place where the visitor would be able to see paintings by Constable, "other great artists of the region" (implicitly, therefore, Thomas Gainsborough and John Nash) and enjoy an "interactive interpretation experience of the 'Life and Times of John Constable'" (modesty forbids my recommending a more domestically viable version of the latter).

Paintings by Constable are abundantly available at the Victoria and Albert Museum, or Tate Britain; and, closer to hand at Christchurch Mansion, Ipswich, in which are to be found the wonderful small paintings of *Golding Constable's Flower Garden* and *Golden Constable's Kitchen Garden*, which the artist had painted from different windows of the family house in 1815. It was clear that no Constables would be lent to Horkesley Park from public collections, and nor, it seems, would loans be available from private sources. By February 2006 Senior Partner Stephen Bunting was saying that he couldn't "fill the place up with Constables, but we shall be able to get an overview of artists of the area."[24] Moreover, as many people pointed out, Horkesley Park lies completely outside Constable Country. It has no connection with it. Those with an interest in Constable can visit East Bergholt,

Flatford, and Dedham and at least experience the modern versions of the landscapes that he painted.

In 2006 the Buntings withdrew their planning application. In 2007 they returned to the fray, mounting what must have been an extremely costly attempt to woo public opinion.[25] The firm had moderated estimates of visitor numbers, and was still referring to the project as "Horkesley Park Heritage and Conservation Centre," although the destruction of productive farmland in linking the center with the Stour Valley below it so that Suffolk Punch carthorses could trundle through it pulling cartloads of tourists seems to have little to do with "conservation." There was still going to be "Fine Art 'outstation' for national and other leading galleries" to "display the works of John Constable and other great artists of the region," although the Buntings were silent on where these would be coming from. The Suffolk Punch was still being saved "from extinction." That the Suffolk Punch Trust at Hollesley in Suffolk is already doing this receives no mention.[26] Despite widespread opposition—Dr. John Constable, the painter's great-great-great-grandson, acidly pointed out that "the project is vulnerable to rapid failure as a heritage park, and would need to be refocused as a dedicated major retail center in order to survive"—the fate of the scheme has still, in early 2010, to be decided.[27] Rather than reuse or convert apparently redundant greenhouses, carry on the firm's admirable tradition of initiative, resourcefulness, and experimentation, a policy entirely in keeping with the diversification which is now entirely characteristic of British agriculture and horticulture, the preferred option was to develop what remains undeveloped country as a heritage-style retail center. Characteristically Blairite in its bland vacuousness, "heritage" is a manufactured and dead history, and the heritage experience exists to be packaged and sold. Constable was simply being used as a brand name, a kind of designer label. In this context his paintings are utterly irrelevant.

In order to do this, Constable's paintings had had to assume the role of the quintessential landscape of nation, the landscape that we all share, an idea that has played a significant part in directing Constable scholarship, coincidentally reinforcing the insistent role of landscape imagery in establishing one view of national identity. Therefore, it is worth reviewing the history of that scholarship, and of the history of landscape imagery more generally. From the late 1960s, arguably inaugurated by John Gage's 1969 exhibition, A Decade of English Naturalism 1810–1820, British landscape became a subject of real interest.[28] That same year the Tate Gallery had published Leslie Parris's and Conal Shields's *John Constable 1776–1837* in their Little Book series, the impact of which was disproportionate to its size, for it presented the artist as complex; his art as responsive to political and cultural histories; and in their small exhibition, Constable: The Art of Nature, held at the Tate in 1971, the same pair included painting treatises and volumes of poetry along with the art to point up the historical interconnectedness of the interest in landscape of which Constable's art was but one manifestation. The catalog to their great 1973 exhibition, *Landscape in Britain c. 1750–1850*, remains the most comprehensive account of landscape in its various manifestations during that period. In 1976 they were joined by the older scholar, Ian Fleming-Williams, in curating the bicentennial Constable exhibition, again at the Tate. Not only did this attract something over 300,000 visitors, it fueled the academic interest in Constable and landscape painting that had already been sparked by those earlier shows.[29]

Scholars began to investigate the ideological underpinning of these works. This might have been an unexceptionable thing to do in the case of Tim Clark, Courbet, and French realist painting of the mid-nineteenth century, but, as we were to discover, it amounted to an unacceptably Marxist "reading in" of meanings to British landscapes in general and paintings by Constable in particular. And such is serendipity that in 1979 Margaret Thatcher won her first general election, and, in 1980, John Barrell published *The Dark Side of the Landscape: The Rural Poor in English Painting 1730–1840*.

Barrell pointed out that paintings such as Constable's (and others') were informed by poetic iconographies, and, in negotiating subjects—landscape and those who worked it, which in reality were highly problematic, for this was a revolutionary era—had to adapt strategies for so doing while remaining aesthetically acceptable. Thus it was in his catalog to his 1982 Tate exhibition, *Richard Wilson: The Landscape of Reaction*, David Solkin explained how Wilson's classical scenes were informed by ideas to do with the exemplary role Roman history played in the self-imagining of the contemporary British patrician, or how to perceive the domestic landscapes as benign and pleasant depended on your point of view. The landowner would perceive things rather differently from the peasant whose exhausting labors had been described so eloquently by the "Peasant Poet" Stephen Duck in "The Thresher's Labour" of 1740.

In his foreword to the exhibition catalog, Tate Director Alan Bowness wrote how Wilson, "the Father of British landscape," had manifested "a frank and personal reaction to the natural beauty of the Roman Campagna," had gone on to transform "the English country house portrait," and, in his native Wales, "painted those . . . grand and powerful British

landscapes which suddenly opened people's eyes." Then he observed that
Solkin's "original and challenging" catalog, "in many respects contradicts
the more traditional view expressed above." That it would "prove a most
original and indispensable contribution to studies of eighteenth-century
British painting" was a commendable endorsement of the imperative to
support a pluralism of views if scholarship is to have any radical relationship with culture more generally.[30]

The director of the Tate Gallery might have been prepared to uphold
civilized values, but the British establishment was not. The row that followed has been well documented, the outrage essentially provoked by the
Tate's having presumed to publish scholarship that undermined any cliché
that historically British society had been homogenous, untroubled, with
the ideologies of a patrician elite gratefully shared by the proletariat on
whom that elite partly depended for the maintenance of its wealth and
status. From some came calls for the Tate to be censored if it was to persist
in publishing that kind of stuff (and here it should be remembered that
from this time Thatcher was engaged in a bitter struggle to compromise
the political partiality of the BBC), and, as has often been observed, from
then on its exhibitions of historical British art tended toward the safely
antiquarian rather than the historically risky.[31] If exhibitions were compromised, books were less so, and a concern with landscape persisted through
the 1980s and into the 1990s.[32]

By now this persistently historical interest in landscape as something
that articulated a politics as well as aesthetics was perhaps becoming a little
quaint, as postmodernism became all the rage; and, for a while, it seemed
that the only thing worth paying any attention to was the body. It might
have been that, in Britain at least, decades of a right-wing authoritarian-
ism that preferred to silence rather than engage in dialogue with dissent-
ing voices meant that an engagement with landscape as a contestable field
could appear irrelevant. At least most of us have bodies, and to understand them as social constructs as much as biological entities, in an era
when postmodernism was denying the possibility of such grand narratives
in politics as much as the politicians themselves were, was one way of making it look as though there were some point to academic activities—activities that in our hearts of hearts we might have been forgiven for suspecting
were as relative and irrelevant as anything else.[33]

Yet, when it came to Constable (on whom I had published a book in
1983) the problems refused to go away.[34] R. B. Beckett's great edition of
Constable's *Correspondence* (with the welcome addition of a further volume
edited by Leslie Parris and Ian Fleming-Williams) meant that we had an

unparalleled resource when it came to finding out a great deal about the painter.[35] Among many other things, it revealed that the artist had a good grounding in Augustan poetry, or that his attitudes toward the countryside in general were those of his class, a respectable, Protestant sort, propertied and substantial but not patrician. It was clear that his politics were conservative—he would be enraged and fearful of political reform in the 1830s— and as clear that his views of what he and his art were aiming to achieve changed as time passed and circumstances altered. It seemed reasonable to assume that these factors would have an impact on his painting: If nothing else this would be to follow the lead of the curators of the 1976 exhibition, or to develop ideas outlined by John Barrell in *The Dark Side of the Landscape*.[36]

The curators of a second Tate Constable retrospective in 1991 believed otherwise; a little surprising, considering one of them was Leslie Parris, who had been so instrumental, along with Conal Shields, in kick-starting serious and innovative scholarship in British landscape painting. One highlight of the show was the recently rediscovered *The Wheatfield* of 1816. Its foreground is occupied by what appear to be two teenage girls and two small children gleaning, while a small boy sits with a collie. In the near distance four male reapers, none of whose faces can be seen, cut the corn. A contrast would be with Peter de Wint's crowds of gleaners in his contemporary *Cornfield* (Victoria and Albert Museum), or George Robert Lewis's strikingly individuated group of standing reapers in his 1816 *Hereford from the Haywood, Noon* (Tate). Constable was being meticulously careful in keeping his laboring poor under control, in place. Yet the catalog entry to the painting ended with the triumphant: "Even *within his own* terms the contrast drawn by John Barrell between the bold figuration of the latter and the—to him—nearly invisible workers in Constable's landscapes of the period clearly requires some qualification now," when in fact it was confirmed. (my emphasis). The real anxiety to neutralize Constable's art led to the abandoning even of the standard scholarly courtesies.

I was among various people taken to task for assuming, both on the basis of Constable's having written "I do hope to sell this present picture— as it has certainly got a little more eye-salve than I usually condescend to give them" and the fact that its subject and handling were a radical departure from what had been developing in the canal scenes, notably *The Leaping Horse* (1825, Royal Academy of Arts), that, in *The Cornfield* (1826, London, National Gallery) whose composition was a deliberate travesty of the picturesque, Constable was making a joke informed by the sarcastic humor noticeable in his contemporary correspondence. This could not do.

The idea that the dead tree at the left foreground would, in an actual land-scape, have been long felled was countered by identifying it as a polled oak, something of which nobody had previously heard. Among others this amazed Stephen Daniels, whose paper, "The Field of Waterloo," delivered at a Constable symposium at the Tate Gallery, compared that tree to the legendary Norwegian Blue Parrot. My own pointing out these and other anomalies provoked some members of the symposium audience to walk out.[37] Stephen Daniels writes how many "of the 1991 catalog entries were intent to straighten out interpretative controversies over Constable, if only by refusing the legitimacy of many readings of the pictures which were not grounded in (what were confidently presented as) physical facts about the places painted or the painted canvas itself."[38]

If the curators found scholarship disagreeable, they dismissed it out of hand as Thatcher had condemned BBC reporting that did not accord with her own views of events as being "left-wing" and, therefore, inadmissible. However, this attitude to scholarly debate, which refused a voice to any history that aspired to be anything more than antiquarian, seemed extra-ordinary in what was supposed to be a vibrantly pluralistic Western democ-racy of the kind which all other countries aspire to achieve for themselves. We need to ask why the curators had taken so extreme a position. And in answering this question, the peculiar status of Constable and his art are of central importance, because this anxious desire to keep Constable simple, instinctive, natural, persists.[39] Investigating this phenomenon takes us back to David Dimbleby and *A Picture of Britain*. One of the laborers help-ing keep the distant view in *The Haywain* open by cutting down the trees and any other impediments to that view called it, as we saw, "an English thing"; and in one of the excellent essays that Tate Britain curators sup-plied for the book of the exhibition and television films, David Blayney Brown, a scholar of admirable acuity, notes that "this scene on the Stour between Suffolk and Essex, with a hay cart crossing the water and a farm-house on its bank, has certainly become a Picture of Britain."[40] This is land-scape as iconic of nation.

That statement should cause pause for thought, for, since 2006, there has been intense debate, in part instigated by reactions on the part of Brit-ish Muslims to the illegal invasion of Iraq and its consequences, as to what Britishness is. This is a country of immense regional variation as much as tribal variety, a place as much of urban squalor as of suburban respectabil-ity or rural prettiness, and a place where the disappearance of traditional manufacturing and other industries has left the populations of whole areas in certain respects adrift, bereft of the occupations that supplied some communal cement. How, then, can one claim that a historical landscape painting can embody the quintessence of nation? To answer that question we need to bear in mind who owns the land thus memorialized. The Duke of Cornwall, Charles Windsor, unsurprisingly gains the bulk of his income from the Duchy of Cornwall: in 2005–2006, £14.1 million became £10.8 million after the voluntary payment of tax at 40 percent. The Duchy itself extends to 54,764 hectares spread over twenty-two counties, mostly in the southwest of England.[41] Other patricians, notably the Duke of Westminster, have vast estates in England and Scotland. Moreover, unlike the rest of the population, the aristocracy, which continues to exercise political power in the unelected House of Lords, still has a radical connection to country life.

I would not wish to make so crude an assertion that those who own large parts of the British Isles would find it both automatic and natural to understand a nation in landscape imagery, and that, therefore, anyone who suggests that the uncomplicated messages such imagery communicates are skewed by historical actualities (much as Constable painted in *The Hay Wain* a peaceful and tranquil countryside, which at that time wasn't) is at the least unwelcome, and that this goes in part to explain the extreme reaction provoked by those who attempt to write about Constable historically. But it does bear thinking about. In this view, the David Dimbleby films that made up *A Picture of Britain* were absolutely enthralling.

The downsides were a persistently irritating musical soundtrack, and the unaccountable speeding up of the clouds in the first program, "The Romantic North." On the positive side, the photography was often breathtakingly good, and Dimbleby, who, to his credit, had pointed out in the book that "the reality" of *The Haywain* "is complex and demands careful study," was prepared to treat his subject with proper seriousness.[42] Hence, in this first program, he went round Derwentwater with West's 1778 *Guide to the Lakes* to hand, filming the views to be had from some of the stations West famously recommended. As historically informative was his taking to the lake in a boat equipped with a cannon and firing it a few times to provoke multiple echoes, thus to duplicate the eighteenth- and nineteenth-century practice. The episode in *The Prelude*, when Wordsworth remembers his illicitly loosing a boat and rowing out one summer's evening to discover the crags and rocks menacing, appearing to stride after him until: "With trembling oars I turned, / And through the silent water stole my way / Back to the covert of the willow tree,"[43] was tenderly recreated. Nor had the filming schedule allowed the program makers the luxury of time, so we witnessed the presenter experiencing characteristically filthy weather.

At a late stage in the film Dimbleby was at Ilkley Moor, in Yorkshire, when in a rather unlikely piece of happenstance, he stumbled upon the Black Dyke Band, one of the finest brass bands in the world, playing "On Ilkley Moor Baht 'At." This was a little disturbing. The Black Dyke had originally been the Black Dyke Mills Band, the musicians workers from the eponymous mills at Queensbury, outside Bradford. The Mills have long closed, and while the Band itself continues to flourish through sales of recordings, its actual deracination testifies to some of the effects of the economic upheavals that have been experienced in Britain over the twentieth century. There was a comparable moment in North Wales in the final program "The Mystical West."[44] In Snowdonia, Dimbleby spoke of the Welsh bards, their historic role, and the legend of their slaughter by Edward I. He then met a blue-blazered male voice choir, clustered on the hillside, singing "Land of My Fathers." This was the Côry Brythioniad Male Voice Choir. In response to Dimbleby's question whether they were all Welsh speakers (they were), one of the choir asked, "Excuse me, what dialect have you got," to which came the reply "I don't have a dialect. I've come hot foot from the BBC," which in turn led to an admission that he indeed spoke BBC English, something which, to his regret, was "dying out," for he had "learned it at my father's knee."

The father, we remember, was the broadcaster Richard Dimbleby, and David had pointed up how authoritative this professional genealogy was in the first of his films, when he had shown a clip of a film he and his brother had made in the Lake District in 1955. This had led him to joke about his accent then, although it is still pretty striking now. Only the patriciate pronounces "Constable" "Cownstable," as Dimbleby does. To someone who is unaware of the subtleties of social distinction and class identification in Britain, it cannot be too much stressed how much accent can tell the attentive auditor. In most countries accent denotes region of origin. In Britain in general and England in particular, it reveals class. Dimbleby, a privileged courtier, shares his accent with members of the royal family. He cannot but speak as a member of the establishment, someone in general ways proprietorial of the countryside he was presenting. The message was reinforced with other cues, some obvious, others less so. Throughout the series Dimbleby drove a short-wheelbase Landrover, which, its registration revealed, was around eight years old. That is, he was driving the kind of useful vehicle that farmers and proper country people use, not the gargantuan, ugly, shiny, intimidating, and brand-new kind of four-wheel drive favored by *nouveaux riches* or people who live in towns.

One virtue of the series was its willingness to inspect what we tend to ignore because of its depressingly derelict character, the wrecked factories and bleak townscapes of the former industrial heartland. Episode 4 concentrated on this.[45] There were fine shots of Matlock, and acknowledgment of the impact of paintings such as Joseph Wright's *Arkwright's Cotton Mills at Night* (1782–1783, private collection). Passing through Belper and Stoke on Trent, Dimbleby established it as "the old industrial Britain," though "it's all in ruins now," which was properly honest. There was a fine section on Coalbrookdale, once famous for the production of iron, though the processes by which this was done now had to be shown in re-creation. Having visited the formerly thriving Dudley, in the West Midlands, and acknowledged the very positive ways in which J. M. W. Turner had responded to a burgeoning manufacturing industry that left some "less thrilled with progress" than him, the presenter stated that: "From the Black Country I'm driving south, out of the darkness and into the light. I'm heading for the Cotswolds." These we will remember as the "charming blend of cottages with honey colored walls and thatched roofs, marked towns with crooked half-timbered houses . . . all set in the gently rolling hills, 'wolds,' that are so typically English in character." Dimbleby, always the visitor from the South, hence the fakery of coming upon indigenous bands or choirs in the middle of scenery, perhaps unconsciously saw this as the light of the real England.

Toward the end of the film Dimbleby spoke of the composer and collector of old folk songs, George Butterworth, shown Morris-dancing in a rare film clip of 1912 which was abruptly followed by scenes of First World War carnage, a war which dealt "death on an industrial scale" to many from throughout the British empire, including Butterworth. He observed how A. E. Housman's 1896 cycle of poems, *A Shropshire Lad* (for Shropshire lies on the northwestern extremity of the region on which he was focusing) was taken by "many soldiers . . . with them to the trenches," and read those famous lines:

Into my heart an air that kills
From yon far country blows:
What are those blue remembered hills,
What spires, what farms are those?

That is the land of lost content,
I see it shining plain,
The happy highways where I went
And cannot come again.[46]

That this was television did not diminish the power of the verse, which, we remember, is portable enough to have been as memorably exploited in respect of the Australian Outback by Nicholas Roeg at the end of his film *Walkabout*, nor its capacity to reinforce the myth that *patria* resides for us all in the blue remembered hills, the spires and farms.

Something of the nature of that identification of person with *patria* had been strikingly articulated in the second program. "The Flatlands" focused on eastern England, in which region lies the village of Grantchester. Grantchester of course means the war poet, Rupert Brooke, and Dimbleby read a fair amount of Brooke's most famous sonnet, "The Soldier," where "there's some corner of a foreign field / That is for ever England" and where there "shall be / In that rich earth, a richer dust concealed; / A dust whom England bore."[47] The Englishman is so identified with place that his body is coeval with it. At this point we appear to have further forgotten the idea of *The Landscape of Britain*. The Brooke segment was tapping into a sentimental Englishness that the fifth of these films, "The Home Front," explored in some detail. It began with a shot of the presenter gazing out at a perspective of white cliffs, and then out to sea: "The white cliffs of the south coast: a symbol of Britain's defiance" (so now "Britain" is Kent). We were to visit the Island Nation, a place which had withstood invasion since 1066.[48] It defined itself by what it was not. Driving up the coast of Sussex toward the town of Bognor Regis, Dimbleby admitted that it "is a bit bleak, I suppose. I like bleak . . . what do you expect? This is the English channel; not the South of France or Southern Spain."

This is the coast that invaders target, where, had it not been thwarted, the Third Reich would have poured its soldiers and violated that "precious stone set in the silver sea."[49] In contrasting its bracing asperity with the torpid louchness of Mediterranean countries, Dimbleby was implying that despite centuries of immigration from Italy, from Germany and Scandinavia and France, the English, if not the Scots or Welsh, or at least the southern English were a breed apart from Continental Europeans. In one segment of the film, Dimbleby visited the house at Felpham in Sussex which William Blake had occupied in 1800, and spoke of how Blake's great poem "Jerusalem" "imagines England as the promised land," and the air was filled with a choir lustily singing that poem to Hubert Parry's 1916 arrangement. Dimbleby joined in, singing badly, and after a helicopter shot of him driving on a suspiciously empty road through invitingly springlike downland, he suggested that, to the Londoner, William Blake, all this must have seemed "like paradise. It still does, really": at which point the choral "Jerusalem" rose to a stirring crescendo. Dimbleby was not the first to imagine England as some "other Eden, demi-paradise," a "fortress built by Nature for herself,"[50] and, after a suggestive investigation of the Battle of Britain through the paintings of then war artist Paul Nash, the film closed with Dimbleby, Vera Lynn, a shot of the White Cliffs, and a Spitfire flying past. After a little persuasion Lynn sang a snatch of "(There'll Be Bluebirds Over) the White Cliffs of Dover."

To those brought up in the England of the 1950s and 1960s, this startlingly *retardaire* iconography remains evocative, even if it should have become so irrelevant that a first impulse is simply to explain it away as a self-indulgence on the part of a presenter who was as integral to the series as the scenery through which he was so often filmed traveling. The little Englander persona appeared out of kilter, too, not least because Dimbleby himself had learned French in Paris and Italian in Perugia, and throughout the series displayed sufficient literary finesse to render it unlikely that he was unaware of the radical content of Blake's "Jerusalem," itself part of the preface to the epic poem, *Milton*. In addition, either he or his producer did take pains to eschew the bland. That very first film ended up in Bronte Country in Yorkshire, and some fine and prolonged shots of wind farms—an element of contentious modernity in a landscape which, despite constantly changing, is more usually presented by its protectors as "timeless." And, though, as I have mentioned, Dimbleby's Britain was curiously uncrowded, it was not altogether a simple place.

In Sussex Dimbleby appeared the traditional patriot on his own turf, at the same time cryptically quoting Kipling on that region as being "the most marvelous of all the foreign lands he'd been in." In Scotland he spoke of her "violent history" and how "Scotland and Ireland have had a very troubled relationship with England," and how artists and writers "create a sense of national identity for their two countries." There was an element of self-contradiction here. He went on to be skeptically amusing on Walter Scott and the invention of Scottishness; and, later, not to decry Yeats, Irish Nationalism, and the Easter Rising of 1916. And while he would from time to time resort to poignant sentimentality in scenery of engaging and sometimes gripping appeal, there remained what was perhaps an honesty that meant that as well as expounding on Elgar's love for the Malvern Hills and the radical relationship his music had with them, he stressed too the composer's increasing unease "with the flag waving" that "Land of Hope and Glory" inspired, and still inspires. "Patriotism," said Dr. Johnson, "is the last refuge of the scoundrel."

In other words, the films of *A Picture of Britain*, while at one level functioning, despite some of the weather, as an enticing travelogue, attempted, in the Reithian way befitting a scion of the BBC, to allow the viewer some literary culture, a capacity to understand ideas, and in general a willingness to accept more than one view of things. Yet the only Asian faces to appear in the series turned up in "The Home Front," in Brighton, where Dimbleby, thronged by cheerful mobs, was eating cockles and speaking, with no apparent irony, of how the influx of daytrippers after the introduction of fast rail travel in 1841 initiated "class warfare" on the beaches. As one would hope, the book, despite appearances, also paid its readers some respect: "despite appearances" because editorial policy had declared war on complex sentences, or on any punctuation beyond the comma or hyphen. Nevertheless, the authors, all Tate curators and distinguished scholars, won through. In her essay for the "Home Front" section, Christine Riding pointed out that Alex Potts and Jane Beckett "have noted (in reference to the late nineteenth century) characterizing 'the English countryside as the essence of Englishness' was 'a defence mechanism, incorporated and mobilised as a national mythology in times of political tension.'"[51] Hence, perhaps, in the troubled times of the Thatcher and Major years it was natural that Constable and his art should be rendered static, comprehensible; their study ringfenced from the type of inquiry that might have them raise awkward ideas about ways of seeing, or the actual histories that underpinned their subjects.

Once the historical is defused in this way, it is not far from becoming heritage, part of some indefinably shared past we are assumed to have but which can have only curiosity value. And, as Shakespeare's Stratford, one great monument to the British heritage industry, is mostly aimed at the tourist dollar rather than a communal celebration of Shakespeare's writings as a living thing, Constable, in one small corner of East Anglia, is looking to be in danger of going the same way.[52] This is entirely appropriate for a neoliberal economics which understands the market as the only model for society and that the consumer as the only public role for the individual. In Manchester the "hundreds of smoking chimneys have been erased from the landscape. The cotton-mills have been converted into canal-side of apartments" and it "has become the pleasure-dome of the North."[53] Its city center is now managed by the Manchester City Centre Management Company rather than any public body which might have civic concerns, and in consequence: "Users of the city are defined as consumers; others, who might endanger those objectives, are ruthlessly marginalised or excluded."[54]

In this view the landscape or paintings of the landscape cannot register. They can hardly articulate ideas of nation when nation is comprised of private individual consumers with no common interest, and where government sees itself as managing the interface between those consumers and global capital rather than with intervening between them by enacting policies. As former British education secretary Charles Clarke observed in 2003, "universities exist to enable the British economy and society to deal with the rapid process of global change" rather than to be "places of learning and scholarship."[55] Likewise, when it comes to culture in the public realm, as "museums have become increasingly complex and costly to manage, and as government support has waned, the temptation is great to follow policies driven not by a mission but by the market."[56] And in this light, Guggenheim director James Krens, who, in partnership with the State Hermitage Museum had, in 2001, opened two museums at the Venetian Resort Hotel-Casino in Las Vegas, stated that his job was to "manage a brand."[57]

In this wise painting is simply cultural product, distinguished, in a properly postmodern way, from no other kind of product so long as it has the proper endorsement, which, among other things, also means that it does not necessarily have to be any good. Which means, as the postmodernists would confirm, that there is no such thing as art, but only visual culture. Glenn D. Lowry, director of the Museum of Modern Art in New York, has quoted John Seabrook on "nobrow culture," which he defines as "an awkward though apt term that describes what happens when the line between art and commerce becomes so blurred . . . that one is indistinguishable from the other."[58] This is counterproductive if, like the museum directors who contributed to the book in which Lowry's essay was printed, your view is that the prime purpose of art is to supply some kind of transcendent experience for the visitor. The person who looks at *The Hay Wain* and is put in mind of the pleasantness of summer days is immediately enjoying a muted version of that kind of experience. To contend that, say, Titian's 1516 *Assunta* in the church of the Frari in Venice is of equal value and interest as a contemporary German woodcut may have some historical justification, but it willfully ignores both the capacity of the former to amaze and move some spectators, and the fact that that experience is now open to any visitor to Venice who is willing to part with a few euros. "It is not," writes Terry Eagleton, "Shakespeare who is worthless, just some of the social uses to which his work has been put"; and it is perverse not to acknowledge that it is partially in its dislocation from the mundane upon which the power of Shakespeare's writing depends.[59] Likewise, we do not see airborne Virgins that often, but are willing to take Titian's on trust.

In "The Home Front," the fifth of David Dimbleby's films in *A Picture of Britain*, Shakespeare's power was evident in the whispers and echoes of John of Gaunt's speech from *Richard II* that could, from time to time, be picked up by the attentive listener. To react to the *way* in which that speech was used was both to acknowledge its persistently seductive power and silently to dispute the character of the Britain that was being pictured. To proclaim the landscape of the South Downs the landscape of nation was to admit to real political power remaining with an inconspicuous landed patriciate. It's their land; therefore, it's their landscape. Yet Dimbleby could not avoid a slippage that revealed some of the innate tensions in all this. That it was also possible to agree that certain paintings offered a transcendent vision of its landscapes, or that certain poems had the power to be deeply moving, was to admit to a politics that allowed for conflicting claims over the images or verses which countered any deadening neo-liberal vision of them as simply commercial counters. Dimbleby, an establishment figure, agreed that he paid young journalists wretched wages, but countered that in return they received a good training. He offered us a picture of Britain that was complex and nuanced and one with which we could engage. In inviting us then to endorse, dispute, refute this notion of a national imagery when the nature of English, if not Welsh or Scots society, makes it virtually impossible to conceive such a concept as viable, he perhaps unwittingly offered a reassurance that the green unpleasant land of neo-liberalism might find opponents in quite unlikely places.

Moreover, the nature of that opposition will be political in essence. If a politics assumes that relations between people are more than material— and here one might suggest that although a market might be an excellent mechanism for buying and selling it might not be so efficacious when it comes to the management of human affairs, with the exception of slave trading—then ideas of how one manages those relations will of necessity be informed by political contingencies. As humanity can be temperamentally fickle, we institute systems of laws; as it sometimes appears capable of acquiring knowledge, we form institutions by which that good might be promoted. Political ideologies arise when it comes to disputing to whose benefits these institutions will be directed. It has long been recognized that creativity and imagination have their places within such a civic framework: The moment in *Casablanca* when Victor Laslo incites the crowds to chorus *The Marseillaise* amounts to more than just a few people singing, just as *The Hay Wain* can be far more than just a painting of a landscape. In allowing that possibility you allow the artwork a status beyond mere commodity. But the first step in restoring what was once assumed to be a normal state of affairs will have to be taken by governments which understand that their duty is to serve their electors rather than merely act as an interface between them and global capitalism.

Notes

1. For potential Australian visitors, for instance, the cover of the "Qantas Holidays Britain & Ireland 2006/7" brochure had a view of Big Ben viewed from within a red telephone box, that for "Creative Holidays Britain & Ireland 06/07" a photograph of a red telephone box, as does that of "Adventure World Britain & Ireland 2006," although this goes one better and sets it alongside a red mailbox and against the honey-colored stone wall of a house or cottage.

2. "Creative Holidays" brochure, p. 6.

3. Taken from the "Qantas Holidays" brochure.

4. "Creative Holidays" brochure, p. 5.

5. This will be discussed later in this essay.

6. David Dimbleby, *A Picture of Britain* with essays by David Blayney Brown, Richard Humphreys, and Christine Riding (London: Tate Publishing, 2005), p. 7.

7. Ibid., p. 9.

8. Barrie Clement, Labour Editor, "Unions Likely to Oppose Dimbleby as BBC Chief," *Independent*, August 11, 2001.

9. Bob Simpson, "Trade Disputes and the Labour Injunction after the Employment Acts of 1980 and 1982," *Modern Law Review* 47 (1984): 577.

10. Clement, "Unions Likely to Oppose Dimbleby."

11. R. B. Beckett, ed., *John Constable's Correspondence IV: Patrons, Dealers, and Fellow Artists* (Ipswich: Suffolk Records Society, 1966), p. 387.

12. Michael Rosenthal, *Constable: The Painter and his Landscape* (New Haven: Yale University Press, 1983), p. 7.

13. Caroline McGhie, "Constable Country's Brush with Controversy," *Financial Times*, January 28–29, 2006.

14. Stephen Daniels, "John Constable and the Making of Constable Country," in *Fields of Vision* (Cambridge: Polity Press, 1993), pp. 200–242.

15. Ibid., pp. 207, 210.

16. Dimbleby, *A Picture of Britain* (book), p.153; broadcast, episode 2: "The Flatlands," broadcast June 12, 2005 (transcript by Michael Rosenthal).

17. All this information is to be found on the laudably informative Horkesley Park Web site: <http://www.horkesleypark.co.uk>.

18. See *Financial Times*, January 28–29, 2006, and the *Guardian* and the *Daily Telegraph*, February 4, 2006.

19. Will Pavry, "This Is Why We Don't Need Heritage Scheme," *Essex County Standard*, January 6, 2006.

20. Ibid.

21. Caroline Davies, "Storm Gathers Over Constable 'Theme Park,'" *Daily Telegraph*, February 4, 2006.

22. *Country Life*, April 6, 2006.

23. For all this information and more, see <http://www.buntingandsons.co.uk>.

24. *Guardian*, February 4, 2006.

25. For all this, see the Buntings' extremely informative Web site, <http://www.horkesleypark.co.uk>.

26. See <http://www.horkesleypark.co.uk>; <http://www.suffolkpunchtrust.org>.

27. Letter in *East Anglian Daily Times*, April 28, 2009; see also <http://www.stourvalley actiongroup.org.uk/Files/EADT28April2009.pdf> and <http://stourvalleyaction group.org.uk> for press more generally; also the Dedham Vale Area of Outstanding Natural Beauty & Stour Valley Project—<http://www.dedhamvalestourvalley.org>— for a letter written to the Principal Planning Officer of Colchester Borough Council on March 31, 2009.

28. The exhibition was held at the Norwich Castle Museum, November 15–December 15, 1969, and at the Victoria and Albert Museum, London, January 15–February 28, 1970.

29. For a comprehensive account of this, see Daniels, "John Constable and the Making of Constable Country," pp. 224ff.

30. Alan Bowness, "Foreword," in David Solkin, *Richard Wilson: The Landscape of Reaction* (exhibition catalog) (London: Tate Gallery, 1982), p. 7.

31. For the reaction to the Solkin catalog, see Alex Potts and Neil McWilliam, "The Landscape of Reaction: Richard Wilson and His Critics," in *The New Art History*, ed. A. L. Rees and Frances Borzello (London: Camden Press, 1990), pp. 106–109; Michael Rosenthal, "Approaches to Landscape Painting," *Landscape Research 9* (1984): 2–12; Daniels, "John Constable and the Making of Constable Country," p. 2. For Thatcher and the BBC, see Stephen Barnett and Andrew Curry Aurum, "The Battle for the BBC," <http://www.bbc.co.uk/historyofthebbc/resources/bbcandgov/pdf/real_lives.pdf>, and Jean Seaton, "Rows and Consequences," *British Journalism Review* 14 (2003): 26–31.

32. These included Ann Bermingham, *Landscape and Ideology: The English Rustic Tradition, 1740–1860* (Berkeley: University of California Press, 1986); Andrew Hemingway, *Landscape Imagery and Urban Culture in Early Nineteenth-Century Britain* (Cambridge: Cambridge University Press, 1992); Daniels, "John Constable and

the Making of Constable Country"; Nigel Everett, *The Tory View of Landscape* (New Haven: Yale University Press, 1994); Charlotte Klonk, *Science and the Perception of Nature: British Landscape Imagery in the Late Eighteenth and Early Nineteenth Centuries* (New Haven: Yale University Press, 1996); and Kay Dian Kriz, *The Idea of the English Landscape Painter: Genius as Alibi in the Early Nineteenth Century* (New Haven: Yale University Press, 1997).

33. For a fine investigation of this, see Terry Eagleton, *After Theory* (London: Allen Lane, 2003).

34. Rosenthal, *Constable: The Painter and His Landscape*.

35. R. B. Beckett, ed., *John Constable's Correspondence*, 6 vols. (Ipswich: Suffolk Records Society, 1962–1968); *John Constable: Further Documents and Correspondence*, ed. Ian Fleming-Williams, Leslie Parris, and Conal Shields (Ipswich: Suffolk Records Society, 1976).

36. Rosenthal, *Constable: The Painter and His Landscape*; for the history of Constable scholarship more generally, see Daniels, "John Constable and the Making of Constable Country," pp. 224–227.

37. Ian Fleming-Williams and Leslie Parris, *Constable* (exhibition catalog) (London: Tate Gallery, 1991), pp. 160–162, entry to No. 76, pp. 301–305, entry to No. 165. See also Stephen Daniels, "The Field of Waterloo," *Rural History* 3 (1992): 139–145; Michael Rosenthal, 'Constable at the Tate: The Bright Side of the Landscape', *Apollo* 134 (August 1991): 77–84, "Constable Then and Now," *Art Monthly Australia* 192 (August 2006): 7–13; John Barrell, "Constable's Plenty," *London Review of Books*, August 13, 1991.

38. Daniels, "John Constable and the Making of Constable Country," p. 229.

39. Ray Lambert, *John Constable and the Theory of Landscape Painting* (Cambridge: Cambridge University Press, 2004)—see my review in *Burlington Magazine* 167 (September 2005): 622.

40. David Blayney Brown, "The Flatlands: 'The Nature of Our Looking,'" in Dimbleby, *A Picture of Britain*, pp. 157–181, 157–158. See also Daniels, "John Constable and the Making of Constable Country."

41. Figures from <http://www.princeofwales.gov.uk>.

42. Dimbleby, *A Picture of Britain*, p. 153.

43. William Wordsworth, *The Prelude* I, ll. 356–388, in *Poetical Works*, ed. Thomas Hutchinson, a new edition revised by Ernest de Selingcourt (London: Oxford University Press, 1969), p. 499.

44. The program was broadcast on July 10, 2005.

45. Broadcast on June 20, 2005.

46. A. E. Housman, *A Shropshire Lad*, XL.

47. Verse transcribed from <http://www.oucs.ox.ac.uk/ww1lit/education/tutorials/intro/brooke/vsoldier.html>, part of the "Virtual Seminar for Teaching Literature," created by the Oxford University Computing Unit.

48. Program broadcast on July 3, 2005.

49. W. Shakespeare, *Richard II*, act 2, scene 2, words spoken by John of Gaunt.

50. Ibid.

51. Christine Riding, "The Home Front: War and Peace," in Dimbleby, *A Picture of Britain*, p. 64. She too goes on to acknowledge the pervasive hold of John of Gaunt's speech.

52. For this see my "Shakespeare's Birthplace at Stratford: Bardolatory Reconsidered," in *Writers' Houses and the Making of Memory*, ed. Harald Hendrix (New York: Routledge, 2008.

53. David Dimbleby, *A Picture of Britain*, commentary to Episode 4, "The Heart of England."

54. UHC Collective, *UHC Collective Works: Manchester 2005–2006* (Manchester: Castlefield Gallery Publications, 2006).

55. Clarke, quoted by Jeevan Vasagfar and Rebecca Smithers, "Will Charles Clarke Have His Place in History?" *Guardian*, May 10, 2003.

56. From the dust cover notes to James Cuno, ed., *Whose Muse? Art Museums and the Public Trust* (Princeton: Princeton University Press, 2004).

57. Ibid., pp. 14, 16.

58. Quoted by Lowry in "A Deontological Approach to Museums and the Public Trust," in Cuno, ed., *Whose Muse?*, p. 146.

59. Terry Eagleton, *The Idea of Culture* (Oxford: Blackwell, 2000), p. 52.

16   The Lie of the Land: Reflections on Irish Nature and Landscape

Nigel Everett

I

In November 2005, Irish State Television showed a documentary, *Land Is Gold*, opening with a broad vista of Derreen, County Kerry. Constituting an entire, oceanic, mountain-bound bay, luxuriant with giant Himalayan rhododendrons, Antipodean ferns, and American conifers, Derreen readily recalls the aesthetics of the sublime—that sense of awed exhilaration most influentially defined by Edmund Burke. Yet the program exists to remind its viewers that this landscape, apparently so quintessentially Irish, should be regarded, beyond its geological framework, as an alien affront. Representatives of Ireland's National Library and National University explain that Derreen was part of the landed empire acquired by Sir William Petty, physician, econometrist, adventurer, and chief cartographer, as well as significant beneficiary, of the Cromwellian confiscation of Ireland. Petty's descendants, earls of Shelburne and marquises of Lansdowne, presided over centuries of hardship, emigration, and famine. All this was a product of the "Anglo-Saxon mindset," reinforced by a new scientific spirit—embodied in Petty, a founding member of the Royal Society for Improving Natural Knowledge—committed to land as a commodity to be appropriated, mapped, secured, and exploited for immediate profit. The old "Gaelic mindset"—devoted to land as a mystical and communal resource—was ill adapted to confront such an assault.

Elsewhere in this volume, Wesley Kort cites Francis Bacon, chief inspiration of the Royal Society, on the "first distemper of learning," when men neglect the study of "matter" for that of "words"—which are "but the images of matter"—and so "fall in love with a picture." In Irish historiography no "picture" recurs more constantly than the politico-racial supplanting of landscapes. William J. Smyth's recent, massively erudite, *Map-Making, Landscapes, and Memory* encapsulates his nation's tragedy as

Gaels "chatting and sporting, loving and fighting in a familiar, warm and wooded land" gave way to the "bare and silent landscape" of English "*conquistadores.*"[1] A Merrie Ireland, prolific with much-loved "native forests" before their extirpation by Englishmen ironically termed "planters," has long constituted a central tenet of Irish nationalism, unquestioned and unquestionable.[2] The fact that Irish literature, from the earliest times, invariably equates such forests with violence might be embraced within Professor Smyth's image of pleasantly fighting Gaels if the prevailing emotions (before the Celtic Twilight cult of armed struggle) were not those of terror, decay, and unheroic death. This is as true of the genial Oliver Goldsmith as the obscure medieval bard who envisaged the descendants of Adam as desperate and embattled souls lost amid a physically dense but spiritually empty wood.[3] Evidence of preplanter Irish entrepreneurs clear-felling vast quantities of timber for shipment to France and Spain is generally ignored, or adduced to underline "Gaelic Resurgence" as the English Pale retreated between the late thirteenth century and the Elizabethan reconquest.[4] Constant legislation, from the mid-sixteenth to early nineteenth centuries, protective of Irish woods and massive schemes of estate planting (not least by the Lansdownes) are easily dismissed as expressions of colonial power, the planting especially insidious as exotic trees supplanted native, with beech no better than spruce.[5]

Edmund Burke's *Reflections on the Revolution in France* (1790) remembers, "sixteen or seventeen years since," a "delightful vision" of Marie Antoinette: "I saw her just above the horizon . . . glittering like the morning-star." Burke's images of Ireland tend to be similarly picturesque, or aspiringly sublime. Around 1760, Burke complained that Ireland was "wholly unplanted," his multiply ironic term for "unimproved"—"the farms have neither dwelling-houses, nor good offices," nor are the lands "almost anywhere provided with fences and communications." In a closely related irony, the "native," that is, Catholic, population had been denied the much-vaunted advantages of primogeniture, a mockery of Gaelic law, or "new species of Statute Gavelkind," dividing their property forever. In the 1770s and 1780s, Burke promoted a kind of Swiftian satire. Opposing the taxation of Ireland's absentee landowners, he became an English Protestant addressing Irish Catholics, alarmed that diminished "connexion" between the two peoples would leave both "barbarized," albeit in different measure. "*We* shall sink into surly, brutish Johns"; "*You* will degenerate into wild Irish"—creatures "as much gazed at" as some "strange animal" from Otaheite. Burke went on to define his homeland as *terra incognita*— "I do not know the map of the country," "have not set my foot in Ireland these sixteen years." "Memory" was Burke's principal resource, recalling an Ireland subject to a "conquest" based on the "total extirpation of the interest of the natives in their own soil." Protestants and Catholics lived in Ireland as "two distinct species," "without common interest, sympathy, or connexion." Even well-disposed members of the "Protestant Ascendancy" might never encounter a Catholic—"unless they happened to talk to their gardener's workmen, or to ask their way, when they had lost it, in their sports." The 1782 grant of Irish legislative independence—on Protestant terms and followed by (naturally humiliating) measures of Catholic "toleration"—confirmed the arrogant illegitimacy of Ascendancy rule. It was a result of militia-led pressure in an act that "did not so much contradict the . . . law, as supersede it"—effectively, a "Revolution."[6]

By the 1790s, Ireland was too thoroughly "planted"; fences were constantly pulled down and breaches made in park walls—"outrages" that "characterize the disorders of an oppressed or a licentious populace." Broadly similar events were occurring in France, as Jacobins leveled official "landmarks," regarded the country as *"carte blanche"* on which to "scribble" at will. In Burke's Ireland, however, Jacobinism was embodied, not in the wreckers of fences and park walls, but a Protestant *"Junto"* determined to secure all power to itself, leaving the wider nation in an equal state of ruin. "Native" rebellion was not only a vindication of "natural" rights, but a form of holy war comparable with Catholic, royalist, and, oddly enough, English resistance to Regicide France.[7]

Burke's map, or rather memory, of Ireland pictured no distressed Protestants, or flourishing Catholics, and largely confined Protestant virtue to accidental conversation with workmen, Catholic vice to complicity with alien rule. It offered, therefore, no help in understanding Catholic participation in the "Revolution" of 1782, or Protestant leadership of the United Irish "rebellions" of 1796–1798. Burke's contemporary picture of India was yet more partial—distance, ignorance (probably absence) of any coherent map, and above all, absolute lack, therefore luxuriance, of memory, allowing an easy conflation with Ireland. India's virtues—those of an ancient civilization, happy, prosperous, united, possessed of highly developed aristocratic, religious, aesthetic, and moral sensibilities—left her hopelessly ill equipped to deal with Englishmen naturally brutish, cynical, and selfish. Just as the Ascendancy constantly proved it "has no root," so Warren Hastings, the chief tool and presiding genius of Anglo-Indian power, ruled by turning vast tracts of India into "a private domain"—"his park" or, wittily, his "warren"—to fund the more lasting comforts of a Gloucestershire estate.[8]

Burke's short way with things English, Anglo-Indian—above all, Anglo-Irish—was most acerbic in his response to the first marquis of Lansdowne. Conor Cruise O'Brien cites Lansdowne as Burke's chief "devil-figure," and joins with his hero in contemplating another Catiline or Borgia, embodying "all the worst passions of the human mind." The grounds of this loathing include elements of personality and ideology—for example, Lansdowne's desire to make peace with revolutionary France—but the main problem (for Professor O'Brien as much as Burke) is one of ancestry. Sir William Petty "acquired his enormous wealth and vast estates in Co. Kerry through services to Oliver Cromwell"; Burke represented the "Irish Catholic gentry," "intensely proud of their Norman blood," contemptuous of "upstarts who had usurped the lands of their betters." Lansdowne—raised in Kerry, seated in Wiltshire, and British prime minister during the "grant" of legislative independence—personified Ascendancy lack of roots.[9]

An obvious irony is Burke's own rootlessness, his comprehensive substitution of memory for map, and not only in matters of religion and race. During the near-famine conditions of the mid-1790s, Burke was one of two especially trenchant commentators on William Pitt's plans for a radical extension of poor relief, in particular measures to strengthen the bargaining position of laborers vis-à-vis farmers. Jeremy Bentham's dismissal of Pitt's scheme was appropriately utilitarian; it would promote unquantifiable expenditures and discourage individual effort. Burke, often regarded as the antithesis of Bentham, was impassioned, Swiftian, and entirely sincere. He was keen to distance "us"—Burke embodied the Buckinghamshire "farming-interest," having "cast a little root" in that county with the purchase of a 600-acre estate—from the "miserable understandings" of day-laborers, well-meaning intellectuals, and politicians. Such men—lacking any practical wisdom—could hardly understand that the "natural" interests of farmers and laborers were "always the same," and that therefore "free contracts" between them were never "onerous to either party." Burke's desire to confine relief to discretionary charity and gin represented an—essentially revolutionary—dismissal of national traditions, not in favor of some Gaelic, Catholic, even feudal, ideal of community, but the crudest psycho-economics.[10]

Sir William Petty, often cited as a pioneer of free-market values, or lack thereof, had adopted very different views. His *Treatise of Taxes* (1662) divided the "public charge" into six components—foreign war and civil strife, the "Governors," education, the Church, maintenance of the poor, and measures to increase employment. The first four should be "lessened"; of the others, "we shall rather recommend the augmentation." Such interventions were a necessary basis for sound private contracts.[11] Petty famously mapped Ireland; his later work sought a loosening of the demarcations he had so assiduously defined. Petty's *Political Anatomy of Ireland* (1672) found most Irishmen living in the Hobbesian "state of nature"—a "brutish nasty condition"—amid a nation actually or potentially three-quarters "profitable"—"good Meadow, Arable and Pasture." Resolution of this paradox depended on a supplanting of received ideas—economic, political, territorial, religious—equally inimical to enterprise and stability, and the encouragement of ambitions as "natural" among Irishmen as any other race—the "Endeavor to get Estates," acquire "fine Houses and Gardens, Orchards, Groves," in short, all the "commodities" of an advancing civilization.[12]

An effective "plantation" of Ireland would require owners of civilized and civilizing demesnes to establish "As many Fruit and Timber-trees, and also Quick-set Hedges, as being grown up, would distinguish the Bounds of Lands, beautify the Country, shade and shelter Cattle, furnish Wood, Fuel, Timber and Fruit"[13] to satisfy an expanded gentry, contented tenantry, and valued class of laborers. None of these groups was to be limited by species—a comprehensive liberalization of social constraints gradually "transmuting one People into the other." Ireland's public space would expand even as her private "Bounds" were defined and matured without being fixed, equitable laws regulating natural fluctuations between, for example, the feckless and astute, regardless of race or religion.[14]

Conor Cruise O'Brien's reference to Petty's "enormous wealth and vast estates" in Kerry conflates cause and effect, assets and income, maps and memory. Petty's Kerry estates were vast, in large part, because "unprofitable"—"unpassable Bogs, Rocks and Shrubs." Petty certainly attempted to make them pay, but signally failed to do so. His wealth elsewhere subsidized estates soon dismissed in economic, but hardly emotional and intellectual, terms as "mere visions and delusions."[15]

II

Sir William Petty's main predecessors in Kerry, the O'Sullivans, had arrived around 1320, steadily supplanting weaker septs (from the Irish *sliocht*, "tribe" or "clan"). In the late sixteenth century, the O'Sullivans fragmented between factions at various times militantly opposed to and supportive of English rule. The "loyalists" eventually triumphed, expelling or killing their rivals, but, duly supporting the Stuarts, they suffered major confiscations under Cromwell. The transfer of O'Sullivan lands to Petty, his local associates, and descendants did not necessarily involve a change in occupation. Under a series of leases granted (1696–1697) by the late Sir William's agent, Richard Orpen, a significant proportion of leading O'Sullivans retained possession of their lands, agreeing, among other things, to build "good houses" and plant a stated (generally significant) number of trees—mainly oak and fruit—as well as Protestants. Given the effectively perpetual, so unenforceable, nature of these leases, it is unclear how many tenants fulfilled (or were expected to fulfill) such obligations.[16]

Beginning around 1710, Sir William Petty's son Henry—from 1719, first earl of Shelburne—undertook litigation to secure the "avoidance" of perpetuities granted (as he claimed) without his direct assent and inimical to effective estate management. By 1721, the bulk of the leases had been renegotiated, and Shelburne had petitioned the king for authority to establish a manorial court at Dunkerron Castle, hoping thereby to bring order to a region "coarse and mountainous," long inhabited by a population that "living very remote from courts of law, and justice, had hitherto acted without any regard to either." Shelburne was particularly keen to restore the area's "considerable woods"—widely supposed (then and now) to have been felled to supply his father's ironworks, but, according to Shelburne, "almost destroyed" by native pilfering and livestock.[17]

On Shelburne's death (1751), his estates passed to a nephew, who became first earl of Shelburne in a new creation. Shelburne settled in Wiltshire, but Adam Smith, writing (in April 1759) as tutor to Shelburne's younger son, emphasized his "very noble and generous work" in Ireland, his refusal to allow vast areas "to lie waste, almost uninhabited and entirely unimproved," and his determination to "introduce arts, industry and independency into a miserable country," hitherto "a stranger to them all." Nothing, Smith surmised, would have given greater pleasure to Sir William Petty, a man whose ideas "are generally equally wise and public spirited."[18]

The second earl of Shelburne—from 1784, first marquis of Lansdowne—succeeded his father in 1761. A prominent Irish absentee, he proposed (with the support of Oliver Goldsmith and, arguably, Adam Smith) the absentee tax satirized by Edmund Burke for threatening to separate surly Johns from wild Irish. Shelburne also espoused active landlordism, defined, in large part, by a rejection of Burke's views regarding the natural identity of interest between farmers and laborers. Too much power had shifted from landowners to an unholy combination of professionals—lawyers, agents, and middlemen—conspiring with "shrewd, sagacious, advantage-taking" farmers. All were inclined to denounce head landlords as "hard," but happy to exploit subtenants and laborers, for Shelburne (as for Goldsmith

and Smith) the true "strength and wealth and glory of the nation." Landlords should intervene in their favor, build model cottages, "soften and lib-
eralize manners," promote "civilization"—and not least, "keep down the
professions."[19]

In 1764, Shelburne commissioned John Powell's "Topographical Map
or Plan" depicting "several Denominations" of "Lands situated at, or near
Neddeen." The project took nearly three years, complicated by largely
"unprofitable" terrain, bounds widely scattered and often disputed. Various O'Sullivans were (not unnaturally) contentious, but the most irksome,
and intricately commingled, party was Trinity College, an (exclusively
Protestant) institution disposed to manage its landed endowment with
litigious neglect. Shelburne's periodic visits, constant agency reports, and
Powell's map confirmed that a century of family ownership, but hardly
control, had left his Kerry estates generally "wild and unimproved either
by Tillage, Manufactures or Arts." The focus on Nedeen—more townland
than town—reflected Shelburne's identification of a potential port central to his plans for local agriculture, commerce, mining, forestry, tourism, and residential development. Nedeen would be renamed Kenmare to
honor Shelburne's friend, the improving (and Catholic) Thomas Browne,
fourth Viscount Kenmare, and (like Kenmare's Killarney) become a resort
of such appeal as to "incline wealthy people to come into the Country,
and build, and employ the natives." Again in common with Lord Kenmare
(and, of course, Sir William Petty) Shelburne tied successful plantation to
careful planting. Tenants would be "bound" to contribute half the cost
of making "bounds" around new plantations, and then "preserve" those
bounds/plantations; in return, they would own half the "woods and timber trees" standing at the expiration of their lease. Within and about Kenmare, great efforts were to be made in "preserving the woods and planting
fit ground"—the agent's "Lodge park or Demesne" setting the standard,
elegantly designed and ornamented with beech, wych elm, and a variety
of apples. In 1799, a Scottish gardener, William Irvine, arrived to manage
a ten-acre nursery at the center of Kenmare; using local seed, he was to
establish saplings of oak, ash, larch, Scots pine, elm, sycamore, black poplar, willow, birch, quickthorn, and holly for distribution throughout Lord
Lansdowne's Kerry estates.[20]

III

From the early fourteenth century to 1809, Derreen was the seat of a hered-
itary O'Sullivan chieftain known as Mac Finin Dubh. No native records of

this era appear to survive, but Sir William Petty's *Civil Survey* (1653–1654) cites a house standing amid twelve acres of "woody pasture," the only woodland of any kind nearby. Under a lease of February 28, 1697, Dermot O'Sullivan, Mac Finin Dubh, retained possession of Derreen, agreeing (among other stipulations) to build "one good house with double chimney," fence two twenty-acre enclosures with "double ditch and quickset of white thorn and ash trees about them," plant 7,000 oaks, and ten acres of apple, pear, or plum trees. How much of this was accomplished is unknown; for much of the following century the wider parish of Tuosist struck Ascendancy observers, at least, as mere "waste." Dr. Charles Smith's *History of Kerry* (1756) dismissed "one continued rock, terminated with bog." In 1773, Joseph Taylor, agent to Lord Shelburne, was disgusted by "the wildest and most villainous Country I ever saw"—"nothing but Rocks and Mountains and only fit to be inhabited by Barbarians."[21]

Estate records of 1777 indicate some patchy progress at Derreen; the house was in good order and accompanied by a new (unspecified) structure sixty feet long. Derreen's woods (mainly oak) were recently "full grown," but badly damaged, eight years earlier, by careless bark-stripping and incursions of cattle. Blame was readily attached to the tenant, Morty O'Sullivan, a Mac Finin Dubh chiefly associated (in the estate records) with smuggling and drink. Sylvester, his son and (from c. 1796) successor, rose within the Ascendancy as an assistant agent to the Lansdowne estates and a captain in the Kerry militia. He also maintained a reputation for "intemperance," possibly confirmed by his sudden, somewhat mysterious, death in September 1809.[22]

Successful woods were harbingers of improvement, and the first Lord Lansdowne's efforts raised hopes, as his son Lord Henry Petty (later third marquis) put it in 1805, that "trees will grow even in the wildest of our mountains." Visiting Kerry in the autumn of 1809, Petty found 850,000 trees established on 340 acres around Kenmare, with plans well advanced to expand "plantations" into a "considerable district" of the wider estates. Petty's wife offered the first Ascendancy record of Derreen's special charms. In October 1809, Lady Louisa Petty sailed from the rising civilities of Kenmare, past the wilds of Tuosist, to land at the hybrid outpost of Kilmakilloge Harbour. She was obliged by the emotions accompanying Sylvester O'Sullivan's wake to observe the scene from a distance:

It is a beautiful bay surrounded by high mountains, whose broken summits make a magnificent boundary, many of them run into the bay forming bold headlands whose forms and tints vary every step you take.

There was some "natural wood" on one side of the bay; within it, at the bottom of a "conical hill," stood Derreen House.[23] Sylvester O'Sullivan died intestate, leaving Derreen to be fought over by rival kinsmen, both in the courts and through more or less militant skirmishes. Peter McSwiney, locally prominent as a sportsman, litigant, and duelist, prevailed in the struggle by forming an alliance with Mary Anne Browne, O'Sullivan's sister and a kinswoman of Lord Kenmare. In May 1815 McSwiney stormed Derreen at the head of eighty armed men, securing his claim by marrying Mrs. Browne's daughter (and his cousin) Lucinda. A miscegenation, like his predecessor, of Burke's "distinct species," McSwiney combined native esteem with Ascendancy duties as an assistant agent to the Lansdowne estates, magistrate, militia captain, and (from 1841 to 1856) Poor Law Guardian. McSwiney's close relationship with Richard White, first earl of Bantry—his reputed godfather and originally ennobled for services against the Franco–United Irish invasion attempt of December 1796—proved especially useful after McSwiney was accused (in March 1812) of murdering James McCarthy, a local (and native) tithe proctor. McSwiney went into hiding, but agreed to be tried (in March 1814) after receiving promises of support from Lord Bantry, who "did not know a more excellent, or a more correct man."[24]

In 1826, steady improvements on the Lansdowne estates were noted by the Reverend Caesar Otway, an anti-Catholic polemicist keen to contrast the deficiencies of Trinity College—"His Lordship's lands were much better cultivated." A worthy peasant found, or created, by Otway explained that Trinity relied on middlemen, whereas Lansdowne, wishing his "tenants to live and thrive," would permit no man "to set and re-set, over and over again, his estate," and "no Jack of a Squireen" to go "riding in topboots over the country," drinking, carousing, and grinding the faces of the poor.[25] A decade later, the Catholic antiquarian John Windele concurred, finding the environs of Kenmare especially remarkable for "an aspect of improvement highly cheering and gratifying." Large tracts of "heath and unreclaimed mountain" had been transformed into "excellent pasture and productive arable land"; extensive plantations were flourishing, and stone houses supplanting "ancient mud-built cabins." The "general comforts," so "civilization," of the Kerry "peasantry" were rising amid an assiduous development of the "resources of the country."[26]

The map and "memoirs" compiled (1841–1846) by the first Ordnance Survey tend to endorse this sense of improvement. Derreen was an "old house of three stories" surrounded by elaborate drives, plantations, and shrubberies, the wider parish of Tuosist "principally" made up of "rocky and mountainous pasture with a considerable quantity of arable land."[27]

Figure 16.1
Robert French, Derreen House and Knockboy Mountain from Derreen Bridge (1841–1917). From an album commissioned by the Lansdowne estate in 1869 (original album at Derreen).

Lord Devon's commissioners, appointed to investigate relations between Ireland's landlords, tenants, and laborers, heard somewhat different views at their Kenmare hearings of September 1844. James M'Lure, a substantial tenant of the Reverend Denis Mahony—peculiarly miscegenous as an Anglican clergyman and Gaelic chieftain seated at Dromore Castle—noted steady growth in the local economy, but also an apparently inexorable proliferation of families living at the margins of subsistence. Lord Lansdowne was genially culpable, his reputation for benevolence over vast estates creating a perfect setting for subdivision by more or less unscrupulous middlemen. James Hickson, Lansdowne's agent since 1809, broadly agreed; his endeavors to combine moderate rents with significant investment (improved dwellings, roads, drainage, and agricultural practice) acted as a magnet for middlemen and a superabundant class of poor "so anxious to get into land," they did not "care the rent they assume." The standard of living on the Lansdowne estates was "generally mending," but highly vulnerable.[28]

Figure 16.2
Derreen Lawn from Derreen House, also from the album commissioned in 1869.

Augustus Maybery, a Protestant landowner, underlined the deficiencies of Trinity College; a recent agent, Edward Orpen, had been "very severe," and "injured the tenants materially," before being replaced by his sister Lucinda, who was much better inclined. Father John O'Sullivan, parish priest of Kenmare, complained that Trinity knew "almost nothing of the state of the tenantry," and the "great distress" abounding on its lands. Even the middlemen suffered; indeed, they were "often more needy than the tenants themselves." Lord Lansdowne's policies were very different—his nature was benevolent, his rents low, and it was his "mode and principle" to evict nobody, including the poorest squatters on subdivided lands. Yet the main beneficiaries of Lansdowne's good intentions were hardly impoverished. Astute farmer-tenants of the Lansdowne estates (the great majority of them O'Sullivan's parishioners) were responsible for many of the "very good and substantial houses" rising around Kenmare, while their laborers were "the most wretched people upon the face of the globe." Father

O'Sullivan did not believe "that any race on the face of the earth could suffer the privations they do under the farmers."[29]

Such ecumenical criticisms suggest various difficulties in Edmund Burke's map of Ireland as a nation of "distinct species," mitigated (presumably) by a natural coincidence of interest (as well as race and religion) between farmers and laborers. Ironically, perhaps, Burkean values triumphed in the curious combination of seismic shock and tectonic drift represented by Ireland's Great Famine. Britain's *Poor Law Amendment Act 1834* was widely condemned by Tories as a "revolutionary" assault on Old England, yet retained the convention (endorsed, among others, by Petty, Locke, and Blackstone) that relief was a "natural" right, and thus a "public charge."[30] Ireland was excluded, as beyond the pale of a mainland nature highly developed, so deeply compromised by tradition. Richard Whately, Oxford economist before archbishop of Dublin (1831–1863), noted the obvious folly of attaching *"certainty of relief"* to "mere *want*"—"I have seen that operate a good deal in England, and I think it would operate with much more rapid and destructive effect in Ireland." Poor Law legislation of 1838, 1844, and 1847 used Irish backwardness to secure a new nature, achieved by targeting not only the "wanting" among the poor—according to the London *Times* a "race savage, reckless, and irreconcilable"—but a landed class (again according to the *Times*) "without social humanity, without legal obligation, without natural shame."[31] Substantial landowners were made entirely responsible for the maintenance of smaller tenants, cottiers, and laborers; poor rates chargeable to more prosperous tenants took legal precedence over rents. Whig ideologists, typically mixing liberal economics with social engineering, calculated that a major (and inevitable) emergency would replace an absurd social pyramid with fertile plains controlled by a "new race" of "capitalist farmers." Most assumed that this new "race" would be predominantly English and Scottish, but ethnic and religious identity were far less important than personal astuteness, cash flow, and commitment to "free contracts."[32]

Throughout the famine, Lord Lansdowne granted James Hickson, as chairman of the Kenmare Poor Law Board, *"carte blanche"* in the payment of relief.[33] Paradoxically, perhaps, the scale of the disaster—personal, dynastic, and public—eventually caused Lansdowne (born 1780) to set aside old-fashioned ideas of benevolence in favor of more modern, species-driven views of natural and social development. Lansdowne was inaugural chairman of the Statistical Society of London, founded in 1834 by the computer-pioneer Charles Babbage. Keen to reconcile religion and science, Babbage invoked his "Calculating Engine" to demonstrate perfect consistencies between divine design and unpredictability, miracles and the doctrine of probabilities, omnipotence and catastrophe. Central to Babbage's concerns was the role of "memory" in evolution (and, a little more arcanely, eternal judgment). The "natural extinction" of species (and races) was hardly the "dominion of chance," but the fulfillment of a logic "implanted" in every atom of the universe, set in motion and periodically "adjusted" to ensure systematic "adaptations" to a "face of nature" constantly improving in "grandeur." Babbage's imagery was appropriately sublime. The "air we breathe" is "one vast library," "testimony" of man's "changeful will" but "accumulated power"; "a forest of oaks waves its luxuriant branches over a spot fertilized by the ashes of a forest of pines."[34]

Hickson retired, exhausted, late in 1849; his successor, William Steuart Trench, inherited rent arrears exceeding £8,000, an "immense mass of confused accounts," widespread "dilapidation, rot, filth, and ruin." Trench announced a "vigorous collection" of rents and arrears, with "allowances" made for "good" tenants, the "bad" "punished by ejectments" and "emigrated" to North America. Such "weeding out" would be accompanied by "extensive improvements," costing £5,150 annually for the foreseeable future. As anxious to thwart as to promote principles of natural selection, Trench confronted the historic menace of subdivision by obliging tenants to make a direct connection between their sexual proclivities, wider comforts, and local land tenure; "fornication" disqualified a tenant, marriage "without leave" brought an increase in rent. Trench's landscape tastes were similarly decorous. In 1850, he ordered the repair of ruined walls and decayed footpaths near Kenmare and, within the town, the re-equipment of Lord Lansdowne's nursery. The following year, Kenmare's "neat appearance" was further enhanced as "ruined houses" were restored by "men of Capital." In 1853, the road between Kenmare and Derreen was dignified by scatterings of elm, ash, rowan, fir, larch, oak, sycamore, poplar, holly, quickthorn, beech, chestnut, birch, and yew.[35]

By the end of 1856, all seemed well. Lord Lansdowne's tenants were paying their rents "cheerfully"; "pilfering and depredations" no longer menaced the estate woods, rapidly approaching 700 acres and financially "self-sustaining" from thinnings and sporting-lets. Not the least success of 1856 was the eviction of Peter McSwiney for rent-arrears (albeit mollified by compensation of £1,200). Trench had identified McSwiney as the last of an "absurd style of aristocracy," for centuries happily "screwing" their undertenants to support a lifestyle devoted to gambling, fighting, litigation, and drink. McSwiney's departure allowed Trench to relet Derreen's agricultural lands—realizing an immediate gain of £143 *per annum*—and offer the "House and Garden and pleasure grounds" to an un-absurd aristo-crat, a "wealthy Nobleman" whose residence would be of "social and pecu-niary advantage to the estate."[36]

Unfortunately, perhaps, Trench's evolutionary triumph was another Kerry delusion; the old pattern of "suicidal" subdivisions and woodland "destruction" was resumed by 1857. Such setbacks favored planting based on a narrower range of species, typically offering quick growth (in several cases, ready self-propagation), (somewhat suburban) amenity, and limited temptations to grazing and theft. In 1863, John Milne, a "forester resi-dent in Kenmare," recommended the ornamentation of walks in Mucksna Wood—"near to Kenmare, and in the eye of every visitor"—using "ever-greens such as Silver Fir, Spruce, Holly, Portugal & Bay Laurel." Mucksna Mountain should be planted to "give a warm appearance to Kenmare," and Derreen stocked with larch, silver fir, and spruce.[37]

Decisive moves to transform Derreen into a holiday home for the Lansd-ownes began in 1864 with "extensive repairs" to the house and the "taking and planting" of "some prominent tracts of land." The plantation of Der-ryconnery, containing Knockatee, "the beautiful mountain rising behind Derreen," required the transplantation of three families. In 1865, 290 acres of mountain about Derreen were "taken up" and a quick "improvement of the scenery" secured by planting forty acres with "good quality" saplings—mainly larch, fir, spruce, and elm. Over £900 was spent building an exten-sion to the house, a new boathouse and pier, and making walks and drives through Derreen Wood—still predominantly oak, but increasingly diversi-fied by exotic trees and shrubs.[38]

Between 1869 and 1871, Derreen was let to James Anthony Froude, no aristocrat, but a historian fully committed to Whiggish theories of evolu-tion—the means of selection (natural or unnatural) being less important than the ends. Froude's two essays, "A Fortnight in Kerry," used Derreen to encapsulate an Ireland still desperately in need of virtues only Anglo-Sax-ons could supply. Peter McSwiney (by now dead) served to represent the old Gaelic order (perhaps "mindset"). "One of the old fire-eaters" (serial duelists), he drank heavily, exploited his undertenants, and occupied a house—"little more than a cottage"—soon reduced (wittily enough) to the condition of a pigsty. Trees grew "close to the door," in total disregard for the beauties of the location, but serving to shield a variety of nefarious pursuits. With McSwiney's departure, many trees were cleared to form an extensive garden, affording fine views over the bay, but otherwise "shut in on all sides" by "primeval forest." Within the forest, everything was "as Nature made it"—"gnarled and moss-clothed trunks of oaks hundreds of years old," massive boulders draped with ferns, banks of strawberries, whortleberries, and London Pride growing "luxuriantly wild." Nature existed, of course, to be improved—not only by discreet landscaping, but by the wholesale introduction of delightful exotics, especially rhododendrons, "scattered under trees where the ground was dry enough to let them grow." The entire scene embodied Froude's perception that Ireland "can never be independent of England"; the Gael was also "luxuriantly wild," but unruly, so destined to be "laid under discipline" by forces of "education and civilization" sufficiently vigorous to "save him from himself."[39]

The 1872 accounts of the Lansdowne estates in Kerry, prepared by Trench's son and successor, John Townsend Trench, describe Derreen as a "formidable" expense, justified by its "rapidly becoming one of the most beautiful spots in Europe." Trench's commentary evokes scenes of "contentment and prosperity" in the wider estates, but the detailed accounts underline an ever-increasing separation—mirrored throughout Ireland—between demesne and tenants, landlords and agriculture.[40] Rationalists—often admirers—of the Great Famine had hoped for such a result, marked by the advance of "strong"—in the event, overwhelmingly native—farmers, mainly engaged in grazing and sufficiently powerful to ensure that output prices rose substantially ahead of rents and wages. Residual laborers remained dependent on potatoes; politicians continued to peddle abstractions, virtually all committed, like Froude, to sound evolution, but offering a rather different view of its necessary outcome. Froude had envisaged improvement through the cultivation of rhododendrons; the proponents of Ireland's various *Land Acts* (1870–1923) pondered a more noxious exotic, denouncing "landlordism" as "the Upas-tree of Ireland."[41]

Addressing the Richmond Commission in July 1880, the fifth marquis of Lansdowne noted that of his 119,000 acres in Kerry half was officially "wasteland"; rents were low, tenant improvements effectively nil, and farming practices "extremely bad." Capital expenditures between 1859 and 1878 had exceeded £28,000, the rent roll, at around £11,000, remaining essentially static despite significant growth in the Irish economy. The estates had failed to generate a satisfactory return, while affording most inhabitants a standard of living entirely unacceptable by English standards. "More landowners," in the sense of enterprising farmer-proprietors, were clearly needed, and Lansdowne would be happy to oblige; significant sales began in 1882.[42]

IV

The fifth marquis of Lansdowne succeeded to his titles and estates in 1866, taking possession of Derreen five years later. Plant species were steadily introduced from every part of the world, valued for their previous unfamiliarity, aesthetic delight, and not least, lack of any obvious utility. The "disastrous winter" (profound frosts) of 1878–1879 constituted a significant setback—"Fuchsias all cut down, Veronicas killed, Flax damaged, Embothrium done for, Eucalyptus all dead, and many pet curios crippled or gone." Yet evidence of failure would be displaced in Lansdowne's absence, the endeavor continue—"scars soon cover in that luxuriant country wherever there is shelter, and I hope to find no great disfigurement when I return in the Autumn." Improved techniques of "acclimatization" secured that aim, the problems of Derreen increasingly focused on "luxuriance" rather than frost.[43]

Froude evoked a landscape "as Nature made it" apart from scatterings of exotics; the style of gardening exemplified by Lansdowne's Derreen was so taxonomically prolific (or promiscuous) as to form, essentially, a new "Nature." The horticultural journalist William Robinson, Dublin-born but rooted in Sussex, offered to illuminate that Nature in a series of works, beginning with *The Wild Garden* (1870), equally remarkable for their popularity and incoherence. Fashionable science—mainly derived from Darwin and Spencer—was invoking a Nature quintessentially feminine in her unpredictability, often feebleness, yet devoted to internecine violence—the "struggle for existence" or "survival of the fittest." A catfighting Nature was clearly in need of manly intervention—order supplanting effusiveness, mountains, forests, wild beasts, and savage races tamed, if not removed. Yet enough Nature must be left to reinvigorate the civilized spirit, remind humanity of its origin and destiny, promote the hard-edged skills—personal as well as organizational—necessary to successful struggle. Opinions differed as to the nature of the skills desired or required—some favored the disciplines of chivalry, others took cunning to be at least as important as intellect, vastly more valuable than cultural achievement or moral scruple. In the bluff and double-bluff of Victorian preoccupations with untrammeled freedom and social engineering, the only (probable) certainty was (real or apparent) paradox. Liberal individualists became proponents of an all-pervasive State; Benjamin Disraeli, whose *Sibyl* (1845) borrowed Burke's "distinct species" (and aristocratic pretensions) to denounce industrial England's "two nations" (without "intercourse" or "sympathy"), devoted much of his literary and political career to equations of "difference" with "superiority," hence "predominance."[44] Critics of Victorianism dismissed a tedious pottage—the seventh earl of Shaftesbury, for example, lamenting the free rein given to commerce, causing many "tares to be sown" and necessitating tortuous schemes of regulation to "uproot" them.[45]

Victorian tastes in gardening veered between parallel extremes. Industrial-scale production of showy hybrids, elaborate stone, iron, and pipe-work supplied the "blazing" parterres and "Babylonian" terraces swooned at and satirized in Disraeli's *Lothair* (1870). Seeking to upstage such taste, Disraeli married his eponymous hero—possessed of ancient lineage, stupendous wealth, and personal culture—to the similarly stupendous Lady Corisande. The couple then devoted themselves to the common good, not least an espousal of rustic virtue and old "cottage flowers"—cabbage roses, lilies, honeysuckles, gillyflowers, jasmines. Of course, being stupendously wealthy, the Lothairs could enjoy tastefully Babylonian terraces as well as cottage flowers, their true sophistication, amid the Victorian bugbear of and genius for "vulgarity," lying in a capacity to embrace both dignity and simplicity.[46]

Promotion of cottage flowers suggested that the "wild" could hardly be far behind—hence the contemporary emergence of *Lothair* and *The Wild Garden*. Some readers assumed that Robinson was commending the survival of the fittest—an attractive idea, perhaps, for a low-maintenance garden—others, an assemblage of old cottage flowers. Still others, noting the paucity of species indigenous to Britain (especially Ireland—devoid, for example, of native beech, maple, lime, and chestnut), found Robinson an unbridled enthusiast for plants, as he put it, "not in our woods." The argument was evidently complicated by the fact that many cottage flowers—including cabbage roses and "common" jasmine—were well-established imports into "our woods."[47] Froude seems to have envisaged a combination of Robinsonian themes—his Derreen mixed the wild and exotic in a triumph of cultural (probably racial) supersession.

Horticultural controversy, as usual, became heated, proponents of the "formal," "traditional," or "English" garden accusing Robinson of valuing plants only if they were ugly and foreign—perhaps Fenian. The horticultural journalist Wyndham Fitzherbert offered to settle the matter in his *Book of the Wild Garden* (1903). Fitzherbert dismissed any inclination to leave some species to "win the mastery," others to "succumb as fate may will." By employing "solicitude" and the "encompassing shield" of a protective, and protected, wood, a gardener might select materials from the totality of nature, arranging them to achieve an "effect of being indigenous to the spot."[48]

Such a wild garden had obvious appeal—innocent of showy hybrids, architectural and mechanical excess, but nonetheless ambitious, the botanical epitome of a world steadily explored, civilized, memorized, and mapped. The perception that many species newly "discovered" and brought to Britain could achieve levels of growth and beauty, sometimes spontaneous and fetching hybridization, unparalleled in their native habitats, was at once gratifying and entirely natural. Ireland—especially her southwest, widely possessed of dramatic landscapes, temperate climates, and extensive demesnes—was ideally suited to this endeavor. So, of course, was an Ascendancy conscious of growing detachment—its roots constantly denied as well as threatened—yet often doggedly committed to Ireland, at least Anglo-Ireland, variously oblivious and skeptical of a nationalism disposed to view Petty-style "transmutation" as dangerous miscegenation, Burke's "distinct species" as overly diverse. The "foreign" was rejected in favor of more or less invented Gaelic games, music, literature, and design, linguistic, often religious, pieties based on similar ideas of clannish self-denial and delight—the whole grounded in a conviction of racial superiority fortified by interminable memories of subjection and rebellion.[49] Ironically, perhaps, Gaelic sanctities were often most eloquently expressed by self-conscious hybrids. W. B. Yeats invoked the purity of the Gaelic wildwood to imagine an Ireland once again free, martial, spiritual, and above all, innocent of the tawdry "materialism" of a world being mapped and homogenized entirely in the interests of commerce.[50]

V

Reflecting, in 1912, on the fate of *RMS Titanic*, Joseph Conrad pondered a culture overly commercial, cosmopolitan, and complacently obsessed with "mere bigness."[51] By the *Belle*/pre-bellum *Epoque*, Derreen had absorbed a myriad of species under the direction of an owner assisted in his horticultural ambitions by service as Governor-General of Canada and Viceroy of India. Luxuriance naturally favored excess, sometimes a Upas-style menace. Examples of *Rhododendron arboreum* achieved such exaggerated size as to constitute an invasion, and were duly eradicated. Gaultherias, myrtles, laurels, and *Rhododendron ponticum*—variously planted for ornament and game-cover—proliferated out of control into the wider woods. They were joined by sika deer, a Japanese species introduced via Scotland in 1899, and only briefly confined by elaborate fences. Shooting and fishing—focused, Edwardian-style, on "record bags"—necessitated a covert culture of land-poisoning, mass slaughter of foxes, eagles, otters, and seals. Other forms of collateral damage arising from this curious pattern of naturalization and genocide included a major impetus to poaching. With guns and explosives readily available, poachers, landowners, magistrates, and politicians equally happy to equate trespass with rebellion, Derreen acquired yet another new species—"nightwatchmen" mounted on bicycles, armed with revolvers, and fortified by whiskey.[52]

As Home Rule approached, Derreen—like the Ascendancy—was readily perceived as anomalous, provocative, and above all impotent. A "big raid" during the night of April 16, 1918, was followed by reports of nocturnal drilling by Sinn Fein. A summer incident of river-poisoning went unchallenged for fear of the "very lawless feeling at present and the unprotected state of the whole place and of the men who are in charge." The winter brought numerous acts of "intimidation and lawlessness," not least the theft of eight substantial oaks in a single night. Lord Lansdowne's agent, Henry Maxwell, declared himself "helpless" in a "country where everybody sides with the wrongdoers, and is ready to shield them."[53]

In March 1922, Maxwell wrote to the Commandant, IRA No. 5 Brigade, based in Cork, calling for "strong measures" to "put a stop" to acts of "wanton destruction" at Derreen. "Valuable plants" were "being taken nightly from the pleasure grounds," including "Chinese Rhododendrons" and "such like," which could be "of no use to any person." Yet Derreen's raiders knew precisely the use of Chinese rhododendrons—they found a ready market in County Cork. Such economically inspired acts mingled with "malicious damage." During the two weeks following May 14, a dance was held in the Derreen garage, the woods were occupied by cattle, and many "valuable shrubs" stolen or "broken." The night of May 25 found the "usual gang" armed with long bamboo canes as they "thrashed all the Roses off the house."[54]

For much of August and September 1922, IRA and Free State forces battled in Kenmare, two Free State officers being famously murdered, more or less in their beds. Both sides, Maxwell reported, were "quite civil" to the Anglo-Irish. Meanwhile, the bulk of west Kerry demesnes suffered more or less systematic destruction. During the night of September 1, Derreen House was emptied of its furniture and linen. The following day, Maxwell found the house occupied by a "very large number" of "wreckers," some "destroying and looting," others "lying about drunk" on Lord Lansdowne's best whiskey. By September 6, the house was entirely gutted, its floors ripped up, windows and doors removed. An adjacent greenhouse had been "smashed," leaving "a number of rare plants lying about." The demesne woods reminded one observer "unpleasantly of a shell-swept area in Belgium."[55]

By 1925, peace had been largely secured, Derreen House rebuilt, and its gardens restored. There were setbacks—in December 1925, for example, Maxwell's successor, William Mansfield, his wife, and driver were returning from a shoot and held up by four masked men armed with double-barreled shotguns. In the absence of any cash, conversation turned to the "agrarian question," and Mansfield was warned "not to come again robbing the poor people." A few weeks later, Mrs. E. Lyne, member of a Gaelic family long-settled in Tuosist, sent Lord Lansdowne a "secret communication" offering to clarify the events of September 1922. Jack Sullivan, she alleged, had "made a fortune in the sale of timber, furniture, works of art, treasures, books" looted by his son—a Derreen employee—after they had been returned (under priestly pressure) by the more respectable locals. Meanwhile, Sullivan had been "picking up rare plants" and selling them in County Cork.[56]

VI

Land Is Gold laments the continuing anomaly of Derreen's occupation by a descendant of Sir William Petty. Irish independence was, after all, an achievement of heroes prepared to confront colonialists—a species of men, such as the fifth marquis of Lansdowne, who were no mere "pansies"—in order to vindicate nobler views of nation, land, and community. The contrast of values is underlined by images of signs epitomizing the Anglo-Saxon mindset—"Private Property," "No Shooting," "Private Fishing," and so on—the commentator neglecting to mention that these have been posted by Gaelic neighbors, not the estate.

Views of history based on racial mindsets elide with notorious ease into lies. Michael Rosenthal, elsewhere in this volume, analyzes the adroitness with which British politico-commercial interests deploy "pictures," of all kinds, to celebrate, shape, and often pervert the national "way of life." He reflects wryly on the fluctuating fortunes and values of scholars seeking to engage with, or challenge, those interests. *Land Is Gold* underlines various realities—among them, the general absence in Ireland of any serious tension between official and academic values, and (despite the program's best intentions) the importance of such unexploited private spaces as Derreen within a State remarkable since its inception for the destruction of cultural capital.

Continued flogging of a dead colonial horse seems an especially feckless pursuit given the recent fate of the Gaelic mindset—swallowed by (or perhaps evolved into) the Celtic Tiger. The Tiger, of course, has recently suffered a reversal, retreating, presumably, into its more or less native forests. In its brightest days of 2005–2007, property speculation constituted around one-quarter of the Irish economy. In an especially triumphant moment, the Irish tricolor was hoisted over London's "ultra-luxurious" Savoy Hotel. The Celtic Tiger was most ravenous as an instrument of displacement. Floodplains, ancient and natural monuments gave way—briefly, as regards many of the floodplains—to houses and shops, cities disgorged into apparently infinite suburbs, immigrants arrived to supply cheaper labor; social inequalities were multiplied, public spaces privatized, private vulgarized before becoming loss-making, and thus nationalized. Further national responses to the fruits of the Celtic Tiger may help to indicate the extent to which he is a colonial exotic, a native force unleashed from the Celtic Twilight, or a not-so-subtle hybrid of these, and other, species.

Notes

1. William J. Smyth, *Map-Making, Landscapes, and Memory* (Cork: Cork University Press, 2006), p. 87.

2. The standard account of Irish forests remains Eileen McCracken, *The Irish Woods Since Tudor Times* (Newton Abbot: David and Charles, 1971).

3. Oliver Goldsmith, *The Deserted Village* (London: W. Griffin, 1770), ll. 341–362; Neil Buttimer, "Gaelic Ireland," *Journal of the Cork Archaeological and Historical Society* 107 (2002): 217–228.

4. For hints, see Alice Stopford Green, *The Making of Ireland and Its Undoing* (London: Macmillan, 1908), pp. 14–38; Michael Dolley, *Medieval Anglo-Irish Coins* (London: Seaby, 1972), pp. 16–41; J. J. Silke, *Kinsale* (Liverpool: Liverpool University Press, 1970), pp. 77–78; Alph O'Brien, "Commercial Relations between Aquitaine and Ireland, c. 1000–c. 1550," in *Aquitaine and Ireland in the Middle Ages*, ed. Jean-Michel Picard (Dublin: Four Courts Press, 1995), pp. 31–80; Smyth, *Map-making, Landscapes, and Memory*, pp. 23–29.

5. See, for example, the abundant Internet documentation for Ireland's Native Woodlands Scheme.

6. Edmund Burke, "Reflections," in *The Works of the Right Honorable Edmund Burke* (London: Rivington, 1815–1827), vol. V, p. 149; "Tracts Relative to the Laws against Popery in Ireland," in *Works*, vol. IX, pp. 327–333, 379–385, 390–391; "Letter to Sir Charles Bingham on the Irish Absentee Tax," in *Works*, vol. IX, pp. 134–147; "Letter to Thomas Burgh," in *Works*, vol. IX, pp. 248–250; "Letter to a Peer of Ireland," in *Works*, vol. VI, pp. 293–296; "Letter to Sir Hercules Langrishe on the Roman Catholics of Ireland," in *Works*, vol. VI, pp. 356–360. (Note that the present essay footnotes entire paragraphs rather than individual quotations.)

7. Burke, "Letter to Sir Hercules Langrishe," in *Works*, vol. VI, p. 313; Michael Biggs, "Putting the State on the Map," *Comparative Studies in Society and History* 41, no. 2

(1999): 374–405; James Conniff, "Reflections on the Coming Revolution in Ireland," *Journal of the History of Ideas* 47, no. 1 (1986): 37–59.

8. Burke, "Trial of Warren Hastings," in *Works*, vol. XV, pp. 339–340.

9. Conor Cruise O'Brien, *The Great Melody* (London: Sinclair-Stevenson, 1992), pp. 235–240.

10. F. P. Lock, *Edmund Burke*, vol. I: *1730–84* (Oxford: Oxford University Press, 1998), p. 249. On Burke's financial "roots" see Dixon Wecter, *Edmund Burke and His Kinsmen* (Boulder: University of Colorado Press, 1939). Bentham's review of Pitt's proposals was published as *Observations on the Poor Bill* (London: William Clowes, 1838); Burke quotations are from "Thoughts and Details on Scarcity," in *Works*, vol. VII, pp. 373–419.

11. E. A. Wrigley, *Continuity, Chance, and Change* (Cambridge: Cambridge University Press, 1988), pp. 121–122.

12. Sir William Petty, *Political Anatomy of Ireland* (Shannon: Irish University Press, 1970), pp. 27, 91–99.

13. Ibid., pp. 29, 121.

14. Ibid., pp. 26–29, 118–123.

15. Sixth Marquis of Lansdowne, *Glanerought and the Petty-Fitzmaurices* (Oxford: Oxford University Press, 1937), p. 211.

16. Gerard J. Lyne, "The Mac Finin Duibh O'Sullivans of Tuosist and Berehaven," *Journal of the Kerry Archaeological and Historical Society* 9 (1976): 32–67.

17. Gerard J. Lyne, "Land Tenure in Kenmare and Tuosist, 1696–c.1716," *Journal of the Kerry Archaeological and Historical Society* 10 (1977): 19–54; "Land Tenure in Kenmare, Bonane, and Tuosist, 1720–70," *Journal of the Kerry Archaeological and Historical Society* 11 (1978): 25–55; Lansdowne, *Glanerought*, pp. 99, 134–135, 164–169.

18. Adam Smith, *Correspondence* (Oxford: Oxford University Press, 1987), pp. 32, 38.

19. Oliver Goldsmith, "The Revolution in Low Life," *Lloyd's Evening Post*, June 14–16, 1762, pp. 14–16; Adam Smith, *Wealth of Nations* (Oxford: Oxford University Press, 1976), pp. 264–266; Lansdowne, *Life of Shelburne*, vol. II (London: Macmillan, 1912), pp. 228–229, 303–307, 336–367.

20. Lansdowne, *Glanerought*, pp. 61–68, 81–91.

21. Charles Smith, *The Antient and Present State of the County of Kerry* (Dublin; printed for the author, 1756), pp. 252–254; Lyne, "Land Tenure in Kenmare, Bonane, and Tuosist, 1720–70," p. 30; Lansdowne, *Glanerought*, p. 158.

22. Lansdowne, *Glanerought*, pp. 165–169.

23. Ibid., pp. 91–96, 117–118, 164–169.

24. Gerard J. Lyne, "Peter McSwiney and the Vexed Succession to the Last Mac Finin Duibh," *Journal of the Kerry Archaeological and Historical Society* 13 (1980): 50–81.

25. Caesar Otway, *Sketches in Ireland* (Dublin: William Curry, 1827), pp. 367–368.

26. John Windele, *Notices of the City of Cork* (Cork: Bolster, 1849), p. 332.

27. *Ordnance Survey Papers* (unpaginated typescript in the Boole Library, University College Cork): Kerry volume, Tuosist.

28. *Report of the Devon Commission* (London: British House of Commons Sessional Papers, 1845), pp. 909–920.

29. Ibid., pp. 917–923.

30. Richard Whateley, *Introductory Lectures on Political Economy*, 2nd ed. (London: B. Fellowes, 1832), pp. 278–279. On Tory views see, for example, Richard Oastler, *Letters to the Duke of Wellington* (London: J. Cochrane, 1835) and Robert Seeley, *Life of Michael Thomas Sadler* (London: Seeley & Burnside, 1842).

31. James S. Donnelly, *The Great Irish Potato Famine* (Stroud: Sutton Publishing, 2002), pp. 98–131.

32. John Stuart Mill, *Principles of Political Economy*, 2nd ed., 2 vols. (London: J. W. Parker, 1849), vol. I, pp. 284–285; William Whewell, *Six Lectures on Political Economy* (Cambridge: Cambridge University Press, 1862), pp. 97–102; R. J. Scally, *The End of Hidden Ireland* (Oxford: Oxford University Press, 1995), pp. 185–186.

33. William Steuart Trench, *Realities of Irish Life* (London: MacGibbon & Kee, 1966), pp. 55–66; Lansdowne, *Glanerought*, pp. 109–111; *Reports of the Lansdowne Estates in Kerry* (ms. Derreen House—hereafter *Reports*), 1850–1851; Gerard J. Lyne, *The Lansdowne Estates in Kerry* (Dublin: Geography Publications, 2001), pp. 34–35, 76, 165–166.

34. Charles Babbage, *Ninth Bridgewater Treatise*, 2nd ed. (London: Frank Cass, 1967), pp. 44, 60, 88–112, 160, 175.

35. *Reports*, 1850–1852; *Glanerought Estate Minute Books* (ms. Derreen House—hereafter *Minutes*), February 6, 1854, March 13, 1861, March 14, 1862.

36. *Reports*, 1850–1853, 1855; *Minutes*, May 12–15, 1854.

37. *Reports*, 1854–1856, 1858–1860; *Minutes*, September 29, 1857.

38. *Reports*, 1860–1863; *Minutes*, October 24, 1863.

39. *Reports*, 1864–1865; James Anthony Froude, *Short Studies on Great Subjects* (London: Longmans, Green, 1871), pp. 180–193, 210–213.

40. *Reports*, 1866–1873.

41. See Samuel Clark, *Social Origins of the Irish Land War* (Princeton: Princeton University Press, 1979) and W. E. Vaughan, *Landlords and Tenants in Mid-Victorian Ireland* (Oxford: Oxford University Press, 1994).

42. *Royal Commission on Agriculture 1881* (London: H.M.S.O., 1881), pp. 725–739.

43. Lansdowne to Peter Fitzgerald, May 5, 1879; Lady Lansdowne to Fitzgerald, September 6, 1879 (Knight of Kerry ms. 2/154, 2/211—courtesy of Sir Adrian Fitzgerald).

44. Todd M. Endelman, "Benjamin Disraeli and the Myth of Sephardi Superiority," *Jewish History* 10, no. 2 (September 1996): 21–35.

45. Edwin Hodder, *Life and Work of the Seventh Earl of Shaftesbury* (London: Cassell, 1888), pp. 312, 357, 476, 641–645.

46. Benjamin Disraeli, *Lothair* (London: Peter Davies, 1927), pp. 196–197.

47. Reginald Blomfield and F. Inigo Thomas, *The Formal Garden in England* (London: Macmillan, 1892), pp. vi–viii, xx, 127, 227–232.

48. Wyndham Fitzherbert, *Book of the Wild Garden* (London: Peter Davies, 1903), pp. 5, 21, 68.

49. See, for example, the Gaelic Athletic Association opposition to "foreign games" and the "Gaelic mindset" exemplified in the writings of Simone Téry, notably *L'Île des bardes* (Paris: Flammarion, 1925).

50. William Butler Yeats, preface to Lady Gregory, *Gods and Fighting Men* (New York: Scribner, 1904).

51. Joseph Conrad, *Notes on Life and Letters* (London: Gresham Publishing, 1925), pp. 213–228.

52. *Reports*, 1892–1893, 1903–1904.

53. Maxwell to Lansdowne, May 26, 1918; to Rochfort, February 5, 1915, August 2, 1918, February 6, 1919 (this and following correspondence at Derreen).

54. Maxwell to I.R.A., March 20, 1922; to Rochfort, May 18, 1922; Arrowsmith to Maxwell, May 26, 1922.

55. Mansfield to Downing, September 18, 1922; to "Issy," September 13, 1922; Lansdowne, *Glanerought*, p. 203.

56. Mansfield to Lord Kerry, December 13, 1924; Mrs. E. Lyne to Lansdowne, January 16, 1926.

Bibliography

Aben, R., and S. deWit. *The Enclosed Garden: History and Development of the* Hortus conclusus *and Its Reintroduction into the Present-Day Urban Landscape*. Uitgeverij: 010 Publishers, 1999.

Abramovitz, Jane. *Unnatural Disasters*. Washington, D.C.: Worldwatch Paper 158, 2001.

Ackroyd, P. *The Life of Thomas More*. London: Random House, 1999.

Acton, Harold. *Tuscan Villas*. London: Thames & Hudson, 1970.

Acton, Harold. *Memoirs of an Aesthete*. London: Methuen, 1948.

Alcock, Susan E., and Robin Osbourne, eds. *Placing the Gods: Sanctuaries and Sacred Space in Ancient Greece*. Oxford: Clarendon Press, 1994.

Anderson, A. O., and M. O. Anderson, eds. *Adomnan's Life of Columba*. Oxford: Clarendon Press, 1991.

Anderson, J. The voyage of Brendan: An Irish monastic expedition to discover the wonders of God's world. *American Benedictine Review* 43 (1992): 262–282.

Appadurai, Arjun. *Modernity at Large: Cultural Dimensions of Globalization*. Minneapolis: University of Minnesota Press, 1996.

Apter, D., and T. Saich. *Revolutionary Discourse in Mao's Republic*. Cambridge, MA: Harvard University Press, 1998.

Arendt, Hannah. *Condition de l'Homme moderne*. Paris: Pocket, 1983.

Arendt, Hannah. *The Human Condition*, 2nd ed. Chicago: University of Chicago Press, 1998.

Armstrong, R., and I. Brady, eds. *Francis and Clare: Complete Works*. New York: Paulist Press, 1982.

Ashcroft, B. The horizon sublime. *Antipodes: A North American Journal of Australian Literature* 19 (2005): 141–151.

Babbage, Charles. *Ninth Bridgewater Treatise: A Fragment*, 2nd ed. London: Frank Cass, 1838/1967.

Bachelard, Gaston. *The Poetics of Space*. Trans. Maria Jolas. Boston: Beacon Press, 1958/1976.

Bacon, Francis. *The Advancement of Learning*. Ed. Arthur Johnston. Oxford: Clarendon Press, 1974.

Baert, Patrick. *Time, Self, and Social Being*. Aldershot: Avebury, 1992.

Barrell, John. Constable's plenty. *London Review of Books*. August 13, 1991.

Barrell, John. *The Dark Side of the Landscape: The Rural Poor in English Painting 1730–1840*. Cambridge: Cambridge University Press, 1980.

Barrell, John. *The Idea of Landscape and the Sense of Place, 1730–1840: An Approach to the Poetry of John Clare*. Cambridge: Cambridge University Press, 1972.

Basso, K. Wisdom sits in places: Notes on Western Apache landscape. In *Senses of Place*, ed. S. Feld and K. Basso. Sante Fe: School of American Research Press, 1996, 53–70.

Baxandall, M. Kunst, Gesellschaft und das Bougier-Prinzip. *Freibeuter* 33 (1987).

Beckett, R. B., ed. *John Constable's Correspondence*. 6 vols. Ipswich: Suffolk Records Society, 1962–1968.

Bede. *Ecclesiastical History*. Trans. L. Sherley-Price. London: Penguin Classics, 1990.

Beevor, Kinta. *A Tuscan Childhood*. London: Viking, 1993.

Bellosi, L. "Castrum pingatur in palatio." 2. Duccio e Simone Martini pittori di castelli senesi "a l'esemplo come erano." *Prospettiva* 28 (1982): 41–65.

Belting, H. Das Bild als Text. Wandmalerei und Literatur im Zeitalter Dantes. In *Malerei und Stadtkultur in der Dantezeit. Die Argumentation der Bilder*, ed. H. Belting and D. Blume. Munich: Hirmer, 1989, 23–64.

Bender, B. Introduction: Landscapes—meaning and action. In *Landscape, Politics, and Perspectives*, ed. B. Bender. London: Berg, 1993, 1–18.

Benjamin, Andrew. *Art, Mimesis, and the Avant-Garde*. London: Routledge, 1991.

Benjamin, Andrew. *Disclosing Spaces: On Painting*. Manchester: Clinamen Press, 2004.

Benjamin, Andrew. *Style and Time: Essays on the Politics of Appearance*. Chicago: Northwestern University Press, 2006.

Benjamin, Andrew. *The Plural Event*. London: Routledge, 1993.

Benterrak, K., S. Muecke, and P. Roe. *Reading the Country*. Fremantle: Fremantle Arts Centre Press, 1984.

Bentham, Jeremy. *Observations on the Poor Bill*. London: William Clowes, 1838.

Berger, John. *Ways of Seeing*. Harmondsworth: Penguin, 1972.

Berleant, A. *The Aesthetics of Environment*. Philadelphia: Temple University Press, 1992.

Bermingham, Ann. *Landscape and Ideology: The English Rustic Tradition, 1740–1860*. Berkeley: University of California Press, 1986.

Berque, Augustin. De paysage en outre-pays. *Revue Le Débat* 65 (1991): 4–13.

Bertelsen, Lars Kiel. The Claude Glass: A modern metaphor between word and image. *Word and Image* 20 (3) (2004): 182–190.

Bian, Y. J. and R. Breiger. Occupation, class, and social networks in China. *Social Forces* 8 (2005): 1443–1468.

Bielawski, E. Inuit indigenous knowledge and science in the arctic. In *Naked Science: Anthropological Inquiry into Boundaries, Power, and Knowledge*, ed. L. Nader. New York: Routledge, 1996, 216–227.

Biggs, Michael. Putting the state on the map. *Comparative Studies in Society and History* 41 (2) (1999): 374–405.

Blomfield, Reginald, and F. Inigo Thomas. *The Formal Garden in England*. London: Macmillan, 1892.

Bloom, Harold. *Where Shall Wisdom Be Found?* New York: Riverhead Books, 2004.

Blumenberg, H. *Der Prozess der theoretischen Neugierde*. Frankfurt: Suhrkamp, 1973.

Borst, A. *Barbaren, Ketzer und Artisten. Welten des Mittelalters*. Munich: Piper, 1988.

Borst, A. *Lebensformen des Mittelalters*. Frankfurt: Ullstein, 1979.

Bourdieu, P. *Outline of a Theory of Practice*. Cambridge: Cambridge University Press, 1979.

Bourdieu, Pierre. *Language and Symbolic Power*. Ed. John Thompson, trans. Gino Raymond and Matthew Adamson. Cambridge, MA: Harvard University Press, 1991.

Bowen, E. G. *Saints, Seaways, and Settlements*. Cardiff: University of Wales Press, 1977.

Bradley, J. "We always look north": Yanyuwa identity and the marine environment. In *Customary Marine Tenure in Australia*, ed. N. Peterson and B. Rigsby. Sydney: University of Sydney Oceania Publications, 1998, 124–141.

Bradley, J. How can a whitefella know it all . . .? Indigenous science/Western science and marine turtles. In *Marine Turtle Conservation and Management in Northern Australia*. Proceedings of a workshop held at Northern Territory University, Darwin, June 3–4, 1997. Darwin: Centre for Indigenous Natural and Cultural Resource

Management and Centre for Tropical Wetlands Management, Northern Territory University, 1997, 25–33.

Bradley, J. Landscapes of the mind, landscapes of the spirit: Negotiating a sentient landscape. In *Working on Country: Contemporary Indigenous Management of Australia's Lands and Coastal Regions*, ed. R. Baker, J. Davies, and E. Young. Melbourne: Oxford University Press, 2001, 295–307.

Bradley, J. Singing through the sea: Song, sea, and emotion. In *Deep Blue: Critical Reflections on Nature, Religion and Water*, ed. Sylvie Shaw and Andrew Francis. London: Equinox Publishers, 2008.

Bradley, J. When a stone tool is a dingo: Country and relatedness in Australian Aboriginal notions of landscape. In *Handbook of Landscape Archaeology*, ed. B. David and J. Thomas. Walnut Creek: Left Coast Press, 2008.

Bradley, J. Wirriyarra Awara: Yanyuwa land and sea scapes. *South Atlantic Quarterly* 98 (2000): 801–816.

Bradley, J., M. Holmes, D. N. Marrngawi, A. I. Karrakayn, J. M. Wuwarlu and I. Ninganga. *Yumbulyumbulmantha ki-awarawu—All Kinds of things from Country—Yanyuwa ethnobiological classification*. Aboriginal and Torres Strait Islander Studies Unit Research Report Series, vol. 6. St Lucia: University of Queensland, 2006.

Bresson, Robert. *Notes on the Cinematographer*. London: Quartet, 1975/1986.

Brinkley, Douglas. *The Great Deluge: Hurricane Katrina, New Orleans, and the Mississippi Gulf Coast*. New York: William Morrow, 2006.

Brooke, Isis. Can Merleau-Ponty's notion of "flesh" inform or even transform environmental thinking? *Environmental Values* 14 (3) (2005): 353–362.

Brown, Charles, and Ted Toadvine, eds. *Eco-phenomenology: Back to the Earth Itself*. New York: SUNY Press, 2003.

Brown, Daniel, Richard Aspinall, and David Bennett. Landscape models and explanation in landscape ecology: A space for generative landscape science. *Professional Geographer* 58 (2006): 369–382.

Brown, David Blayney. The Flatlands. "The nature of our looking." In *A Picture of Britain*, with essays by David Blayney Brown, Richard Humphreys and Christine Riding, ed. David Dimbleby. London: Tate Publishing, 2005, 157–181.

Brown, P. *Society and the Holy in Late Antiquity*. Berkeley: University of California Press, 1989.

Brown, P. *The Making of Late Antiquity*. Cambridge, MA: Harvard University Press, new edition 1993.

Brueggemann, W. *The Land: Place as Gift, Promise, and Challenge in Biblical Faith.* Philadelphia: Fortress Press, 1977.

Buchanan, I. *Michel de Certeau: Cultural Theorist.* London: Sage Publications, 2000.

Buku-Larrngay Mulka Centre. *Saltwater People: Yirrkala Bark Paintings of Sea Country. Recognising Indigenous Sea Rights.* Yirrkala: Buku-Larrngay Mulka Centre in Association with Jennifer Isaacs Publishing, 1999.

Burckhardt, J. *The Civilization of the Renaissance in Italy.* Trans. S. G. C. Middlemore and I. Gordon. New York: American Library, 1960.

Burel, Françoise, and Jacques Baudry. *Landscape Ecology: Concepts Methods and Applications.* Enfield, NH: Science Publishers, 2003.

Burgi, Mattias, Anna Hersperger, and Nina Schneeberger. Driving forces of landscape change: Current and new directions. *Landscape Ecology* 19 (2004): 857–868.

Burke, Edmund. *The Works of the Right Honourable Edmund Burke,* 15 vols. London: Rivington, 1815–1827.

Burke, Edmund. *A Philosophical Enquiry into the Origin of Our Ideas of the Sublime and Beautiful.* Ed. James T. Boulton. Notre Dame: University of Notre Dame Press, 1759/1993.

Busch, W. *Landschaftsmalerei.* Berlin: Riemer, 1997.

Buttimer, Anne. Grasping the dynamism of the lifeworld. *Annals of the Association of American Geographers* 66 (1976): 277–292.

Buttimer, Neil. Gaelic Ireland. *Journal of the Cork Archaeological and Historical Society* 107 (2002): 217–228.

Buwarrala Akarriya. (Journey East). Video. Marndaa Productions and Australian Broadcasting Commission, 1989.

Cabrales Barajas, L. F., and E. Zamora Canosa. Residential segregation and urban fragmentation: Closed neighbourhoods in Guadalajara. *Espiral* 7 (2001): 223–253.

Cache, Bernard. *Earth Moves: The Furnishing of Territories.* Cambridge, MA: MIT Press, 1995.

Cane, A., ed. 2002. *Mario Praz, Belleza e bissarria, Saggi scelti.* Milan: Mondadori, 323–324.

Carli, Enzo. *The Landscape in Art.* New York: William Morrow, 1980.

Carlson, Allen. *Aesthetics and the Environment.* London: Routledge, 2000.

Carter, Ian. *Railways and Culture in Britain: The Epitome of Modernity.* Manchester: Manchester University Press, 2001.

Carter, P. *The Road to Botany Bay*. London: Faber and Faber, 1987.

Casey, Edward S. *Getting Back into Place: Towards a Renewed Understanding of the Place-World*. Bloomington: Indiana University Press, 1993.

Casey, Edward S. How to get from space to place in a fairly short stretch of time: Phenomenological prolegomena. In *Senses of Place*, ed. S. Feld and K. Basso. Sante Fe: School of American Research Press, 1996, 13–52.

Casey, Edward S. *Re-Presenting Place: Landscape Painting and Maps*. Minneapolis: University of Minnesota Press, 2002.

Casey, Edward S. Smooth spaces and rough-edged places: The hidden history of place. *Review of Metaphysics* 51 (2) (1997): 267–296.

Casey, Edward S. *The Fate of Place: A Philosophical History*. Berkeley: University of California Press, 1998.

Casey, Edward S. *The World at a Glance*. Bloomington: Indiana University Press, 2007.

Casey, Edward S. Tijuana: Bordertown and estuary. In *The World on Edge*. In preparation.

Cennini, Cenino. *Das Cennino Cennini Handbüchlein der Kunst*. Ed. W. Verkade. Strasbourg: Heitz, 1916.

Chadwick, N. *The Celts*. London: Penguin, 1971.

Chan, T. W., T. L. Liu, and T. W. P. Wong. A comparative analysis of social mobility in Hong Kong. *European Sociological Review* 11 (1995): 135–155.

Chew, M. The dual consequences of dual localization: How exposed short stockings subvert and sustain global cultural hierarchy. *Positions—East Asia Cultures Critique* 11 (2003): 479–509.

Choay, F. Le règne de l'urbain et la mort de la ville. In *La Ville: Art et architecture en Europe, 1870–1993*. Paris: Éditions du Centre Georges Pompidou, 1994.

Christie, M. Aboriginal science for the ecologically sustainable future. *Australian Teachers Journal* 37 (1991): 26–31.

Christie, M. Transdisciplinary research and Aboriginal knowledge. *Australian Journal of Indigenous Education* 35 (2006): 78–89.

Clark, Samuel. *Social Origins of the Irish Land War*. Princeton: Princeton University Press, 1979.

Clarke, Kenneth. *Landscape into Art*. London: Readers Union/John Murray, 1953.

Clement, Barrie. Unions likely to oppose Dimbleby as BBC chief. *Independent*, August 11, 2001.

Clifford, Sue, and Angela King, eds. *Local Distinctiveness: Place, Particularity, and Identity*. London: Common Ground, 1993.

Coates, Peter. *Nature: Western Attitudes since Ancient Times*. Berkeley: University of California Press, 1998.

Colten, Craig. *An Unnatural Metropolis: Wresting New Orleans from Nature*. Baton Rouge: Louisiana State University Press, 2005.

Combe, William. *Tour of Doctor Syntax in Search of the Picturesque*. London: Routledge and Son, 1812/1878.

Conisbee, Philip, and Denis Coutagne, et al. *Cézanne in Provence*. New Haven, CT: Yale University Press, 2006.

Conniff, James. Reflections on the coming revolution in Ireland. *Journal of the History of Ideas* 47 (1) (1986): 37–59.

Conrad, Joseph. *Notes on Life and Letters*. London: Gresham Publishing, 1925.

Cortone, N. and N. Lavermicocca. *Santi di strada: Le edicole religiose della cittá vecchia di Bari*, 5 vols. Bari: Edizione BA Graphis, 2001–2003.

Cosgrove, D. E. *Geographical Imagination and the Authority of Images*. 2005 Hettner-Lecture, Department of Geography, University of Heidelberg. Stuttgart: Franz Steiner Verlag, 2006.

Cosgrove, D. E. *Social Formation and Symbolic Landscape*. Totowa, NJ: Barnes & Noble, 1984.

Cosgrove, D. E., and S. Daniels. Spectacle and text: Landscape metaphors in cultural geography. In *Place/Culture/Representation*, ed. J. Duncan and D. Levy. London: Routledge, 1993, 57–78.

Cosgrove, D. E., and S. Daniels, eds. *The Iconography of Landscape: Essays on the Symbolic Representation, Design, and Use of Past Environments*. Cambridge: Cambridge University Press, 1988.

Cronon, William. The trouble with wilderness; or, Getting back to the wrong nature. In *Uncommon Ground*, ed. W. Cronon. New York: W. W. Norton, 1995, 69–90.

Cuno, James, ed. *Whose Muse? Art Museums and the Public Trust*. Princeton: Princeton University Press, 2004.

Curtius, E. R. Rhetorische Naturschilderung im Mittelalter. In *Landschaft und Raum in der Erzählkunst*, ed. A. Ritter. Darmstadt: Wissenschaftliche Buchgesellschaft, 1975, 69–112.

Cutter, Susan, and Christopher Emrich. Moral hazard, social catastrophe: The changing face of vulnerability along the hurricane coasts. *Annals of the American Academy of Political and Social Science* 64 (2006): 102–112.

Czerwinski, P. Per visibilia ad invisibilia: Texte und Bilder vor dem Zeitalter von Kunst und Literatur. *Internationales Archiv für Sozialgeschichte der deutschen Literatur* 25 (2000): 1–94.

Daniels, Stephen. John Constable and the making of Constable Country. In *Fields of Vision*. Cambridge: Polity Press, 1993, 200–242.

Daniels, Stephen. The field of Waterloo. *Rural History* 3 (1992): 139–145.

David, B., and H. Lourandos. Landscape as mind: Land use, cultural space and change in north Queensland prehistory. *Quaternary International* 59 (1999): 107–123.

David, B., and M. Wilson. Re-reading the landscape: Place and identity in NE Australia during the late holocene. *Cambridge Archaeological Journal* 9 (1999): 163–188.

Davies, C. Virtual space. In *Space: In Science, Art, and Society*, ed. François Penz, Gregory Radick, and Robert Howell. Cambridge: Cambridge University Press, 2004.

Davies, C. Storm gathers over Constable "Theme Park." *Daily Telegraph*, February 4, 2006.

Davis, W. A. *Inwardness and Existence: Subjectivity in/and Hegel, Heidegger, Marx, and Freud*. Madison: University of Wisconsin Press, 1989.

Debarbieux, Bernard. The mountain in the city: Social uses and transformations of a natural landform in urban space. *Ecumene* 5 (1998): 399–431.

Debarbieux, Bernard, and Charles Perraton. Le parc, la norme et l'usage: Le parc du Mont-Royal ou l'expression de la pluralité des cultures à Montréal. *Géographie et Cultures* 26 (1998): 109–127.

de Certeau, M. *Culture in the Plural*. Trans. T. Conley. Minneapolis: University of Minnesota Press, 2001.

de Certeau, M. *The Practice of Everyday Life*. Trans. Steven Rendall. Berkeley: University of California Press, 1988.

de Certeau, M. *The Practice of Everyday Life*, vol. 2: *Living and Cooking*. Trans. Timothy J. Tomasik. Minneapolis: University of Minnesota Press, 1998.

Delumeau, J. *Angst im Abendland*, vol. 1. Reinbek bei Hamburg: Rowohlt, 1965.

Deleuze, Gilles, and Felix Guattari. *A Thousand Plateaus*. Trans. B. Massumi. Minneapolis: University of Minnesota Press, 1987.

de Luc, J. A. *Lettres physiques et morales sur l'histoire de la terre et de l'homme, addresées à la Reiune de la Grande-Bretagne, à la Haye*. Paris: Duchesne, 1779–1780.

de Monte Imperiali, Manfredus. *Liber de herbis et plantis*. Salerno, c. 1350.

Derrida, Jacques. *Margins of Philosophy*. Trans. A. Bass. Chicago: University of Chicago Press, 1985.

Devlin-Glass, F. An atlas of the sacred: Hybridity, representability, and the myths of Yanyuwa country. *Antipodes: A North American Journal of Australian Literature* 19 (2005): 127–140.

Dewey, John. *The Public and Its Problems*. Denver: Alan Swallow, 1927.

Dimbleby, David, ed. *A Picture of Britain*, with essays by David Blayney Brown, Richard Humphreys, and Christine Riding. London: Tate Publishing, 2005.

Dinzelbacher, P., and H. Kleinschmidt. Seelenbrücke und Brückenbau im mittelalterlichen England. *Numen* 31 (1984): 242–287.

Dinzelbacher, P. *Mittelalterliche Visionsliteratur. Eine Anthologie*. Darmstadt: Wiss. Buchges, 1989.

Disraeli, Benjamin. *Lothair*. London: Peter Davies, 1927.

Dixon-Hunt, John. *Gardens and the Picturesque*. Cambridge, MA: MIT Press, 1992.

Dolley, Michael. *Medieval Anglo-Irish Coins*. London: Seaby, 1972.

Domer, Dennis. Inventing the horse farm. *Kentucky Humanities* (October 2005): 3–12.

Donald, S. Landscape and agency: Yellow earth and the demon lover. *Theory, Culture & Society* 14 (1) (1997): 97–112.

Donald, S., and Y. Zheng. A taste of class: Manuals for becoming woman. *Positions—East Asia Cultural Critique* 17 (3) (2009): 489–521.

Donnelly, James S. *The Great Irish Potato Famine*. Stroud: Sutton Publishing, 2002.

Dürer, A. In *Schriften, Tagebücher, Briefe*. Ed. M. Steck. Stuttgart: Kohlhammer, 1961.

Duncan, James. *The City as Text: Politics of Landscape Interpretation in the Kandyan Kingdom*. Cambridge: Cambridge University Press, 1990.

Dutton, Ralph. *The English Garden*, 2nd ed. London: Batsford, 1950.

Eagleton, Terry. *After Theory*. London: Allen Lane, 2003.

Eagleton, Terry. *The Idea of Culture*. Oxford: Blackwell, 2000.

Elgood, George. *Italian Gardens*. London: Longman, 1907.

Ellul, J. *The Meaning of the City*. Grand Rapids: Eerdmans, 1970.

Elvin, M. *The Retreat of the Elephants: An Environmental History of China*. New Haven: Yale University Press, 2005.

Endelman, Todd M. Benjamin Disraeli and the myth of Sephardi superiority. *Jewish History* 10 (2) (September 1996): 21–35.

Engel, J. Ronald. *Sacred Sands: The Struggle for Community in the Indiana Dunes*. Middletown: Wesleyan University Press, 1983.

Entrikin, J. Nicholas and Stanley Brunn, eds. *Reflections on Richard Hartshorne's "The Nature of Geography."* Washington, D.C.: Occasional Publications of the Association of American Geographers, 1989.

Entrikin, J. Nicholas. Place destruction and cultural trauma. In *Culture, Society, and Democracy: The Interpretive Approach*, ed. I. Reed and J. V. Alexander. Boulder, CO: Paradigm Press, 2007, 163–179.

Everett, Nigel. *The Tory View of Landscape*. New Haven: Yale University Press, 1994.

Fearnly-Whittingstall, Jane. *The Garden: An English Love Affair*. London: Weidenfeld Nicolson, 2002.

Fechner, R. *Natur als Landschaft. Zur Entstehung der ästhetischen Landschaft*. Frankfurt: Lang, 1986.

Feld, Steven. *Sound and Sentiment: Birds, Weeping, Poetics, and Song in Kaluli Expression*. Philadelphia: University of Pennsylvania Press, 1990.

Feldges-Henning, U. *Landschaft als topographisches Porträt. Der Wiederbeginn der europäischen Landschaftsmalerei in Siena*. Bern: Benteli, 1980.

Ferguson, E., and A. J. Malherbe, eds. *Gregory of Nyssa: The Life of Moses*. New York: Paulist Press, 1978.

Fitzherbert, Wyndham. *Book of the Wild Garden*. London: John Lane, 1903.

Flasch, K. *Das philosophische Denken im Mittelalter von Augustin bis Macchiavelli*. Stuttgart: Reclam, 1986.

Fleming-Williams, Ian, and Leslie Parris. *Constable*. Exhibition catalog. London: Tate Gallery, 1991.

Fleming-Williams, Ian, Leslie Parris, and Conal Shields, eds. *John Constable: Further Documents and Correspondence*. Ipswich: Suffolk Records Society, 1976.

Forman, Richard. *Land Mosaics: The Ecology of Landscapes and Regions*. Cambridge: Cambridge University Press, 1995.

Forman, Richard, and Michael Godron. *Landscape Ecology*. New York: John Wiley and Sons, 1986.

Friedländer, M. J. *Essays über die Landschaftsmalerei und andere Bildgattungen*. Den Haag: Stols, Cassirer, 1947.

Frisby, David. *Cityscapes of Modernity*. Cambridge: Polity, 2001.

Froude, James Anthony. *Short Studies on Great Subjects*. London: Longmans, Green, 1871.

Frugoni, C. *A Distant City: Images of Urban Experience in the Medieval World*. Princeton: Princeton University Press, 1991.

Gadamer, Hans-Georg. *Truth and Method*. Trans. J. Weinsheimer and D. G. Marshall. New York: Continuum, 2005.

Ganss, G. E., ed. *The Constitutions of the Society of Jesus*. St. Louis: The Institute of Jesuit Sources, 1970.

Gauchet, Marcel. Les lettres sur l'histoire de France d'Augustin Thierry. In *Les Lieux de Mémoire*, vol 2: *La Nation*, ed. Pierre Nora. Paris: Gallimard, 1992, 247–316.

Gerhardt, Christoph. Gab es im Mittelalter Fabelwesen? *Wirkendes Wort* 38 (1988): 156–171.

Gibson, J. J. *The Ecological Approach to Visual Perception*. Hillsdale, NJ: Erlbaum, 1986.

Gilpin, William. *Three Essays*. London: R. Blamire, 1792.

Ginzburg, C. Hoch und niedrig. Erkenntnisverbote im 16. und 17. Jahrhundert. *Freibeuter* 10 (1981): 9–23.

Glacken, Clarence. *Traces on the Rhodian Shore: Nature and Culture in Western Thought from Ancient Times to the End of the Eighteenth Century*. Berkeley: University of California Press, 1967.

Glanerought Estate Minute Books (ms. Derreen House), 1854–1863.

Goethe, J. W. von. Selections from *Maxims and Reflections*. In *Scientific Studies*, ed. and trans. Douglas Miller. New York: Suhrkamp, 1988, 303–312.

Gohau, Gabriel. *Une histoire de la géologie*. Paris: Points Seuil, 1990.

Goldsmith, Oliver. The revolution in low life. *Lloyd's Evening Post*, June 1762.

Goldsmith, Oliver. *The Deserted Village*. London: W. Griffin, 1770.

Golley, Frank. Historical origins of the ecosystem concept in ecology. In *Ecosystem Concept in Ecology*, ed. E. Moran. Washington, D.C.: American Academy for the Advancement of Science Publications, 1983, 33–49.

Golley, Frank. Introducing landscape ecology. *Landscape Ecology* 1 (1987): 1–3.

Gombrich, R. H. *Art and Illusion: A Study in the Pyschology of Pictorial Representation*. London: Phaidon, 1968.

Goodman, D. S. G., ed. *The New Rich in China: Future Rulers, Present Lives*. London: Routledge, 2008.

Gorky, Maxim. Newspaper review of the Lumière Program at the Nizhni-Novgorod Fair, *Nizhegorodski listok*, July 4, 1896. In *In the Kingdom of Shadows: A Companion to Early Cinema*, ed. Colin Harding and Simon Popple. London: Cygnus Arts, 1996.

Gosden, Christopher. *Social Being and Time*. Oxford: Blackwell, 1994.

Gottmann, Jean. *La Politique des Etats et leur géographie*. Paris: Armand Colin, 1952.

Graham, Georgina. *In a Tuscan Garden*. London: John Lane, 1902.

Green, Alice Stopford. *The Making of Ireland and Its Undoing*. London: Macmillan, 1908.

Gregg, R. C., ed. *Athanasius: The Life of Anthony*. New York: Paulist Press, 1980.

Grosz, Elizabeth. Chaos, territory, art, Deleuze, and the framing of the earth. *IDEA Journal* 6 (2005): 15–25.

Grümmer, G., ed. *Von seltsamen Ländern und wunderlichen Völkern. Ein Reisebuch von 1356*. Leipzig: Brockhaus, 1986.

Grünter, R. Landschaft. Bemerkungen zur Wort- und Bedeutungsgeschichte. In *Landschaft und Raum in der Erzählkunst*, ed. A. Ritter. Darmstadt: Wissenschaftliche Buchgesellschaft, 1975, 192–207.

Gurevich, A. *Categories of Medieval Culture*. Trans. G. L. Campbell. London: Routledge & Kegan Paul, 1985.

Gurevich, A. *Medieval Popular Culture*. Trans. J. Bak and P. Hollingsworth. Cambridge: Cambridge University Press, 1988.

Hägerstrand, Torsten. Space, time, and human conditions. In *Dynamic Allocation of Urban Space*, ed. A. Karlqvist, L. Lundqvist, and F. Snickars. Lexington, MA: Lexington Books, 1975, 3–14.

Hansen, David. *John Glover and the Colonial Picturesque*. Hobart: Tasmanian Museum and Art Gallery, 2003.

Harding, Colin, and Simon Popple, eds. *In the Kingdom of Shadows: A Companion to Early Cinema*. London: Cygnus Arts, 1996.

Hartshorne, Richard. *The Nature of Geography: A Critical Survey of Current Thought in Light of the Past*. Lancaster, PA: Association of American Geographers, 1939.

Harvey, David. *Justice, Nature, and the Geography of Difference*. Oxford: Blackwell, 1996.

Haywood, Mark. Claife Station: Looking at the world through coloured glasses. Paper presented at the Romantic Spectacle Conference, July 2006, Roehampton.

Hazlitt, William. *The Complete Works of William Hazlitt*, vol. X. London: Dent, 1932.

Heaney, Seamus. *Seeing Things*. London: Faber and Faber, 1991.

Heaney, Seamus. *Preoccupations: Selected Prose, 1968–1978*. London: Faber, 1980.

Heidegger, Martin. *Poetry, Language, Thought*. New York: Harper & Row, 1971.

Heidegger, Martin. *Being and Time*. Trans. John Macquarrie and Edward Robinson. Oxford: Blackwell, 1927/1962.

Hemingway, Andrew. *Landscape Imagery and Urban Culture in Early Nineteenth-century Britain*. Cambridge: Cambridge University Press, 1992.

Hewitt, Kenneth, ed. *Interpretations of Calamity: From the Point of View of Human Ecology. The Risks and Hazards Series*, vol. I. Boston: Allen & Unwin, 1983.

Heyd, Thomas. Thinking through botanic gardens. *Environmental Values* 15 (2) (1996): 197–212.

Hill, Geoffrey. *Collected Poems*. Harmondsworth: Penguin, 1985.

Hillier, J., ed. *Cahiers du cinéma: 1960–1968—New Wave, New Cinema, Re-evaluating Hollywood*. Cambridge, MA: Harvard University Press, 1986.

Hobhouse, P. *Plants in Garden History*. London: Pavilion Books, 1992.

Hobhouse, Penelope. *The Story of Gardening*. London: Dorling Kindersley, 2002.

Hodder, Edwin. *Life and Work of the Seventh Earl of Shaftesbury*. London: Cassell, 1888.

Hoveyda, Fereydoun. Sunspots. In *Cahiers du cinéma: 1960–1968—New Wave, New Cinema, Re-evaluating Hollywood*, ed. J. Hillier. Cambridge, MA: Harvard University Press, 1986.

Hsi, Kuo. *An Essay on Landscape Painting*. Trans. S. Sakanishi. London: Murray, 1949.

Hughes, K. *Early Christian Ireland: Introduction to the Sources*. London: Hodder and Stoughton, 1972.

Hussey, C. *The Picturesque*. 1927. London: Frank Cass, 1983.

Huxley, Aldous. *Those Barren Leaves*. 1928. London: Chatto & Windus, 2005.

Ingold, Tim. *The Perception of the Environment: Essays on Livelihood, Dwelling, Skill*. London: Routledge, 2000.

Jackson, John B. *The Necessity for Ruins*. Amherst: University of Massachusetts Press, 1980.

Jackson, John Brinkerhoff. *Discovering the Vernacular Landscape*. New Haven: Yale University Press, 1984.

Jacobs, Jane. *The Death and Life of Great American Cities*. New York: Random House, 1961.

Jaffee, V. "Every man a star": The ambivalent cult of amateur art in new Chinese documentaries. In *From Underground to Independent: Alternative Film Culture in Contemporary China*, ed. Y. J. Zhang and P. G. Pickowicz. Lanham: Rowman & Littlefield, 2006, 77–108.

James, Henry. *Italian Hours*. Boston: Houghton, 1909.

James, Henry. *Letters*, vol. 1. Cambridge, MA: Harvard University Press, 1974.

Kearney, A. An archaeology of engagement: Yanyuwa Country and the lived cultural domains in archaeology. In *The Social Archaeology of Indigenous Societies: Essays on Aboriginal History in Honour of Harry Lourandos*, ed. Bruno David, Ian McNiven, and Bryce Barker. Canberra: Aboriginal Studies Press, 2005.

Kearney, A., and J. Bradley. Landscape with shadows of once living people: Kundawira and the challenge for archaeology to understand. In *The Social Archaeology of Indigenous Societies: Essays on Aboriginal History in Honour of Harry Lourandos*, ed. Bruno David, Ian McNiven, and Bryce Barker. Canberra: Aboriginal Studies Press, 2005, 182–203.

Kearney, M. An archaeology of engagement: Yanyuwa Country and the lived cultural domains in archaeology. PhD diss., Melbourne University, 2004.

Kemp, M., ed. *Leonardo on Painting*. New Haven: Yale University Press, 2001.

Kessler, P. *Oracle Bones: A Journey between China and the West*. London: John Murray Publishers, 2007.

Kimberley, Jonathan. *Jonathan Kimberley—Ur-Landscape: Post-Landscape (Blue Tier)*. Exhibition catalog. Hobart: Bett Gallery, 2005.

Klonk, Charlotte. *Science and the Perception of Nature: British Landscape Imagery in the Late Eighteenth and Early Nineteenth Centuries*. New Haven, London: Yale University Press, 1996.

Koschorke, A. *Die Geschichte des Horizonts. Grenze und Grenzüberschreitung in literarischen Landschaftsbilder*. Frankfurt: Suhrkamp, 1990.

Krall, Florence R. *Ecotone: Wayfaring on the Margins*. Albany: SUNY Press, 1994.

Kriz, Kay Dian. *The Idea of the English Landscape Painter: Genius as Alibi in the Early Nineteenth Century*. New Haven: Yale University Press, 1997.

Lambert, Roy. *John Constable and the Theory of Landscape Painting*. Cambridge: Cambridge University Press, 2004.

Langton, M. The edge of the sacred, the edge of death: Sensual inscriptions. In *Inscribed Landscapes: Marking and Making Place*, ed. B. David and M. Wilson. Honolulu: University of Hawaii Press, 2002, 253–269.

Lansdowne, Sixth Marquis of (Henry William Edmund Petty FitzMaurice). *Glanerought and the Petty-Fitzmaurices*. Oxford: Oxford University Press, 1937.

Lansdowne, Sixth Marquis of (Henry William Edmund Petty FitzMaurice). *Life of Shelburne*. 2 vols. London: Macmillan, 1912.

Larner, J. The artist and the intellectuals in fourteenth century Italy. *History* 54 (180) (1969): 13–30.

Latour, Bruno. *We Have Never Been Modern*. Trans. Catherine Porter. Cambridge, MA: Harvard University Press, 1993.

Layton, R. Representing and translating people's place in the landscape of Northern Australia. In *After Writing Culture: Epistemology and Praxis in Contemporary Anthropology*, ed. A. James, J. Hockey, and A. Dawson. London: Routledge, 1997, 122–143.

Le Blond, Aubrey. *The Old Gardens of Italy*. London: John Lane, 1912.

Lee, Vernon. *Genius Loci*. London: John Lane, 1908.

Leeman, Richard. *Cy Twombly: A Monograph*. London: Thames & Hudson, 2004.

Lefebvre, Henri. *Critique of Everyday Life*, vol. II: *Foundations for a Sociology of the Everyday*. Trans. John Moore. London: Verso, 2002.

Lefebvre, Henri. *Rhythmanalysis: Space, Time, and Everyday Life*. 1992. Trans. Stuart Elden and Gerald Moore. London: Continuum, 2004.

Lefebvre, Henri. *The Production of Space*. Trans. Donald Nicholson-Smith. Oxford: Blackwell, 1991.

LeGates, Richard T., and Frederic Stout, eds. *The City Reader*, 2nd ed. London: Routledge, 1996.

Le Goff, J. *The Medieval Imagination*. Chicago: University of Chicago Press, 1988.

Le Goff, Jacques. *The Medieval Imagination*. Chicago: University of Chicago Press, 1988.

Leopold, Aldo. *A Sand County Almanac: And Sketches Here and There*. 1949. Oxford: Oxford University Press, 1989.

Lewis, Pierce. *New Orleans: The Making of an Urban Landscape*, 2nd ed. Santa Fe: Center for American Places, 2003.

Lock, F. P. *Edmund Burke*, vol. I: *1730–84*. Oxford: Oxford University Press, 1998.

Locke, John. *An Essay Concerning Human Understanding*. Ed. Peter H. Nidditch. Oxford: Clarendon Press, 1975.

Loudon, Jane. *Gardening for Ladies*. London: John Murray, 1843.

Louth, A. *The Wilderness of God*. London: DLT, 1991.

Lowry, Glenn D. A deontological approach to museums and the public trust. In *Whose Muse—Art Museums and the Public Trust*, ed. J. Cuno, Princeton: Princeton University Press, 2004, 129–150.

Lucas, Joseph. *Our Villa in Italy*. London: Unwin, 1913.

Luhan, Mabel Dodge. *European Experiences*. New York: Harcourt, Brace, 1935.

Lyne, Gerard J. Land tenure in Kenmare and Tuosist, 1696–c.1716. *Journal of the Kildare Archaeological Society* 10 (1977): 19–54.

Lyne, Gerard J. Peter McSwiney and the vexed succession to the last Mac Finin Duibh. *Journal of the Kerry Archaelogical and Historical Society* 13 (1980): 50–81.

Lyne, Gerard J. The Mac Finin Duibh O'Sullivans of Tuosist and Berehaven. *Journal of the Kerry Archaelogical and Historical Society* 9 (1976): 32–67.

Lyne, Gerard J. *The Lansdowne Estates in Kerry*. Dublin: Geography Publications, 2001.

Maier, A. Das Problem der "species sensibiles in medio" und die neue Naturphilosophie des 14. Jahrhunderts. In A. Maier, *Ausgehendes Mittelalter: Gesammelte Aufsätze zur Geistesgeschichte des 14. Jahrhunderts*, vol. 2. Rome: Edizioni di storia e letteratura, 1967.

Malpas, Jeff. *Place and Experience: A Philosophical Topography*. Cambridge: Cambridge University Press, 1999.

Malpas, Jeff. *Ethos and Topos: On the Ethics and Politics of Place*. In preparation.

Marsh, H., W. J. Freeland, C. J. Limpus, and P. C. Reed. *The Stranding of Dugongs and Sea Turtles Resulting from Cyclone Kathy, March 1984: A Report of the Rescue Effort and the Biological Data Obtained*. Darwin: Conservation Commission of the Northern Territory, 1986.

Marx, Leo. *The Machine in the Garden: Technology and the Pastoral Ideal*. New York: Oxford University Press, 1964.

Massey, Doreen B. *For Space*. London: Sage, 2005.

McCarthy, Mary. *The Stones of Florence*. London: Harcourt, Brace, 1959.

McCracken, Eileen. *The Irish Woods Since Tudor Times*. Newton Abbot: David and Charles, 1971.

McDannell, C., and B. Lang. *Heaven: A History*. New Haven: Yale University Press, 1988.

McGhie, Caroline. Constable Country's brush with controversy. *Financial Times* (January 2006): 28–29.

McGrath, A. *A Brief History of Heaven*. Oxford: Blackwell, 2003.

McIntosh, Robert. *The Background of Ecology: Concept and Theory*. Cambridge: University Press, 1985.

McNiven, I. Saltwater people: Spiritscapes, maritime rituals, and the archaeology of Australian indigenous seascapes. *World Archaeology* 35 (2003): 329–349.

McNiven, I. Sentient Sea: Seascapes and spiritscapes. In *Handbook of Landscape Archaeology*, ed. B. David and J. Thomas. Walnut Creek: Left Coast Press, 2008.

McVey, K., ed. *Ephrem the Syrian: Hymns*. New York: Paulist Press, 1989.

Meeks, Wayne. St. Paul of the cities. In *Civitas: Religious Interpretations of the City*, ed. Peter S. Hawkins. Atlanta: Scholars Press, 1986.

Meinig, D. W., ed. *The Interpretation of Ordinary Landscapes*. New York: Oxford University Press, 1979.

Melville, Herman. *Moby-Dick.*. Ed. Harrison Hayford and Hershel Parker. A Norton Critical Edition. New York: W. W. Norton, 1851/1967.

Mill, John Stuart. *Principles of Political Economy*, 2nd ed., 2 vols. London: J. W. Parker, 1849.

Minteer, Ben. *The Landscape of Reform: Civic Pragmatism and Environmental Thought in America*. Cambridge, MA: MIT Press, 2006.

Mitchell, Don. *The Lie of the Land: Migrant Workers and the California Landscape*. Minneapolis: University of Minnesota Press, 1996.

Mitchell, W. J. T. *Landscape and Power*. Chicago: University of Chicago Press, 1994.

Mitchell, W. J. T. *Landscape and Power*, 2nd ed. Chicago: University of Chicago Press, 2002.

Monumenta Historica Societatis Jesu. *Monumenta Nadal*. Rome: Institutum Historicum Societatis Iesu, 1905.

Morphy, H. Colonisation and construction of place: The politics of landscape in Northern Australia. In *Landscape, Politics and Perspectives*, ed. B. Bender. Oxford: Berg, 1993, 205–243.

Morphy, H. Landscape and the reproduction of the ancestral past. In *The Anthropology of Landscape: Perspectives on Place and Space*, ed. E. Hirsch and M. O'Hanlon. Oxford: Clarendon Press, 1995, 184–209.

Morphy, H. *Ancestral Connections: Art and an Aboriginal System of Knowledge*. Chicago: University of Chicago Press, 1991.

Morris, R. *Churches in the Landscape*. London: Dent, 1989.

Mowaljarlai, David. Aboriginal law. ABC (Australian Broadcasting Corporation) radio feature, <http://www.abc.net.au/rn/talks/8.30/lawrpt/lstories/lr311001.htm>.

Mowaljarlai, David, and Jutta Malnic. *Yorro Yorro: Everything Standing Up Alive*. Broome: Magabala Books, 1993.

Muecke, Stephen. *Ancient and Modern: Time, Culture, and Indigenous Philosophy*. Sydney: UNSW Press, 2004.

Myers, Frank. *Pintubi Country, Pintubi Self: Sentiment, Place, and Politics among Western Desert Aborigines.* Berkeley: University of California Press, 1991.

Neiman, Susan. *Evil in Modern Thought: An Alternative History of Philosophy.* Princeton: Princeton University Press, 2002.

Netting, R. *Cultural Ecology.* Sydney: Cummings Publishing, 1977.

Newman, Barnett. *L'inhumain: Causeries sur le temps.* Paris: Galilée, 1988.

Nicholls, Christine, and Ian North. *Kathleen Petyarre: Genius of Place.* Kent Town, South Australia: Wakefield Press, 2001.

Nichols, Rose Standish. *Italian Pleasure Gardens.* New York: Dodd, Mead & Co., 1902/1928.

Nicolson, M. H. *Mountain Gloom and Mountain Glory.* New York: W. W. Norton, 1959/1963.

Oastler, Richard. *Letters to the Duke of Wellington.* London: J. Cochrane, 1835.

O'Brien, Alph. Commercial relations between Aquitaine and Ireland, c. 1000–c. 1550. In *Aquitaine and Ireland in the Middle Ages,* ed. Jean-Michel Picard. Dublin: Four Courts Press, 1995.

O'Brien, Conor Cruise. *The Great Melody.* London: Sinclair-Stevenson, 1992.

Olwig, Kenneth Robert. *Landscape, Nature, and the Body Politic.* Madison: University of Wisconsin Press, 2002.

Ordnance Survey Papers—Kerry/Tuosist. Typescript, Boole Library, Cork.

Orestano, Francesca. The Revd William Gilpin and the picturesque; Or, Who's afraid of Doctor Syntax? *Journal of Garden History* 31 (2) (2003): 163–179.

Origo, I. *Der Heilige der Toskana. Leben und Zeit des Bernadino von Siena.* Munich: Beck, 1989.

Origo, Iris. *Images and Shadows.* London: John Murray, 1970.

Otway, Caesar. *Sketches in Ireland.* Dublin: William Curry, 1827.

Ouida (Marie Louise de la Ramée). *Friendship.* London: Methuen, 1914.

Pächt, O. Early Italian nature studies and the early calendar landscape. *Journal of the Warburg and Courtauld Institutes* 13 (1950): 13–47.

Paget, (Lady) Walburga. *My Tower.* London: Hutchinson, 1923.

Paget, (Lady) Walburga. *The Linings of Life.* London: Hurst & Blackett, 1923.

Paine, Thomas. *The Age of Reason, Being an Investigation of True and Fabulous Theology.* New York: Prometheus Books, 1794–1795/1984.

Palang, Hannes, and Gary Fry, eds. *Landscape Interfaces: Cultural Heritage in Changing Landscapes*. Dordrecht: Kluwer Academic, 2003.

Palang, Hannes, Helen Sooväli, Marc Antrop, and Guhild Setten, eds. *European Rural Landscapes: Persistence and Change in a Globalising Environment*. Dordrecht: Kluwer, 2004.

Panofsky, E. *Perspective as Symbolic Form*. Trans. C. Wood. New York: Zone Books, 1991.

Parkes, Don, and Nigel Thrift. *Times, Spaces, and Places: A Chronogeographic Perspective*. Chichester: John Wiley, 1980.

Pavry, Will. This is why we don't need heritage scheme. *Essex County Standard*. January 6, 2006.

Perry, E. J. Studying Chinese politics: Farewell to revolution? *China Journal* 57 (2007): 1–22.

Perry, E. J. *Challenging the Mandate of Heaven: Social Protest and State Power in China*. Armonk, NY: M. E. Sharpe, 2002.

Perry, E. J. *Patrolling the Revolution: Worker Militias, Citizenship, and the Modern Chinese State*. Lanham: Rowman & Littlefield, 2006.

Petrarca, F. *Rerum familiarium I–VIII*. Trans. A. Bernado. Albany, NY: SUNY Press, 1975.

Petty, Sir William. *Political Anatomy of Ireland*. Shannon: Irish University Press, 1970.

Plano Carpini, John of. *Kunde von den Mongolen*. Trans. F. Schmieder. Sigmaringen: Thorbecke Verlag, 1245–1247/1997.

Polo, Marco. *The Travels of Marco Polo*. Trans. T. Waugh. London: Sidgwick & Jackson, 1984.

Pordenone, Oderico da. *Die Reise des seligen Odorich von Pordenone nach Indien und China*. Trans. F. Reichert. Heidelberg: Manutius-Verlag, 1314/18–1330/1987.

Potts, Alex, and Neil McWilliam. The landscape of reaction: Richard Wilson and his critics. In *The New Art History*, ed. A. L. Rees and Frances Borzello. London: Camden Press, 1990, 106–109.

Povinelli, E. Might be something; the language of indeterminacy in Australian land use. *Man* 28 (1993): 679–704.

Pratt, Mary Louise. Scratches on the face of the country; or, What Mr. Barrow saw in the land of the Bushmen. In *"Race," Writing, and Difference*, ed. Henry Louis Gates, Jr. Chicago: University of Chicago Press, 1986, 138–162.

Price, Uvedale. *On the Picturesque*. Edinburgh: Caldwell, Lloyd & Co., 1794/1842.

Quest-Ritson, Charles. *The English Garden: A Social History*. London: Penguin, 2001.

Raberg, Per. *The Space of Man: New Concepts for Social and Humanistic Planning*. Stockholm: Almquist and Wiksell International, 1987.

Raedts, P. The medieval city as a holy place. In *Omnes Circumadstantes: Contributions towards a History of the Role of the People in the Liturgy*, ed. C. Caspers and M. Schneiders. Kampen: Uitgeversmaatschappij J. H. Kok, 1990.

Raffestin, Claude. Écogénèse territoriale et territorialité. In *Espaces, jeux et enjeux*, ed. F. Auriac and R. Brunet. Paris: Fayard-Fondation Diderot, 1986, 175–185.

Raison, Laura. *Tuscany: An Anthology*. London: Cadogan, 1983.

Raitz, Karl. Gentleman farms in Kentucky's inner bluegrass: A problem in mapping. *Southeastern Geographer* 15 (15) (1975): 33–46.

Raitz, Karl. Negro hamlets and agricultural estates in Kentucky's inner Bluegrass. *Geographical Review* 64 (1974).

Ray, Gene. Reading the Lisbon Earthquake: Adorno, Lyotard, and the contemporary sublime. *Yale Journal of Criticism* 17 (2004): 1–18.

Reichler, Claude. *La découverte des Alpes et la question du paysage*. Lausanne: Georg, 2002.

Relph, Edward. *Place and Placelessness*. London: Pion, 1976.

Relph, Edward. *Rational Landscape and Humanistic Geography*. London: Croom Helm, 1981.

Report of the Devon Commission. London: British House of Commons Sessional Papers, 1845, 909–920.

Reports of the Lansdowne Estates in Kerry. Ms. Derreen House, 1850–1865.

Rewald, John, ed. *Paul Cézanne Letters*, 4th ed. New York: Da Capo, 1976.

Rhodes, Robin Francis. *Architecture and Meaning on the Athenian Acropolis*. Cambridge: Cambridge University Press, 1995.

Richards, S. *Le Corbusier and the Concept of the Self*. New Haven: Yale University Press, 2003.

Ricoeur, P. *The Conflict in Interpretation: Essays in Hermeneutics*. Ed. D. Idhe. Evanston: Northwestern University Press, 1974.

Ritter, J. 1974. Landschaft. Zur Funktion des Ästhetischen in der modernen Gesellschaft. In *Subjektivität. Sechs Aufsätze*. Frankfurt: Suhrkamp, 141–164.

Robinson, William. *The Wild Garden*. London: J. Murray, 1870.

Rose, Deborah Bird. Indigenous ecological knowledge and the scientific community. In *Bushfire '97 Proceedings: Australian Bushfire Conference*, July 8–10. Darwin, Northern Territory, 1997, 69–74.

Rose, Deborah Bird. *Country of the Heart: An Indigenous Australian Homeland*. Canberra: Aboriginal Studies Press, 2002.

Rose, Deborah Bird. *Dingo Makes Us Human: Life and Land in an Aboriginal Australian Culture*. Cambridge: Cambridge University Press, 1992.

Rose, Deborah Bird. *Nourishing Terrains: Australian Aboriginal Views on Landscape and Wilderness*. Canberra: Australian Heritage Commission, 1996.

Rose, Deborah Bird. *Reports from a Wild Country: Ethics for Decolonisation*. Sydney: UNSW Press, 2004.

Rosenthal, Michael. Approaches to landscape painting. *Landscape Research* 9 (1984): 2–12.

Rosenthal, Michael. Constable at the Tate: The bright side of the landscape. *Apollo* 134 (August 1991): 77–84.

Rosenthal, Michael. Constable then and now. *Art Monthly Australia* 192 (August 2006): 7–13.

Rosenthal, Michael. *Constable: The Painter and His Landscape*. New Haven: Yale University Press, 1983.

Rosenthal, Michael. Review of Ray Lambert, *John Constable and the Theory of Landscape Painting*. *Burlington Magazine* 167 (September 2005): 622.

Rosenthal, Michael. Shakespeare's birthplace at Stratford: Bardolatory reconsidered. In *Writers' Houses and the Making of Memory*, ed. Harald Hendrix. New York: Routledge, 2008.

Ross, Janet. *Italian Sketches*. London: Kegan Paul, 1887.

Ross, Stephanie. *What Gardens Mean*. Chicago: University of Chicago Press, 1998.

Rowntree, L. The landscape: A view from geography. In *Tracking Knowledge in North Australian Landscapes: Studies in Indigenous and Settler Ecological Knowledge Systems*, ed. Deborah Bird Rose and A. Clarke. Darwin: North Australia Research Unit, 1997, 1–18.

Royal Commission on Agriculture 1881. London: H.M.S.O., 1881, 725–739.

Rudwick, Martin. Minerals, strata, and fossils. In *Cultures of Natural History*, ed. N. Jardine, J. A. Secord, and E. C. Sparry. Cambridge: Cambridge University Press, 1996.

Russell, J. Burton. *A History of Heaven: A Singing Silence*. Princeton: Princeton University Press, 1997.

Sack, Robert. *A Geographical Guide to the Real and the Good*. New York: Routledge, 2003.

Sack, Robert. *Homo Geographicus: A Framework for Action, Awareness, and Moral Concern.* Baltimore: Johns Hopkins University Press, 1997.

Said, Edward. *Culture and Imperialism.* New York: Knopf, 1994.

Samuel, F. *Le Corbusier: Architect and Feminist.* Chichester: Wiley, 2004.

Sauer, Carl O. The morphology of landscape. In *Land and Life: Selections from the Writings of Carl Ortwin Sauer.* 1925. Ed. John Leighly. Berkeley: University of California Press, 1963, 315–350.

Sauer, Carl. Now this matter of cultural geography: Notes from Carl Sauer's last seminar at Berkeley. Ed. James Parsons. In *Carl O. Sauer: A Tribute,* ed. Martin Kenzer. Corvallis: Oregon State University Press, 1987, 153–163.

Scally, R. J. *The End of Hidden Ireland.* Oxford: Oxford University Press, 1995.

Schama, Simon. *Landscape and Memory.* London: HarperCollins, 1995.

Schatzki, T. R. Living out of the past: Dilthey and Heidegger on life and history. *Inquiry* 46 (2003): 301–323.

Schatzki, T. R. *The Site of the Social: A Philosophical Exploration of the Constitution of Social Life and Change.* University Park, PA: Pennsylvania State University Press, 2002.

Schein, Richard H. The place of landscape: A conceptual framework for interpreting an American scene. *Annals of the Association of American Geographers* 87 (4) (1997): 660–680.

Scholte, B. Toward a reflexive and critical anthropology. In *Reinventing Anthropology,* ed. D. Hymes. New York: Pantheon, 1972, 430–457.

Scully, Vincent. *The Earth, the Temple, and the Gods: Greek Sacred Architecture.* New Haven: Yale University Press, 1962.

Sears, John F. *Sacred Places: American Tourist Attractions in the Nineteenth Century.* New York: Oxford University Press, 1984.

Seaton, Jean. Rows and consequences. *British Journalism Review* 14 (2003): 26–31.

Seeley, Robert. *Life of Michael Thomas Sadler.* London: Seeley & Burneside, 1842.

Seidel, M. Castrum pingatur in palatio. 1. Ricerche storiche e iconografiche sui castelli dipinti nel Palazzo Pubblico di Siena. *Prospettiva* 28 (1982): 14–41.

Seidel, M. Wiedergefundene Fragmente eines Hauptwerks von Ambrogio Lorenzetti. *Pantheon* 36 (1978): 119–127.

Selections from the Carmina Burana. Ed. B. Radice, trans. D. Parlett. Harmondsworth: Penguin, 1986.

Serres, Michel. *The Natural Contract.* Trans. Elizabeth MacArthur and William Paulson. Ann Arbor: University of Michigan Press, 1995.

Sharp, N. *Saltwater People*. Crows Nest: Allen & Unwin, 2002.

Sheldrake, Philip. Reading cathedrals as spiritual texts. *Studies in Spirituality* 11 (2001): 187–204.

Sica, Gracia Gobbi. Florence between the 19th and 20th centuries. In *Of Queen's Gardens: The Myth of Florence in the Pre-Raphaelite Milieu and in American Culture*, ed. Margherita Ciacci and Grazia Gobbi Sica. Livorno: Sillabe, 2004.

Silke, J. J. *Kinsale*. Liverpool: Liverpool University Press, 1970.

Simpson, Bob. Trade disputes and the labour injunction after the Employment Acts of 1980 and 1982." *Modern Law Review* 47 (1984): 577–587.

Sitwell, Sir George. *On the Making of Gardens*. London: Duckworth, 1909.

Smith, Adam. *Correspondence*. Oxford: Oxford University Press, 1987.

Smith, Adam. *Wealth of Nations*. Oxford: Oxford University Press, 1976.

Smith, Charles. *The Antient and Present State of the County of Kerry*. Dublin: Printed for the author, 1756.

Smith, Neil. There's no such thing as natural disaster. In *Understanding Katrina: Perspectives from the Social Sciences*. Social Science Research Council. <http://understandingkatrina.ssrc.org/Smith>.

Smyth, William J. *Map-making, Landscapes, and Memory*. Cork: Cork University Press, 2006.

So, A. Y. The changing pattern of classes and class conflict in China. *Journal of Contemporary Asia* 33 (2003): 363–376.

Solkin, David. *Richard Wilson: The Landscape of Reaction*. Exhibition catalog. London: Tate Gallery, 1982.

Spirn, Anne Whiston. *The Language of Landscape*. New Haven: Yale University Press, 1998.

Sprigge, Sylvia. *Berenson: A Biography*. London: Allen & Unwin, 1960.

Stanner, W. E. H. The dreaming. In *Traditional Aboriginal Society*, 2nd ed., ed. W. H. Edwards. Melbourne: MacMillan Education Australia, 1998, 227–238.

Steinberg, Theodore. What is natural disaster? *Literature and Medicine* 15 (1996): 33–47.

Steinberg, Theodore. *Acts of God: The Unnatural History of Natural Disaster in America*. Oxford: Oxford University Press, 2000.

Stierle, K. *Petrarcas Landschaft. Zur Geschichte ästhetischer Landschaftserfahrung*. Krefeld: Scherpe, 1979.

Strang, V. *Uncommon Ground: Cultural Landscapes and Environmental Values*. Oxford: Berg, 1997.

Switzer, Stephen. *Iconographia Rustica*. Cowbridge: D. Brown, 1718.

Tacon, P. Socializing landscapes: The long term implications of signs, symbols, and marks on the land. *Archaeology in Oceania* 29 (1994): 117–129.

Tamisari, F. Names and naming: Speaking forms into place. In *The Land Is a Map: Place Names of Indigenous Origin in Australia*, ed. L. Hercus, F. Hodges, and J. Simpson. Canberra: Pandanus Press, 2002, 87–102.

Tamisari, F., and J. Bradley. Place and event. In *Animal Names*, ed. A. Minelli, G. Ortalli, and G. Sanga. Venice: Instituto Veneto Di Scienze Lettere Ed Arti, 2005, 237–250.

Teo, S. Cinema with an accent: An interview with Jia Zhangke, director of *Platform*. *Senses of Cinema* 15 (2001), <http://archive.sensesofcinema.com/contents/01/15/zhangke_interview.html>.

Téry, Simone. *L'Île des bardes*. Paris: Flammarion, 1925.

Thomas, Dylan. *Collected Poems, 1934–1952*. London: Dent, 1966.

Thomas, J. *Time, Cultur,e and Identity*. London: Routledge, 1996.

Thomas, Nicholas. *Possessions: Indigenous Art/Colonial Culture*. London: Thames & Hudson, 1999.

Tilley, C. A. *Phenomenology of Landscapes: Place, Paths and Monuments*. Oxford: Berg, 1994.

Toland, John. *Christianity Not Mysterious*. London: Sam Buckley, 1696.

Tomba, L. Creating an urban middle class: Social engineering in Beijing. *China Journal* 82 (2004): 1–26.

Townsend, Dabney. The picturesque. *Journal of Art Criticism* 55 (4) (1997): 365–376.

Traherne, Thomas. *Centuries of Meditation*. London: Mowbray, 1975.

Trench, William Steuart. *Realities of Irish Life*. London: MacGibbon & Kee, 1966.

Troll, C. Die geographische Landschaft und ihre Erforschung. *Studium Generale* 3 (1950): 163–164.

Trollope, Frances. *A Visit to Italy*. London: Richard Bentley, 1842.

Tuan, Yi-Fu. Foreword. In Kenneth Olwig, *Landscape, Nature, and the Body Politic: From Britain's Renaissance to America's New World*. Madison: University of Wisconsin Press, 2002.

Tuan, Yi-Fu. *Cosmos and Hearth: A Cosmopolite's Viewpoint.* Minneapolis: University of Minnesota Press, 1996.

Tuan, Yi-Fu. *Space and Place: The Perspective of Experience.* Minneapolis: University of Minnesota Press, 1977.

Turner, Sandra. Review of *Landscape Ecology: Concepts, Methods and Applications* by F. Burel and J. Baudry. *Landscape Ecology* 20 (2005): 1031–1033.

Turner, Victor W. *The Ritual Process: Structure and Anti-Structure.* Chicago: Aldine, 1966.

UHC Collective. *UHC Collective Works: Manchester 2005–2006.* Manchester: Castlefield Gallery Publications, 2006.

Vasagfar, Jeevan, and Rebecca Smithers. Will Charles Clarke have his place in history? *Guardian,* May 10, 2003.

Vaughan, W. E. *Landlords and Tenants in Mid-Victorian Ireland.* Oxford: Oxford University Press, 1994.

Vivian, T., ed. *Journeying into God: Seven Early Monastic Lives.* Minneapolis: Fortress Press, 1996.

Voltaire, François Marie Arouet de. The Lisbon Earthquake: An inquiry into the maxim, "Whatever is, is right." In *Candide and Related Texts.* Trans. David Wootton. Indianapolis: Hackett, 2000, 99–107.

Walder, A. G. Social dimensions of China's economic transition: Organization, stratification, and social mobility. *Asia Pacific Research Center Working Paper.* Stanford: Stanford University, 2003.

Walder, A. G. Privatization and elite mobility: Rural China 1970–1996. *Asia Pacific Research Center Working Paper.* Stanford: Stanford University, 2002.

Walker, G. S. M., ed. *Sancti Columbani Opera.* Dublin: Dublin Institute for Advanced Studies, 1957/1970.

Walsh, M. The land still speaks? Language and landscape in Aboriginal Australia. In *Tracking Knowledge in North Australian Landscapes: Studies in Indigenous and Settler Ecological Knowledge Systems,* ed. Deborah Bird Rose and A. Clarke. Darwin: North Australia Research Unit, 1997, 105–119.

Walter, François. *Les figures paysagères de la nation.* Paris: EHESS, 2004.

Wang, J. Bourgeois bohemians in China? Neo-tribes and the urban imaginary. *China Quarterly* 183 (2005): 532–548.

Wang, J. Youth culture, music, and cell phone branding in China. *Global Media and Communication* 1 (2005): 185–201.

Wang, S., and Z. Zhang. The new retail economy of Shanghai. *Growth and Change* 36 (2005): 41–73.

Wang, S., et al. The uneven distribution of cultural capital: Book reading in urban China. *Modern China* 32 (2006): 315–348.

Watelet, Claude-Henri. *Essay on Gardens: A Chapter in the French Picturesque.* 1774. Ed. and trans. S. Danon. Philadelphia: University of Pennsylvania Press, 2003.

Watkins, Mary, and Helene Lorenz. *Toward Psychologies of Liberation.* New York: Palgrave Macmillan, 2008.

Watson, G., and D. Chambers. *Singing the Land, Signing the Land.* Melbourne: Deakin University Press, 1998.

Wecter, Dixon. *Edmund Burke and His Kinsmen.* Boulder: University of Colorado Press, 1939.

Westcoat, James. Common themes in the work of Gilbert White and John Dewey. *Annals of the Association of American Geographers* 82 (1992): 587–607.

Wharton, Edith. *Italian Villas and Their Gardens.* New York: The Century Co., 1904.

Whateley, Richard. *Introductory Lectures on Political Economy,* 2nd ed. London: B. Fellowes, 1832.

Whewell, William. *Six Lectures on Political Economy.* Cambridge: Cambridge University Press, 1862.

White, Gilbert F. *Human Adjustments to Floods: A Geographical Approach to the Flood Problem in the United States.* Chicago: University of Chicago, 1945.

White, J. *The Birth and Rebirth of Pictorial Space.* London: Faber & Faber, 1972.

Williams, Raymond. *Culture and Society: 1780–1950.* New York: Columbia University Press, 1983.

Williams, Raymond. *The Country and the City.* London: Chatto & Windus, 1973.

Wilson, Edward O. Foreword. In *Land Mosaics: The Ecology of Landscapes and Regions,* ed. Richard Foreman. Cambridge: Cambridge University Press, 1995.

Windele, John. *Notices of the City of Cork.* Cork: Bolster, 1849.

Winter, Deborah, and Sue Koger. *The Psychology of Environmental Problems.* Hillsdale, NJ: Lawrence Erlbaum, 2003.

Wolfe, P. On being woken up: The "Dreamtime" in anthropology in Australian settler culture. *Comparative Studies in Society and History* 133 (1991): 197–224.

Wordsworth, William. *The Prelude* I, ll.356–388. In *Poetical Works,* ed. Thomas Hutchinson, a new ed. revised by Ernest de Selingcourt. London: Oxford University Press, 1969.

Wozniakowski, J. *Die Wildnis. Zur Deutungsgeschichte des Berges in der europäischen Neuzeit.* Frankfurt: Suhrkamp, 1987.

Wright, John Jr. *Lexington: Heart of the Bluegrass.* Lexington: Lexington Fayette County Historical Commission, 1982.

Wrigley, E. A. *Continuity, Chance, and Change.* Cambridge: Cambridge University Press, 1988.

Yanyuwa families, J. Bradley, and N. Cameron. *"Forget about Flinders": A Yanyuwa Atlas of the South Western Gulf of Carpentaria.* Gold Coast, Queensland: J. M. McGregor, 2005.

Yeats, William Butler. Preface to Lady Gregory, *Gods and Fighting Men.* New York: Scribner, 1904.

Zhang, Y. J. My camera doesn't lie? Truth, subjectivity, and audience in Chinese independent film and video. In *From Underground to Independent*, ed. Y. J. Zhang and P. G. Pickowicz. Lanham: Rowman & Littlefield, 2006, 23–45.

Zhen, Zhang, ed. *The Urban Generation: Chinese Cinema and Society at the Turn of the Twenty-First Century.* Durham: Duke University Press, 2007.

Contributors

Andrew Benjamin is Professor of Critical Theory and Philosophical Aesthetics at Monash University, where he is also Director of the Research Unit in European Philosophy. His most recent books are *Of Jews and Animals* (2010) and *Writing Art and Architecture* (2010).

John J. Bradley is Associate Professor in Anthropology and Indigenous Studies at the Centre for Australian Indigenous Studies at Monash University. He is also Deputy Director of this center. He has worked with issues in indigenous Australia for the last thirty years. His most recent book is *Singing Saltwater Country* (2010).

Isis Brook a philosopher and aesthetician, is Head of Learning and Technology at Writtle College, Essex, and has published on phenomenology, place, gardens, and Goethe's epistemology. She is also the Managing Editor of the journal *Environmental Values*.

Katie Campbell is Lecturer in Landscape History at Bristol University; she also runs the university's Institute of Garden and Landscape History. Her most recent book is *Paradise of Exiles: The Anglo American Gardens of Florence* (2009).

Edward S. Casey is Distinguished Professor of Philosophy at SUNY, Stony Brook, and the current President of the American Philosophical Association, Eastern Division. He has written *Getting Back into Place* (1996), *The Fate of Place* (1998), and *Representing Place in Landscape Painting and Maps* (2002), among many publications. Most recently, he published *The World at a Glance* (2007), and is now engaged in a sequel to be entitled *The World on Edge*.

Bernard Debarbieux is Professor of Cultural and Political Geography at the University of Geneva (Switzerland). He has worked on the cultural meanings and political shaping of mountains in the West, and, more generally speaking, on theories of modern territoriality.

Stephanie Hemelryk Donald is Dean of Media and Communication at RMIT University and Honorary Professor of Chinese Media Studies at the University of Sydney. She works on the comparative politics of visual communication, with a current focus on historical trauma, mobility and cosmopolitanism, branding cities, and children's film.

J. Nicholas Entrikin is Vice President for Internationalization and Professor of Sociology at the University of Notre Dame. He is also Professor Emeritus of Geography at UCLA. He is the author of *The Betweenness of Place* (1991), coeditor of *The Marshall Plan Today: Model and Metaphor* (2004), and editor of *Regions* (2008).

Nigel Everett is an independent historian of British and Irish landscape. Publications include *The Tory View of Landscape* (1994), *Wild Gardens—the Lost Demesnes of Bantry Bay* (2000), *A Landlord's Garden: Derreen, Co. Kerry* (2001), and a forthcoming history of Irish woodlands.

Ross Gibson is Professor of Contemporary Arts at the University of Sydney. He was founding Creative Director for the establishment of the Australian Centre for the Moving Image and Senior Consultant Producer for the establishment of the Museum of Sydney. His recent works include the books *Seven Versions of an Australian Badland* (2002) and *The Summer Exercises* (2009), the video installation *Street X-Rays* (2005), and *Conversations II*, a three-month durational work for the 2008 Biennale of Sydney.

Wesley A. Kort is Professor in the Department of Religion and the Graduate Program in Religion at Duke University. He is the author of nine books and many published essays that relate literary and religious studies to one another. His most rec ent book is *Place and Space in Modern Fiction* (2004).

Jeff Malpas is Professor of Philosophy and ARC Professorial Fellow at the University of Tasmania; he is also Distinguished Visiting Professor at La Trobe University in Melbourne. He is the author of *Place and Experience* (1999) and *Heidegger's Topology* (2006), and the editor of *Dialogues with Davidson* (2011).

Michael Rosenthal was Professor of the History of Art at the University of Warwick. He has a particular interest in landscape, cultural politics, and the art of colonial Australia. His books include *The Art of Thomas Gainsborough: "a little business for the Eye"* (1999).

Theodore R. Schatzki is Dean of Faculty and Professor of Philosophy in the College of Arts and Sciences at the University of Kentucky. He is the author of *Social Practices* (1996), *The Site of the Social* (2002), *Martin Heidegger: Theorist of Space* (2007), and *The Timespace of Human Activity* (2010).

Philip Sheldrake is William Leech Professorial Fellow in Applied Theology in the Department of Theology and Religion at the University of Durham; he is Honorary Professor at the University of Wales Lampeter and is a regular Visiting Professor at the University of Notre Dame and Boston College. He is the author or editor of several books, including *Spirituality and History* (1991/1996), *Spirituality and Theology* (1998), and *Spaces for the Sacred: Place, Memory, Identity* (2001).

Reinhard Steiner is Professor of Art History at the University Stuttgart. He is the author of *Egon Schiele, 1890–1918: The Midnight Soul of the Artist* (1991), as well as many essays on the history and theory of expression in painting and sculpture, and on conceptual problems of the historical mediation of artistic production and aesthetic experience.

Index

Note: Page numbers in italics indicate figures.